QUEEN ELIZABETH

From a painting of the Holbein School.

The
MIRACLE
OF ENGLAND

*AN ACCOUNT OF HER RISE TO PRE-EMINENCE
AND PRESENT POSITION*

By ANDRÉ MAUROIS

Translated by Hamish Miles

HARPER & BROTHERS *Publishers*
New York and London
MCMXXXVII

This story is published in
England under the title of
A HISTORY OF ENGLAND.

To

SIMONE ANDRÉ-MAUROIS

CONTENTS

[vii]

Contents

Contents

ILLUSTRATIONS

LIST OF MAPS

Prefatory Note

AT THE end of this book the reader will find a list of the books to which I have had constant recourse. Long though it is, that list is of course too brief to be regarded as even a sketch bibliography of the subject. Omissions must be explained by the strict necessities of selection rather than by any adverse judgment on my part.

It was impossible, in the range of a single volume, to narrate the history of Scotland and of Ireland along with that of England. The relations between the three countries have been explained whenever it seemed necessary, but in the narrowest compass. For the same reason the history of the British Empire has here been dealt with only in its relation to the internal history of England.

I am greatly indebted to Mr. A. V. Judges, Lecturer at the London School of Economics, of the University of London, who was good enough to read my typescript, and whose criticisms I took fully into account. And my friend and translator, Hamish Miles, has been, as ever, a most valued counsellor.

A. M.

Book I

ORIGINS

CHAPTER I

The Situation of England

"WE MUST always remember that we are part of the Continent, but we must never forget that we are neighbours to it." Bolingbroke's words define the primordial facts of England's position. So close to the Continent does she lie that from the beach at Calais the white cliffs of Dover are plainly visible, tempting the invader. For thousands of years, indeed, England was joined up with Europe, and for long ages the Thames was a tributary of the Rhine. The animals which returned to roam the country after the Ice Age, and the first hunters who followed on their tracks, crossed from Europe on dry land. But narrow and shallow as the straits are which now sever the island of Britain from Belgium and France, they have nevertheless shaped a unique destiny for the country which they protect.

"Insulated, not isolated." Europe is not so far away that the insularity of English ideas and customs could remain unaffected. Indeed, that insularity is a human fact rather than a phenomenon of nature. In the beginnings of history England was invaded, like other lands, and fell an easy victim. She lived then by husbandry and grazing. Her sons were shepherds and tillers of the soil rather than merchants or seamen. It was not until much later that the English, having built powerful fleets, and feeling themselves sheltered within a ring of strong sea defenses, realized the actual benefits of insularity, which freed them from fears of invasion and, for several centuries, from the military requirements which dominated the policy of other nations, and so enabled them safely to attempt new forms of authority.

By a fortunate chance, the most accessible part of England was the low-lying country of the southeast, which confronts the Continent. If the land had happened to slope in the other direction, if the Celtic and Scandinavian sea-rovers had chanced upon forbidding mountains on their first voyages, it is probable that few of them would have attempted invasion, and the history of the country would have been very different. But their vessels came with the inflowing tides deep into well-sheltered estuaries; the turfed chalk ridges made it possible to explore the island without the dangers of marsh and forest; and the climate, moreover, was more kindly than that of other lands in the same latitude, as Britain lies in a gulf of temperate winters produced by the damp mild mists of the ocean. Thus every feature of the coastline seemed to encourage the conqueror, who was also the creator.

This accessible part of England lies exactly opposite the frontier which severs the Germanic from the Roman languages (nowadays, the Flemish from the French), and was thus destined to be open equally to the bearers of the Roman and Latin culture, and to those of the Teutonic. History would show how England characteristically combined elements from both these cultures, and out of them made a genius of her own. "Her East coast was open to Scandinavian immigrants, her South to Mediterranean influences reaching her through France. To the Teutons and Scandinavians she owes the greater part of her population, numerous traits of character, and the roots of her speech; from the Mediterranean peoples she received the rest of her language, the chief forms of her culture, much of her organising power." In this respect England differs profoundly from France or Italy, in both of which the Latin basis is always dominant, despite certain Germanic contributions, and also from Germany, where Latin culture was never more than an ornament, and often was indignantly rejected. England was thrice subjected to contact with the Latin world—by the Roman occupation, by Christianity, and by the Normans —and the impress left by these Latin influences was deep.

Paradoxical it may seem, but it is true to say that England's position on the globe changed between the fifteenth and seventeenth centuries. To the races of antiquity and the peoples of the Middle Ages, this mist-clad country represented the farthest fringe of the world: *Ultima Thule*, magical and almost inhuman, on the verge of hell itself. Beyond those rocks battered by ocean billows lay, to the west, the sea that had no end, and northward, the everlasting ice. The boldest of the bold ventured thither because they could find gold and pearls, and later wool; but how could

ENGLAND IN THE ANCIENT WORLD
THE ROMAN EMPIRE UNDER TRAJAN.

OCEANUS

BRITANNIA

GERMANIA

SARMATIA

MARE CASPIUM

BELGICA

Lutetia

ATLANTICUS

AQUITANIA

Danubius F

PONTUS EUXINUS

ITALIA

HISPANIA

ROMA

THRACIA

ASIA

MESOPOTAMIA

MARE

INTERNUM

MAURETANIA

AFRICA

AEGYPTUS

ARABIA

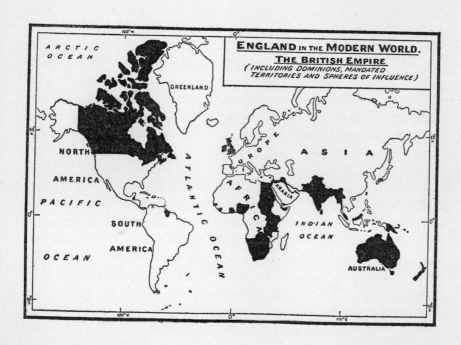

ENGLAND IN THE MODERN WORLD.
THE BRITISH EMPIRE
(INCLUDING DOMINIONS, MANDATED
TERRITORIES AND SPHERES OF INFLUENCE)

ARCTIC OCEAN

GREENLAND

EUROPE

ASIA

NORTH

AMERICA

ATLANTIC OCEAN

AFRICA

ARABIA

PACIFIC

INDIAN OCEAN

SOUTH

AMERICA

OCEAN

AUSTRALIA

they imagine the prodigies which the future held for these islands? Those were days when all human activity was founded, directly or indirectly, on the Mediterranean basin. It needed the barrier of Islam, the discovery of America, and above all the emigration of the Puritans, to shift the great trade routes, and to make the British Isles, confronting a new world, into the most advanced maritime base of Europe.

Finally, it was in the eighteenth and nineteenth centuries that England's insular position, after allowing her behind the shield of her fleet to attain a higher degree of domestic liberty than Continental peoples could reach, enabled her through that same maritime instrument to conquer a worldwide empire. The mastery of the seas, which solved the problem of national defense inherent in England's geographical situation, serves as one key to her political and imperial history. And the invention of the airplane is for her the most important and the most perilous development of our times.

CHAPTER II

The First Traces of Man

THE first page of England's history is not, as has often been said, a blank. It is rather a page inscribed with the letters of several alphabets to which we have no key. Some parts of the country, especially the rolling chalk Downs of Wiltshire, are scattered with monuments of prehistoric origin. Near the village of Avebury can be seen the vast ruins of a megalithic structure, a cathedral in scale. Great avenues lead up to circles built of more than five hundred monoliths, and a rampart with a grassy inner ditch incloses a spacious circle. Today, standing on that earthwork, one can see a few hundred yards away an artificial mound which overlooks the surroundings levels, and must have required as much toil and faith and courage for a primitive people to raise as was needed by the Egyptians to erect the monuments of Gizeh. On every ridge hereabouts lie the irregular outlines of turf-covered barrows, some oval, some circular, which are the graves of chiefs. Inside their stone chambers have sometimes been found skeletons, pottery, and jewelry. These heroic burial-grounds, the simple, majestic shapes of earthworks rising on the skyline, the bold definite contours of ramparts, circles, and avenues, all indicate the presence of a civilization already well developed.

Time was when historians chose to portray these primitive Britons as overawed by the forests of the weald, haunted by gods and beasts, and wandering in small groups of hunters and shepherds who took refuge on the hills. But such monuments as those at Avebury and Stonehenge seem to prove the existence of a fairly numerous population fully two thousand years before the Christian era, customarily united for common action under an accepted authority. Grassy tracks ran along the ridges and served the earliest inhabitants as roadways, many of which converged

[7]

on Avebury and Stonehenge, which must have been highly important centers. Many of these roadways retained their importance for travelers into modern times; and nineteenth-century cattle-drovers and the Englishman's motor-car today have followed the ridgeway tracks which overlook valleys once blocked by swamp or forest to early wayfarers. Thus, ever since those mysterious ages, certain unalterable features of human geography have remained fixed. Many of the sacred places of these primitive people have become places of enchantment for their posterity. And already, too, nature was foreshadowing the positions of towns yet to be. Canterbury was the nearest point to the coast, on that line of road, from which it was possible to reach certain ports so as to fit in with the tides; Winchester occupied a similar situation to the west; London itself retains few traces of prehistoric life, but was soon to become conspicuous because it offered convenient shelter, at the head of the safest estuary, at the mouth of a stream, and was also the nearest point to the sea where it was possible to throw a bridge across the river Thames.

Whence came those clans who peopled England after the disappearance of palæolithic man and at the end of the Ice Age, bringing with them cattle, goats, and swine? Their skeletons show two races, one with elongated, the other with broad, skulls. It used to be held that the long skulls were found in oval barrows, the broad ones in round barrows. This was convenient, but inaccurate. Unfortunately, the round barrows revealed long skulls, and it calls for a great many intellectual concessions to distinguish two distinct civilizations in the megalithic remains of England. The name of Iberians is generally given to these primitive inhabitants, and they are supposed to have come from Spain. Spanish or not, they were certainly of Mediterranean origin. The traveler returning from Malta is struck, at Stonehenge, by the resemblance between the megalithic monuments of two places so far apart. It is more than likely that in prehistoric times there existed in the Mediterranean, and along the Atlantic seaboard as far as the British Isles, a civilization quite as homogeneous as the European Christendom of the Middle Ages. This civilization was introduced into England by immigrants, who retained contact with Europe through traders coming in search of metals in Britain, and bartering the products of the Levant or amber from the Baltic. Gradually the islanders, like the inhabitants of the Continent, learned new technical devices, the arts of husbandry, the methods of building longboats and manipulating bronze. It is important to have some picture of how slowly the progress of men moved during these long centuries. The thin coating of historic time is laid over deep strata of pre-history, and there were countless generations who left no tangible or visible traces beyond some rough-hewn or up-ended stones, tracks, or wells, but who bequeathed to mankind a patrimony of words, institutions, devices, without which the outcome of the adventure would have been inconceivable.

CHAPTER III

The Celts

BETWEEN the sixth and fourth centuries before the Christian era, there arrived in England and Ireland successive waves of pastoral and warrior tribes who gradually supplanted the Iberians. They belonged to a Celtic people who had occupied great tracts in the Danube basin, in Gaul, and to the north of the Alps. They probably began to move because shepherd races are doomed to follow their flocks when hunger drives these towards fresh pastures. Doubtless human causes also intervened: an adventurous chief, the desire for conquest, the pressure of a stronger people. These migrations were slow and steady. One clan would cross the Channel and settle on the coast; a second would drive this one farther inland, the natives themselves being pushed always farther back. These Celtic tribes had a taste for war, even amongst themselves, and were composed of tall, powerful men, eaters of pork and oatmeal pottage, beer-drinkers, and skillful charioteers. The Latin and Greek writers depicted the Celts as a tall, lymphatic, white-skinned race, with fair hair. Actually there were many dark Celts who in the Roman triumphs were sorted out and made to dye their hair, so as to produce prisoners in conformity with popular ideas for the parades in the metropolis. The Celts themselves had formed an ideal type of their own race, to which they strove to approximate. They bleached their hair and painted their bodies with coloring matter; whence it came about that the Romans later styled the Celts in Scotland, Picts, (*Picti,* the painted men).

In this slow and prolonged Celtic invasion, two main waves are distinguished by historians: the first, of the Goidels, or Gaels, who gave their language to Ireland and the Scottish Highlands; and the second, of the Bretons or Brythons, whose tongue became that of the Welsh and the Bretons in France. In England the Celtic speech later vanished under the Germanic irruptions. There survived only a few words of domestic life, preserved, we may suppose, by the Celtic women taken into the households of the conquerors, such as "cradle" and certain place names. "Avon" (river) and "Ox" (water) are Celtic roots. "London" (the Latin Lundinium) is supposed to be a Celtic name analogous to that of the Norman village of Londinières. At a much later date certain Celtic words were to reënter England from Scotland (such as "clan," "plaid," "kilt") or from Ireland ("shamrock," "log," "gag"). The word "Breton," or "Brython," signified "the land of the tattooed men": when the Greek explorer Pytheas landed in these islands in 325 B.C., he gave them the name of *Pretanikai nēsoi*, which they have ever since, more or less, preserved.

Pytheas was a Greek from Marseilles, an astronomer and mathematician, dispatched by a merchant syndicate to explore the Atlantic. He was the first to turn the beam of history on to an obscure region then regarded as on the farthest bounds of the universe. In these fabulous islands Pytheas found a comparatively civilized country, whose people grew corn, but had to thresh it in covered sheds because of the damp climate. The Britons whom he saw drank a mixture of fermented grain and honey, and traded in tin with the ports of Gaul on the mainland. Two centuries later another traveler, Poseidonius, described the tin-mines and how the ore was conveyed on horses or donkeys, then by boat, to the isle of Ictis, which must have been Mont-Saint-Michel. This trade was large enough to justify the use of gold coinage, copied by the Celts from the "staters" of Philip of Macedon. The first coin struck in England bore a head of Apollo, symbolic enough of the Mediterranean origins of her civilization.

The evidence of Julius Cæsar is our best source for the Celts' mode of life. They had nominal kings, it is true, with local influence, but no serious political sway. Every town or township—every family, almost— was divided into two factions, the leading men of each giving protection to their partisans. These people had no sense of the State, and left no political heritage: both in England and France, the State was a creation of the Latin and Germanic spirits. United, the Celts would have been invincible; but their bravery and intelligence were nullified by their dissensions. The Celtic clan rested on a family, not a totem, basis, which forges strong links but hampers the development of wider associations. In countries of Celtic origin the family has always remained the unit of social life. Amongst the Irish, even where they have settled in America, politics remain a clannish concern. Even in Cæsar's time these clans had a strong liking for colors, emblems and blazonry. The Scottish clan tartans are probably of Celtic origin. According to Cæsar the rural community life with communal fields and pastures, so important later in English history, is essentially Germanic, and certainly would hardly have fitted in with the network of factions described by him. In any case, for these partly nomadic people, agriculture was less important than hunting, fishing, and stock-rearing. In Wales, until the Middle Ages, the population kept moving their settlements in search of new hunting-grounds, new pasture, and even new farmland.

The most highly honored class was the priestly one of the Druids, who approximate most closely to the Brahmans of India or the Persian Magi. The hunger strike, a device which reappeared in Ireland in modern times, recalls the *dharna* of the Hindus, where the Brahman fasts at his adversary's door until he has obtained his desire: there is a mental affinity between a Gandhi and a MacSweeney. In Cæsar's time the most famous Druids were those of Britain, who forgathered every year at a central point, possibly Stonehenge, although their holy of holies was the island of Mona (Angelsey). It was to Britain that the Druids of the Belgians or Gauls went to seek fuller knowledge of the doctrine, and there they learned numerous verses in which the sacred precepts were embodied. Only one of these sentences, preserved by Diogenes Laertius, has survived: "Worship the gods, do no mean deed, act with courage"—more or less the Kipling creed. The Druids taught "that death was only a change of scene, and that life is continued with its forms and possessions in the World of the Dead, which consists of a great store of souls awaiting disposal. . . . This population of souls does not seem to have been confined to the human race, and they apparently believed in the transmigration of souls," which is another feature in common with the East.

The Celts of Britain and the Belgians across the Channel were in close and constant touch. At the time of the Roman invasion the British Celts sent aid to their kin on the Continent, but Cæsar noted that the island Celts were not so well armed as the Gauls. The Gaulish Celts had abandoned their archaic war chariots, since they had found quite good horses in the plains of the Midi. But the Britons, not yet having horses which could carry fighting-men, still fought like the Homeric warriors.

The Celts

In Britain as in Gaul, the quick-witted, adaptable Celts were swift to imitate the Roman civilization when it had defeated them. "It was Gaulish teachers, trained in the Druidic school, who gave Gaul her classic culture. . . . Later, in the Middle Ages, the Irish monks were to revive in Europe the study of Greek and Latin literature." But the Celts were not merely good transmitters of a foreign culture. They had their own artistic tastes, and the spiral ornamentation of their weapons, their jewels and pottery, shows that they were more fanciful than the Romans ever were. They gave to European literature an Oriental sense of mystery and a dramatic conception of fatality which are peculiarly their own. The Celtic genius left its mark in Europe chiefly, perhaps, through the story of Tristram and Yseult, and by that of King Arthur. In the formation of modern England, too, the Celtic elements, with their strong admixture of Iberian blood, preserved in the western and northern parts of the British Isles, have played a great part: in the twentieth century we find men of Celtic stock from Scotland, Wales, and Ireland presiding over British Cabinets and commanding British armies.

CHAPTER IV

The Roman Conquest

IT IS difficult for a weak people, living within reach of a great military power, to keep its freedom. With Gaul subdued, Britain became the natural objective for the Roman armies. Julius Cæsar needed victories to impress Rome, and money to reward his legions and partisans; and in these fabulous islands he hoped to find gold, pearls, slaves. Furthermore, he thought it advisable to overawe these British Celts who had sided with those of the Continent against his arms. Late in the summer of the year 55 B.C. he decided to carry out a short reconnaissance across the Channel. He sought information first from traders in Gaul, but through ignorance or willful enmity they misled him. The favorite device of Cæsar was to work from inside, moving through one tribe to the next, using one against another. But in this improvised venture he was pressed for time. Sending forward a vessel to choose a suitable landing-place, he started off himself with two legions. The expedition was not too successful. The Britons, on the alert, were waiting in force on the shore. The legionaries, compelled to leap from their transports into quite deep water, were battered by the waves, and under their heavy load of arms could hardly get a foothold. Cæsar had to order the galleys of archers and slingers to set up a covering barrage of projectiles. The strength of the Romans lay in the great superiority of their discipline and military science over those of the Britons. Immediately after landing, these experienced legionaries were able to build a camp, protect their vessels, and make a "tortoise" with their joined shields. The Celts had mustered thousands of chariots. When this mounted infantry attacked, the fighting-men left the chariots, whilst the charioteers withdrew a short distance, in readiness to pick up their men again in case of defeat or withdrawal. But notwithstanding some success, Cæsar soon realized that his small army was not secure. Heavy seas had already destroyed some of his transports, and the equinoctial tides were at hand. Taking advantage of a slight success to secure hostages and promises, he secretly raised anchor soon after midnight. He had saved his face. And on the strength of this inglorious expedition he sent the Senate a dispatch in such glowing terms that a *supplicatio* of twenty days was voted to celebrate his victory.

But Cæsar was too much of a realist to disguise the failure to himself. He had learned about the nature of the country, the harbors, and the British tactics, saw that a conquest would need cavalry, and decided to return in the following year (54 B.C.). This time he found the Britons united by the pressure of danger and obeying one chief, Cassivelaunus, whose territory lay north of the Thames. The Roman army advanced in that direction, and when Cæsar reached the northern bank of the river he entered dexterously on negotiations. Taking advantage of the smolder- ing jealousies of the Celtic chieftains, some of whom he incited against Cassivelaunus, he secured the submission of several tribes, defeated others in the field, and finally, treating with Cassivelaunus himself, fixed an annual tribute to be paid to the Roman people by Britain. In point of fact this tribute was not paid after the year 52, and for a long time Rome's interest in the Britons was distracted by her civil war. Cicero mocked at this "conquest" which yielded nothing but a few slaves, laborers of the coarsest type, with not one of them literate or a musician, and at an achievement which had been a move in internal policy rather than an imperial victory.

For a century after Cæsar's departure Britain was forgotten. But mer- chants came thither from Gaul, by now thoroughly Romanized, and the Imperial coinage was current. The poet Martial, in the first century of the Christian era, boasted of having readers there, and spoke with en- thusiasm of a young British woman who had married a Roman and was very popular when he brought her back to Italy. In the time of Claudius, various groups urged a conquest of Britain: generals with an eye on fame and gain, traders who declared that mercantile security required the presence of the legions, administrators who deplored the bad influence wielded in Gaul by the Druids, whose center of activity was still in Britain, and a host of officials hoping to find posts in a new province. In the year 43 A.D., accordingly, Claudius sent over an expedition of four legions (II, Augusta; XX, Valeria Victoria; XIV, Gemina Martia Victoria; and the famous IX, Hispana, of the Danubian army), totaling about 50,000 men, inclusive of auxiliaries and horsemen. With such a force the conquest appeared easy enough, and resistance did not prove serious until the mountain regions of Wales and Scotland were reached. From the island of Mona (Angelsey), a center of Druidism, came forth a terrifying host of warriors in whose midst women with flying hair brandished blazing torches, whilst the serried ranks of white-robed Druids raised their arms in invocation of the gods. In the southeast, which seemed to be pacified, the conquerors were momentarily imperiled by a violent rising led by a queen, Boudicca, or Boadicea, provoked by the injustices of the first Roman administrators. But it was ended by a massacre of the Britons. By the beginning of the second century all the rich plains of the south were in subjection.

Roman methods of occupation varied little: they built excellent roads enabling the legions to move swiftly from place to place, and fortified centers to hold fixed garrisons. Most English towns with names ending in *"chester"* or *"cester"* were Roman camps (*castra*) in the time of the occupation. Veterans of the legions, after their term of service, began to retire to the small British towns of Camulodunum (Colchester) and Verulamium (St. Albans). Towns like Lincoln, Gloucester, and York were originally only garrison towns. London (Londinium) grew large in Roman times because the conquerors made it a center through which passed all the roads linking north with south, the principal one being Watling Street, running from London to Chester. The excellent harbor of London was used for bringing over supplies for the armies.

In towns built in their entirety by the Romans, the streets intersected each other at right angles, the baths, the temple, the forum, and the basilica occupying their traditional places. Before long the south of England was sprinkled with small Roman houses. Wall-paintings and mosaic floors showed classic scenes—the stories of Orpheus or Apollo. Soldiers and officials made their modest attempts to reconstruct the backgrounds of Italy in this misty clime. At Bath (Aquæ Sulis)—which, it has been said, was the Simla of Roman Britain, while London was its Calcutta or Bombay—they built a completely Roman watering-place. To this new life the Celts, or some of them at least, adapted themselves.

London, Restitutus, is known to have attended the synod of Arles along with two others from that country. Small and poor his see must have been, for the faithful had not been able to pay for their bishop's journeying and a subscription had to be opened for him in Gaul.

The south and central parts of Britain were thus becoming part and parcel of the Empire. But in the north the Roman dominion made no headway. On the edge of rough heather moorlands lived the half-savage tribe of the Brigantes, and still farther north another Celtic group, the Picts, both equally refractory to all peaceful penetration. These dissident, uncompromising tribes, attracted by the comparative wealth of the Celto-Roman townships, kept making profitable forays into the south, and easily escaped the pursuing Roman generals. Thanks to a skillful combined action by land and sea forces, Agricola thought he had overcome them, but whenever the Romans penetrated Scotland their overlong lines of communication became too vulnerable, and a raid of Brigantes led to a massacre of legionaries. It was in consequence of one such disaster, in which the IX legion perished, that the Emperor Hadrian himself came to Britain in the year 120, bringing the VI Victrix legion. He abandoned the idea of subduing the north, and fortified the frontier by building between the Tyne and the Solway Firth a line of fourteen forts, joined at first by a continuous earthwork, and soon by a stone wall, to be permanently garrisoned. In fact, Hadrian abandoned a conquest of the refractory, and confined himself, in Caledonia as in Europe, to holding them back. This "wisdom" was in time to bring about the fall of the Roman Empire.

CHAPTER V

The Romans Depart

AFTER the third century the Roman Empire, despite certain impressive counterstrokes, was threatened by a threefold crisis, economic, religious, and military. Roman capitalism had blindly exploited the resources of the provinces; the conflict of paganism with Christianity had sundered emperors and citizens; and military power had collapsed. The system of the continuous frontier (a line of forts linked by a rampart) had broken down. In Britain it had seemed slightly more effective than elsewhere, the line of defense being short. On the Continent it had proved necessary to substitute mobile troops for the fortified lines. But even the legions found it impossible to battle against the barbarian horsemen. Sword and javelin had soon to give way to bow and lance, and the victories of the Goths, warriors trained on the Russian steppes, the land of great horsemen, foretold the advent of mounted troops in place of the legionaries. This fundamental change affected the art of war for twelve or thirteen centuries, predominance passing from infantry to cavalry. And to meet the urgent need of a cavalry force, the Empire sought the aid of the barbarians, themselves, at first only as auxiliaries, but later as enlisted legionaries, until at last the legions contained none else. By the middle of the fourth century "soldier" had become synonymous with "barbarian," and the virtues of the armies were no longer Roman in character.

To Britain the barbarian cavalry had no access, and so the Pax Romana survived there longer than in the Continental provinces of the Empire. The first half of the fourth century, indeed, saw in Britain the apogee of its Roman civilization. But there, as elsewhere, the army ceased to be Roman. The garrison of the Wall consisted of local units which were land of the dead. At the time of the great invasion of Rome in 410, Stilicho, overwhelmed by Vandals and Burgundians, made one last appeal for reinforcements from Britain. The soldiers who responded, and disappeared, were not Romans, but Britons. The province was now almost bare of its defenders.

What happened thereafter? The Picts and Scots seem to have become bolder, and to combat them, says the chronicler, a British chief, Vortigern, summoned Saxon auxiliaries, Hengest and Horsa, to whom he offered land as payment for their swords. Having once set foot on the island, they turned against their master, and Germanic invaders, attracted by this fruitful and ill-defended land, became more and more numerous. The year 418 is noted in the Anglo-Saxon Chronicle as that in which "the Romans gathered together all the treasure that was in Britain. Hiding part of it underground, they bore away the rest into Gaul." In our own day some of these treasures have been unearthed, caches of gold and silver objects. The discoveries of archæology all point to a land then in a state of terror. Villas and destroyed houses show signs of fire; doors have been hastily walled up; skeletons have been found uncoffined. The Venerable Bede describes these invasions: "Public as well as private structures were overturned; the priests were everywhere slain before the altars. . . . Some of the miserable remainder, being taken in the mountains, were butchered in heaps. Others, spent with hunger, came forth and submitted themselves to the enemy for food, being destined to undergo perpetual servitude if they were not killed even upon the spot. Some, with sorrowful hearts, fled beyond the seas. Others, continuing in their own country, led a miserable life among the woods, rocks, and mountains." Most of the Celts fled into the mountainous districts of the west, where they are still living today. To these fugitives the Saxons gave the name "Welsh," that is, foreigners (German, *Welche*). Other Celts moved away towards Armorica, one of the most remote parts of Gaul, and there created Britanny. Between Britanny and Britain there was a lasting link. "Tristan is a Breton; Lancelot came from France to the court of Arthur, and Merlin plied between both countries."

The conquest of Britain by the Germans was slow, and hampered by moments of courageous defense. In 429 St.-Germain, Bishop of Auxerre, visited Verulamium to direct the fight against the Pelagian heresy—a proof that the Britons still had leisure for theological concerns. During his stay the town was threatened by Saxons and Picts, and St.-Germain took command of the troops, prepared an ambush, and at the right moment hurled the Christians against the Barbarians to the cry of "Alleluia!". He was victorious. In the sixth century a mythical sovereign named Arthur (Artorius), who was later to inspire the poets, is reputed to have gained triumphs over the invaders. But thenceforward the Angles, Saxons, and Jutes were masters of the richest parts of the country. It is certainly surprising that the Celto-Roman civilization vanished in England so quickly as it did. In Gaul, and in the south of France particularly, Roman towns and monuments have remained standing. Low Latin provided the chief elements of the French language. But in England the language retained few traces of the Roman occupation. English words of Latin origin are either words acquired by the learned at a later date, or French words dating from the Norman Conquest. Among the few vocables originating in the first Roman conquest can be seen "Cæsar," a universal word, "street" (*via strata,* which is also seen in the place-name "Stratford") "mile" (the Roman *mille*), "wall" (*vallum*), and the termination "chester," as mentioned before. An Emperor, roads, a wall—was this all that Rome bequeathed after four centuries to the most distant of her provinces?

"The important thing about France and England is not that they have Roman remains. They are Roman remains." In the heritage of Rome England found, as all Europe found, Christianity and the idea of the State. The Empire and the Pax Romana were to remain the blessed dream of the best among the barbarian sovereigns. In Ireland and Wales there remained priests and monks who were to save the Roman culture. The chronicler Gildas (c. 540) quotes Virgil and refers to Latin as *"nostra lingua."* The old theory, dear to the Saxon historians, of a total destruction of the Romanized Celts is almost inconceivable. The fact that the few Celtic words surviving in England have reference to domestic life seems to show that the invaders married native women. Many of the men, no doubt, became slaves, but the Celts were no more obliterated than the Iberians had been. The profound difference between the modern Englishman and the German arises partly from the Norman Conquest having been for him a second Latin conquest, and partly from the fact that the blood of the Germanic invaders received a fairly strong admixture of the blood of their predecessors.

CHAPTER VI

Angles, Jutes, Saxons

"TALL and fair of body, with fierce blue eyes and ruddy fair hair; voracious, always hungered, warmed by strong liquors; young men coming late to love, and having no shame in drinking all day and all night"—these Saxons and Angles had violence in their temperament, and kept it. After fifteen centuries, notwithstanding the strict rules of a code of manners sprung from that very violence, their character was to remain less supple than that of Celts or Latins. In the days of those invasions they held human life cheap. War was their delight, and their history has been compared to that of the kites and crows. But "this native barbarism covered noble inclinations," and there was "a quality of seriousness which saved them from frivolity. Their women were chaste, their marriages pure. The man who had chosen his leader was true to him, and loyal towards his comrades though cruel to his foe. The man of this stock could accept a master, and was capable of devotion and respect." Having always known the tremendous forces of nature, more so than the dweller in gentler climes, he was religious. A sense of grandeur and melancholy haunted his imagination. The solitudes which he had known in the Frisian marshlands and the great coastal plains were not like those which engendered the harsh poetry of the Bible, but they prepared him to understand it. When the Bible came in time to his ken, the Scriptures filled him with a deep and lasting passion.

It is fairly easy to picture the landings of the Saxon bands. Sailing with the tide into an estuary, the barbarians would push on upstream, or follow a Roman road, to find a Roman villa ringed by tilled fields, or the huts of a Celtic hamlet. Silence. A corpse before the door and the other inhabitants in flight. The hungry band halts; a few fowls and cattle are left; here they can stop, and as the land is already cleared, they will stay. But the Saxons refrain from occupying the Roman villa: it is partly burned down, and in any case, perhaps, these superstitious barbarians dread the ghosts of murdered masters. Still less will these open-air men—peasants, hunters, and woodmen—go and inhabit towns. The Roman townships were soon left abandoned. In a new land these Germans follow their old usage, and build their cabins from the felled trees. The head of the tribe, the noble, will have a hall of tree-trunks built for him by his men. In parceling out the land the band follows the Germanic tradition. The village ("town" or "township," from the Saxon *tun*, hedge or fence) will own the fields collectively, but every man is to have his share marked out. Before the coming of the Romans, the Celts tilled the land in primitive fashion, clearing a field, sowing, reaping, and then moving on when the soil became exhausted. These Saxons have better methods. The arable land of the community, in the east and midlands is divided into two or three great fields, one of which is left fallow each year to allow the soil to recuperate. The grass is burnt in clearing the ground, and the ashes manure it. Then each of the communal fields is divided into strips, separated by narrow belts of grass. The strips allotted to each family are scattered in different parts of the large fields, so that each has a share of the good and the bad soil. Meadowland likewise is shared out until the haymaking. And lastly a communal woodland is inclosed, where the swine find acorns and men cut their fagots. Such, at any rate, is the general picture we can reconstruct from the evidence of later agricultural custom.

The cell of Anglo-Saxon life, then, is the village, a community of between ten and thirty families. It is administered by the *moot*, a small assembly meeting under some tree or on a hillock, and determining the partition of the fields, the number of cattle which may properly be grazed on the common meadows, and the payment of the communal herdsmen. Here too are appointed the village *reeve*, who is at once a mayor and an administrator of the common domain, the *woodreeve*, who looks after the woods, and the plowman who is to turn over the common arable land. Generally the village has its *thane*, the noble war-chieftain with rights to levy dues in kind or labor. In these primitive times social classes are simple and ill-defined. Beneath the noble is the freeman, owing nothing to the noble for his lands except the *trinoda necessitas*, that is, service under arms, the upkeep of roads and bridges. Then come various classes, varying with locality and period, but with the common feature that the men belonging to them pay a rent, in kind or services. And lastly are the slaves who disappear in the tenth and eleventh centuries.

It is probable that when the Anglo-Saxons arrived, each new tribe that landed had its chief or king, whose thanes were bound to him by personal loyalty. Gradually, wider states were formed, by conquest, marriage, or fresh clearings of the land. An embryonic central power contrived to impose that modicum of administrative structure without which it would have been impossible to muster an army or levy a tribute. In the seventh century England still had seven kingdoms. In the eighth, three survived—Northumbria, Mercia, and Wessex. By the ninth, there was only Wessex. The king in each kingdom came always of one sacred family, but from its members the *Witan*, or council of elders, could within certain limits make a choice. This body was not a representative assembly, an anticipation of Parliament or the House of Lords; it was not even an assembly of hereditary peers. The king summoned to it the leading chiefs, and later, after the conversion of the Germans, the archbishops, bishops, and abbots. This council of elders, few in number, was also the supreme judicial body. It could depose a bad king, or refuse—especially in time of war—to intrust the realm to a minor. The monarchy was thus partially elective, though from within a definite family. The kingdom was divided into *shires*, the boundaries of these Anglo-Saxon divisions corresponding nearly everywhere to those of the present-day counties. At first the shire was primarily a judicial unit, with a court of justice to which every village sent its representatives several times a year. Before long the king was represented by a sheriff, whilst the *ealdorman* appeared as a local governor, at the head of military and judicial administrations. The shire was composed of *hundreds* (groups of one hundred families, or groups furnishing one hundred soldiers), and these in turn were made up of *tuns* or townships. In the sixth century these divisions were vague, and became definite only after several centuries of organization.

Justice was in the hands of an assembly, the shire court, and not as under the Romans, of a magistrate representing the central power. We do not know how this body gave its judgments, probably by discussion, followed by the verdict of a majority. The commonest crimes were homicide, robbery under arms, and violent quarrels. Penalties rose with the numbers of offenders. The laws of the Saxon Ina, in the late seventh century, laid it down that men were "thieves" if their group consisted of seven or fewer; from seven to thirty-five constituted a "band"; over thirty-five, an "army." Crimes were also deemed to be graver if they violated the King's Peace, that is to say, if committed in his presence or neighborhood. A man who fought in the king's house could lose all his property, and his life was in the king's hands; fighting in a church involved a fine of one hundred and twenty shillings, and in the house of an *ealdorman*, the same sum, payable to king and *ealdorman* in equal parts. Fighting in the house of a peasant was punished by payment of one hundred and twenty shillings to the king and six to the peasant. Every man had to have another as surety, who should be responsible for him if he could not be brought to justice. A *wergild* also was allotted to every man, this being the sum which must be paid to his family if he should be killed, and which he himself might have to pay to the king as the price of his own life. The *wergild* of a noble was six times that of a freeman, and his oath was of correspondingly higher value. *Wergild* is the sign of a society in which the tribe, the blood-group, is more important than the individual; friendship, hatred, and compensation are thus all collective.

The scales of justice at this stage weighed oath against oath, not proof against proof. Plaintiff and defendant had to bring men prepared to swear in their favor. The worth of the oath was proportionate to the extent of the witness's property. A man accused of robbery in a band was obliged, if he were to clear himself, to produce sworn oaths to the total value of 120 "hides" (the "hide" being the unit of land necessary to produce a family's living). These sums of oaths may seem strange, but we should bear in mind the formidable gravity of perjury to men who believed in the individual miracle, and also the fact that in a small community neighbors are always more or less cognizant of the truth. A notorious evil-liver would not find witnesses. Failing proof by witnesses, recourse was had to trials by ordeal, such as by water (the accused man being bound hand and foot and flung into a pool of water, previously blessed, and regarded as innocent if he sank straight down, because the water consented to accept him), or by red-hot iron (which he had to carry a certain distance, his guilt or innocence being determined by the appearance of the burns after a certain number of days).

These are characteristics of a brutal and crude society, but one with a strong sense of honor and with institutions containing the seeds of a strong local life. "If Hengest and Horsa did not, as has been claimed for them, bring over the seed of the Declaration of Right of 1689, nor that of the Act of 1894 establishing the rural district councils, they nevertheless introduced several valuable customs to England." And if, throughout their national life, the Anglo-Saxons retained a fondness for "committees," groups of men trying to solve the problems of everyday life by public discussion, this was due in part to their early custom of deliberation in the village moots and shire courts, and of dealing on the spot with numerous administrative and judicial questions, without reference to a central authority.

CHAPTER VII

The Conversion of the Anglo-Saxons

THERE was a rude beauty in the religion of the Anglo-Saxons. It derived from the mass of legends recounted in the Edda, the Bible of the north. The gods, Odin, Thor, Freya (who gave their names to the days of the week), lived in Valhalla, the paradise to which the Valkyries, the warrior virgins, carried off men who died fighting in the field. Thus the brave were rewarded, the traitors and liars punished, the violent forgiven. But in transportation across the North Sea this religion had lost much of its strength. Its true habitation was the forests and rivers of Germania, and in Britain Weyland the Smith was merely an exile. Amongst the Saxons the priestly class had been small in number and weak in organization, and seems to have put up no energetic resistance to the introduction of Christianity into England. The sole utterance of a barbarian high priest preserved for us by the Venerable Bede is a skeptical and disheartened admission of defeat. In any case, from the sixth century, the kings of the Angles and Saxons knew that their racial brothers in Gaul and Italy had become converted, and the example encouraged them. In the Church of Rome could be seen the still potent glamour of the Empire; it had inherited the ancient culture and the Mediterranean spirit of organization. These small Anglo-Saxon courts received the Christian missions with tolerance, often with respect.

The conversion of England was the work of two groups of missionaries, one from the Celtic countries, Ireland in particular, and the other from Rome itself. After the departure of the Romans, Wales had remained largely Christian. In Ireland, St. Patrick—the Roman Patricius—had converted the Celtic tribes to the faith, and founded monasteries which later became the refuge of scholars from the Continent in flight from the

[30]

The Pope had given them sage counsel: they must, above all things, interfere as little as possible with the usages of the pagan folk. "A man does not climb to the top of a mountain by leaps and bounds, but gradually, step by step. . . . Firstly, let there be no destruction of the temples of idols; only the idols should be destroyed, and then the temples should be sprinkled with holy water and relics placed within them. . . . If these temples be well built, it is good and profitable that they pass from the cult of demons to the service of the true God; for so long as the nation may see its ancient places of prayer, so long will it be more disposed to repair thither as a matter of custom to worship the true God." This conciliatory method worked, and the Kentish King was converted. The Pope sent to Augustine the *pallium*, symbol of authority, giving him power to set up bishops in England, and advising him to choose Canterbury as his temporary archbishopric, and move to London as soon as London became converted. But nothing endures like the provisional, and Canterbury has ever since been the ecclesiastical capital of England. Bede preserves a series of questions sent to the Pope by Augustine, which shows the concerns of a great Church dignitary in the year 600: how should the bishops behave towards their clergy, and into how many portions should the gifts of the faithful be divided? Or, to what degree of kinship could the faithful intermarry, and was it lawful for a man to marry his wife's mother? Could a pregnant woman be baptized? How long must she wait after confinement before coming to church? How soon after the birth of a child could a woman have carnal relations with her husband? These, he said, were all matters upon which the wild English required knowledge.

The conversion of England to Christianity proceeded by local stages, and we have the record of one of these conversions, that of Edwin, King of Northumbria. It shows how thoughtfully, and often how poetically, these men with their sense of sublimity debated religious matters. The King summoned his chief friends and counselors to hear the Christian missionary, Paulinus, who expounded the new doctrines. Then the King asked them their several opinions, and one of them answered: "The present life of man, O King, seems to me, in comparison of that time which is unknown to us, like to the swift flight of a sparrow through the room wherein you sit at supper in winter, with your commanders and Ministers, and a good fire in the midst, whilst the storms of rain and snow prevail abroad; the sparrow, I say, flying in at one door, and immediately out at another, whilst he is within, is safe from the wintry storm; but after a short space of fair weather he immediately vanishes out of your sight, into the dark winter from which he had emerged. So this life of man appears for a short space, but of what went before, or what is to follow, we are utterly ignorant. If, therefore, this new doctrine contains something more certain, it seems justly to deserve to be followed." To which the pagan high priest replied: "I have long since been sensible that there was nothing in that which we worshiped. . . . For which reason I advise, O King, that we instantly abjure and set fire to those temples and altars which we have consecrated without reaping any benefit from them." Conversion of the kings entailed that of their subjects, so that the influence of the missionaries increased by rapid strides.

The headway made by the Church of Rome in England was to cause a clash with the old British Church of the unconquered west. Augustine, having received papal authority over all the bishops of Britain, summoned the Celtic bishops. They came, but in high dudgeon, and at once showed resentment because Augustine, to emphasize his status, did not rise to receive them. He required of them three concessions: to celebrate Easter at the same time as other Christians, to use the Roman rite of baptism, and to preach the Gospels to the Anglo-Saxon pagans, which the Celts had always refused to do, because, in their hatred of invaders who had massacred their forbears, they had no wish to save their barbarian souls. The Britons yielded on none of these points and broke with Rome, declaring that they would recognize only their own primate. Strain developed between their priests and their Roman brethren. They did not give the kiss of peace to Catholic priests and refused to break bread with them. The Celtic monks, forgetting their grievances against the Anglo-Saxons in their hatred of Rome, set about converting the pagans; they succeeded with the humbler classes, while the Roman Church influenced chiefly women, sovereigns, and men of rank. When both Churches were preaching the faith in the same court, the divergent doctrines caused complications. In one and the same family Easter might have to be twice celebrated in one year. A king might have completed his Lenten observance and be celebrating his Easter, whilst his queen was observing Palm Sunday and still fasting.

Finally King Oswy of Northumbria, a convert of the Scots, became influenced by the reasoning of his son Alfred, who had been taught by a Roman monk. To clear up the situation he convoked a synod at the abbey of Whitby, where both parties should expound their teachings. Oswy opened the debate with sound sense, saying that servants of the same God should obey the same laws, that there was certainly no true Christian tradition, and that it was the duty of every man to declare whence he held his doctrine. To which the Scots mission replied that they had received their Easter from St. John the Evangelist and St. Columba, the Romans declaring that theirs was derived from St. Peter and St. Paul and was so observed in all lands—in Italy, Africa, Asia, Egypt, and Greece—everywhere, indeed, except amongst these obstinate men in their two islands at the back of beyond, who made bold to defy the rest of Christendom. There followed a long and learned discussion, which the Catholic Wilfrid concluded by arguing that even if their Columba had been a saintly man, he could not be set above the very prince of the apostles, the one to whom Our Lord had said: "Thou art Peter, and upon this rock I will build my church; and the gates of hell shall not prevail against it." When Wilfrid had thus spoken, the King asked the Irish bishop, Colman, whether these words had in truth been spoken by Our Lord. Loyally he admitted that they had. The King asked whether he could prove that any such powers had been given to Columba. "No," said Colman. "Are you both agreed," went on Oswy, "in holding that the keys of the Kingdom of Heaven were intrusted to St. Peter?" "We are," they answered. Whereupon the King declared that as Peter was the guardian of the gates of heaven, he himself would obey the decrees of Peter, lest he might appear before these gates and find none willing to open them to him, the keeper of the keys being his adversary. This was approved by all present, and they resolved thenceforth to give obedience to the Pope.

CHAPTER VIII

Christian and Germanic Forces

FROM the eighth century the whole of England formed part of the Roman Church. Her kings looked for support to the Church, not only as believers, but also because of their realization that from this great body, inheritor of the Imperial traditions, they could derive the hierarchy, the organic form, and the experience which they lacked. Bishops and archbishops were for many years to be the kings' natural choice as Ministers. And the Church likewise upheld the monarchies, being in need of a temporal authority to impose her rules.

The Papacy, too, was strengthened by the foundation in England and Germany of new and obedient Churches. The Eastern Churches were disputing the supremacy of the see of Rome; the Church in France was occasionally too independent, but the English bishops spontaneously requested the constant intervention of the Holy Father, who dispatched to England virtual pro-consuls of the faith, men who stood in relation to ecclesiastical Rome very much as the great organizers of the provinces had stood to Rome as the center of the Empire. The universality of the Church is nobly displayed in the spectacle of a Greek from Asia Minor, Bishop Theodore of Tarsus, and an African, the abbot Hadrian, introducing to England a Latin and Greek library, and setting up in Northumbria monasteries which rivaled in their learning those of Ireland. It was a strange paradox that the Mediterranean culture came to be preserved for the Gauls by Anglo-Saxon monks. At the time when the Saracens were thrusting into the heart of France, and when the classic age seemed to be ending in Europe, the Venerable Bede, a monk in this almost barbarian land, was writing in Latin his delightful ecclesiastical history of the English nation. Bede himself was the master of Egbert, who was in turn the teacher of Alcuin; and Alcuin it was who, summoned by Charlemagne, checked the intellectual decadence of France.

Thus England has her place in the history of the Latin and Christian civilization. But from the nature of the Anglo-Saxons, from their earlier traditions and tastes, that civilization bred certain individual traits. The seventh and eighth centuries in England were an age of saints and heroes, bold and turbulent spirits capable at once of great sacrifices and great crimes. In time to come, the blend of the morality of the Nordic warrior with that of Christianity was to shape the heroes of the chivalrous romances. But in dark and primitive ages the balance between the two forces was unsteady. At one time these Saxon kings would be turning monks or starting on pilgrimage to Rome; Sebbi of Essex entered a monastery in 694, as did Ethelred of Mercia ten years later; the latter's successor, Conrad, ended his days in Rome, as also did Offa of Essex. At another time, sovereigns were being murdered, kingdoms laid waste, towns sacked, and townsmen massacred. The Church had to combat the taste for the epic bellicose poems sung by the gleemen to the harp after banquets in the houses of nobles, or recited in villages by wandering minstrels. The Anglo-Saxon priests themselves took only too much delight in these pagan poems. In 797 Alcuin had to write to the Bishop of Lindisfarne: "When the priests dine together, they should read nothing but the Word of God. It is fitting on such occasions to listen to a reader and not a harpist, to the discourses of the Fathers, not to heathen poems." But the love of this Nordic poetry was so deep then that one Saxon bishop went forth from Mass in disguise to chant the deeds of a sea-king.

Rich though Anglo-Saxon poetry was, the only complete work extant is *Beowulf*, an epic on Nordic themes but refashioned by an English monk between the eighth and tenth centuries, and adapted to Christian conceptions. It has been described as an Iliad with a Hercules as its Achilles. The theme is that of Siegfried—the slaying of a monster by a hero. Beowulf, a prince of Sweden, crosses the seas and comes to the castle of the King of the Danes, where he learns that it is haunted nightly by a monster, Grendel, which devours the lords whom it finds. Beowulf slays Grendel, whose mother then seeks vengeance; the hero pursues her into the hideous regions where she dwells, and so rids the world of their race. Returning to Sweden, he himself becomes king, and in the end dies from a wound from the poisoned tooth of one last dragon he seeks to fight. He dies nobly: "For fifty years have I ruled this folk. No folk's king among the neighbor lands durst bring their swords against me or force me into dread of them. I have accomplished the allotted span in my land, safeguarded my portion, devised no cunning onslaughts, nor sworn many oaths faithlessly. Mortally stricken, I can rejoice now in these things. Wherefore the ruler of mankind can lay no blame on me for slaying of my blood-kin, when my last breath is drawn. . . . Hasten now that I may behold the riches of old, the treasure of gold . . . that after winning wealth of jewels I may more gladly leave the life and the land which long has been my ward."

In reading *Beowulf*, or other fragments of Anglo-Saxon poetry, one is first struck by the melancholy tone. The landscapes are desolate, regions of rock and marsh. Monsters inhabit "the chill currents and the terror of waters." "A somber imagination collaborated with the sadness of a northern nature to paint these powerful pictures." They are the creations of a people living in fierce climes. Whenever the poet speaks of the sea, he excels himself. *Beowulf* contains a description of the departure of a band of warriors for a sea-roving expedition, with the foam-covered prows of their bird-like ships, the gleaming cliffs, the giant headlands, which is all worthy of the greatest epic poets. But nowhere does the Anglo-Saxon poet reach the serenity of Homer. In the Iliad the pyres of the slain burn on the plain; in *Beowulf* the corpses are fought over by ravens and eagles. In these unsunned minds a certain joy in horrors seems to mingle with the nobility of feeling. But the society described has more refinement than that of the Germania painted by Tacitus. It has nothing in common with the Anglo-Saxon "democracy" imagined by the English historians of the nineteenth century. In the world of Beowulf, king and warriors are in the foreground; the halls of princes are rich with thrones, tapestries, ornaments of gold. The king is all-powerful, so long as he keeps the support of his companions. Towards these he is generous, showering lands and gifts upon them. Every man in these poems has a lord to whom he owes fealty, and who in return must treat him generously. Whosoever offends his lord must away to foreign lands. Traitors and felons are utterly scorned. The wives of chiefs are respected, and are always present at banquets. But love is grave and joyless: "this ancient poetry has no love-song; love here is neither a diversion nor a ravishment of the senses, but a pledge and a devotion."

As poetry it has been justly compared to the Homeric. Both, indeed, present features of what may be called the heroic ages. In completely primitive societies, the bonds of tribe or family were the strongest. It was a man's family who had to avenge him or be responsible for his wrongdoing. In heroic societies the family tie begins to slacken. The individual breaks free from the tribe. Freed from that terror of nature which overwhelms primitive man, he gives free course to his craving for power. Individual passions overcome political intelligence. It is a time of battles fought by men singly, of wars waged for honor. And yet, as every society must needs keep a hold on individuals, loyalty and friendship forge a new link. The hero is immoderate, but a bold man and true, which makes a character of sufficient merit for the Christian moralist to find in it elements of real nobility. Before long the generosity of the hero will be exercised for the benefit of the Church. A pious king will give lands to bishops and monasteries. It remains, obviously, for violence to be disciplined, or turned to aid just causes. Christian humility and modesty, mingled with the heroic passions, were to engender between the tenth and the thirteenth centuries a type unknown to the ancients, still sinning often enough through cruelty, but striving after purity—the knight of chivalry. And Beowulf, fighting against the monsters from hell, is already almost a Christian knight. His end is the end of Lancelot. In the admirable figure of King Arthur we shall see the finest possible product of the blending of Roman civilization, barbarian honor, and Christian morality.

CHAPTER IX

The Danish Invasions and Their Results

IT WAS in 787 that the Anglo-Saxon Chronicle recorded the first arrival in England of three shiploads of Norsemen, coming from the "land of robbers." The nearest village reeve, not knowing who these men might be, rode out to meet them, as was his duty, and was killed. Six years of silence follow this murder, and then, from the year 793, the short yearly entries of the Chronicle nearly always contain mention of some incursion of the "pagans." Sometimes they have sacked a monastery and massacred the monks, sometimes the pagan armies have spread desolation across Northumbria. Occasionally the chronicler notes with gladness that some of the pagan ships have been shattered by stormy seas, that the crews were drowned, and that survivors who struggled ashore were put to death. Gradually the strength of these enemy fleets increased. In 851, for the first time, the pagans wintered on the Isle of Thanet, and in that year, too, three hundred of their vessels sailed up the Thames estuary, their crews taking Canterbury and London by storm. In the years that follow, the "pagans" are given their real name—the Danes; and the Chronicle speaks only of the movements of "the army," meaning the army of these Norsemen, which at times mustered 10,000 men.

The tribes then inhabiting Sweden, Norway, and Denmark, all of one race, were indeed pagans: they had barely been touched by the old Roman Empire, and not at all by that of Christian Rome. But they were not barbarians. Their painted ships, the carved figures of their prows, the literary quality of their sagas, and the complexity of their laws all show that they had been able to create a civilization characteristic of themselves. These vikings obeyed the chiefs of their bands and were doughty fighters, but did not like fighting for fighting's sake. They gladly used guile instead of force when they could. In their warring and pillaging alike they were traders and, if they found themselves confronted on the strand by too large a crowd of inhabitants, were quite ready to barter their whale-oil or dried fish for honey or slaves.

Why did these Northern peoples, who for so many centuries had seemed to be ignorant of England, suddenly begin these invasions at the same time as they were attacking Neustria, the western kingdom of the Franks? It has been suggested that Charlemagne's pressure on the Saxons drove the latter back towards Denmark, and thus, by showing the Norsemen the danger in which they stood from the Christian powers, provided the driving force of their thrusts. It is perhaps equally simple to suppose that chance, a craving for adventure, and the desire of bold seamen to push ever farther, all conspired. It was customary amongst them, as later amongst the Knights of Malta, for a young man to make some expedition to prove his courage. Their population was growing fast. Younger sons and bastards had to seek their fortune in new lands. But their fine ships, long and narrow, carrying a single red sail seldom hoisted, with the alternating black and yellow shields of the warriors set along the sides, and the figure of a sea monster on the prow, were hardly suited to the open sea. Like all the warships of antiquity, they were rowing-boats, and the range of such a vessel is perforce limited. If a voyage requires more than half a day at sea, a double crew of oarsmen is needed. Each crew weighs as much as the other; weapons are heavy; and this leaves a scant margin for stores. The ships themselves must be light, and so cannot withstand the heavy seas of an ocean voyage. It took the vikings several centuries of experience, and doubtless innumerable shipwrecks, to learn the best coastwise routes and the favorable seasons. Gradually they learned to move quickly from isle to isle, catching the fine weather, and to build larger boats; and they began to be seen throughout the world. The Swedes headed for Russia and Asia; Norwegians discovered the way to Ireland round the north of Scotland, and even landed in Greenland and touched America in search of furs; the Danes naturally chose the inner passage, nearer their own country, which led to the coasts of Scotland, Northumbria, and Neustria.

There may be matter for surprise in the swift success of these expeditions, originally composed of small bands and attacking kingdoms which ought to have been able to put up an easy defense. But it should be remembered that the vikings held the mastery of the sea. Neither Saxons nor Franks had tried to build a fleet. The ruler of the sea is immediately ruler of the islands and can use them as naval bases. The earliest Danish attacks were made on those rich monasteries which the first monks, in their desire for solitude, had placed on islands like Iona and Lindisfarne. The faithful had made gifts of jewels and gold to the monks. The vikings sacked these treasuries, slew the monks, and occupied the islands. However near these might be to the mainland, the invaders were there impregnable. And in this way Thanet became their base on the English coast, as Noirmoutier did off the French coast and the Isle of Man in the Irish Sea. It must also be borne in mind that mastery of the sea enabled them to choose their point of attack. If they found the enemy too strong at one point, it was easy to reëmbark and seek a better chance, especially as the means of communication among their victims were primitive and joint understanding rare. How could a Saxon king oppose them? He assembled the *fyrd*—a militia of freemen. But they were a throng of peasants armed with boar-spears—sometimes even, when the reserves were called up, with pitchforks—slow to muster, difficult to feed, and unable to stay long under arms because of the claims of their farming. They were unworthy opponents for the northern warriors, who were well armed, wore protective mail and metal helmets, and wielded the battle-ax to rare advantage. The only Englishmen capable of standing up to them were the king's companions (the *comitati*, or *gesiths*), but these were few in number, and in any case the Danes were constantly improving their tactics. They soon learned, on landing, to seize the local horses, equip a mounted body of soldiery, and then hurriedly build a small fort. The Saxon rustics and woodmen, who had never built fortified towns and had lost their seafaring tradition, and were disunited to boot, let the invader conquer nearly the whole country. Ireland, then in the throes of anarchy, was the first to be subjugated; then Northumbria; then Mercia. Soon Wessex itself was partly lost, and it looked as if the whole of England would become a province of the Norsemen's Empire.

The Danish invasions resulted directly in hastening the formation in Saxon England of a class of professional soldiers. There might have been three solutions to the problem of the country's defense: (1) the *fyrd*, or mass levy of freemen, to which the kings long resorted; in spite of the inadequacy already indicated; (2) mercenaries, paid troops, such as were used by the later Roman emperors, and again by Kings Canute and Harold; but the Saxon princes had no revenues sufficient to maintain such an army; and (3) a permanent army of professional warriors, paid by grants of land in lieu of money payments. The last was the solution gradually adopted throughout Europe between the end of the Roman Empire and the tenth century, because, in default of strong States, no other method was possible. It was formerly taught that feudalism was imported into England by the Normans during the eleventh century; but one historian has amusingly remarked that it was introduced by Sir Henry Spelman, a seventeenth-century scholar who was the first to systematize a vague body of custom. In point of fact, feudalism was originally not a deliberately selected system, but the outcome of manifold natural changes. At the time when the Saxon tribes reached England, peasant and fighting-man were one and the same. The freeman was free because he could fight. When warlike equipment, after the Danish forays, became too burdensome for the average peasant, soldiering could not be anything but the profession of one class.

How came the free husbandman to admit the superiority of that class? Because he could not dispense with it. Attachment to a superior has great advantages in times of trouble: not only is he a well-armed captain, but he defends the title-deeds of his men. So long as the central State is strong—as the Roman Empire had been and the Tudor dynasty would be—individuals count upon that State and admit their duties towards it. When the State weakens, the individual seeks a protector nearer at hand and more effective, and it is to him that he owes military or pecuniary obligations. A personal bond replaces the abstract. In the welter of the small English kingdoms, endlessly warring with one another and being laid waste by piratical raids, the hapless peasant, the churl or *ceorl*, could maintain his land or preserve his life only by the aid of a well-armed soldier, and agreed to recompense him in kind or services or money for the protection he could give. Later, this working practice was to engender a doctrine, "no land without a lord." But in origin feudalism was not a doctrine, but rather, as it has been described, a disintegration of the right of property together with a dismemberment of the rights of the State. Guizot wrote that it was a mixture of property and suzerainty. More accurately, it is the joint passing of property and suzerainty, for a time, to the man who is alone capable of defending the first and exercising the second. Like all human institutions, it was born of necessity, and it disappeared when a renewal of the central government's strength made it useless.

A further effect of the Danish invasions was to end the rivalries between the Anglo-Saxon kingdoms. Pressure from without always imposes a sense of unity on peoples of the same culture, but rent by old grievances. Some of the Anglo-Saxon kings had already styled themselves kings of the whole of England: these were known by the special name of *bretwaldas*. Egbert of Wessex (802-839)—himself the descendant of the semi-mythical conqueror Cedric—the earliest "sovereign" from whom descends the line of the present King of England, was the eighth *bretwalda*. These Saxon kings were not so powerful as their Norman successors proved to be. But they prepared the ground for the latter. In contrast with Continental developments, they were already turning their nobles into an aristocracy of service rather than of birth. The thanes held their lands from the king because, as warriors, administrators, or prelates, they were his servants. With the king they were nothing, but without them the king could do nothing. He took important decisions only with them, in his Council. The Saxon king was not absolute, any more than the Saxon kingship was absolutely hereditary. And finally, after the conversion to Christianity, the king was the sacred chief, protected and counseled by the Church. He was bound, more than any man, to respect the Church's commands. The image of the just sovereign, duly taking counsel with his wise men for the common weal, was to be firmly engraved upon the English mind, even before the Conquest, by great Saxon sovereigns like Alfred; and throughout the course of England's history, whenever it threatened to be dimmed or effaced, that image was opportunely revived, by an Edward I, a Henry VII, or a Victoria.

CHAPTER X

_____

From Alfred to Canute

ALFRED is a sovereign of legend, whose legend is true. This wise and simple man was at once soldier, man of letters, sailor, and lawgiver, and he saved Christian England. He had all the virtues of devout kings, without their weakness or their indifference to mundane matters. His adventure partakes of the fairy-tale and the romances of chivalry. Like many a romantic hero, he was the youngest son of a king, Æthelwulf, and in these days of invasion he was brought up with the din of battle in his ears and the memory of three of his brothers slain. Sickly and sensitive, he had the energy of the weak who strive after strength. An excellent horseman and great hunter, he also knew from childhood the desire for learning. "But, alas! what he most longed for, training in the liberal arts, was not forthcoming according to his desire, for in that day good scholars were non-existent in the realm of Wessex." In old age he told how the grief of his life had been that when he had youth and leisure for learning he could find no teachers, and when at last he had gathered learned men round him, he had been so busied with wars and the cares of governance, and with infirmities, that he could not read his fill. In childhood he had made a pilgrimage to Rome, where the Pope "hallowed him as king," and then, back in England, won distinction alongside of his brothers in the struggle against the Danish "army." When the last of his family had been slain, Alfred was chosen as king by the Witan, in preference to his nephews, who were too young to rule in time of war.

The first year of his reign saw him in battle against the Danes, but having a mere handful of men, he was worsted. He purchased peace from the invaders by payment of a tribute, as the Saxon and Frankish kings had so often done. But success in blackmail was bound to encourage the aggressor in his devices. The Danes occupied the north and the east of the country, and with this conquest behind them a fresh horde, under the pagan king Guthrum, again invaded Wessex. Panic reigned at first. Alfred had to flee almost alone into the Isle of Athelney, where he and his companions built a small fort in the marshes. Near this spot, during the seventeenth century, a beautiful jewel of enamel, gold, and crystal, was unearthed, bearing the inscription *"Ælfred mec Heht gewyrcan"* ("Alfred Fashioned Me"). For a whole winter the king remained hidden in the swamps, and the Danes believed that they were masters of Wessex. Towards Easter he left his hiding-place and, at the place known as "Egbert's Stone," secretly convoked the *fyrd* of Somerset, Wiltshire, and Hampshire. The Saxon peasants were overjoyed to find their king alive, and marched at once with him against the Danes, who were pursued to their strongholds, beseiged, and forced by starvation to surrender. Alfred spared their lives, but insisted that the "army" should evacuate Wessex, and that Guthrum and the leading Danish chiefs should be baptized. Three weeks later Guthrum and twenty-nine other chiefs received baptism, Alfred himself being their sponsor. A pact was then signed, fixing a frontier between Wessex and the Danelaw. The Danes thereafter remained masters of the east and the north, and Alfred was able to reign in peace over the territories south of that line.

Alfred the Great affords an example of the immense part which can be played by one man in a people's history. Only his tenacity prevented the whole country from accepting the pagan domination, which would have meant for England, not her end, but a totally different destiny. Alfred's mind was at once original and simple; he transformed the land and sea forces as well as justice and education. Increasing the effectives of the army, he summoned to the rank of thane all freemen possessing five hides of land, and those merchants of the ports who had made at least three voyages on their own account, requiring from this lesser nobility services of knighthood. The Anglo-Saxon armies had always been handicapped by their short term of service. Alfred created classes which could be called upon to relieve each other in turn. He ordered the restoration of the fortifications of the old Roman towns, and had the very modern idea of setting up two echelons for defense, mobile and territorial. Knights living near a burgh, or fortified town, were to proceed thither in time of war, whilst those living in the open country formed the mobile force. He created a fleet, the vessels of which, though few, were of his own design and more trustworthy than the ships of the vikings. He composed a code which incorporated the various rules of life then accepted by his subjects, from the Mosaic Commandments to the laws of the Anglo-Saxon kings. He sought to change none, he said, because he could not be sure that change would please his posterity. He therefore maintained the old *wergild* system, or the redemption of crime, except in cases of treason. The traitor to king or lord would henceforth find neither pardon nor chance of redemption. A man could not even defend his kindred against his lord. And this was the triumph of the new feudal conceptions over the old tribal ideas.

Alfred was hard put to it to revive the pursuit of learning in a country where it had been ruined by wars and woes. He said himself that, when he came to rule his kingdom, it probably contained no man south of the Thames who could translate his prayers into English. The King set up great schools where the sons of nobles or rich freemen might learn Latin, English, horsemanship, and falconry. He likewise commanded the preparation of an Anglo-Saxon Chronicle, which should record the chief happenings of each year, and is so valuable to us today. It is possible that he himself dictated the history of his own time. He wrote much, but as a translator—and a very scrupulous one—rather than an author, seeking first the sense word by word, or, as he said, thought by thought, and then transposing it into good English. Into a subject which interested him he would interpolate passages of his own composition. His aim in these translations was to bring such texts as he considered useful within the reach of a people who had lost their Latin. He translated Bede's *Ecclesiastical History*, the *Universal History* of Orosius, the *Pastoral Care* of Gregory the Great (of which he provided fifty copies for the bishops and monasteries of the realm), and above all, the *Consolation of Philosophy* of Boethius, which this philosopher-king must indeed have appreciated.

It is both strange and satisfying to contemplate this sovereign burdened with cares, ruling his sorely menaced country, and writing so simply of how he "turned into English the book that is called *Pastoralis*." Artists as well as scholars he encouraged. Speaking of the famous Weyland, or Wieland, the Smith, he calls him "a wise man" and adds: "Wise I call him, because a good workman can never lose his skill, and that is a property whereof he can no more be deprived than the sun can change its place." Then the legends of his childhood return to his memory, and with an anticipation of Villon he wonders "where now are the bones of Wieland?" Finally, according to his biographer, he was anxious that the hours of devotions should be strictly observed in the monasteries, and conceived the idea of placing four candles in a horn lantern, carefully weighed so as to burn six hours each, so that their successive lighting might show almost exactly the correct time. This learned and devout soldier was also a man of invention.

After the death of this great monarch, the prestige of the Anglo-Saxon sovereigns was further enhanced by his successors, trained in his school. They first recovered Mercia, then Northumbria, from the Danes. King Athelstan (924-941) could truthfully style himself "king of all the Britains." The Danes settled in East Anglia intermingled with the Anglo-Saxon inhabitants, and began to adopt their language. But peace in England depended on two conditions—a strong king and the cessation of invasions. The piratical forays had apparently slowed down because the Norsemen, in their own lands, were engaged in internal struggles to create the kingdoms of Norway and Denmark. When this period of conflict ended, voyages of adventure were resumed, all the more actively as many malcontents wished to escape from the new-made monarchies. The Anglo-Saxon Chronicle, through the second half of the tenth century, shows the same baleful process at work as in the earlier onslaughts: first a few raiders, with seven or eight vessels, then whole fleets, then an army, then "the army." This new invasion coincided with the reign of an inept king —Ethelred. Instead of defending himself, he reverted to the cowardly method of buying off "the army" for a heavy tribute, to pay which he had to levy a special tax, the Danegeld, a land tax of three or four shillings on each hide of land. The Danes' appetites, of course, were whetted; they became more and more exigent; and after the death of Ethelred's son, Edmund Ironside, who had tried to fight but was murdered, the Witan could find no solution but that of offering the crown to the leader of "the army," Canute, the twenty-three-year-old brother of the King of Denmark. "The whole country," says one chronicler, "chose Canute, and submitted of its own accord to the man whom it had lately resisted."

The choice turned out well. Canute had been a stern, even a cruel, foe, but he was intelligent and moderate in his ideas. A foreigner wishing to become an English king, he began by marrying the queen dowager,

Emma of Normandy, a woman older than himself but who linked him to his new kingdom. He made it clear at once that he would draw no lines between English and Danes. What was more, he put to death those of the English nobles who had betrayed his adversary, Edmund Ironside. How could a man who had deceived his master become a loyal servant? He disbanded his great army and kept only twoscore ships, the crews of which, some 3,200 men, formed his personal guard. These were the "housecarls," picked troops who, contrary to feudal usage, received payment in money and not in land. To pay them Canute continued to levy the Danegeld, and bequeathed to the Conqueror this land tax, which the people themselves accepted. In 1018, at Oxford, Canute summoned a great assembly at which Danes and English pledged respect to the old Anglo-Saxon laws. An astonishing figure, this princely pirate who transformed himself when hardly more than twenty into a conservative and impartial king. A convert to Christianity, he showed such piety that he declined to wear his crown, and had it suspended above the high altar at Winchester as a sign that God alone is King.

King of England in 1016, and King of Denmark by the death of his brother two years later, Canute conquered Norway in 1030 and, at the cost of surrendering the English rule over much country north of the Tweed, he received the homage of the Scottish king at about the same time. Once again England found her lot involved with the Nordic peoples. If Canute's achievement had endured, and if William of Normandy had not come to confirm the Roman Conquest, how would the history of Europe have shaped itself? But the Anglo-Scandinavian empire lacked the breath of life. Made up of stranger nations, and divided by dangerous seas, it existed only through one man. Canute died at forty, and his creation perished with him. After some struggles between his sons, the Witan again showed its power of choice by reverting to the Saxon dynasty and choosing as king the second son of Ethelred, Edward. These alternations buttressed the authority of the Witans, and royalty, a mere elective magistracy, lost much of its prestige. Certain earls were by now ruling several shires, and, if they had not been destroyed by the Norman Conquest, would have become real local sovereigns and dangerous rivals to the King himself.

CHAPTER XI

The Norman Conquest

THE Rollo who obtained the Duchy of Normandy from Charles the Simple in 911, by the verbal agreement of Saint-Clair-sur-Epte, sprang from the same race as the conquerors of the Danelaw. But after a century these two stems of a single breed had diverged so widely that Danes in England were calling Danes in France "Frenchmen." The English Danes had encountered a European civilization which was still feebly rooted, and they left their mark upon it; but the Norman Danes, confronted by Rome in the form of France, had imbibed the Latin spirit with surprising speed. From the end of the tenth century the Normans at Rouen spoke nothing but French, and the heir to the duchy had to be sent to Bayeux in order to learn his ancestral tongue. The blend of the old Roman order with youthful Norman energy had given excellent results. "O France!" wrote one chronicler, "thou layest stricken and low upon the ground. . . . But behold, from Denmark came forth a new race. . . . Compact was made, peace between her and thee. This race will lift up thy name and dominion to the skies."

The "Duke of Normandy's peace," that respect for law which he had soon contrived to impose on his territories, roused the admiration of the chroniclers. They recount how Duke Rollo hung some gold rings in an oak tree in the forest of Roumare (*Rollinis mare*) which remained there for three years. The old pirate chiefs—now barons, or *jarls*—naturally chafed under this strictness, and continued to wage their private feuds with singular violence and cruelty. But the dukes had their way. Normandy had no great vassals. None of its lords became strong enough to withstand the Duke, who was directly represented in each district by a viscount; and a viscount was not a mere bailiff of royal domains, but a real governor. The Duke of Normandy levied money taxes and had a genuine financial administration known as the Exchequer. Of all his contemporary sovereigns, he approximated most closely to the head of a modern State.

The Normans adopted the ceremonial and hierarchy of Continental chivalry much sooner than did the English. As in England, feudalism had developed in Europe through the need for local defense, but by the eleventh century it was regulated with more precision. Under the Duke of Normandy stood the barons, who in turn had power over the knights, a knight being the owner of land the tenure of which involved military service. At his baron's summons, the knight had to present himself armed and mounted, and to remain in the field for forty days. This was a short time, but suited to short campaigns. For a lengthy enterprise like the conquest of England special agreements had to be made. The baron himself had to answer his duke's call to arms, bringing with him the knights dependent on him. In Normandy as elsewhere, feudal ceremonies included a symbolic act of homage: the vassal knelt with his weapons laid aside, placed his joined hands between those of his lord, and declared himself his man for a certain fief. The lord raised him and kissed him on the mouth, and then the vassal took the oath of fealty on the Gospel. To release oneself, an act of "de-fiance" (*diffidatio*) was required, but permitted only in defined circumstances.

In these chivalrous ceremonials the Church was closely involved. After the conversion of the Normans their dukes had won especial favor from the Pope by their zeal in restoring the monasteries and churches destroyed by their fathers. They were born architects, with a sense of the planned unity of buildings which reflected their feeling for unity in governance, and were among the first to build great cathedrals. They summoned men of learning from afar. Lanfranc, for instance, a scholar of Padua, came to teach at Avranches and there became famous. Smitten with shame at his ignorance of religious matters, he wished to become a monk in the poorest of monastic houses, and entered one built on the banks of the Risle by Herlouin, at a place still called Bec-Hellouin. There he founded a school whose fame attracted Bretons, Flemings, and Germans to its courses of study. And from that lovely valley he was to set out to become Abbot of Caen, and then Archbishop of Canterbury.

But how came it that a Duke of Normandy, in the eleventh century, conceived the idea of making himself King of England? After the death of Canute's ineffectual progeny, the Witan had proclaimed as king the natural heir of the Saxon sovereigns, Edward, named the Confessor by reason of his great piety, of whom his biographer naïvely remarks that he never spoke during divine service unless he had a question to propound. Edward the Confessor seems to have been a gentle, virtuous man, but childish and lacking in will. Despite a vow of chastity he took in marriage the daughter of the most powerful of his *ealdormen*, Godwin, formerly a local lord but who had become predominant in Wessex. A marriage of this kind suited Godwin's ambitions very well, as he hoped to play the part of the mayor of the palace in his son-in-law's house. Who could tell? Had not the Capets once supplanted their royal masters? Edward's upbringing in Normandy had made him more Norman than English; he spoke French; he was surrounded by Norman counselors; he chose a Norman, Robert of Jumièges, as Archbishop of Canterbury. He was visited by his cousin from Rouen, William the Bastard (later to be known as the Conqueror), who always maintained that Edward, during this visit, promised him the succession to the throne. Edward could not, in fact, offer a crown which was dependent, not on himself, but on the choice of the Witan; but it is possible that he made the offer to William, as he also did, apparently, to Harold, son of Godwin, and to Sweyn, King of Denmark. The kindly busybody Edward has been compared to a rich uncle who promises his fortune to several nephews. He had vowed to make a pilgrimage to Rome, but received a dispensation from the Holy Father on condition that he founded an abbey. He accordingly built one at Westminster, and moved his own residence near to this, from its old position in the City of London. This act of piety of the Confessor's had great and unpredictable consequences, for the removal of the royal palace from the City fostered an independent spirit among the citizens of London which, in time, exercised a great influence on the nation's history. Edward the Confessor died in the summer of 1066, leaving memories cherished by his people. For a long time it was "the laws of Edward" which every new sovereign had to swear to observe, although Edward himself had made no new ones. But he was the last Saxon king before the Conquest, and thus became to the subject English a symbol of an independent England.

William the Bastard, Duke of Normandy, was the natural son of Duke

Robert and the daughter of a tanner in Falaise, Arletta by name. Acknowledged by his father, he succeeded him. At first the barons had caused much vexation to this sovereign who was both a bastard and a minor, and William's apprenticeship was hard. But he emerged from the ordeal not only master of his duchy, but having increased it by the conquest of Maine. He had made Normandy tranquil and prosperous. A man of dogged will, he knew how to hide his feelings and bide his time in days of failure. When his resolve to marry Matilda, daughter of Count Baldwin of Flanders, was countered by the Pope's ban on a union within forbidden degrees of kinship, William was patient, and then forced the marriage. He stormed against Lanfranc, the prior of Bec, for venturing to condemn this defiance of a pontifical decree, but then made use of the same Lanfranc to negotiate a pardon from the Pope, which in the end he obtained on condition that he build those two noble churches of Caen, the Abbaye-aux-Hommes and the Abbaye-aux-Dames. During the parleys this highly skillful prior of Bec had become intimate with the most powerful man in Rome, the monk Hildebrand, who was later to become Pope Gregory VII. Two ambitions were coming into harmony: William aspired to the crown of England, and in this great project the Pope could help him; Hildebrand hoped to make the Pope the suzerain and judge of all the princes of Christendom, and this candidate for a throne offered pledges to Rome which a lawful king would have declined to give.

What claims had William to the English crown? Genealogically, none. The Duke of Normandy's only relative in common with Edward the Confessor had been a greataunt, and he himself was a bastard. Besides, the English crown was elective, and at the disposal only of the Witan. Edward's promise was a poor agreement, as Edward had promised to various claimants something which he had no right to pledge. But Lanfranc and William, who always subtly lent a moral covering to their desires, had engineered a diplomatic machination against the only possible rival, Harold, son of Godwin and brother-in-law of Edward. The hapless Harold had been made prisoner by the Count of Ponthieu after being shipwrecked on his coasts, but was freed by William and conveyed to Rouen. There the Duke let him understand that he had full liberty, on the sole condition that he should do homage to him and become in the feudal sense "his" man. In this ceremony Harold had to give an oath, the exact details of which are unknown. It may have been to marry William's daughter, or to support William's claim to the English throne. Whatever it was, he swore something which afterwards was held against him. The chronicler even avers that the Normans had hidden two sacred reliquaries underneath the table when the oath was taken, and our knowledge of William makes the story quite probable.

Was an oath given under duress valid? Once free, Harold did not regard himself as bound; and again the choice of a king of England was not in his hands. When Edward died the Witan showed no hesitation between a bold and well-beloved lord, Harold, and a mere child, Egbert's only descendant, Edgar the Atheling. Within twenty-four hours Harold, the elected king, was crowned in the new Abbey of Westminster. There had been no question at all of William. But immediately a well-staged propagandist campaign was launched in Europe, and especially at Rome, at the instigation of William and Lanfranc. The Duke of Normandy called upon Christendom to take cognizance of the felonious act whereof he was the victim. Harold, he maintained, was his vassal, was violating both feudal law and a solemn oath, and had filched a crown promised to one who was, however remotely, of the blood royal and no mere usurper like the son of Godwin. William's bad faith is beyond doubt; he, of all men, knew how the oath had been obtained, and what his claims were really worth. But the facts, as presented with skill and judged by feudal standards, seemed to press strongly against Harold. That age had its principles of feudal law, as ours has those of international law; those who had least respect for them accused others of violating them. In any case, Rome supported the Duke of Normandy because he had undertaken to adopt the ideas of Hildebrand and to reform the Church in England. The Pope declared in William's favor and, in token of his blessing on the enterprise, sent him a consecrated banner and a ring containing a hair of St. Peter. For so difficult a campaign the ordinary forty days' service of the Norman knights would not have sufficed. Harold's *house-carls* formed an excellent and dangerous body of troops. When William first laid his plan before the assembled barons at Lillebonne, it was coldly received. Everything looked hazardous. But William had the knack of transforming an act of international brigandage into a real crusade. And a profitable one: to all his Norman vassals he promised money and lands in England. His brother Odo, Bishop of Bayeux, more soldier than prelate, recruited fighting-men, and William sent invita-

tions throughout Europe. Adventurous barons came from Anjou, from
Brittany and Flanders, even from Apulia and Aragon. It was a slow
mobilization, but that mattered little, as the fleet had to be built before
embarkation could be started. The Bayeux Tapestry shows how forests
were felled for the building of the seven hundred and fifty vessels then
necessary to transport 12,000 or 15,000 men, of whom 5,000 or 6,000 were
horsemen. Early in September, 1066, the fleet was ready. For a fortnight
longer William was delayed by contrary winds; but, as often happens in
human history, this unwelcome delay brought him an easy victory.
For in the meantime there had arrived on the Northumbrian coast the
King of Norway with three hundred galleys. At the bidding of the
traitorous Tostig, Harold's brother, he too had arrived to claim the
crown of England. Harold, who was awaiting William off the Isle of
Wight, had to hasten north with his *house-carls*. He inflicted total defeat
and destruction on the Norwegians, but on the morrow of his victory
learned that William had landed unopposed on the shore of Pevensey, on
September 28th. The wind had changed.

By forced marches Harold came south. Things were starting ill for
him. His guard had been broken by the clash with the Norwegians. The
north-country thanes had done their fighting and showed little ardor to
follow him. The bishops were perturbed by the papal protection granted
to William. The country contained a "Norman party," formed of all the
Frenchmen introduced by Edward the Confessor. The only battle of the
war was fought near Hastings, where two types of army were confronted. Harold's men formed the traditional mounted infantry of their
country, riding when on the move and dismounting to fight. The Normans, on the other hand, charged on horseback, supported by archers.
The first charges of the Norman horsemen failed to seize the ridge held
by the English, but William, a good tactician, used the classic feint of
armies and beat a retreat. Harold's footmen left their position in pursuit
of him, and when the Normans saw the English troops fully committed
to this, their cavalry swung around and closed in on the flanks of the
English foot. In the massacre Harold himself fell. The superiority of
cavalry, already well established in Europe, was confirmed by this battle.

William's character is further clarified by the subsequent military and
diplomatic moves. Instead of attacking London directly, he encircled
the town, surrounding it with a belt of ravaged country, and awaited the

inevitable surrender. Instead of proclaiming himself King of England, he waited for the crown to be offered to him, and even then made a show of hesitation. He tried characteristically to "put his possible adversaries in the wrong," and wished to appear in all men's eyes as the lawful sovereign. At last, on Christmas Day, 1066, he was crowned at Westminster. At the gates of the City, he had already laid the first stones of the fortress on the left bank of the Thames which was to become the Tower of London.

What did these Normans find in England? A peasant people of pioneering Saxons and Danes, living in village communities, cut off from each other by woods and heaths, and grouped around the wooden church and their lord's hall. The Celts of Wales and Scotland did not form part of the kingdom conquered by William. The Saxons, like the Romans, had abandoned the attempt to conquer the Celtic tribes of the north and west. The Danes in the east had thrown in their lot with the Saxons, but with fresher memories than the latter of their piratical past, they remained more independent. For a strong king, this realm of England, much smaller than France, would be comparatively easy to rule. It had long possessed institutions of its own—a system of taxation in the *geld*, and a mass levy in the *fyrd*. These instruments were to be used by the Norman kings, but from these kings came most of the institutions which made England distinctive in its originality. The Saxon kings did not summon a parliament; they did not try offenders by royal judges with the assistance of a jury; they did not found universities properly so called. The only Saxon institutions which survived were those regulating local and rural life. The fine old Saxon words designating the tools of husbandry, the beasts of the field, or the fruits of tilling, have to this day retained their bold and simple forms. Village assemblies became transformed into parish bodies, wherein Englishmen were to continue their apprenticeship in the art of governance by committees and compromise. The boundaries of parishes and counties were to remain almost unaltered. But although the village cells which composed the frame of England were in existence in the year 1066, it was to be the Norman and Angevin kings, during the next three centuries, who would give that frame its form and organs.

Book II
THE FRENCH KINGS

propriety. He first deprived traitors of their la   l, traitors being those
who had fought for Harold—a legal fiction which just held water because
he, William, declared himself to be the lawful overeign. He then took
advantage of the numerous revolts, and annexed new territories for the
Crown. With appalling severity he crushed a rising in the north, burning
villages far and near, and then raised the superb castle of Durham to
dominate that ravaged land, flanking it with a cathedral worthy of his
abbeys at Caen. In the end, the last of the Saxon rebels, Hereward the
Wake, was overcome, and he organized the kingdom. For himself he
kept 1,422 of the manors which had become "lawfully" vacant, and this
insured him unrivaled military power and wealth. After William, the
two lords most generously provided for were his two half-brothers, Robert
of Mortain, and Odo, Bishop of Bayeux, who received 795 and 439
manors, respectively. Other domains were much smaller. The unit of
land was the "knight's fee," which sent one knight to the king in time
of war. William created numerous domains counted as from one to five
knights' fees, the holders of which were to form as it were a feudal "plebs,"
which the great lords could not draw into league against the King. The
greater domains themselves were not in single hands, but made up of manors scattered throughout the country. Thus, from the first, there was no suzerainty comparable to that exercised in France by a Count of Anjou
or a Duke of Brittany. After conquest and partition, the country was held
by about five thousand Norman knights, who were at once landed proprietors and an army of occupation. In principle the loyal English had
the same rights as these Frenchmen; in practice, all important posts were
held by Normans. The indispensable Lanfranc, summoned from Caen,
became Archbishop of Canterbury. The day of the Ceolfrids and Wil-
frids and Athelstans was over; their places were taken by Goeffreys and
Roberts and Simons. The Conqueror's companions formed the new nobility of England.

As in India or Morocco today, two languages were simultaneously
used in one country. The ruling classes, the Court, the lords and judges
spoke French; the higher clergy spoke French and Latin; and to this
day, after nine centuries, some of the old French formulas of the Norman
kings are used in England—*"Le roi s'avisera . . ."*—*"Le roi remercie ses
bons sujets, accepte leur bénévolence et ainsi le veult . . ."* The local representatives of the King and the lords had to speak both languages, as

the common folk still spoke English. For almost three centuries English was to remain a language with neither literature nor grammar, only spoken and spoken by the populace. It developed quickly, however, because only the upper classes are conservative in speech. English was a Germanic tongue, with complex inflections. But the common people simplify, and English, once freed from the tutelage of gentility, soon acquired its wonderful suppleness. Words uttered by untutored men or foreigners preserve only their accented syllable: whence comes the great number of single-syllabled words which gives English poetry its peculiarly rich quality. Meanwhile, in contact with their masters, the Saxon and Danish peasants were learning a few words of French, which became English almost without change. There were ecclesiastical terms like "prior," "chapel," "mass," "charity," "grace"; military, such as "tower," "standard," "castle," "peace" and words like "court," "crown," "council," "prison," "justice," complete a truthful sketch of the administrative relation between the two classes. A curious fate befell the French word *preux*, applied to a valiant knight, its English version, *proud,* coming to mean haughty or disdainful—the master's point of view, and the servant's.

The results of men's actions are unpredictable. Just as the clouding-over of the English language produced its peculiar beauty, so the Conquest became the starting-point of English freedom. The King of France, "poor in his domains" and ringed around by domineering vassals, had painfully to conquer his own kingdom, and having done so, to impose a stern discipline upon it, the King of England, who had distributed the lands himself, safeguarded his interests, and from the first prevented the growth of any large domains which might rival his own. Born of a conquest, English royalty was vigorous from the start. The indisputable strength of the central power made it comparatively tolerant. In France the King's bureaucracy had to assert its authority by force, not always successfully or universally, and the unity of law was only finally established by the Revolution. In England the Crown was secure, and this enabled it to organize the Saxon heritage of local liberties, and to oblige the barons to respect them.

The Norman King had a court, the *Concilium* or *Curia Regis*, which corresponded roughly to the Saxon Witan. Three times a year, as Alfred or Edward the Confessor had done in days gone by, William "wore his crown" at Westminster, Winchester, and Gloucester, and there held "deep converse with his wise men." But whereas the Saxon Witan in the days of the powerful *Ealdormen* had been masters of the king, the Norman Council generally confined itself to listening and approval. Barons, bishops, and abbots attended, not as a national duty, but as a feudal duty to their suzerain. These convocations were irregular: sometimes the Council consisted of a hundred and fifty prelates and magnates, at others the King was content to consult on some question with only those of his counselors who happened to be present when it arose. This lesser Council also varied in composition. But the presence of the sovereign sufficed to make any decision valid. In his absence—and being also Duke of Normandy he had frequently to cross the Channel—a Justiciar administered the realm, guided by a few trusted men like Lanfranc and Odo of Bayeux.

The Norman Conquest was not followed by a ruthless breach with the past. Such a break would not have been possible. How could five thousand men, however well armed in comparison, have dictated to a whole people and forced them to abandon the habits they had acquired during century after century? On the contrary, William the Conqueror who regarded himself as the heir of the Saxon kings, was glad to make appeal to their laws and judgments. He preserved all such of the Saxon institutions as served his plans.

The *fyrd* was to become a useful weapon against the barons when the peasantry came to regard themselves as allies of the Crown—an alliance which was soon reached. In the Saxon sheriffs the Norman King recognized his viscounts, and found an instrument of government. He therefore appointed a sheriff for each shire, intrusting him with the collection of taxes, the administration of the court of justice in the shire (which now was called the county), and in general with the representation of the central power. William did not suppress the manorial courts, but he controlled them. The office of sheriff was not hereditary and this functionary was himself supervised occasionally by envoys of the King, comparable to the *missi dominici* of Charlemagne. At a time when the lords on the Continent had both greater and lesser rights of justice in their own hands, their counterparts in England saw their courts passing more and more under the control of a strict sovereign. The sheriff punished abuses of power and noted signs of popular discontent. The whole policy of the Norman monarchs was one of checking the barons by securing the support of the freemen, until the people and barons in unison came in their turn to curb the power of the Crown. The English nobility, it has been pointed out, is a unique example of an aristocracy obliged to join hands with the populace to play a part in the State. That alliance was a factor in the growth of parliamentary institutions.

It would be misleading, not to say crude, if we conceived the image of a royal power constantly concerned with checkmating rebellious lords. Hostility could not have been a normal relation between William and his companions, as he needed them and they needed him. We should not, therefore, picture feudal England in such simple terms as those of the king using the support of the people to curb the barons. Actually, mediæval society was comparatively stable; the barons collaborated with the King; and it was from among them that he chose his agents, thus introducing the aristocracy with the great administrative and local parts which it has since filled, even to our own day. Some of the baronage may have been turbulent, but most of them were loyal, and helped the King to suppress rebellion. A period of general revolt, as at the time of Magna Carta, meant that the king had overstepped his rights and that the barons were acting in self-defense, sometimes with the support of the knights and burgesses. But these troublous times were brief, and although they fill the pages of history with their hubbub, they must not blind us to the long, tranquil years during which king, nobles, and common people behaved as members of a united body, and during which a civilization was being unobtrusively built up.

For a king to be able to impose his will on a warlike nobility impatient of all trammels, two conditions are essential: the sovereign must have armed force, and must possess an assured revenue. In his opposition to the barons William could count on the main body of the knights, on his own vassals, and before long on the *fyrd*. At Salisbury, in 1086, he took oaths of homage directly from the vassals of his vassals, so that a troth pledged to the king outweighed any other loyalty. As regards revenue, the Norman King was well provided. He had, to start with, the revenue of his private domain—1,422 manors, with farms as well. William's lands brought him eleven thousand pounds annually (some say seventeen thousand), twice as much as Edward the Confessor had enjoyed, and to this were added the feudal revenues ("reliefs") due from vassals; "aids" in the case of crusade, ransom, marriage of the suzerain's

THE NORMAN EMPIRE
(ENGLAND AND NORMANDY)

POSSESSIONS OF WILLIAM I......
DEPENDENT ON   „   ......

SCOTLAND

IRELAND

WALES

ENGLAND

London

ROMAN EMPIRE

NORMANDY   Paris

BRITTANY   MAINE

F R A N C E

Scale of Miles
0   50   100

daughter, entry into chivalry of an eldest son; "wardship" of the property of minors; the Danegeld, a legacy of the Saxon kings; payments made by burgesses of towns and by Jews; and finally, fines. The exchequer accounts show that under William's successors these fines were numerous, and sometimes curious. We read how Walter de Caucy paid fifteen pounds for leave to marry when and whom he might choose; how Wiverone of Ipswich paid four pounds and one silver mark to marry only the man she might choose; how William de Mandeville gave the king twenty thousand marks to be able to marry Isabel, Countess of Gloucester; how the wife of Hugo de Neville gave the king two hundred pounds for leave to lie with her husband (who must have been a prisoner of the king). Behind these accounts one can detect a robust, roguish humor in that Norman Court. Lastly, the king sold liberties; under Stephen, London gave a hundred silver marks to choose her sheriffs; the Bishop of Salisbury gave a palfrey to have a market in his city; some fishermen paid for the right to salt their catch; and the profits of justice increased with the prestige of the royal Courts.

The Conqueror had previously pledged his word to the Papacy for the reform of the Church in England. With the help of Lanfranc, even greater as statesman than as churchman, he kept his word. The ignorant and licentious clergy had lost the respect of the faithful; priests wore lay clothes and drank like lords; bishops used unlawful means of procuring advancement. Orders came from Rome, where Hildebrand had become Pope Gregory VII in 1073, that Lanfranc should compel the celibacy of the clergy, that the investiture of bishops should remain in Papal hands, and that the King of England, who owed the throne to him, should do him homage. Lanfranc and William moved cautiously. It would have been dangerous to impose strict celibacy on the Saxon priests; allowances would have to be made for the customs and moral standards of this newly acquired country. The Italo-Norman Lanfranc was already writing "we English" and "our island." He disallowed the celebration of further marriages of priests, forbade bishops and canons to have wives, but authorized parish priests already married to remain so. He admitted that only Rome could depose bishops, but maintained the elective principle, and that of investiture by the Crown. On the other hand, he submitted his own dispute with the Archbishop of York to Rome, and obtained a confirmation of Canterbury's primacy. In the end, the King, writing a "firm and respectful" letter, declined to regard himself as the Pope's vassal. The whole negotiation was marked by great deference on the part of the King, and by courtesy and goodwill on that of the Pope; but one can feel the pressure of inevitable quarrels between the Papacy and the civil power.

Two of Lanfranc's reforms were to have important repercussions in days to come. Firstly, he initiated the custom of holding "convocations," or ecclesiastical assemblies, at the same time as the great Council. Many of the prelates sat both in the feudal body, as temporal lords, and in the clerical synod, too. Both assemblies were presided over by the King, but the fact that they were distinct was later to prevent the growth in the English Parliament of a direct clerical representation like the clerical Estate in France. Secondly, Lanfranc and William wished to have rights over the Church in England similar to those of the Duke over the Church in Normandy: namely, that the King's consent was necessary for the recognition in England of any Pope; that no negotiation should be carried on with Rome unknown to himself; that the decisions of English ecclesiastical councils could be valid only with his approval; and that barons and royal officials could not be judged by ecclesiastical courts without the King's consent. The conflict between Church and State was already taking shape.

William's prompt affirmation of his conqueror's authority over nobles and ecclesiastics laid the foundations of a great monarchy. But he was not an absolute sovereign. His coronation oath bound him to maintain the Anglo-Saxon laws and usages; he had to respect the feudal rights granted to his companions; he feared and revered the Church. William the Conqueror could not conceive the idea of absolute monarchy as it was later envisaged by Charles I or Louis XIV. The Middle Ages did not even imagine a State in the modern sense of the word; a country's equilibrium, as they saw it, was not insured by a central keystone, but by a network of coherent and mutually strengthening local rights. The Norman King was very strong; his will was circumscribed by no written Constitution; but if he violated his oath of suzerainty his vassals would feel justified in renouncing their feudal oath. Insurrection remained a feudal right, and a day was to come when the barons exercised it. The gradual emergence of the rules forming the Constitution came from the need for replacing insurrection by some simpler and safer means of calling an unjust sovereign to order.

CHAPTER II

Results of the Conquest—Feudalism and Economic Life

FROM the days of the Saxon kings there had been peasants and lords, cottages and manors; but the Saxon temper was willing to let custom be added to custom and form a complex economic network. The Normans, with their clear constructive minds, introduced a more rigid structure, based on the axiom that there could be no land without its lord. The apex of the economic, as of the political, hierarchy was the king. He was the landlord of the whole realm, and for the Norman spirit to be completely satisfied by this logical edifice, it was taken for granted that the king himself derived his kingdom from God. The king, however, kept only part of his lands, granting the remainder in fief to great landlords and to single knights, against military service and specified dues. Supposing, for instance, that the king granted one hundred manors to a baron in return for the promise of fifty knights in time of war, this baron would retain forty of these manors to keep up his own mode of life and that of his dependents, and would give sixty in fief to lesser vassals in return for the service of sixty knights. (The tenant-in-chief would insure his personal standing and avoid fines for failure in his commitments by taking care always to have rather more soldiers at his disposal than he promised to the king.) In principle, and ruling out serious crimes, all these fiefs were hereditary, in order of primogeniture, which would avoid breaking up of estates. The lord and the knight were themselves unable to practice, as a modern landowner might, agriculture on a large scale, because they would have had no market for their produce; they reserved only a home farm, and granted the remainder to peasants in return for dues in kind and in labor. In Saxon times the peasant hierarchy had been as complex as that of the nobility, since the acquisition of rights created different forms of status. Distinctions were then drawn between freemen, *socmen* (hardly distinguishable from freemen), *cottarii* and *bordarii*. The Norman lords were almost blind to these subtleties, and took small account of them. It is not hard to imagine how difficult it would be for a Saxon socman to explain his privileged status to an impatient conqueror ignorant of his language. And it is noticeable that during the two decades after the Conquest, except in the Daneland of the northeast, the freemen almost totally vanish. All the peasants become either *villeins* (who till a *virgate*, or about thirty acres), or *cotters* (who have only four or five acres). Times were bad for the survival of the small free, and semi-free, cultivators. In the years of the Norman land settlement many of them disappeared. In Cambridgeshire there were nine hundred socmen in the time of Edward the Confessor: in 1086 there were two hundred.

We know exactly the composition of the different classes in the nation twenty years after the Conquest, as in 1085 William the Conqueror "wore his crown at Gloucester and held deep converse with his wise men." There he showed that the Danegeld of the previous year had yielded disappointing returns. It was a lucrative imposition (in 991 it had produced ten thousand pounds, in 1002 twenty-four thousand, in 1018, under Canute, seventy-two thousand), but for effective collection it was essential to have an accurate account of all the lands of the realm. At this Council of Gloucester it was accordingly resolved that certain barons, appointed as special commissioners, should traverse the whole country. Their instructions were that the king's barons should require by oath from the sheriff of each shire, from all barons, and from their Frenchmen, and from the priest of each hundred, and from six villeins of each village, a statement of the name of the castle and of its occupant now and in the reign of King Edward; how many hides of land and how many plows on the domain; how many freemen, slaves, socmen, how much woodland and meadow; how many mills and fishponds. All of which was to be set down as it was in the time of King Edward, as it was when King William granted the domain, and as it was at the time of the survey in 1086. It was also to be declared how much more now than formerly could be extracted from the domain. The commissioners completed their task, and the summary of their survey formed what is called Domesday Book.

Statistical surveys of this kind had certainly been made in the days of the Saxon kings, as they would have been necessary for the raising of a tax like the Danegeld, but these Norman reports are meticulous in their detail: At Limpsfield in Surrey "there are on the home farm five plough teams: there are also 25 villeins and 6 cotters with 14 teams amongst them. There is a mill worth 2s a year and one fishery, a church and four acres of meadow, wood for 150 pigs and two stone quarries, each worth 2s a year, and two nests of hawks in the wood and ten slaves. In King Edward's time the estate was worth £20 a year, afterwards £15, now £24." Not even the most isolated man escapes the Conqueror's inquisition: "Here [in Herefordshire] in the midst of the woodlands, and outside the district of any hundred, lives a solitary farmer. He owns a plough team of eight oxen and has his own plough. Two serfs help him to cultivate the hundred or so acres that he has reclaimed. He pays no taxes and is the vassal of no man." The horror of the Saxon chronicler for this Norman precision is touching, and slightly comical: "So skilfully," he says, "was this statement drawn up by his commissioners that there was not one yard of land, no (and it is shameful to say that the King was not ashamed to do this), not even one ox nor one cow, nor one pig, that were not inscribed on his roll." Adding up the figures set out in the Domesday Book, we find nearly 9,300 tenants-in-chief and vassals, representing the nobility and the ecclesiastical dignitaries; 35,000 freemen and socmen, nearly all in the north and east; 108,000 villeins; 89,000 cotters; 25,000 slaves (who become serfs during the next century): in all, nearly 300,000 families, which enables us to estimate the whole population at a million and a half, perhaps two million, with women and children.

The economic unit of feudalism was the manor, just as its political unit was the knight's holding of land, sending a single horseman to the king's army. The size of the manor varied, but in many cases it corresponded to a present-day village. Frequently manors were separated by intervening forests or heaths, connected to their neighbors only by tracks which winter made impassable. In the center was the hall, later the castle, belonging to the lord of the manor and surrounded by his farm or private land. When the lord held several manors, he went from one to another to make use on the spot of the dues paid to him in kind. In his absence he was represented by a seneschal, or bailiff. The communal fields and meadows preserved the same aspect as in the times of the Saxon masters. The villeins were obliged to have all their corn ground by the lord's mill; but many of them surreptitiously ground their own, although they were fined if detected. The peasants were headed by the reeve of their own election, who, caught between the bailiff and the villagers, led a difficult life. Many local disputes were judged by the manor court, which was held every three weeks in the hall, or under an oak tree traditionally so used, and was presided over by the lord of the manor or his representative. In principle only trifling offenses were there dealt with: "William Jordan in mercy for bad ploughing on the lord's land. Pledge, Arthur. Fine, 6d. . . . Ragenhilda of Bec gives 2s, for having married without licence. Pledge, William of Primer. . . . The parson of the Church is in mercy for his cow caught in the lord's meadow. Pledges, Thomas Ymer and William Coke. . . . From the whole township of Little Ogbourne, except seven, for not coming to wash the lord's sheep, 6s 8d. . . . Twelve jurors say that Hugh Cross has right in the bank and hedge about which there was a dispute between him and William White." Only to a few manors had the king granted the right of trying more serious crimes. Theoretically a manor was supposed to be self-sufficing, having its own cordwainer, its wheelwright, its weavers. The weavers spun the wool. Nothing was bought from outside but salt, iron or steel tools, and millstones. These last were rarities, coming sometimes from near Paris, and the bailiff had to go to the port where they were landed to negotiate their purchase and arrange for their conveyance. To pay for these imports the manor exported wool and hides. All other produce was locally consumed, except where a market was near at hand.

The position of the villeins might seem to our day to be none too happy. The villein was bound to the soil, and could not go away if he were discontented. He was sold with the property. Even an abbot did not scruple to buy and sell men for twenty shillings apiece. We find a rich widow making a gift of villeins: "Know all present and future that I, Dame Aundrina de Driby, formerly wife to Robert de Driby, in my lawful power and free widowhood, have given, granted, quit-claimed, and by this my present deed confirmed, for myself and my heirs, to my well-beloved and faithful Henry Cole of Baston and his heirs, for their service, Agnes daughter to Jordan Blanet of Baston, and Simon Calf dwelling at Stamford, with all their chattels and live-stock, and suits and issue, and all claim of serfdom and villeinage which I or my heirs have or might have had therein." The villein could give his daughters in marriage only with the lord's consent, and had to pay for that. If he died the lord could claim a death duty of the best head of cattle, or the most handsome object, left by the dead man; and after the lord, the parish priest had the right to claim his share of the heritage. Thus, the receipts of an abbey will show cows, goats, and pigs received in payment of these claims on death. The socman took a share only in unusual work, such as carting corn to market for the lord, but the villein worked on the manorfarm for two or three days a week, and also gave other days for sheep dipping or shearing, gathering acorns, or making hay. He paid a small tribute in kind: merely a dozen eggs at Easter, a slab of honey, a few chickens, a load of wood. Furthermore, the lord could levy an annual "tallage," of varying value, from his serfs. This body of dues seems heavy enough, but was perhaps no more of a burden than the more modern type of farming lease which hands over half of the produce to the landowner. In lieu of half of his produce, the lord required about half of the peasant's time. Reeves and bailiffs quarreled hotly about these exactions of labor and after long bargaining they came to understandings, sometimes for better, sometimes for worse. Summer was bound to weigh heavily on the villein, as it still does on farm workers, "but winter was of necessity quiet, and the Church kept watch over Sundays and over the countless saints' days." Finally, every lord was bound to respect manorial usages, the traditional rights of the village which the peasants themselves undertook to keep alive. At a later date all these rights and obligations were inscribed in the manorial records. About the middle of the thirteenth century it became customary to hand to tenants on their request a copy of the pages in that register touching upon their lands and rights. Those in possession of such copies were termed "copyholders," in contrast to the "freeholders," whose property was absolute and unencumbered.

An outstanding grievance of the native English against the Conqueror or his Normans was the creation of royal forests. As Duke of Normandy, William had had vast forests where he could hunt the stag and boar. As King of England he wished to provide for his favorite pastime, and not far from Winchester, his capital, he planted the New Forest, thus destroying (according to the chroniclers) sixty villages, many fertile fields and churches, and ruining thousands of inhabitants. The figures seem exaggerated, but those royal forests were certainly a lasting grievance. In the twelfth century they covered a third of the area of the kingdom, and were protected by ruthless laws. In William's day anyone killing a hind or a stag had his eyes put out. To kill boars or hares meant mutilation. At a later date, the slaying of a deer in the royal forest was punished by hanging. In this respect the Conqueror's private passions outweighed his political judgment.

At first the Conquest hardly changed the lot of the small Saxon towns. Those which resisted were dismantled; here and there the King's men razed houses to make room for a Norman keep; but, as amends, the Conqueror's peace allowed merchants to grow rich. The liberties of London had been prudently confirmed: "William, King, greets William, Bishop, and Godfrey, Portreeve, and all the burghers within London, French and English, friendly. And I give you to know I will that you be all those laws worthy that you were in the days of King Edward. And I will that every child be his father's heir after his father's day. And I will not suffer that any man offer you any wrong. God keep you."

New craftsmen came over from Normandy in the train of the armies, among them Jewish traders. The position of these last could only be precarious in a Christian community, whose transactions were all based on religious oaths. As their Sabbath did not coincide with the Christians' Sunday, they could not easily undertake farm work, or even shopkeeping; and as ordinary livelihoods were thus barred to them, they sought refuge in moneylending, a trade forbidden to Catholics by the Church. The Gospels, literally interpreted, did not admit that money, which is sterile, could produce interest. In the twelfth century a Norman baron in need of money to go campaigning had to apply to the Jews, who exacted enormous usurious charges. Doubly hated as enemies of Christ and as professional creditors, these hapless creatures, living in special quarters, the Jewries, were the natural victims of any wave of popular anger. Their sole protector was the king, to whom they belonged, body and goods, like serfs. The royal city of Winchester was the only one in which a Jew could be a citizen, and was styled the English Jerusalem. The title deeds of Jews were kept in a special room of the Palace of Westminster, and their debts, like the king's, were privileged. One Jew, Aaron of Lincoln, became a real banker in the time of Henry II, of such importance that for the liquidation of his affairs after his death a special department of the Exchequer had to be set up, the *Scaccarium Aaronis*. In return

[73]

for this protection, the King called for money from the Jews when he required it. In normal years they provided about £3,000 to the Exchequer, one seventh of Henry II's total revenue: "it was in the Hebrew coffers that the Norman kings found strength to hold their baronage at bay."

The Saxon and Danish peasantry were doubtless as angry as the chronicler when the Norman kings began with such humiliating precision to reckon up men's wealth, levy strict exactions, and establish their barons all up and down the country. But at least this new order provided security. With a strong king, under the feudal system, the common man might not be free to move as he listed, or sell his goods or change his occupation; but his place in the social framework was uncontested. His land could not be sold without himself, and he was not a victim of economic crisis or sale at a loss. Nobody could lawfully deprive him of the means of producing food for himself and his wife. His obligations to his lord might be burdens, but they were at least clearly defined, and the lord had to respect custom. The villein was not so well protected against judicial error as the ordinary man today, but the Norman kings were at pains to provide safeguards for him. It would be too simple, of course, to suppose that men then were contented with their lot; humanity has always been divided, more or less equally, into optimists and pessimists. But most Englishmen in the twelfth century hardly conceived of a social structure other than what they knew. Although they did not hesitate to criticize the mode of life of the priesthood, they were sincerely religious, and regarded a king duly anointed and crowned as a sacred figure. The personal bond between them and their lord seemed perfectly natural, and with enduring memories of past dangers, of piratical raiders and sacked villages, the existence of a military class seemed to them necessary. It was during the thirteenth century that the feudal system, in a society where that system had made life more secure, began to appear burdensome and useless. And before much longer, like all systematic regimes, it was to die of its own success.

Chapter III

The Conqueror's Son

For twenty-one years William reigned over England with effective firmness, "wearing his crown" thrice a year, at Christmas and Easter and Whitsun, combating the overweening barons, hunting the stag, and crossing occasionally to Normandy to guard against the encroachments of the King of France. But during one of these campaigns, when he had just regained Mantes, this great man was mortally injured. His horse stumbled, and a blow from the pommel of his saddle bruised him internally, from which he died. His end had pathos. He had loved nobody but his wife Matilda, who was already dead, and possibly, in his gruff way, his Minister, Lanfranc, who was not with him. Of his three sons, whom he had not associated with his rule, the second was his favorite; and to him, William Rufus (so called because of his red complexion), he left the English crown. To Robert, the eldest, whom he held in scant esteem, he reluctantly bequeathed Normandy, declaring that with such a sovereign the duchy would fare ill. Henry, the youngest, received only 5,000 silver marks. And thus the Conqueror died, being buried in the church of St. Stephen at Caen, in only a small concourse. The swollen body burst its coffin, and so, remarks the chronicler, "he who living had been dight with gold and precious stones was now mere rottenness." His three sons had already hurried off to secure their shares of the heritage. Rufus embarked for England with a letter from his father to Lanfranc, who agreed to crown him at Westminster. This time there was no election by the Council, and the barons simply accepted their king from the archbishop. That was a sign of the growing power of the Church.

William Rufus was no fool, but he was a boor. This fat, clumsy, brutal youth, stammering his sarcasms, cared only for soldiers. At a time of universal piety he flaunted his dislike of priests, and took a crude delight in blasphemy. When certain monks complained that they could not pay an excessive tax, he pointed to their sacred relics and asked if they had not those gold and silver boxes full of dead men's bones. His delight was in the Christmas and Easter banquets that he gave his barons, to heighten the splendor of which he employed the London craftsmen for two years in building Westminster Hall, then regarded as the most magnificent building in the country and destined, in the reconstructed form in which Richard II left it, to become the seat of the Courts of Justice. The Court of William Rufus was "a Mecca of adventurers," and to maintain the hundreds of mercenary knights from overseas he levied taxes contrary to usage, in spite of his coronation oath to respect the laws of the land. "But who can keep to all he promises?" he said, cynically. He successfully fought down several baronial risings, aimed at supplanting him by his brother, Robert of Normandy. The weak and paltry Robert, always crippled by debt, had not fathered this project, but in him the barons found a sovereign more malleable than William Rufus. It is noteworthy that the king had to call upon the English *fyrd* in order to bring his Norman companions to their senses. He promised the Saxon peasantry remission of taxes, and with simple credulity they fought to support him. When he felt himself on firm ground in England, he aimed at regaining Normandy from his brother. The Conquest had left a difficult position. The vassal lords of the King of England were likewise those of the Duke of Normandy, in respect of their demesnes on the Continent, and this twofold suzerainty gave rise to confusion. Rufus failed to master Normandy by force, but when his brother Robert left for the First Crusade, Rufus lent him 10,000 marks, and received the duchy as a pledge. Rufus himself never went on a Crusade, nor did his subjects show any more enthusiasm; England never beheld the spectacle which was seen in the French countryside, of serfs leaving for Jerusalem, dragging their wives and children in carts. A few devout, or adventurous, Norman lords took the Cross; but the common people went on tilling their fields.

Conflict became inevitable between the Roman Church, as reorganized by Gregory VII and the lay monarchies. The Pope's ambition, to reform the Church so as to fit it for reforming the world, was a noble one. The clergy, he felt, had lost their prestige through excessive contact with secular society. If a churchman were dependent on lords or kings, he could not combat sin or impiety with the same uncompromising courage as if his allegiance were only to his spiritual heads. This was the underlying significance of the so-called Conflict of Investitures which disturbed England and Europe. A bishop had two aspects: he was a Prince of the Church, and as such depended only on the Pope and God; but he was also a temporal lord, the owner of great fiefs, and so had to do homage to the king, his suzerain. Many bishops felt humiliated by this temporal subordination, believing that they held their lands in the name of God and the poor. But if they had refused homage after their election, the king, for his part, would have refused the episcopal lands.

A Papal surrender in this matter of the Investitures would have endangered the Church, by placing it in the hands of creatures of the lay power, and possibly of simoniacs and heretics. If the king yielded, he would be encouraging within his realm a rival power which he could not control. The danger was all the greater because this power seemed to be developing hostility towards the monarchy. Many theologians were then arguing that any lay government was the intervention of men ignorant of God and led by the devil. "The authority of laws . . ." wrote John of Salisbury, "is naught unless it keeps the image of the divine law, and the desire of a prince is of no worth if it conforms not to the discipline of the Church." Such claims made it look as if the Pope aspired to universal mastery. Kings were bound to resist it, but it was dangerous for them to come into conflict with the Vicar of God, revered by their own subjects. The Germanic Emperor who made the attempt had had to bow low at Canossa. The Conflict of Investitures may not have been the first clash of Church with State, as the State did not yet exist; but it was a clash between Church and Monarchy, both claiming to be creations of the same God.

During his lifetime, Lanfranc's prestige maintained the balance. After his death in 1089, the king tried not to replace him. He chose as his private counselor one Ranulf Flambard, a low-born and ill-bred man, and did not nominate an Archbishop of Canterbury. He thus retained the archiepiscopal revenues, a device which he found so profitable that when he died eleven great abbeys and ten bishoprics were vacant. But as regards the see of Canterbury the strongest pressure was put upon William by the Church and by the barons, to make him appoint Anselm, prior of Bec-Hellouin. Like Lanfranc, Anselm was an Italian, but much less interested in temporal affairs than his predecessor; he was a saintly man, to whom earthly life appeared as a swift, empty dream, meaningless except as preparatory to eternal life. Only a grave illness made the King consent in a moment of fear to invest Anselm, himself openly reluctant. The archbishop had literally to be dragged to the King's bedside, and there forcibly invested with ring and crozier while bishops intoned the *Te Deum*. But Anselm had the firmness as well as the modesty of a saint, and was resolved to have the dignity of the Church respected in his own person. Between King and archbishop began a struggle, now hidden, now open. Rufus did not disguise his hatred of this archbishop who looked him in the eyes and blamed him for his vices. Anselm challenged the King by recognizing Pope Urban, against whom the Germanic Emperor had tried to set up an anti-Pope, and after this defiance had to flee the country. Once again the see of Canterbury was left vacant and the King drew its revenues, but he had uneasy dreams, and for all his sarcasms was concerned about his salvation. He had no time to insure it, for in the year 1100, when hunting in the New Forest, he was killed by an arrow piercing his heart. Whether this was accident or crime was never known.

In these stern times an heir could afford no sacrifice to propriety. Prince Henry, the Conqueror's third son, left his brother's body where it lay and hurried off to Winchester to secure the keys of the royal treasury. He arrived just in time, as almost immediately there appeared the treasurer, William of Breteuil, who claimed it in the name of Robert, Duke of Normandy, the lawful heir. But at headlong speed Henry arranged his own proclamation as king by a small group of barons, and was crowned by the Bishop of London in default of an archbishop: all of which was irregular, but accepted. Robert was far away, a foreigner, and ill-famed. Henry was reported to be energetic and instructed, especially in matters of law. Furthermore, he won popularity immediately on his accession by granting a charter, one of those electoral undertakings which in those days, except for insurrection, were the sole method of curbing the royal prerogative. By his charter Henry I pledged himself to respect "the laws of Edward the Confessor, to abolish the evil customs introduced by his brother Rufus, never to leave ecclesiastical benefices vacant, and to raise no more irregular feudal taxation." These first actions of his roused confidence; he cast Ranulf Flambard into prison, recalled Anselm, and, to crown all, married a wife of

WILLIAM THE CONQUEROR

From *Heads of the Kings of England*,
a book of engravings by George Vertue.

IOHANNES REX ANGL.
DNS HIB.

JOHN I

From *Heads of the Kings of England*,
a book of engravings by George Vertue.

royal blood—Edith-Matilda, daughter of Malcolm III of Scotland and descendant of Ethelred. This "native" marriage quickened the irony of the Norman nobility, who nicknamed the king and his queen "Godric" and "Godgifu," parodying the outlandish Saxon names; but it delighted the Anglo-Saxon people, who gladly hailed the king's eldest son as "the Atheling," the ancestral style of the firstborn of the Saxon kings. After this marriage, which augured well for the fusion of the two races, Henry's position in England was so strengthened that revolt on the part of Robert's partisans was useless. In 1106 Henry conquered Normandy by a victory at Tinchebrai, an English victory gained on Norman soil—a revenge, so to speak, for Hastings. He made a peace of compromise with the Papacy, after long discussion of the Investitures, renouncing his claim to hand personally to the bishop the ring and crozier, but winning his counter-claim, that the duly invested bishop should do homage to the sovereign for his temporal fiefs. Henry had prudently resisted the suggestions of the Archbishop of York, who advised resistance. "What need had English-men to receive the will of God from the Pope of Rome?" urged this prelate. "Had they not the guidance of Scripture?" The Protestant spirit was already stirring in this English archbishop.

After his victory over the insurgent barons, Henry I enjoyed a tranquil reign, and he took advantage of the calm to organize his realm. He was conspicuous as a jurist, and thanks to him, the royal courts of justice were developed at the expense of the feudal. Nearly every crime was hence-forward regarded as a breach of the King's Peace, and accordingly brought before the king's courts. The jury, as yet in its infancy, an insti-tution borrowed by the Normans from the Franks, represented an ancient method of determining facts by the evidence of those who were capable of knowing the truth. At the time of the Domesday Book, William I had summoned local juries to determine proprietary rights in each village; and gradually the Norman and Angevin kings came to muster similar juries to decide questions of fact in all criminal cases. Then individuals requested the service of the royal jury, a right which the king granted, but for which he required payment. Step by step the feudal jurisdiction of the lords was supplanted by local courts, presided over at first by the sheriff and then more and more by judges of the royal court, with a jury's assistance.

The central administration, meanwhile, was becoming more complex.

There were a Justiciar (Ranulf Flambard, and then Roger of Salisbury), a Treasurer, and a Chancellor. Originally the Chancellor was only the head of the royal chapel, but as the clerks of this chapel could write, they were intrusted with the copying and editing of documents, with the result that the importance of their chief was speedily enhanced. He was given charge of the royal seal. (It was not until the days of King John that, side by side with this, the privy seal, intrusted to the Keeper of the Privy Seal, was established.) Financial affairs were administered by the Court of Exchequer, which met at Winchester at Easter, Whitsun and Michaelmas. All the sheriffs of the country had to submit their accounts to it, and they sat there at a large table—the Chancellor, the Bishop of Winchester, and a clerk to the Chancellor, who, in the absence of the latter on other duties, came in time to take his place and become known as Chancellor of the Exchequer. The covering of the table was marked out with horizontal lines crossed by seven vertical lines, for pence, shillings, pounds, tens of pounds, hundreds, thousands, and ten thousands of pounds. This squared design gave the name "Exchequer." The sheriffs entered in turn and each declared his various expenditures on the Crown's behalf. A clerk set out counters in the several columns to represent these sums. (The figure 0, that ingenious Eastern symbol, was not yet known to the English.) The sheriff then declared his receipts, likewise represented by other counters placed over the others and canceling the first. The surplus counters showed the sum due to the Treasury, and the sheriffs had to pay the sum in silver pennies, while the clerks of the Great Roll, or Pipe Roll, noted the sums on rolls of parchment, which are still extant from the year 1131. The receipt given to the sheriff consisted of a strip of wood called a tally, cut to measure a hand's-breadth for one thousand pounds, one inch for a hundred pounds, and so on. After which it was cut in two, one half acting as a receipt to the sheriff, the other as a means of checking for the Exchequer. If proof of payment had at any time to be given, all that was needed was the fitting together of the two pieces. The coinciding of the notches and the grain of the wood made fraud impossible, and the method was so reliable that it was used by the Bank of England until the nineteenth century. (It is still used in France by village bakers.)

The King's Peace and the new dynasty had never been so strong and secure when an unpredictable accident ruined all hopes. William the

Atheling, the heir to the throne, was returning from Normandy with a band of his friends, in a vessel called the *Blanche Nef*, which sank as a result of the faulty steering of a drunken pilot. When King Henry was told next day, he fell in a swoon of grief. At no price would he leave his kingdom to Robert's son, William of Normandy, whom he hated, and in 1126 he named as his successor his daughter Matilda, widow of the German Emperor Henry V. To insure the loyalty of the barons, he made the Great Council do homage to her. Then, to protect the frontiers of Normandy, he married the future Queen of England to Geoffrey of Anjou, the duchy's most powerful neighbor. This foreign marriage was not liked by the English, many of whom regretted having plighted their oath to a woman. It was obvious that the death of Henry I would bring troubles.

These three Norman kings, the Conqueror, Rufus, and Henry, had served their adopted country well; they had imposed order, kept the turbulent barons in check, balanced the claims of Church and Crown, systematized public finance, and reformed justice. The English owed much to them, and knew it. The Anglo-Saxon chronicler, who could not be suspected of Norman sympathies, recorded the death of Henry I and added: "A good man he was; and there was great dread of him. No man durst do wrong with another in his time. Peace he made for man and beast. Whoso bare his burthen of gold and silver, durst no man say ought to him but good." The King's Peace—that was the crowning glory of the monarchy, and the achievement which, at the end of the fifteenth century, was to insure its triumph.

CHAPTER IV

Anarchy: Henry II: Thomas Becket

THERE followed nineteen years of anarchy, which taught the people of England the blessings of a strong and comparatively just government. Against Matilda, now wife of the Count of Anjou, another claimant rose when Henry I died—Stephen of Blois, grandson of the Conqueror through his daughter Adela. The citizens of London, with a small band of barons in Stephen's pay, proclaimed him king, and the country was split into partisans of Matilda or of Stephen. He blundered at the start. "When the traitors understood," says the chronicler, "that he was a mild man, and soft, and good, and no justice executed, then did they all wonder." Everywhere fortified castles sprang up, unsanctioned by the crown. The city of London, copying new Continental customs, assumed extensive powers of self-government. The untrammeled lords became simply bandits, employing the peasants on forced building labor and filling their completed castles with hardened and harsh old soldiers. Resistance was met with monstrous tortures: men were hung head down and roasted like joints, and others thrown, like fairy-tale heroes, into dungeons crawling with vipers and toads. But strangely enough, these bandit noblemen, fearful of damnation, were at the same time endowing monasteries. Under Stephen alone over one hundred monastic houses were built.

A typical adventurer of this time was Geoffrey de Mandeville, who betrayed Matilda and Stephen successively, secured the hereditary sheriff-doms of several counties from both claimants, and died by a fortunate stray arrow in 1144. Land passed out of cultivation; towns were put to sack; religion was the only refuge left. Never had men prayed so much; hermits settled in the woods; Cistercian monks cleared forests in the north, and London saw new churches rising everywhere. England seemed to feel, it has been said, as if God and all His angels were asleep, and that they must be roused by redoubled fervor. At last, in 1152, Matilda's young son, Henry, whose father's death had left him Count of Anjou, came to an understanding with Stephen. The Church this time usefully arbitrated, and formulated a treaty which was signed at Wallingford and confirmed at Westminster. Stephen adopted Henry, gave him a share in the administration of the realm, and made him his heir. Peace and unity throughout the land were sworn to by Stephen and Henry, the bishops and earls and all men of substance. In 1154, Stephen died and Henry became king. He was greeted with gladness, "for he did good justice and made peace."

Henry Plantagenet, who thus became Henry II of England, came of a powerful family with a dark history. His Angevin ancestors included Fulke the Black, who was reputed to have had his wife burned alive and forced his son to crave his forgiveness crouching on all fours and saddled like a horse. One of his grandmothers, the Countess of Anjou, had the name of being a witch, who once flew off through a church window. His son Richard was later to say that such a family was bound to be divided, as they all came from the devil and would return to the devil. Henry himself was a hard man, of "volcanic force," but cultivated and charming in manner. A stocky, bull-necked youth, with close-cropped red hair, he had taken the fancy of Queen Eleanor of France when he came to do homage to King Louis VII for Maine and Anjou. She was as hot-headed as the young Angevin, and already married to a man who was, she sighed, "a monk and not a king." She and young Henry understood each other instantly. She obtained a divorce, and two months later, at the age of twenty-seven, married this lad of nineteen, to whom she brought as dowry the great Duchy of Aquitaine, which included Limousin, Gascony, and Périgord, with suzerain rights over Auvergne and Toulouse. Through his mother, Henry II already owned the Duchy of Normandy, and through his father, Maine and Anjou; he was becoming more powerful in France than King Louis himself. Of his thirty-five years on the throne he was to spend only thirteen in England. He was in France continuously from 1158 to 1163. In fact, he was an emperor, viewing England as only a province. He was French in tastes and speech, but this Frenchman was one of the greatest of English kings.

Like his ancestor the Conqueror, Henry II was helped by being a foreigner in England. He had energy, he was zealous for order, and he was coming to a country which had fallen into feudal anarchy; he would hew the living rock and restore the Norman order. The rebels dared not resist the master of so many provinces abroad, from which he could bring armed forces if need be, and Henry forced them to pull down or dismantle the castles built without license. Taxes were again collected and the sheriffs were made subject to dismissal. The feudal term of forty days' service was inadequate for the Angevin ruler's campaigns in Aquitaine and Normandy, and for this was substituted the tax known as scutage, which enabled him to pay mercenaries. This left many of the English nobility to become unused to war, and they took to jousts and tourneys instead of real fighting. The bellicose lord hardly survived, except in the Border counties, and thereafter it was in the counties palatine, facing Scotland and Wales, that all the great risings broke out. But although Henry's quality as a foreigner gave him this freedom of action and ideas in English affairs, his heterogeneous domains abroad weakened him. The bond between Normandy, Aquitaine, and England was artificial. Henry II, no doubt, often dreamed of becoming at once King of France and King of England. In that event, England would have become a French province, perhaps for several centuries. But, as so often happens, facts overcame wishes. The King's zeal for order involved him in the conflicts within England; and so time, and his life, went past.

When the young king from abroad came to the throne, Theobald, Archbishop of Canterbury, was eager to see a trusty man at the King's side, and commended to him one of his clerks, Thomas Becket, who won Henry's favor and was in time made Chancellor. This high office was then gaining importance at the expense of the Justiciar. Becket was a pure-blooded Norman of thirty-eight, the son of a rich City merchant. Of gentle upbringing, he had become clerk to Archbishop Theobald after the ruin of his family, his patron having come from the same village as his father. As Becket's gifts seemed administrative rather than priestly, the kindly disposed archbishop handed him on to the king, and immediately the sovereign and his servant became inseparables. Henry valued this young Minister, good horseman and falconer, able to bandy learned jokes with him, and astoundingly able in his work. It was in large measure due to Becket that order was so speedily restored after the death of Stephen. Success made the Chancellor proud and powerful. Campaigning in the Vexin in 1160, he took seven hundred horsemen of his own retinue, twelve hundred more hired by himself, and four thousand soldiers, a veritable private army. Becket himself, notwithstanding his priesthood, dismounted a knight in single combat during this campaign.

On Theobald's death, Henry II resolved to give the see of Canterbury to Becket. There was some grumbling from the monks to whom the election properly belonged; Becket was not a monk, and seemed to be more soldier than priest. Indeed, he had not till then taken priest's orders. The Chancellor himself, showing the King his lay vestments, said, laughing, that Henry was choosing a very handsome costume to put at the head of his Canterbury monks. Then, when he had accepted, he warned the King that he would hate his archbishop more than he would love him, because Henry was arrogating to himself an authority in Church matters which he, the Primate, would not accept. There is much that is remarkable in this great temporal lord who turned ascetic immediately on becoming an archbishop. Henceforth he devoted his life to prayer and good works. On his dead body were found a hair shirt and the scars of self-discipline. The see of Canterbury had made the gentle Anselm into a militant prelate, and of Becket, the King's servant and Chancellor, it made a rebel, then a saint. Reading his life, one feels that he sought to be, first the perfect Minister, then the perfect churchman, such as the most exacting onlooker might have imagined either. It was an attitude compounded of scruples and pride.

The line of conflict between King and Church lay no longer on the question of Investitures, but on the analogous one of the ecclesiastical courts. In separating civil and religious courts, the Conqueror and Lanfranc had wished to reserve for the latter only cases of conscience. But the Church had gradually made all trials into religious cases. If property rights are violated, this became perjury, a case of conscience. Accused parties were only too glad to have recourse to this milder jurisdiction, which sentenced men neither to death nor to mutilation, seldom even to prison, as the Church had not its own prisons, but to penance and fines. The clerks were answerable only to tribunals of their own category, and so a murderous clerk nearly always got off easily. This was a grave matter when even a lawyer's scrivener was a clerk in the ecclesiastical sense. Any scamp might enter the minor orders and avoid the law of the land.

Furthermore, the court of Rome reserved the right of calling an ecclesiastical case, and then the fines were not paid to the Exchequer. If this intrusion into lay matters had not been checked, the King would no longer have been master in England. Henry II insisted that a clerk found guilty by an ecclesiastical court should be degraded. After this, being a layman again, he could be handed over to the secular arm. Thomas refused, arguing that a man could not be twice punished for one crime. The King was angered, and summoned a council at Clarendon, where, under threat of death, Becket signed the Constitutions of Clarendon, which gave the victory to the King. But the archbishop did not hold himself bound by a forced oath. Pope Alexander gave him dispensation. Condemned by a court of barons, Thomas proudly left England, bearing his crozier, beaten but not tamed, and from his haven at Vézelay began to hurl excommunications at his foes.

Powerful as Henry II was, he was not strong enough to face an excommunication with impunity, or to risk his kingdom being placed under Papal interdict, which would mean seeing his people deprived of the sacraments. In a time of universal faith, the popular reaction might well have swept away the dynasty. But compromise was difficult. The King could not drop the Constitutions of Clarendon without humiliation; and the archbishop refused to recognize them. In the end Henry met Becket at Freteval, made a show of reconciliation, and required him only to swear respect for the customs of the realm. But Becket had hardly landed in England when there reached him, at his own request, Papal orders to turn out those bishops who had betrayed their primate during his disgrace. Now, it was a law established by the Conqueror that no subject was entitled to correspond with the Pope unless by royal leave. The King heard this news when feasting at Christmas near Lisieux. He was furious, exclaiming that his subjects were spiritless cowards, heedless of the loyalty due to their lord, letting him become the laughing-stock of a low-born clerk. Four knights who overheard him went off without a word, took ship for England, came to Canterbury, and threatened the archbishop. He must absolve the bishops, they declared. Becket, the soldier-prelate, replied boldly and proudly. And a little later the altar steps were smeared with his brains, his skull cleft by their swords.

When the King learned of this crime, he shut himself up for five weeks in despair. He was too clever to be blind to the danger. The people might have wavered between the King and the living archbishop, but with a martyr they sided unreservedly. For three hundred years the pilgrimage to Canterbury was an enduring feature of England's life. All the King's enemies were heartened, and rallied. To parry the most urgent, he mollified the Pope by renouncing the Constitutions of Clarendon, and then promised to restore to the see of Canterbury its confiscated wealth, to send money to the Templars for the defense of the Holy Sepulcher, to build monasteries, and to combat the schismatic Irish.

But his own wife and children rose against him. He had, it is true, treated his sons well. The eldest, Henry, he had had crowned King of England during his own lifetime, and to the second, Richard, he made over the maternal inheritance of Aquitaine and Poitou. They both refused his request to hand over a few properties to their youngest brother, John, and at Eleanor's instigation took the head of a league of nobles against their father. After two generations the internal family feuds of the Angevin house were reviving. Some touch of genius these Plantagenets had always had; but they came from the devil and to the devil they were returning. In this peril Henry II showed his energy. He returned forthwith from the Continent to crush the revolt. After landing he came through Canterbury, dismounted, walked to the tomb of Becket, knelt for a long time in prayer, and, divesting himself of his clothes, submitted to discipline from threescore and ten monks. After this he triumphed everywhere; the nobles gave in, his sons did him homage. When order was restored the question of the ecclesiastical courts was apparently settled. Henry maintained his claim to try clerks charged with treason and offenses against the laws of his forests. Those accused of other serious offenses (murder and crimes of violence) were now left to the bishops' courts. But there was a vague borderland which later generations took long to define; and, anyhow, this compromise was a poor one, as for many years English subjects guilty of murder or theft were to plead benefit of clergy. And to reach this halting settlement the two outstanding men of the time had ruined two lives and a great friendship.

CHAPTER V

Henry II as Administrator: Justice and Police

THE history of England has this essential feature—that from the time of Henry II the kingdom had achieved its unity. The task before her kings was easier than it was for those of France. Thanks to William the Conqueror, no English lord, however great, was the sovereign of a petty territory with its own traditions, history, and pride. The Saxon kingdoms dropped into oblivion. Wales and Scotland, which would have been difficult to assimilate, were not yet annexed; and in a comparatively small territory any rebel could be speedily reached. The Church, despite Becket's resistance, seemed by the end of the reign to be in submission to the King, who controlled all ecclesiastical links with Rome, supervised the selection of bishops, and patiently sought to reconcile the monks of Canterbury and the bishops, who disputed the right of electing the archbishop. The Primate, indeed, was now his servant: one ecclesiastical chronicler remarks with asperity that probably the archbishop would take no step save by the King's order, even if the Apostle Paul came to England to require it of him. In fact, one century after the Conquest, the fusion of conquerors and conquered was so complete that an English freeman could hardly be distinguished from one of Norman origin. Both languages existed side by side, but corresponded to class divisions rather than racial differences. The cultured Saxons made a point of knowing French. Mixed marriages were frequent. "A strong king, a weak baronage, a homogeneous kingdom, a bridled Church"—these things enabled Henry II to make his court the single animating center of the country.

That court was one of the most lively in the world. The King had a cultivated and inquiring mind, and gathered men of learning and erudition round him, such as the theologians Hugh, Bishop of Lincoln, and

who had been authorized to use the King's jury, or on questions touching the Jews. Sometimes judge and jury visited the prison together, or reported on the sheriff's administration. Finally, the jury had to charge any local suspects of felony, and jurors neglecting this duty were fined. Later this prosecuting rôle devolved upon a more numerous jury, termed the grand jury, the petty jury thereafter considering the truth of the charge, a development which strengthened the safeguards of the accused party.

Naturally enough, Englishmen generally preferred trial by a jury of neighbors, enlightened as to facts by witnesses, to being subjected to dangerous ordeals by fire or water. Henry II wisely ordained that a notorious rogue should be banished from the realm, even if absolved by ordeal. In 1215 the Pope forbade trial by fire and water, and was obeyed. Ordeal by battle survived much longer: it had not been abrogated in 1818, when a man accused of murder claimed to have his case so tried. In setting up these courts, King Henry was not solely moved by the desire to provide his subjects with a sound justiciary: he enriched the Exchequer with the fines formerly levied by feudal courts. Moreover, the royal judges themselves were not always honest or beyond reach of purchase; their circuits were designed as much for the raising of the King's revenues, by stern means, as for the administration of justice. But, slowly and indirectly, common sense and mercy gained ground.

The system of itinerant judges soon engendered the Common Law, identical and universal in application. Feudal and popular courts had followed local usage, but a judge moving from county to county tended to impose the best usage on all. Local customs were not destroyed, but were cast, as it were, into the melting-pot of the Common Law. The central court of justice recorded precedents, and thus, very early, a body of law took shape in England which covered the majority of cases. Side by side with the Common Law there was to grow up (and still survives) a complementary legal system, that of the equity courts, which, by virtue of royal prerogative, do not judge according to custom, but afford remedies to the inadequacies or injustices of custom. The principle of equity is this, that in certain circumstances the King can mitigate the rigidity of the Common Law in order to insure justice being done.

Something should be said regarding the classification of crimes. The most dreadful of crimes was high treason, an attempt to slay or dethrone the King (treason towards the State was inconceivable to the mediæval mind). The penalties for treason strike us as cruel, but it must be borne in mind that on the King's person depended the peace and safety of the realm. The traitor was dragged at a horse's tail to the place of execution, and there hanged, drawn and quartered, the pieces of his body being publicly exposed. London Bridge was long adorned with the heads of traitors. Petty treason was the murder of a master by his servant or a husband by his wife, and this too was punished by death. Heresy and witchcraft, treasons towards God, were theoretically mortal offenses likewise, but were not often so in fact before the fifteenth century, when the perturbation caused by the growth of heresy revived religious cruelty. Amongst felonies were classed homicide, armed attack, and theft. These were punished by death or mutilation—the loss of a hand, or ears, or of eyes. A man wounded in the wars, if prudent, furnished himself with a paper vouching for his infirmity, as otherwise, arriving in a village with only one arm or one leg, he might be chased forth as a convicted felon. Lesser offenses were punishable by public exposure in the pillory or stocks, which delivered the offender to public scorn and often to blows. Scolds or chatterbox women were fastened to a chair slung at the end of a pole, and ducked in a pond.

The maintenance of order is a function which, in modern societies, appertains to two distinct bodies: the justiciary and the police. The police prevent disorder and arrest offenders. Who performed these tasks in the Middle Ages? Order was assured by the coöperation of all. Henry II had restored the *fyrd*, and by the Assize of Arms in 1181 insisted that every freeman should be in possession of military equipment which he must swear to devote to the King. This equipment varied in completeness with the means of the individual, the poorest having only a lance, an iron casque, and a padded jerkin. A system of collective responsibility made the supervision of malefactors quite easy. The master of a house was responsible for every villein in his household, and any others had to enroll themselves in groups of ten. On his enrollment the man knelt down and swore on the Gospels to obey the chief of his group, to refrain from thieving or the company of thieves, and never to receive stolen goods. In the event of a crime being committed, the group was often responsible for bringing the man to justice; otherwise, they were collectively sentenced to pay a fine. When a criminal escaped, the men of the village pursued him to the bounds of their hundred, blowing on horns and shouting—the "hue and cry." At the boundary the pursuers passed their responsibility to the next hundred—a system of policing by relays. If the criminal succeeded in finding refuge in a church he was protected by the right of sanctuary, and could then summon the coroner, representing the Crown, and before him "renounce the realm." In this ceremony the offender vowed to leave England and never return. The coroner named a port, and he left at once, carrying a wooden cross which indicated his plight to all and sundry. He had to go direct to the port and take the first vessel sailing, and if none was sailing at once the man had to walk knee-deep into the sea every morning in token of his good faith. A breach of the oath outlawed him, and he could be slain at sight. This right of sanctuary gave rise to many abuses, and the citizens of London complained that certain churches, especially round Westminster, were inhabited by bands of criminals living there in immunity, and emerging at night to rob honest folk.

But all in all, a "good peace" prevailed through most of the country in the twelfth century, and this was in great measure due to the King. Judges were honest only when a strict sovereign kept them in hand. A lay judge who jested about the slowness of ecclesiastical courts was answered by a priest: "If the King were as far away from you as the Pope from us, you would do little work"; and the judge smilingly acknowledged the thrust. If the villein welcomed his royal and ordered time, many nobles, and even many clerks, mourned the good days when the Duke of Normandy was not yet King of England. "Nothing so much moves the heart of man as the joy of liberty, and nothing enfeebles it more than the oppression of slavery," said Giraldus Cambrensis to the lawyer Glanville. If a king showed weakness, or became weakened by adventures abroad, a reaction from the barons would be the inevitable result. But on Henry II's death England could show the strongest government in Europe. It has been well said that it revived the Carolingian practices, and at the same time, in the accuracy of its mechanism, the strictness of its tone and bearing, it shows affinities with the Roman State, or even with the modern State.

CHAPTER VI

The Sons of Henry II

KING HENRY's end was tragic. He would gladly have shared his empire between his sons, but they hated one another and they all betrayed him. "You must know," said one of them to a messenger from the King, "that it is implanted in us by ancestral heritage, as our own nature, that every brother of our blood shall fight against his brother, and every son against his father." The eldest two, Henry and Geoffrey, died before their father, Geoffrey leaving a son, Arthur of Brittany; the third, Richard, plotted against his father with the new King of France, Philip Augustus, a cold, able young man, firmly resolved to regain his suzerainty over these Angevins and making skillful use of their dissensions. Henry II, the saddened and lonely old King, cared now only for his fourth son, John. He had left England and Normandy to Richard, and wished to keep Aquitaine for John: a plan which infuriated Richard, who, more closely linked with his mother, Eleanor of Aquitaine, than with his father, attached more importance to that province than to all the rest of the kingdom. Suddenly he did homage to the King of France for all his father's Continental territories, from the Channel to the Pyrenees. Henry II, caught in Le Mans by Philip Augustus and his own son, had to flee the blazing town, which was the city of his birth and the burial-place of his father, the Count of Anjou. As he left it he blasphemed against God. As he galloped in flight by the footpaths, his own son Richard was chasing him. At Chinon the King was so ill that he had to halt, and there he was rejoined by his Chancellor, who returned from a mission to Philip Augustus bearing a list of the English traitors whom he had found at the French court. It was headed by John, his favorite son. Seeing his father in danger, John too had turned traitor. "You have said enough!"

cried the King. "I care naught now for myself nor for the world!" After which he became delirious, and died of a hæmorrhage. Henry II had been a great king, a cynic, a realist, and stern, but on the whole a well-doer. His reign had lasted from 1154 to 1189.

A statesman (it has been said) was now succeeded by a knight-errant. Richard I, styled by some as Cœur de Lion, or Lion-heart, and by Bertrand de Born of Périgord, "Richard Yea-and-Nay," inherited certain traits from his father—the violence of the Plantagenets, their immoderate love of women, and their courage. But Henry II's aims had been practical and cautious. Richard pursued adventure and despised prudence, in a life that seemed a frenzy of violence and fury. A poet and troubadour, friendly with all the warrior squires of Périgord, he wished to play the romantic knight in real life. In the early days of feudalism, knighthood had been no more than the obligation to serve as a horseman in return for a grant of land. But by Church and poets this contract, and the word itself, had been enhanced by loftier associations. The dubbing of a knight had become a Christian ceremony. The young knight bathed to symbolize his purification, as later did the Knights of the Order of the Bath; his sword was laid on the altar; and he kept a vigil of arms in the castle chapel. The sword was two-edged, as the knight must smite the rich oppressor of the poor and likewise the strong oppressor of the weak. Unhappily, the people of England found that knights often acted very differently from this exalted doctrine. They brawled drunkenly instead of combating the enemies of the Cross, and ran to seed in idleness and evil living, degrading the very name of chivalry. In fact, notwithstanding some fine characteristics, no warriors were ever more cruel than certain mediæval knights. In France there were occasions when they massacred the populations of whole towns, men, women, and children. The Church had made laudable efforts to make war more humane, but nothing resulted from them but a certain courtesy towards women of the same class or towards their fellow-knights when captive or disarmed. And of this superficial courtesy and essential cruelty, Richard Cœur de Lion offered a twofold example.

The great chivalrous episode of Richard's reign was the Third Crusade, in which he took part with Philip Augustus of France. England had hardly been affected by the First and Second Crusades, to which some single adventurers, but no sovereign, had gone. The ecclesiastical accounts of the time show traces of numerous Englishmen who expiated an offense by a vow to go on the Crusade, but at the last moment regretted their oath and were dispensed from it by a payment. Archbishop Giffard, releasing one penitent from his vows, added that he was to spend the sum of five shillings sterling, of his own goods, to come to the help of the Holy Land when it should be asked of him on the Pope's behalf. One knight, for adultery committed with the wife of another, pledged himself to send a soldier to the Holy Land at his expense, and to pay one hundred pounds should he fail to do so. Towards the end of Henry II's reign the victories of Saladin and the fall of the Kingdom of Jerusalem had so deeply impressed Christendom that the King raised heavy contributions, through the Saladin tithe, which was notable as the first direct taxation imposed on all property, movable and immovable, and no longer only on land. But this tax was intended to subsidize foreign armies rather than to send Englishmen to the East. Henry II promised to go himself, and the Patriarch of Jerusalem ceremonially brought him the keys of the Holy Sepulcher. But the King never embarked, and to the reproaches of Giraldus Cambrensis answered that the clergy valiantly incited him to expose himself to danger, receiving no blows themselves in battle and bearing no burden which they could possibly avoid. There was nothing enthusiastic or romantic in Henry II. But Richard was different—having once received his father's inheritance, he drained the Treasury dry, sold a few counties, and took ship.

Richard and Philip Augustus, outwardly friends but actually rivals since Richard's succession to his father, set off together for Jerusalem. By the time they left Sicily they had quarreled. Richard lost much time in waiting for the small fleet which the Cinque Ports should have fitted out for him. (These five ports of Hastings, Dover, Sandwich, Hythe, and Romney played the same part for the navy as did the knights' fiefs for the army: the King granted the Cinque Ports valuable privileges in return for their furnishing him with ships in time of war.) King Richard's expedition gave him the chance of showing his courage, but did not free the Holy Sepulcher. He roused hatred by his insolence and cruelty. When Saladin refused to ransom his prisoners, he cut their throats. Long years after that campaign, says Joinville, the Saracens still frightened their naughty children by the threat of fetching King Richard to come and kill them. And in the meantime Philip Augustus, who had gone home, was preparing war against his rival.

Despite their failure, and the abstention of most of the English nobility, the influence of the Crusades on England's history, as on that of Europe in general, was profound. It was in the main by contact with the Orient that the Western spirit became properly aware of its essential nature and of its resistances. The wars of the Medes had coincided with the noblest period of Greek thought, and similarly the Crusades were the beginning of a European renaissance. For three centuries they determined the commercial and maritime centers of the world. Marseilles, Genoa, and Venice, starting-points for the Crusaders, became great cities. Hostelries were built there by the pilgrims. The Mediterranean was safeguarded by the military Orders of the Templars and the Knights of St. John of Jerusalem, who built the first great Christian fleets. It was also during the Crusades that Christian gentlemen, in England as in France, began to wear beards and paint arms on their shields, to recognize one another in a throng of many nations. The vocabulary of Europe was enriched with countless new words. And the failure of the Crusades was to have an influence on England's maritime future, as the barriers of Islam, closing down, forced men to seek other routes for trading with the East.

The art of war progressed little during these conflicts. The mediæval knights were not tacticians. At sight of the enemy they drew themselves up in three large masses (*batailles*), pointed their lances forward, put their shields in position, and charged the opposing *batailles*. There were no reserves, as it was deemed insulting to deprive a knight of the start of an engagement. A battle was simply a mêlée of horses and men, in which foot soldiers played no part. The Crusades, however, showed the European knights the importance of siege warfare. The fortifications of Acre checked the Christian armies and, according to Michelet, caused them to lose over a hundred thousand men. The advantage then lay with the defenders, not the assailants, of a stronghold. The catapults and trebuchets of the time were powerless against walls fifteen or thirty feet thick. A well-built castle, with no openings on the ground level, had a capacity of resistance limited only by its supplies. But it could be sapped, unless it stood upon rock, and the pioneers labored under a roof-covering which protected them from the garrison's archers. To counter this form of attack the brattice was invented, a long wooden gallery jutting out over the attacking force, on whom incendiary substances could thus be showered. But the brattice itself was exposed to fire; stone machicolations and flanking towers did away with dead angles, and again strongholds became impregnable. Only the invention of artillery was to nullify the military value of the castle fortress, the capture of Constantinople by Mohammed II being the first prominent achievement of artillery.

Richard was regarded by the crowned heads of Europe as a dangerous man, and on his way home from the Crusade was treacherously made prisoner by the Duke of Austria and handed over to the Emperor Henry VI, who ignored the Crusaders' privilege and kept him in captivity. News reached England that her King was a prisoner, gayly enduring his captivity by making his guards drunk, and that his ransom would be one hundred thousand pounds. To raise this vast sum, the Ministers, who did their best to replace an absentee sovereign, tried hard to spread the burden over all classes of society (1193). They demanded scutage of twenty shillings for each knight's land, a quarter of every layman's revenue, a quarter of the clergy's temporal goods, and one-tenth of the spiritual revenues. The churches were asked for their plate and jewelry, monastic Orders for one year's wool shearings. Normandy had to pay the same taxes. In spite of these overwhelming dues, the sum raised was insufficient. But the Emperor agreed to give King Richard provisional liberty. In the King's absence his brother John had tried to seize power, but had been repulsed by the energy of Hubert Walter, Archbishop of Canterbury, who showed himself as good a soldier as he was a Minister.

Richard was welcomed back with enthusiasm and pomp by the citizens of London. But instead of showing proper gratitude for this surprising loyalty, he at once proclaimed fresh taxes. The plight of the realm was dangerous. Philip Augustus had invaded Normandy, Aquitaine was in revolt, Anjou and Poitou were drifting towards France. To defend Normandy Richard built one of the greatest fortresses of the time, Château-Gaillard, which commanded the valley of the Seine. "I shall take it, be its walls of iron!" cried Philip Augustus. "And I shall hold it," retorted Richard, "be they of butter!" He had not time to keep his word. One of his vassals, the Viscount of Limoges, found a gold ornament, probably Roman, in a field near his castle of Chalus; Richard maintained a claim to it as King. A quarrel over this trifling incident grew into a war, and whilst besieging Chalus, Richard was struck by an arrow. The wound festered and the King died in his tent on April 6, 1199. *"Telum Limogiae occidit leonem Angliae."* His body was buried at Fontevrault, and his heart in his "faithful city of Rouen." This absentee King was to lie forever far from his realm: he hardly belongs to English history. "A bad son, a bad brother, a bad husband, and a bad king," it has been said. But in judging Richard allowance should be made for his legend, his popularity, and the loyalty of his people. Like certain *condottieri* of the Renaissance or certain libertines of the eighteenth century, he must have been a singularly complete type, nowadays condemned, but at that time accepted by popular opinion.

CHAPTER VII

Magna Carta

MEDIÆVAL peoples forgave their kings much, because the worst king was better than the shortest spell of anarchy. The Norman dynasty had conquered the English with the aid of their barons, and then their barons with the aid of the English. King John succeeded in uniting all his subjects against himself. In the sparkle of his intelligence he was a true Plantagenet, excelling in military and diplomatic tactics, a great charmer of women, a fine huntsman, but cruel and mean-souled. There had been greatness in Henry II and Richard; but John was merely odious. This betrayer of his father and brothers was suspected throughout Europe of having caused the murder of his nephew, Arthur of Britanny, who might have disputed his succession. Philip Augustus, his continental suzerain, summoned him before his court, and then, after delays, declared him guilty of felony and deprived him of all his French fiefs. With feudal right thus on his side, the King of France proceeded to take back his domains from John, one by one. Normandy was reoccupied by France in 1204, despite a skillful maneuver on John's part to save Château-Gaillard; in 1206 he lost Anjou, Maine, Touraine, and Poitou. Ten years after the death of Henry II the Angevin empire had virtually come to an end. There remained Aquitaine, but this proved difficult to keep because the English barons, who had always been ready to fight for Normandy, where they held fiefs, were very reluctant to pursue an adventure in Gascony, of little utility to themselves, and in the service of a hated king.

At war with the King of France, and quarreling with the English baronage, John Landless also got into difficulties with the Church. The Archbishops of Canterbury generally acted as chief Ministers to the King, and the sovereign quite naturally claimed the right of choosing his

Primate. But, as we know, the bishops of the realm and the monks of Canterbury both laid claim to this right. Under John, all three parties appealed to Rome, and Pope Innocent III responded unexpectedly by appointing over the heads of King, monks and bishops, his own candidate, Stephen Langton, a priest admirable for character and learning, who had been long resident at Rome. John was furious and refused recognition to a prelate whom he declared to be known only because he had always lived among his enemies; and he confiscated the properties of the Archbishopric. The Pope countered by the customary sequence of pontifical sanctions. He placed England under an interdict; the church bells were dumb, and the dead were left without Christian burial. The faithful were in sore torment. But the strength of the royal institution was such that no rebellion took shape. A year later the Pope excommunicated King John. Finally he deposed him, and authorized Philip Augustus to lead a crusade against this contumacious England. The position was becoming dangerous. Already the Scots and Welsh were becoming active on the Borders. The King yielded. He humbled himself before the Papal legate, and received Langton with a respectful, hypocritical welcome. Then, feeling secure in the saddle again, he tried to fabricate a Continental coalition with the Count of Flanders and Otto of Brunswick against Philip Augustus. Something unknown in baronial history happened when his barons refused to follow him. They first said they would not serve under the orders of an excommunicated king (absolution had not yet been granted to John), and then pleaded their poverty. John had to postpone his departure, and kept his allies placated with subsidies. Next year (1214) this coalition was shattered at Bouvines, a battle which was at once the triumph of the Capets (whom it enabled to unify the Kingdom of France), and the safeguard of English liberties: because, if John had returned home victorious at the head of his Brabant mercenaries, he would have taken cruel vengeance on the English lords for their refusal to serve. Only Gascony and the port of Bordeaux were left of his French possessions. English historians may well regard this defeat as a happy date in England's history: it destroyed the prestige of John, and heralded Magna Carta.

A clash was not inevitable between John and the baronage. They had endured the despotism of Henry II, a powerful, victorious king who held such wide popular respect that none dared resist him. But why should they have tolerated the abuses of a defeated king so universally despised? In 1213 Archbishop Langton, the brain of the conspiracy, quickened feeling by a secret gathering of barons to whom he read the forgotten charter of Henry I which promised respect for the rights and usages of the King's subjects. At another meeting the barons swore on the relics of St. John that they would grant peace to the King only if he gave his oath to observe this charter. In 1215 they addressed an ultimatum to John, and declared their "defiance" (*diffidatio*), which a vassal had to signify to an unworthy suzerain before taking arms against him. The King tried to persuade the freemen to his side and to bring in mercenaries, but was forced to realize that the whole country was against him. The citizens of London welcomed the small baronial army with enthusiasm. In such circumstances John's ancestors would have summoned the *fyrd*, but times had changed. Henry II's reforms had weakened the nobles and brought them closer to their tenants. Conflicts between manor and village were now less frequent. The Papal interdict had left a deep mark on a religious people. This appeal to ancient liberties was welcome to all classes, and the King's passionate wrath was futile. What could he do? The capital was in rebel hands, the whole administration at a standstill. Without his Exchequer, John had no revenues. He had to yield. The King agreed to meet the barons on the meadow of Runnymede, between Staines and Windsor, and there signed the Great Charter.

The importance of Magna Carta has been sometimes exaggerated, sometimes underrated. It should be remembered, first and foremost, that this is a document drawn up in 1215, that is to say, at a period when modern ideas of liberty had not even taken shape. When the King in the thirteenth century granted the privilege to a lord of holding his own court of justice, or to a town of electing its own officials, these privileges were then styled "liberties." The Great Charter declared in general terms that the King must respect acquired rights. The average man of our own times believes in progress and demands reforms; to the man of 1215 "the golden age was in the past." The barons did not regard themselves as making a new law; they were requiring respect for their former privileges. Their only problem was how to compel the King to respect the privileges of feudalism. But by a happy chance in the mode of wording, they did not set the problem in those terms, and their text enabled future generations to read into Magna Carta these more general principles:

that there exist laws of the State, rights pertaining to the community; that the King must respect these; that if he violated them, loyalty was no longer a duty and the subjects had a right of insurrection. The true significance of the Charter, therefore, resides in what it implies rather than what it is. To succeeding generations it was to become, in the modern sense, a "charter of English liberties," and until the fifteenth century every king had to swear, several times during his reign, that he would respect its text. Under the Tudors the Charter was to be forgotten, until it reappeared, as a counterblast to the theory of divine right, in the time of James I.

It has been customary also to read into Magna Carta the modern principle of "no taxation without representation." Actually the barons only insisted that, if the King wished to raise extraordinary "aids," not provided for by the customary feudal contract, he could not do so without the approval of the Great Council, that is to say, of the barons and tenants-in-chief. But it was not laid down that the villeins must be represented before they could be taxed. The baronage apart, the only case provided for was that of the City of London, which, having sided with the revolt, secured a status as a collective tenant-in-chief. Lastly, it has been said that the Charter contained in embryo the law of habeas corpus. The text runs: "No freeman shall be taken, or imprisoned . . . or exiled, or any otherwise destroyed . . . but by lawful judgment of his Peers, or by the Law of the Land." This is of very limited range as intended by the barons of Runnymede, who simply meant that a lord could be tried only by his peers, or a freeman by freemen, a formula planned by its sponsors to check the King's judges, but which in effect was to prove a protection to the English nation when the villeins themselves had become freemen. A committee of twenty-five members, all barons except the Mayor of London, was intrusted with the hearing of complaints against the Crown. The King was to bid his subjects swear obedience to these twenty-five, and if he himself refused to follow the advice of this body, the barons would have the right to take up arms against him.

The Charter may not be the modern document which it has sometimes been held to be, but clearly it marks the end of the untrammeled monarchy of the Anglo-Norman period. If Henry II had passed on his genius to his sons, and if the barons had not constituted the most powerful armed force in the realm, England from the twelfth century might have been ruled by an absolute and irresponsible monarch. Magna Carta revived the feudalistic concept of a limited monarchy. The English constitution is the "daughter of feudalism and the common law." The former contributed the idea of usage and acquired rights which must be respected; the latter, spread through the land by Henry II's judges, unified the nation in respect for certain protective rules which were binding on even the King himself. But in 1215 such ideas, clear enough to us, were not within reach of the masses. So little was the Charter a document voicing the people's cause, that it was not translated into English until the sixteenth century.

No sooner had King John accepted its terms than his thoughts turned to evasion. His fury was such that he writhed on the ground, biting pieces of wood. "They have set five-and-twenty kings over me!" he cried. Then, reverting to his sly, perfidious diplomacy, he turned to Pope Innocent III, with whom he had been reconciled, seeking dispensation from his oath to respect the accursed Charter; and the Pope, outraged by this armed rebellion inspired by an archbishop of his own choosing, excommunicated the citizens of London. On Langton's advice they rang the bells and said Mass as if nothing had happened. Papal authority over England, too far a country, was already weakening. Philip Augustus, determined, like William the Conqueror, to cloak his ambitions under a guise of legality, took advantage of events to try to have his son Louis, whose wife was a niece of John's, proclaimed King of England. John, he said, had been condemned to death for the murder of Arthur of Britanny, and so had lost his rights to the throne. This judgment having been given before the birth of his son, the lawful heir to the English crown was Louis of France. In 1216 Louis landed in Kent, and set out with the support of numerous English barons in search of the King. But fate speedily ended this drama. John died on October 19, 1216, from a surfeit of peaches and fresh cider.

CHAPTER VIII

The Communities: (I) Towns and Corporations

To APPREHEND the slow change from feudal to parliamentary control after Magna Carta, we must examine the birth in mediæval England of certain new forces—the communities. Feudal law protected the warrior landlord, and indirectly his serfs. But a gradually prospering society, untroubled now by invaders, could not remain a nation of soldiers and farmers. The town-dwellers, traders, students, and all who did not fit into the feudal framework, could only find security in association. The burgesses of a town, the craftsmen of a guild, the students of a university, the monks of a monastery began to form communities which insisted on their rights. Even at Runnymede, as we saw, the City of London had taken rank as a tenant-in-chief.

During the Saxon invasions most of the smaller Roman towns had fallen into decay, but a few survived. London, Winchester, York, and Worcester, for instance, had never ceased to be towns. In the thirteenth century London had about 30,000 inhabitants, but the other towns were very small. Originally many of these had taken shape round a monastery. Some were places where a river was crossed, as indicated by so many names ending in "ford" or "bridge"; others were road junctions, or ports; and nearly all were fortified points. The word "burgess" comes from "burgh," a fort, reminding us that a town was for long a place of refuge, having its earthwork or stone walls, its drawbridge, and sometimes, in Norman days, its royal fortress. The smaller landowners had houses there in case of war or times of danger, which they let in periods of tranquillity. Incased within its walls, a mediæval town could not expand; its houses were small, its streets narrow. Thatched roofs frequently caused fires. Dirt was prevalent. The first public well in London dates from the thirteenth century, and its water was reserved for the poor to drink, as all who could drank beer. Ordure lay in the streets, and the stench was vile. Occasionally some contagion carried off part of the population. Every town was partly rural: even within its walls London had its kitchen gardens, and the mayor was constantly forbidding citizens to allow pigs to wander about the streets. When the King dissolved Parliament during the fourteenth century, he dismissed "the nobles to their sports, the commons to their harvests," drawing no line between knights and burgesses. The town, in fact, took part in the harvesting; courts and universities were suspended from July to October, to make way for the toil of the fields; and hence come the annual "long vacations."

At the time of the Conquest every town was dependent on a lord; its taxes were levied by the sheriff, and a townsman was answerable to the manor-court. Gradually the burgesses, as they grew richer, purchased "liberties," that is to say, privileges. There is a twelfth-century story telling how two poor fellows were ordered by the manor-court to settle a question of property by combat, and how they fought from morning till the sun was high in the sky. One of them, tired out, was driven back to the edge of a deep ditch and was about to fall into it when his adversary, whose pity overcame his acquisitiveness, called out a warning. Whereupon the burgesses of the town compassionately bought from their lord for an annual rent the right to settle such disputes themselves.

In the thirteenth century the French invented the "commune," or free town, a kind of conspiracy of townsmen under a vow of mutual protection. The name and the idea at once crossed the Channel, to the alarm of the lords. When the town attained the status of a tenant-in-chief it found its place in the feudal structure, having its own court, presided over by the mayor, and its own gallows, raising its own taxes, and being in due course summoned to Parliament. Towns, in France as in England, came to have their own seals, arms, and mottoes, because they were themselves lords. The individual, in the Middle Ages, only participated in the governance of the country if he were a noble, but the "communities" were independent powers, and as such recognized by the law. The House of Commons emerged, not as a House of Communes, but a House of Communities—of counties, towns, and universities. England did not pass from the personal and feudal bond to a patriotic and national bond, but rather to a bond between the King and the "states" or commons of the realm.

To see in our own day a town of the twelfth or thirteenth century, one might view the *sukhs* of Fez or Marrakesh. The people are grouped in their several quarters according to their vocations. There is a street of butchers, another of armorers, another of tailors. The guild, or corporation, had the twofold object of protecting its members against outside competition, and of imposing on them rules to safeguard the consumer. Mediæval ideas on trade were in direct opposition to those of the modern liberal economists. The Middle Ages did not admit the idea of competition, nor that of the open market. To buy in advance simply to sell again was an offense, and to buy wholesale so as to sell retail likewise. If one member of a guild made a purchase, any other member, if so minded, could buy also at the same price. No stranger was entitled to settle in a town to practice his calling without license. Guild membership was an hereditary privilege. At first, poor artisans could become master-craftsmen by serving an apprenticeship of six or seven years. Later in the sixteenth century, the guilds in the larger towns restricted some of their choicer privileges to wealthy members, although never altogether excluding any who had truly served apprenticeship. The Middle Ages recognized no law of supply and demand. Any merchandise was thought to have its just price, scaled to enable the seller to live decently without leaving him an excessive profit.

Merchants, of course, were not saints, and had countless tricks for evading the control of guild or municipality. Bakers kneaded loaves of short weight, or when their customers brought their own dough to be baked, kept a small boy hidden beneath the counter to steal handfuls before it was placed in the oven. Such fellows were punished in the pillory, the fraudulent loaves being strung round their necks. A seller of bad wine had the residue of the stuff poured over his head. Rotten meat was burned under the nose of its vender, that he might smell it for himself. But gain is as strong a stimulant to fraud as to laborious toil. Notwithstanding strict rules, merchants grew rich. In 1248 the prosperity of London outraged the feelings of King Henry III, who, having had to sell his plate and jewels to make up deficiencies of taxation, learned that they had been bought by merchants of his capital. "I know," said he, "that were the treasures of imperial Rome for sale, this town would buy them all! These London clowns who style themselves barons are disgustingly rich. This city is a bottomless well." Throughout the Middle Ages the political strength of London was great. Its armed citizens, and the bands of apprentices ever ready to join in a riot, were a contribution to the armies, now checking, now upholding, the sovereign.

The trading methods of the Middle Ages were later severely judged by eighteenth-century economists, and the corporations, like all such bodies of men, were bound to cause abuses. But the system had great advantages in its day. The suppression of middlemen and the ruling out of speculation made rural life excellently stable, until the middle of the fourteenth century. Mediæval times knew little of the artificial rises and falls that we know. A study of old building costs leaves one amazed at their lowness. It has been estimated that the tower of Merton College, Oxford, cost £142, a low price even when the fullest allowance is made for changed values of money. The difference comes from the small number of middlemen. If a rich man wished to build a great house or a church, he might rent a quarry, cut timbers from his own trees, buy winches, and become his own contractor. If a burgess wanted a silver cup, he bought the metal, agreed with a silversmith for the style of its engraving and weighing the finished article, obtained back the unused portion of his silver. The guild protected both vender and buyer against the excess of competition. It was a regulative instrument.

Foreigners were not themselves entitled to engage in retail trade, but must deal with English merchants, burgesses of a town. The league of Flemish towns, and the famous Hanseatic League (Hamburg, Bremen, and Lübeck), had their own warehouses in London. That of the Hansa towns, the Steelyard, was fortified, and the celibate German merchants lived there together under a corporate rule, like Templars or Knights of St. John. They bought metals and wool from the English, and imported silks, jewels, and spices which they had from the East by way of Bagdad, Trebizond, Kiev, and Novgorod. The French merchants of Amiens and Corbie also maintained collective organizations in London. These foreigners, however—French, Germans, Genoese, Venetians—were authorized to attend the great fairs. To hold a fair was a seigniorial privilege granted to certain towns and abbeys, its object being the double one of enabling English producers to find more buyers than there were in the town markets, and allowing the country dwellers to obtain goods not to be found in their small local towns. Most villages before the eighteenth century had no shops. At the fair the bailiff bought his salted fish, sold the manor wool, and found the tar he needed for his ewes. For the great Stourbridge fair a veritable town of wood used to arise, and men came to it from as far off as London. The Lombard moneychangers were there with their balances; Venetian merchants spread out their silks and velvets, their glass and jewelry. Flemings from Bruges brought their lace and linen. Greeks and Cretans displayed their raisins and almonds, and a few rare cocoanuts, highly prized, the shells of which were mounted in tooled silver. The Hamburg or Lübeck merchant paid with Eastern spices for the bales of wool clipped on English grazings. Noblemen bought their horses and furred gowns. Exchequer clerks moved about, collecting the import duties. But before long the king was to simplify their task by appointing a single town through which certain exports from the kingdom must pass, called the "staple" town, which was first Bruges, then Calais. In this way did commerce and industry begin to develop in mediæval England; but their part in a country still feudal and agricultural was as yet comparatively modest. Classes, like districts, mingled freely. The spirit of Oxford was independent, and when Simon de Montfort opened his bold fight against absolutism, the students enrolled in his party. Any political or religious quarrel might start a university riot. In 1238 a Papal Legate, whose followers had insulted some young clerks, was chased through the streets by Englishmen, Irishmen, and Welshmen, who killed his cook. "Where is he?" they kept crying. "Where is that usurer, that simoniac, robber of revenues and insatiate of money, who plunders us to fill strangers' coffers?" The King had to send his men-at-arms to Oxford to deliver the Roman prelate and calm down the students. Before long the Church had to reckon with the danger to unity of faith presented by this body of young rhetoricians, so easily beguiled by any new doctrine. And to recover its grip on the universities, the Church had to make use of new religious orders.

CHAPTER IX

The Communities: (II) The Universities

FROM the eleventh to the thirteenth century Christendom was like a spiritual empire. The clerks of all countries in Europe spoke Latin; the Church taught one single faith; the Crusades were joint enterprises of the Christian kings; the militant orders, such as the Templars, were international armies. Although communications were slower than in our day, intellectual contacts seem to have been then more close and more frequent than now. A famous master, whether Italian, French, or English, attracted students from every country, and was understood by them because he taught in Latin. A scholar such as John of Salisbury (1120-1180) took his first lessons in logic under Abelard in Paris, went on to Chartres to follow the courses of William de Conches, crossed the Alps ten times in search of the truths of Rome, and finally became a teacher in England. Institutions which succeeded in one country were soon imitated in all others: as witness the free towns or the universities. But these institutions were highly original; not since Greek antiquity had any epoch enriched society with organs so novel.

The ancients had no universities. The Greeks founded schools of philosophy, such as the Academy, but would not have thought of collecting, as Oxford was to do, three thousand students in one town. This was due in part to the smallness of their cities, but chiefly to the absence of an organized Church, which could offer a living to young men instructed in its discipline. The word *universitas* originally signified any corporate body. It was by analogy with the trade guilds that men spoke, in the thirteenth century, of the "community," or "university," of masters and students. This "university," was, literally, a corporation which defended its teachers and pupils against the ecclesiastical authorities on the one hand, against the town burgesses on the other. The schools of advanced education which grew up from about the year 1000 at Salerno, then at Pavia, Bologna, and Paris, officially bore the name of *studium,* or *studium generale.* They taught civil law, canon law, Latin, Aristotelian philosophy, medicine, and mathematics. At Paris the success of Abelard made dialectics triumph. The student learned, rather as with the ancient Sophists, the art of argumentation for or against a theory, or the reconciliation of Aristotle with Christian doctrine.

The memorials of John of Salisbury enable us to see that, by the twelfth century, it was understood by able minds that dialectic, useful enough for enlivening and sharpening the wits, and also for the enrichment of an abstract vocabulary, nevertheless led to no positive truth. When the aged English student returned to Paris after his journeying, he said: "I took pleasure in visiting the Mont-Sainte-Geneviève and those former companions whom I had left, who were still kept there by dialectic, and to talk again with them regarding our old subjects of discussion. They seemed not to have attained their goal by unraveling the old questions, nor even to have added to their knowledge the shadow of a proposition. . . . They had advanced only in one manner: they had unlearned moderation and forgotten modesty, so that it was impossible to hope for their cure. Thus experience taught me one certain truth, namely that although dialectic may aid other studies, it remains sterile and dead if it pretend to be self-sufficient." But we must not judge scholastic logic too hardly: it taught men to use their minds with precision. The debt of Galileo to Aristotle is greater than appears at first sight. The idea that the works of God are rational and can be formulated in universal laws made scientific research a possibility.

In England the taste for classic studies was never wholly extinct. The Irish monasteries kept the torch alight during the Saxon invasions; then came the noble period of Northumbrian culture; and when the Danes had destroyed the School of Bede and Alcuin, Alfred rescued what he could of the classical culture. The Normans had elementary schools where the children learned Latin hymns, and sometimes how to read; monastic schools provided for postulants to the secular clergy; and grammar schools, often likewise under the tuition of monks, taught Latin grammar—often with the aid of bodily punishments. But ignorance was deep, even amongst the clergy, in the thirteenth century. In 1222 Archbishop Langton bade the bishops examine the priests of their dioceses and make sure that they understood the Scriptures. The report of William, Dean of Salisbury, is deplorable. One curate, questioned about the Canon of the Mass and about the prayer *"Te igitur clementissime Pater . . ."* did not know the case of *te*, nor what word governed this pronoun. "And when we bade him look closely which could most fittingly govern it, he replied, *'Pater,* for He governeth all things.' We asked him what *clementissime* was, and what case, and how declined; he knew not. We asked him what *clemens* was; he knew not. . . . He is amply illiterate." The poet Langland (*c.* 1332-1400) makes a priest say:

> "I have be prest and persoun passynge thretti wynter,
> Yet can I neither solfe ne synge, ne seyntes lyves rede;
> But I can fynde in a felde or in fourlonge an hare,
> Better than in *beatus vir*, or in *beati omnes*. . . ."

When Louis de Beaumont became Bishop of Durham in 1316, he knew no Latin and could not read his profession of faith on his consecration. Reaching the word *metropolitanus*, he was unable to pronounce it after several attempts, and at last exclaimed in French, "Take it as read!" The universities tried to produce clerks with better title to the name, the first in England being that of Oxford.

For a long time Oxford had been one of the chief towns of the kingdom. Before the foundation of the university itself, eminent masters were teaching in the churches. When Giraldus Cambrensis, the friend of Henry II, had completed his history of the conquest of Ireland, he resolved to read it publicly at Oxford, where the most famous clerks in England were to be found. The reading took three days; on the first day he entertained and fed the poor of the town; on the second, the doctors and clerks; on the third, the burgesses and soldiers. "This was a noble and costly action, but the older times of poetry were thus in some measure revived." Oxford became a real university when Henry II, at loggerheads with Becket, recalled the English clerks from Paris. As for Cambridge, numerous students and masters migrated there from Oxford in 1209, in protest against the injustice of the Mayor of Oxford, who had caused three innocent students to be hanged for the murder of a woman. In Scotland, the first university was that of St. Andrews, founded early in the fifteenth century.

The students of Oxford and Cambridge in the Middle Ages were not young men of good family coming there to learn the gentlemanly life and make acquaintance with the cream of their generation, but poor clerks preparing for ecclesiastical or administrative careers. Some were so poor that they owned but one gown between three of them, and ate only bread and soup. Shielded by "benefit of clergy," these clerks often enough lived an unholy life of quarrelsome violence and loose morals. The colleges were founded to give the protection of a stricter discipline to those young men who had previously lodged with townspeople. Study did not thrive. Roger Bacon complained that students preferred the inanities of Ovid to the wisdom of Seneca. Soon even Ovid went unread, and the teaching of classical Latin died. As in Paris, the fashionable training after the rediscovery of Aristotle by Edmund Rich was in dialectics and logic.

The mediæval spirit was metaphysical, not positive. But here and there, in a few minds, the sense of scientific method had been quickened by contact with Arabic science through the Crusades, and by reading of the classics. The most famous of these early European savants was Roger Bacon, "the prince of mediæval thought," as Renan called him. He went from Oxford to Paris, where he taught geometry, arithmetic, and the art of observing with instruments. He certainly had an intuitive awareness of the critical method. "As regards reasoning," he wrote, "sophism and demonstration are to be distinguished only by verifying the conclusion by experiment and practice. The most certain conclusions of reasoning leave something to be desired if they are not verified. . . . There are a thousand radical errors arising from pure demonstration (*de nuda demonstratione*)." And, condemning the contemporary cult of scholasticism, Bacon urged that the most important secrets of wisdom remained beyond the reach of most scholars, from lack of a suitable method. But who then cared about scientific observation? Even medicine was theoretic, teaching the doctrine of the "humors." Bacon was defeated by poverty and forced, following the counsel of his friend Bishop Grosseteste, to become a Franciscan in order to live. As a rule of the Order did not permit him to own ink, pen, or books, he requested a special dispensation from the Pope, which Clement IV granted. Roger Bacon must have had prodigious energy to write, without an amanuensis, his *Opus Majus*, a sort of *Discours de la Méthode* reviewing all the sciences, a veritable encyclopædia of the thirteenth century.

The universities played an important part in the political awakening of England. At Oxford, students from Scotland and the southern counties, from Wales and East Anglia, met and mixed.

CHAPTER X

The Communities: (III) The Mendicant Monks

THE Church takes as her earthly mission the taming and controlling of human passions, but she is constantly threatened by the aggressive reactions of these passions. Hence came the successive reforms represented by the rules of St. Benedict, of Cluny, and of Citeaux. Popular faith during the thirteenth century remained simple and strong, but the Church frequently fell below men's expectations. In spite of the stern measures of Gregory VII, many of the lesser clergy in England were still married or lived in concubinage. Vows of poverty were no better observed than those of chastity. Anthony Bek, a bishop in the early years of the thirteenth century, had a train of sevenscore knights, and nothing was too costly for him: "He once paid forty shillings in London for forty fresh herrings, because the other great folk there assembled in Parliament said that they were too dear and cared not to buy them. He bought cloth of the rarest and costliest, and made it into horse-cloths for his palfreys." Simony was prevalent: churches, livings, preferment, all were bought and sold. An abbot presenting himself at Rome, and not too sure of his Latin, spent a goodly sum in mollifying his examiners (*"examinatores suos emollire"*). The parish priests, who should have received the tithes paid by the faithful, were often robbed by an abbey which took over, with the rectorial rights, all the larger tithes (corn and wool), leaving the hapless vicar only the lesser tithes of vegetables and fruit. The monks may not have been so vicious as the satirists depicted them, but they were far from being models of virtue. In vain did St. Bernard forbid the Cistercians to raise over-ornate buildings: their magnificent abbeys in England are proof at once of their excellent taste and ineffectual rule.

Two Orders of thirteenth-century origin gave a better response than the older monastic Orders to men's constant need for fervor—the Franciscans and the Dominicans. These "mendicant" Orders were composed not of monks, but of friars, who were ready to leave the monastery and live in the world, amongst their fellow-men, in absolute poverty and with total rejection of worldly goods. The rule of the Order founded by St. Francis in 1209, required that they should live on alms. So fast did they multiply that by 1264 the General of the Franciscans ruled 8,000 houses and 200,000 brothers. The preaching friars created by St. Dominic in 1215 had a different aim. This Spanish priest had observed the progress of the Albigensian heresy in the south of France, and the sanguinary campaigns of Simon de Montfort (father of the English statesman), and suggested to the Pope that he might wage war on heresy by words, not by the sword. Innocent III authorized the Order, the development of which was as prodigious as that of the Franciscans, and its members were soon in every country.

When the Dominicans and Franciscans reached England in 1221 and 1224 they quickly began a wide range of activity. Here they had no heresy to combat. But ignorance and disaffection were equally dangerous foes. Papal prestige had been affected by an excessive use of excommunication. Men remembered that London had defied the interdict of Rome and forced its priests to celebrate the Mass. To retain her hold over England, the Church would have to find new missionaries who could influence the common people. Her great part in the formation of English society had sprung from the fact that she was the only link between the rude peasantry and the culture of the outside world. This mission had to be completed. The isolation and ignorance of villagers was a tragic aspect of the Middle Ages. But could the parish priest secure a bond? He was equally ignorant and hardly less isolated. The monk, again, lived a conventual life which, even if it might be holy, was still self-centered. The mendicant monk, moving from town to country, but living at other times with his brethren and renewing his stock of ideas, could fulfill this function. And he did so.

A first band of Franciscans crossed the Channel in 1224, nine in number. Their journey to England had been charitably arranged by the monks of Fécamp, in Normandy. They went straight to London, where they were given a small room in a school. There they could be seen round a fire, drinking lees of beer—"So bitter that some preferred plain water," says one record of the time with pitying dismay—and with it only some coarse bread, and porridge when there was no bread. At Cambridge they were given ten marks by the king to rent some land, where they built a chapel, "so miserably poor that a single carpenter in one day made and set up fourteen pairs of rafters." For a long time the rule of absolute poverty was observed by the Franciscans. When the brethren wished to build a real monastery, the English Provincial protested that he had not entered into religion to build walls, and pulled down a stone cloister which the citizens of Southampton had built for his Order. And when his monks asked for bolsters, he said: "You have no need of these hillocks to raise your heads nearer to heaven." It is easy to imagine the effect on the common people of Orders so wholehearted in their rejection of this world's riches.

Amongst the rules laid down by St. Francis, the first to be abandoned by his disciples was that of contempt for knowledge. To a novice who asked for a psalter, Francis replied, "I am your breviary." He was in despair when told that his Order had produced great men of learning, and he would probably not have authorized Roger Bacon, as Clement IV did, to possess ink and pen. But the very success of their preaching obliged Franciscans and Dominicans, at the least, to study theology: they had obviously to prepare to refute objections. They soon became the fortunate rivals, in the universities, of the secular clergy. Monks and priests eyed askance these mendicant friars, whose bare feet and wretched victuals were a silent condemnation of rich living and abbatial abundance. But the poor students welcomed them with a trust not now extended to a comfortably placed clergy. At Oxford the Franciscan school attained a splendid reputation. It produced the greatest three minds of the time— Roger Bacon, Duns Scotus, and William Ockham—and raised the University of Oxford to the level of the Sorbonne.

These first mendicant Orders were joined by two others during the century—the Augustinians and Carmelites. Then, as time went on, like the monks before them, the four Orders of friars neglected the disciplines which had been their greatness. In the fourteenth century the "begging brother," too plump, too well fed, was a favorite target of the satirist. As soon as they in their turn yielded to human nature, and dodged the rule forbidding them to own a horse by riding on an ass, or lived in comfortable cloisters built for them by rich sinners, or wore warm clothes, or sometimes indulged in the refined luxury of education, they lost their dominion over the poor. In vain did a man, whose fat pink cheeks betokened much good cheer, preach that the Apostle Paul lived *"in fame et frigore."* Chaucer's friar in the *Canterbury Tales* is already akin to the monks of Rabelais. Actually most of the brothers were good-hearted men, but the contrast between precept and practice could only provide fuel for the indignation of the pure of heart. Besides, in a country which had become aware of its national originality since the end of the Norman and Angevin empires, these friars being representative of the last wave of Continental deposits and claiming to depend directly on the Pope, were a vexation to many of the faithful. The conflict between the Church of Rome and the Church of England was not yet ready to break out, but from that time the deep causes of rupture lay sown in the most exacting consciences; and there they were to germinate.

CHAPTER XI

Henry III and Simon de Montfort

WHEN the death of King John in 1216 left as lawful king a boy of nine, Henry III, the barons who had rallied to Louis of France from hatred of John now instantly rallied to the Crown. A sense of nationality was becoming strong in this nobility, foreign though its own origins were. The loss of Normandy had severed the Norman barons from the domains in France, and tied them more closely to England. During the King's minority the security of the country was assured by sound soldiers, William the Marshal and Hubert de Burgh, and at last, in 1227, the young King came of age. Henry III was neither cruel nor cynical like his father. His piety and simplicity recalled rather Edward the Confessor, whom he held in great admiration, and in whose honor he rebuilt Westminster Abbey. But he was ill equipped to rule England at that juncture. At a time when all the essential forces of the country were trying to impose checks on the royal power, Henry stood for absolutism. In a period of nationalism, he was not English. Having married Eleanor of Provence, he had gathered round him the Queen's uncles, one of whom, Peter of Savoy, built the Palace of Savoy beside the Thames below Westminster. Along with his wife's kinsmen, the King favored also his mother's relatives, who hailed from Poitou. Barons and burgesses alike began to grumble, muttering "England for the English," and the newest Englishmen among them were not the least vehement. Finally, the devout young King, in gratitude to the Pope for protection during his minority, acknowledged himself as vassal of the Holy Father, and encouraged Roman encroachments at the expense of the English clergy. The Pope fell into a habit of giving the wealthiest posts in England to Italian favorites, even before they fell vacant. When these "provisors" became titular holders, they stayed quietly in Rome, appointed vicars, and drew the revenues of their English property. Anger was rife among the native clergy, and there was a rising tide of hostility towards Pope and king.

For thirty years the unpopularity of Henry III waxed slowly greater. Seven confirmations of the Great Charter did not bring him to observe it. During the twelfth century prices throughout Europe had risen, because a revival of confidence brought money back into circulation. This rise automatically increased the expenses of government; but the barons were not economists, and the King's requests for fresh subsidies encountered increasing ill-will. Unable to bring himself to renounce the great Angevin dreams, he tried to reconquer a French empire, and was beaten at Taillebourg in 1242. The limits of England's patience came when he accepted from the Pope—who, on his own diplomatic chessboard, was playing the King of England against the Emperor—the Kingdom of Sicily for his second son, Edmund. This onerous gift had to be conquered, and for this expedition the barons refused all aids, unless the King would accept reforms. The Great Council met at Oxford in 1258; contrary to custom, the barons attended it armed. "Am I then your prisoner?" asked the King, nervously. They insisted on his accepting the Provisions of Oxford, which intrusted the governance of the realm to a reforming council, which would control the Exchequer and appoint the Justiciar, the Treasurer, and the Chancellor. If it had lasted, an oligarchy would have supplanted the monarchy.

The King gave his word, but soon fell back on his father's tactics and obtained Papal release from his pledge. The barons protested, and it was agreed that both sides should accept the arbitration of the saintly King Louis of France, whose prestige in Europe stood very high. The King and his son, Edward, went themselves to defend their cause at the conference at Amiens. Louis decided for them, and declared the Provisions of Oxford null and void, as running counter to all his political ideas, and confirmed Henry's claim to employ foreigners as counselers or Ministers. The judgment, however, a somewhat obscure pronouncement, upheld Magna Carta. The more conservative barons accepted the award of Amiens, but a younger and bolder party maintained that the arbitration was contradictory, that it was impossible at once to confirm Magna Carta and annul the Provisions which were its application, and that the struggle should continue. This party was headed by the most remarkable man of the time—Simon de Montfort, Earl of Leicester.

This champion of English liberties was a Frenchman; but his paternal inheritance had included the earldom of Leicester, formerly confiscated by King John. It had been restored to him by Henry III, who became intimate with him, and in 1238 Montfort had married the King's sister, to the indignation of English feeling. The brothers-in-law quarreled. Henry was impatient and frivolous, Simon impatient and in earnest, and there was endless bickering. Simon went on the Crusade, and after his return governed Gascony, where he restored order, but with such brutality that Gascon envoys lodged plaints against him at the English court. The King called upon his brother-in-law to justify his actions. Simon replied that a man of such nobility as his should not be perturbed about "foreigners." The dispute grew warmer, and Henry uttered the word "traitor." "There is a lying word!" said Montfort. "If you were not my sovereign you would rue the day when you spoke it." Supplanted in Gascony by Henry's son Edward, Montfort returned to England in wrath and rancor, and soon took the lead in the reforming faction. He was a close friend of the great Bishop Grosseteste's, and his enthusiasm was infectious. Impressed by the evils besetting the realm, the Earl of Leicester was the soul of the aristocratic opposition which sought to control the royal authority at the Council of Oxford. After the award of Amiens that opposition was divided, and many of the nobles yielded. Montfort showed his usual violent vexation: "I have been in many lands," he said to his trusted friends, "and nowhere have I found men so faithless as in England; but, though all forsake me I and my four sons will stand for the just cause." And in spite of defections, he resumed the struggle.

The characteristic of this period was the awakening of new social strata into political life. Two groups are particularly interesting because of the rôle they were soon to play—the country knights and the town burgesses. The former class had greatly expanded in the preceding hundred years. After 1278 any freeman whose revenue amounted to £20 was a knight and subject to the military obligations of knighthood. As prices rose, numerous small landowners found themselves willy-nilly in possession of a knight's fee. During the whole of the thirteenth century the small country gentleman, busy with his land and local affairs (the future squire), a very different man from the warrior and courtier barons, had quickly multiplied; and these knights formed a comfortable, respected class, accustomed to playing a considerable part in county life, especially since the advent of the itinerant judges. It will be remembered that, for the formation of juries, the sheriff first obtained the appointment of four knights, who then chose two knights from each hundred. Here, then, was a group of men of good standing in their neighborhood, who were naturally appealed to when it was required to ascertain the feelings of the counties. In 1213 King John had admitted four knights from each shire to a Great Council. In 1254 Henry III, being in need of money and finding the higher nobility hostile, had consulted the county courts through the sheriffs, and had their replies brought to the Great Council by two knights from each shire. It was doubtless hoped that these rustics, overawed by the royal majesty, would not dare to say nay.

The presence, in exceptional circumstances, of a few knights in the Council did not, of course, suffice to make that body into a modern Parliament. The word "parliament" had been used in England since 1239, but signifying originally only a "spell" or "bout" of speaking. A parliament then was a debate of the Council, and the Council itself remained, as before, a court of law, composed of the greater barons (*barones majores*), collectively convoked by the sheriff. In 1254 the knights were present simply as bearers of information, and did not form part of the Council. But the bold ideas of Simon de Montfort were to go much farther. After the award of Amiens the great rebel totally defeated the royal troops at Lewes, where he had against him his nephew Edward, and part of the baronage, but had on his side the younger nobility, the London burgesses, enthusiastic if ill-armed, the students of Oxford, and especially the excellent Welsh archers, who were thus indirectly defending the independence of their principality. Simon counted strategy among his gifts. He captured the King and heir-apparent, and in 1264, resolving on a reform of the realm, summoned in the King's name a Parliament which was to be attended by four trusty knights from each county, elected to handle the affairs of the kingdom along with the prelates and magnates.

Contemporary writings show that political thought was then becoming very bold. One writer said: "Those who are ruled by the laws know those laws best and since it is their own affairs which are at stake, they will take more care." Simon de Montfort, the real head of the government, placed power in the hands of a Council of nine members, appointed by three Electors; the latter could be deprived of their function by the Council. It was the sketch of a constitution almost as complex as that of Siéyès. Simon de Montfort was certainly far from imagining what the British Parliament would one day become, and it is anachronistic to view him as the first of the Whigs. But this great man understood that new forces were rising in the land, and that the future belonged to those who could harness them.

The invincible Earl Simon was determined to lean more strongly on the new classes, and the celebrated Parliament of 1265 included two knights from each county, and two citizens from each city or borough, the latter being summoned by a writ dispatched, not to the sheriff, but directly to the town. This time all the elements of the future Parliament were brought together—lords, county members, borough members. But it cannot be said that the House of Commons, properly speaking, dates from this experiment, because the town and county representatives were there only in a consultant capacity. Their attendance strikes us as important because we know its consequences. To contemporaries, no doubt, it seemed natural; the rebel was summoning his partisans.

But there was one man at least who watched with interest and reluctant admiration the new policy carried out by the Earl of Leicester. This was Edward, the heir to the throne. Inferior in character to his uncle, devoid of the zealous idealism which made Simon a noble figure, Edward was better equipped for success. Simon de Montfort, obsessed by the greatness of his plans, refused to allow for the pettiness of men. Edward was uninventive, but superior in practical application. Having escaped by a trick (he pretended to try the horses of his gentlemen-guards and, picking the fastest, galloped off), he rallied the barons from the western and northern borders, fell upon Montfort and, applying the tactical lessons received from him, defeated the Earl at Evesham. Montfort dispassionately admired the maneuver that was his undoing: "By St. James!" he cried, "they come on in good order, and it was from me they learned it. Let us commend our souls to God, for our bodies are theirs!" For a whole morning he fought heroically, and then, in a darkness of storm-clouds which men regarded as a prodigy, was slain. His enemies mutilated his corpse, but Edward allowed the Franciscans to bury what remained; and for many years the relics of Simon de Montfort were venerated by the people as those of a saint.

With Simon de Montfort vanished the last of the great Frenchmen who helped to fashion England. Before long the sons of the Norman nobles were learning only English. Godric and Godgifu had won. But the part played by these Norman and Angevin kings had been a great one. When William the Conqueror landed, he found a country of set-tlers, a crude local justice, a licentious and contumacious Church. His vigor, the vigor of Henry I, the vigor of Henry II, had established a new country. Many of the institutions imposed or preserved by these kings are extant today—the jury, the assizes, the Exchequer (at any rate in name), and the universities. Even the perfidious King John and the weak Henry III played quite useful parts. The Great Charter granted by the former and confirmed by his heir proclaimed the trans-mutation of feudal usage into national law respected by the king. The period between 1066 and 1272 is one of the most fruitful in English history. The Norman colony founded by the five thousand adventurers of the Conquest developed on lines so original that, during subsequent centuries, after one last effort to unite the two realms of France and England, it cut every link with the Continent. A rough analogy of this astonishing turn of events might be found if we suppose that Lyautey, conqueror of Morocco, had there founded a dynasty accepted by the Arabs,[1] and that his descendants gave that empire stronger laws and a more solid prosperity than those of the home capital.

[1] The difference, of course, being that Normans and Saxons were, after all, the same in race and religion.

Book III

THE PEAK AND DECLINE OF FEUDALISM

Edward I. Legal Reform. Home Administration

Such modernism and insularity were the more surprising as the king remained temperamentally feudalistic, and in his tastes was a Plantagenet. A vigorous, superbly built man, with the long muscular body of a horseman, he delighted in the hunt and tourney. He would make no concessions in the forest laws. His homeward journey from the Crusade was like the wandering of a knight-errant of romance. On the way he redressed wrongs, attacked a brigand in Burgundy, and fought with the Count of Châlons. When he conquered Wales he asked for King Arthur's crown, and staged a banquet of the Round Table. Towards the King of France, his suzerain for Gascony, he was at pains to observe with punctilio the code of an irreproachable vassal. He did homage, and submissively accepted his lord's decisions. His motto was *"Pactum Serva"* (*"Keep Troth"*). It may have turned out that he changed his mind, after thus pledging his word; and he then showed wonderful skill in twisting texts to reconcile promises and desires. One contemporary said of Edward that he wished to be lawful, but whatever he liked he declared lawful. Nor did he scruple to slip out of a troublesome oath by the classic device of the Plantagenets—a Papal absolution. All in all, however, Edward was shaped on a good model; he had noble instincts, and he showed an aptitude, rare in the monarchs of his time, for profiting by the lessons of experience. The revolt of the barons taught him that the age of despotism in England was over, that the monarchy could now be consolidated only by gaining the support of these new classes which were gathering strength. Hot-tempered and proud, obstinate and sometimes harsh, but industrious, honest, and reasonable, this knightly king was also a statesman.

Nearly all of the legal structure which frames contemporary France dates from Napoleon; but in England the statutes of Edward I, except where abrogated, still have the force of law. At the beginning of his reign Edward, like the Conqueror before him, had a survey made throughout the kingdom to ascertain exactly by what rights—*"Quo Warranto"*—the private lords held their part of the public power. This investigation roused much anger among the barons. John de Warenne, the Earl of Surrey, asked by the royal lawyers to show his warranty, unsheathed a rusty sword and answered: "Here is my warranty: my ancestors, who came with William the Bastard, conquered their lands with the sword, and with the sword will I defend them against all who desire to seize them. For the king did not conquer his lands by himself, but our ancestors were his partners and helpers." This was a vexing reply for a knightly king. But Edward I already knew that in England written charters have longer prospects than the rights of the sword.

Thanks to the king's firm self-mastery, the reign passed without any disastrous clash with the Church. The civil and religious powers quarreled frequently, but their disputes never reached the violent pitch of those between William Rufus and Anselm or Henry II and Becket. The gravest came in 1296, when Pope Boniface VIII by the bull *Clericos laicos* forbade the clergy to pay taxes to lay authorities. In just annoyance, Edward I ordered the seizure of Church property and the wool of the monks. The regular clergy sided with Rome; the parish priests, more English than Roman in outlook, proved amenable to the king's reproaches. A reconciliation took place, but such disputes lessened Papal prestige in England. The captivity of the popes in France from 1305 to 1378 was to deal that prestige a still graver blow, by putting the Pope within the enemy's power. With the fourteenth century, the new national sense and traditional Catholicism became hard to reconcile in English eyes. In 1307 the Statute of Carlisle forbade any subject, and the clergy in particular, to pay taxes or to apportion revenues or benefices outside the realm.

This, had it ever come into full operation, meant drying up the most bountiful stream of payments flowing into the Pontifical treasury. But it was essential that the king should be ruthless in protecting his revenue. Governmental expenses grew with multiplicity of functions, and the old taxes and feudal aids no longer met the case. The king's additional resources were "scutage," a payment in lieu of military service, which raised difficulties in collection and disappeared in 1322; the tax on chattels and landed property amounting generally to one-fifteenth for the country and one-tenth for the towns; and the customs, paid for the right of importing or exporting merchandise. These duties were levied chiefly on the export of wool and hides, the chief products of the country, and on the importation of wines.

Edward I willfully divested himself of one of his main ancestral resources by his expulsion of all Jews from England in the year 1290. The failure of the Crusades had resulted in a revival of popular hatred against the only Infidels within reach of reprisals, and powerless to defend themselves. They were accused of every crime. Their baronial creditors wished to be rid at once of debts and creditors. The action taken by the king was less inhumane than previous persecutions. He allowed the Jews to take their chattels with them, and hanged certain mariners who murdered their passengers on the crossing. The trade of moneylending was carried on in England after the expulsion of the Jews by Christians from Cahors in France, the *"caorsins"* as they were called, who had found a trick for evading the laws of the Church. They lent without charge for a short term, and then, when the time expired and the loan remained unpaid, demanded an indemnity for the time following the date of repayment. This was called "interest," from the phrase, *"id quod interest."* Gradually the trade of banking became accepted. It was practiced by many Italians, and moneychangers from Lombardy gave their name to Lombard Street in London. Then the English themselves became adept in the money market, and when the Jews returned to England in the days of Cromwell they found amongst the Gentiles prosperous rivals who were at once formidable and tolerantly indulgent.

CHAPTER II

The Origins and Growth of Parliament

IT WAS under Edward I that there first appeared a Parliament composed of two Houses, but the creation of parliamentary institutions was not a deliberate act. Against unforeseen difficulties a series of expedients was set up by the sound sense of the kings, the power of the barons, and the resistance of the burgesses. From these clashes Parliament was born. Summoned by the king as an instrument of government, it became, first for the barons and then for the nation, an instrument of control. Its origin lies in the Great Council of the Norman sovereigns, the shade of which still haunts the Palace of Westminster today. As we enter the House of Lords, the throne reminds us that the king presides over this assembly. In practice he does so only when he comes there to read the Speech from the Throne. On the woolsack sits the Lord Chancellor. Why is he there? Because it is he who convokes this House, in the name of the king. And whom does he convoke? The right to be summoned to the Council remained ill-defined until the fourteenth century. A peer of the realm is, literally, a gentleman entitled to be judged only by his peers, or equals; but there were thousands of such gentlemen in 1305, whereas the Council then consisted of only seventy members, five being earls and seventeen barons, the rest being ecclesiastical or royal officials.

After Simon de Montfort and his disciple, Edward I, the custom grew up of consulting in grave emergency not only the baronage, but representatives of the "commons"—two knights from each shire, two citizens from the principal towns. This convocation had a double object: the King had realized that a tax was more acceptable if the taxpayer had previous warning; and as the difficulty of communications made it almost impossible to gauge the state of public opinion, he thought it well to explain occasionally how matters stood in the kingdom, to men who came from all the counties and could then create a favorable atmosphere by their reports and descriptions. At first this method was not a new privilege granted to the knights and citizens; indeed, it was only a convenient way of impressing them and extracting money. Some knights, when elected to Parliament, fled to escape the burdensome duty. Besides, these deputies for shires and towns took no part in the Council's deliberations. They listened in silence. It was a Speaker (then a Crown officer) who advised the Council of their assent or dissent. But they soon took to discussion among themselves, and towards the end of the century the chapter-house of the monks of Westminster was allotted as their place of meeting. These first meetings of the Commons, it should be remembered, were secret; they were tolerated, but had no legal standing. The origin of the House of Lords is a court of law; that of the House of Commons, a clandestine committee.

The convoking of the different "Estates" of a kingdom (military, priestly, and plebeian), in order to obtain their consent to taxation, was not peculiar to England in the fourteenth century. Like the corporations, it was then a European idea. Nearly all the sovereigns of the time used this method of making the increasingly heavy taxation acceptable. But the primordial structure of English society soon caused the Parliament to assume a different form from that of the States-General in France. In England, as in France, the king began by asking each of the three Estates to tax itself; but this he soon dropped, because the threefold division did not correspond with the actual mechanism of England. First: the bishops belonged to the Council, not as bishops, but as tenants-in-chief and feudal lords, and so the rest of the clergy ceased to be represented in Parliament. The priesthood preferred to vote its taxes in its own assemblies, the Convocations of Canterbury and York. Alarmed by the frequent conflicts of Pope and king, they were anxious to stand clear of the civil power, and their abstention headed England towards the system of two Chambers. Second: the knights might have sat with the bishops and barons, but in the county assemblies and assize courts they had found themselves in constant touch with the burgesses. As a landed revenue of only £20 had come to mean that its owner was thereby a knight, the type of man and mode of life associated with the word had both changed. This class of knight was glad to ally itself by marriage with the well-to-do merchants, and in any case was more agricultural and commercial than military. Experience showed that the knights were more at ease with the burgesses. Like the latter, they were convoked by the sheriff, and were likewise representative of communities. From the union of the petty nobility with the burgesses was born the House of Commons.

Here, then, were two peculiar circumstances: the deliberate abstention of the clergy, and the association of the knights and burgesses, engendered a Parliament consisting of an Upper and a Lower Chamber. This combination of knights with citizens is a capital fact in history. It explains why England, unlike eighteenth-century France, was never divided into two hostile classes. In the beginning the feudal system in France and Europe was the same as in England. From Poland to the Irish Sea, it has been said, the resemblance is complete—the lord, the manor-court, enfeoffment, the feudal classes, the kingship, all bear a family likeness. But whereas in England during the fourteenth century there was a blending of classes, in France a barrier was rising between the nobility and the rest of the country. It was not that the English nobility remained open while the French was closed. No class was more open than the nobility of France. Numerous offices ennobled those who purchased them. But although this barrier was easily surmountable, it was "fixed, visible, patently recognizable, and detestable to those who were left outside." In France the nobility was exempt from taxation, and the son of a gentleman was by right a gentleman. In England, only the baron who owned a barony, the head of the family, was entitled to be summoned to the House of Lords by individual convocation; his eldest son was still free to go to the House of Commons to represent his county, and soon solicited this honor. The rights of primogeniture and the legislation of Edward I concerning entailed estates obliged thousands of younger sons to seek their own fortune. "If the English middle classes, far from making war against the aristocracy," wrote Tocqueville, "remained closely linked with it, that did not primarily come about because the aristocracy was open, but rather because its form was indefinite and its limits unknown—less from ability to enter it than from men not knowing when they were in it."

If the English kings had supposed that by summoning these two Chambers of barons, knights, and burgesses, they were creating a power which would slowly appropriate all royal prerogatives, their policy would doubtless have been different. Devices would probably have been contrived to enfeeble, or perhaps stifle, the Parliament in its infancy. The kings of France played the three Estates each against the other, convoked those of the provinces, and instituted a standing army and a perpetual *taille* (a tax levied without consent); and by so doing they built up in three centuries a monarchy far more independent of the nation than that of England. But neither the French kings nor the English Parliament were deliberately molding the future. Destiny alone made their paths diverge. How could Edward I foresee the future power of Parliament? If it was to become a rival to the king, it would have to obtain: first, the spending control, as well as the voting, of taxation; second, the right of making laws, which in Edward's time belonged solely to the king (the Commons could only present petitions); an idea which would have been inconceivable to all the members of the 1305 Parliament. Policy was the king's concern, and he alone was responsible for that. Now, as the king was inviolable and could not be taken to task, a conflict of Parliament with Crown could be resolved only by a dismissal of Parliament or a deposition of the king— that is to say, anarchy. To escape this dilemma, the fiction of Ministerial responsibility was in time invented. But this difficult conception could only be reached by stages. Its earliest form was judicial, not political, and consisted of the accusation of Ministers by the Commons before the Lords, the latter acting, as in the primitive period of the Council, as a high court of justice. This rudimentary form of Ministerial responsibility was to be styled "impeachment," an act of prevention. This, and its graver form "attainder" (a law of condemnation voted by both Houses without granting the accused the benefit of judicial process), were cruel and often unjust measures. But there may well have been less danger then in unjustly punishing a Minister than in justly dethroning a king.

CHAPTER III

Edward I, Wales, and Scotland: Edward II

EDWARD was the first Plantagenet to bear an English name, and also the first to try to complete the conquest of the British Isles. His youth had trained him for this task. In 1252 his father had given him Ireland, the earldom of Chester (lying on the marches of Wales), the royal lands in Wales itself, the Channel Islands, and Gascony. The gift was less generous than it seems. Ever since the Celts had fled before the Saxon pressure into the hills of Wales and Scotland, they had maintained their independence and continued their internecine bickerings. The Saxon kings in time adopted towards them the passive method of Hadrian, that of wall-building, and about the end of the eighth century built Offa's Dyke, designed to hold back as well as possible the dwellers in the Welsh mountains. At the time of the Conquest, Norman adventureres carved out domains for themselves in the Welsh valleys, where they built "mottes" and keeps, and the malcontent tribes fled into the hills. There they preserved their own language and customs. Poetry, music, and the foreign occupation, imbued the Welsh with a real national sense. In the mountainous region of Snowdon the tribes united under a Welsh lord, Llewelyn ap Iorwerth, who styled himself Prince of Wales. He had dexterously played the double rôle of national prince and English feudal lord, supported the barons at the time of Magna Carta, and so insured himself of their support. His grandson, Llewelyn ap Griffith (1246-1282), took up the same attitude in Simon de Montfort's day, and gave powerful aid at the victory of Lewes. When Edward was still only Earl of Chester he had made unavailing efforts to impose English customs on the Welsh, who rebelled and repulsed him. The young Edward ruined himself in this struggle, but it taught him to understand Welsh methods of fighting, and especially the value of their archers, who used a long bow, the range and strength of which were much greater than an ordinary bow; and it taught him that against them it was useless to oppose feudal cavalry, whom they routed with their arrows. These lessons he was to remember.

Henry III had given him Ireland as well. But there all military enterprise seemed useless. Ireland, the ancient cradle of the saints, had been partially taken from the Christian Celts by the invading Danes, who had, however, only occupied the ports on the east coast, while the Celtic tribes in the interior of the island continued their feuds. When the Church in Ireland ceased to be part of the Church of Rome, the country became quite detached from European affairs. It lived on the margin of the world. When Henry II sought the Pope's pardon after the murder of Becket, he sent over to Ireland Richard de Clare, Earl of Pembroke, known as Strongbow. But here, as in Wales, the Normans had only established themselves within the shelter of their castles. Round Dublin lay an English zone known as the Pale, beyond which the English had no hold. Norman barons owning castles beyond the Pale acquired after a few generations the language and manners of the Irish themselves. These barons, who enjoyed sovereign rights, desired the coming of an English army no more than did the native-born tribes. Theoretically they recognized the suzerainty of the King of England; actually, they maintained a regime of political anarchy. England, it has been said, was too weak to conquer and rule Ireland, but strong enough to prevent her from learning to govern herself.

On Edward's accession, Llewelyn in Wales made the mistake of supposing that he could continue his rôle in England as arbitrator between sovereign and barons. Edward I was not Henry III, and soon tired of the Welshman's tricks. In 1277 he prepared an expedition into Wales under his own leadership. Broad roads were cut through the forests; the Cinque Ports supplied a fleet, which hugged the coast in touch with the army, insuring its food supplies. Llewelyn with his brother David and their partisans were surrounded in Snowdonia, and had to surrender as winter approached. Edward then tried a policy of pacification, treating Llewelyn and David with courtesy, and set about administering Wales on the English model. He created counties and courts, and sent thither itinerant judges to apply the Common Law. The Welsh protested and clung to their ancient usages, but Edward was narrow as well as strong and refused to tolerate customs which he regarded as barbarous. He maintained his laws, and a rising followed. Llewelyn and David broke their troth, and the King, ruthless to the faithless, this time fought them to the death. Llewelyn was killed in battle, and David was hanged, drawn, and quartered. In 1301 the King gave his son Edward, born in Wales and reared by a Welsh nurse, the title of Prince of Wales, which has remained the title of the ruling sovereign's eldest son. Although English laws and customs were there and then introduced, the principality remained outside the kingdom proper, and did not send representatives to Parliament. It was Henry VIII who in 1536 made England and Wales one kingdom.

Edward I had conquered the Celts of Wales, but against those of Scotland he failed. There a feudal monarchy had established itself, and a civilization analogous to the Anglo-Norman. One Scottish province, that of Lothian, had English inhabitants; many barons had property on both sides of the border; a fusion seemed easy enough. When King Alexander II of Scotland died, leaving the throne to a granddaughter living in Norway, Edward wisely suggested marrying her to his son, and so uniting the two kingdoms. The idea seemed congenial to most of the Scots, and a ship was sent to Norway to bring the child across. To divert the Maid of Norway on her voyage, the ship had a store of nuts and ginger, figs and cakes, but the delicate child did not survive the wintry crossing. She died at sea, and immediately the great Scottish lords were disputing the Crown. Two of them, John de Baliol and Robert Bruce, both kinsmen of the dead king, and both of French descent, seemed to have equally good claims. Edward was chosen as arbitrator, and awarded the kingdom to Baliol, who was crowned at Scone. But the English king, carried along by this appeal to his authority, insisted that the new king and the Scottish nobles should acknowledge his status as suzerain.

The Scots had supposed that such a suzerainty would remain nominal. When Edward declared that a litigant losing his case in a Scots court could henceforth appeal to the English tribunals, Baliol made alliance with the King of France, then opposing Edward in Gascony, sent his defiance to the King of England, and refused to obey a summons from his suzerain. "Ha, the false fool! What folly is his!" cried Edward. "If he will not come to us, we will come to him!" And he marched into Scotland, made Baliol prisoner, carried off the Stone of Destiny from

Scone—traditionally the pillow of Jacob when he dreamed of the descending angels—and fashioned it into part of a sumptuous chair which ever since has been used at coronations of the kings of England.

Whenever Edward I was victorious he began with acts of mildness. As in Wales, so now in Scotland, he embarked on the enforcement of the English laws which he liked and admired. He encountered an unexpected resistance, not from the barons, but from the Scottish people, who rose in revolt under Sir William Wallace. In vain did Edward win the day at Falkirk in 1298; in vain did he hang his prisoners, even Wallace himself; in vain did he spread ravage and desolation across the border country. In days gone by the Romans had been forced to admit that a victory in Scotland was never more than a prelude to defeat. Lines of communication were too long, the climate was too harsh, the country too barren. Froissart gives glimpses of these woeful marches of the English army, "There were such marshes and savage deserts, mountains and dales . . . that it was great marvel that much people had not been lost . . . they could not send to know where they were, nor where to have any forage for their horses, nor bread nor drink for their own sustenances"; and in the other camp, the Scottish army, "right hardy and sore travailing in harness and in wars . . . no carts nor chariots . . . no purveyance of bread nor wine, for their usage and soberness is such in time of war . . . they make a little [oatmeal] cake to comfort their stomachs." In 1305 Edward imagined himself master of the whole country; but in 1306 Robert Bruce headed a fresh revolt of Scotland, and was crowned at Scone.

By now the King of England was old and infirm, but he vowed with a strange mystical oath, "before God and the swans," to crush this Scots rebellion, and thereafter bear arms no more against Christian men, but go and await his death in the Holy Land. This last Scottish campaign finished him. Feeling death near, he bade his sons farewell. He asked that his heart be sent to the Holy Land with a hundred knights, that his body should not be buried until the Scots were beaten, and that his bones be carried into battle, so that in death, as in life, he might lead his army to victory. The epitaph for his tomb, he had composed himself: *"Edwardus primus Scotorum malleus hic est. Pactum Serva."*

Pactum Serva—no pledge was ever kept less loyally than that of Edward II to his father. He instantly abandoned the conquest of Scotland,

and when events forced him to resume the attempt, was beaten at Bannockburn in 1314. He was a strange man, a mixture of vigor and effeminacy, who had an entourage of curious favorites, grooms and young workmen, being particularly attached to a young Gascon named Piers Gaveston, whose flippancies infuriated the court as much as they amused the King. Edward II took no interest in the affairs of the kingdom, his tastes being only for music and manual work. When he married he instantly abandoned his wife for his friend Piers. Knowing his own timidity, he made inquiries of the Pope as to whether it would be sinful to rub his body with an oil which gave courage. The anger of the barons at last rose to boiling-point, and they murdered Gaveston. The Bishop of Oxford chose the text: "I will put enmity between thee and the woman . . . it shall bruise thy head. . . ." Events justified the prophecy. Queen Isabella, who had taken a lover, Roger Mortimer, Earl of March, headed a revolt against her husband and captured him. The Parliament of 1327 forced him to abdicate in favor of his son, who was proclaimed king as Edward III. The deposed king died later in the year, horribly murdered by his guards in Berkeley Castle. For some years the real power was wielded by the Queen-Mother and Mortimer. But the young Edward III was a different man from his father. He soon rebelled against the tyranny of Mortimer, arrested him, and put him to death (1330). Thereafter he strove to be a strong ruler, as strong as his grandfather, the Hammer of the Scots.

Parliament demurred less to the king's demands and willingly voted him armies. The mixture of commercial with chivalrous motives lends a fantastical air to all this period of history. The proud Edward III, who swore "by the heron" at the Round Table that he would conquer France, and those solemnly eccentric knights who for a vow's sake would keep an eye covered with red cloth, are not so foolish as to serve at their own charge. The pious simplicity of the Crusades does not belong to this age. These knights, at bottom, are the hireling agents of the London and Ghent merchants." But the merchants of Ghent felt scruples about declaring war on their suzerain, the King of France, which were all the more troublesome because they were pledged to pay two million florins to the Pope if they committed this breach of faith. Their leader, Jacob van Artevelde, found the means of reconciling respect for treaties with their violation. He advised the King of England to join the arms of France to his own, and thus it was the ally of the Flemings, no longer their enemy, who became for them the real King of France and the object of their oath.

The Hundred Years' War, then, was a dynastic war, a feudal war, a national war, and above all an "imperialist" war. The idea of the English merchants in presenting the King with 20,000 bales of wool to pay for a campaign, was to reserve for themselves the two zones of influence necessary to their trade—Flanders as the buyer of wool, and the Bordeaux country as the producer of wine, the money received at Bruges and Ghent paying for the casks coming from Bordeaux. Further, it should be added that this war was popular in England because it led the armies into a rich country which provided abundant booty. Edward III and his barons were "the flower of chivalry," but the blazonry of their shields signalized a pillager's progress, the deplorable stages of which can be followed in Froissart. "Thus the Englishmen were lords of the town three days and won great riches, the which they sent by barks and barges to St. Saviour, where all their navy lay . . . clothes, jewels, vessels of gold and silver, and of other riches. . . . Louviers was the chief town of all Normandy of drapery, riches, and full of merchandise. The Englishmen soon entered therein, for as then it was not closed; it was overrun, spoiled, and robbed without mercy: there was won great riches. . . . All England was filled with the spoils of France, so that there was no woman who did not wear some ornament, or hold in her hand some fine linen or some goblet, part of the booty sent back from Caen or Calais." It is curious to note, so early in her history, that the main characteristics of England's policy are already discernible, imposed upon her by her situation as well as by the nature of her people. Firstly, we find England in need of mastery of the sea, without which she can neither pursue her trade, nor send troops to the Continent, nor keep in touch with those already sent. From the earliest days of this war the sailors from the Cinque Ports had the upper hand, and they were victorious at the battle of Sluys. So long as England kept her naval superiority, she was easily victorious; but later, when Edward III neglected his fleet, French and Spaniards united, and England's maritime inferiority marked the beginning of her failure. Secondly, we see England able to send abroad only comparatively small armies, and seeking to form Continental leagues against her adversaries, backed by her money. Thus, at the start of the Hundred Years' War, the English king tried to unite against France not only with the Flemings, but also with the Emperor, "sparing to this end neither gold nor silver, and giving great jewels to the lords and ladies and damsels."

Failing to form this coalition Edward was about to make the move of attacking in Guyenne, when Sir Geoffrey of Harcourt pointed out that Normandy lay undefended. Hence, in 1346, came the landing at La Hogue, with a thousand ships, 4,000 knights, and 10,000 English and Welsh bowmen. It was a heartrending sight, this passage of an army through that rich province where no war had been seen for several generations, and whose inhabitants had lost the art of defense. The sole plan of the English king at this juncture was to lay waste northern France as widely as possible and withdraw through Flanders before the King of France had mustered an army. But beyond Rouen Edward found all the bridges on the Seine destroyed, and he could cross only at Poissy. This gave Philip time to summon his vassals, and he awaited the English in a position between the Somme and the sea. At that moment the invaders felt themselves lost. But their victories at Crécy (1346), and later at Poitiers (1356), astounded them, and filled them with boundless pride. In 1347, too, they seized Calais, which gave them control over the Channel, and they kept the town for two hundred years, after expelling nearly all the inhabitants and replacing them with English.

Why were the English consistently victorious in these campaigns? The history of warfare is that of a long struggle between onslaught and projectile. Onslaught may be in the form of a cavalry charge, an infantry at-

EDWARD I

From an old engraving.

GEOFFREY CHAUCER

tack, or an attack by armored cars. The projectile may be a stone from a sling, an arrow, a cannon-ball, a bullet, a shell, a torpedo. The success of the feudal regime had been sanctioned by the predominance of horsemen cased in steel as shock troops. Feudalism was to collapse before the royal artilleries (*"ultima ratio regum,"* the last argument of kings), and before two forms of popular infantry—the English bowmen and the Swiss pikesmen and halberdiers. It was not until the end of the thirteenth century that the bowmen took an important place in the English armies. The short bow of the Saxon peasants had a short range, and its arrows had insufficient power of penetration to stop a cavalry charge. The cross-bow, introduced to England as to France by foreign mercenaries, seemed so dangerous a weapon in the twelfth century that the Church had called, without success, for its suppression. But the cross-bow was slow to reload. Between two shots a horseman could reach the line. On the other hand, the long bow which Edward I had discovered during his Welsh campaigns quickly shot a projectile which carried a hundred and sixty yards, and could pin to the saddle the thigh of a horseman wearing coat of mail. Edward I was an excellent army commander, and on the battlefield had been able skillfully to group light cavalry along with bowmen of the Welsh type. By an Assize of Arms he had made the use of the long bow compulsory on all small landowners. Tennis, bowls, skittles, and other games were made illegal, so that practice with the long bow should become the only pastime of able-bodied subjects. Any proprietor with revenue from his land of forty shillings had to own his bow and arrows, and fathers had to teach archery to their children. So it was fairly easy, when the king needed bowmen for his campaigns in France, to recruit them, either from volunteers or by requiring a certain number from each county. The victories of Edward III were due to superiority in armament.

It is erroneous to picture the King of France, at the outset of this war, as more "feudal" than his adversary. No sovereign could have been more feudal than Edward III, who rejoiced in all the stagecraft of chivalry, was punctilious in courtesy, sighed for fair ladies, vowed to create the Round Table anew, and to this end built the great round tower of Windsor Castle and founded the Order of the Garter, consisting of two groups of twelve knights, one commanded by the King himself, the other by his son, the Black Prince. But for all his relish in the game of chivalry, which was like that of his grandfather, Edward III was a realist sovereign. He chose as his motto, "It is as it is." He proved a good administrator, although not all the credit was his, because he had inherited a powerful monarchy. His taxes came in freely, especially when the waging of a popular war was in the forefront. Even the peasantry in England had hated the French for three centuries past, because of ancestral memories rooted in the Conquest and the long domination of a foreign nobility and a foreign tongue. In France, on the contrary, hatred of England in the countryside was not engendered until this war. The King of France could not at first count upon his people against the invader. The villager was indifferent. The King could not fall back on borrowing from rich merchants, nor on confiscating wool. Many of the provincial Estates refused to vote the taxes, and when they did so the taxpayers showed marked resistance. This opposition to taxation delivered the kingdom into English hands. Lacking money, the King of France could not muster troops. Whether he wished it or not, he had to be content with the feudal cavalry, already out-of-date and contemptuous of infantry. Even after Crécy the French nobles refused to admit the idea of a villeins' victory. As a charge on horseback was no longer admissible, they tried at Poitiers themselves to charge on foot; but this attack, for all its bravery, was shattered on the lines of the bowmen.

After the battle of Poitiers in 1356, when the King of France, John the Good, was made prisoner by the Black Prince, the eldest son of Edward III, the lesson was at last learned. The French army refused to fight in the open, and shut itself up inside strongholds. It could then smile at an adversary not armed for siege warfare. The peasants began to weary of the invasion. They harried the English, and did not hold captured lords to ransom, as professional soldiers did, but killed them if the opportunity arose. The English army wandered hither and thither, powerless to show fight, and the long-drawn campaign caused grumbling. At last, in 1361, the King of England made peace at Brétigny, and after asking for the whole realm of France, was content with Aquitaine, the county of Ponthieu, and Calais. It was a bad peace, as it did not solve the only grave question, which concerned the sovereignty of the English over provinces no longer wishing to be English. In Périgord and Armagnac there were murmurs, justifiable enough, that the King of France had no right to hand over his vassals. The notables of La Rochelle said, "We submit to the English with our lips—with our hearts, never!" This resistance held the seeds of future wars, and foreshadowed the final liberation of France.

CHAPTER V

The Black Death and Its Consequences

THE start of the Hundred Years' War was a time of seeming prosperity for England. Purveyors, armorers, and shipbuilders made fortunes. Soldiers and their families were enriched by the pillage of Normandy. The king's need of money enabled towns and individuals to buy privileges cheap. For a century past the lot of the villein had been rapidly changing. The system of dues payable by labor had been burdensome to the peasant, preventing him from tilling his own land. But it was no longer easy for the lord's bailiff, who had to superintend the work of intermittent and irresponsible laborers. In the thirteenth century two new methods made their appearance: either the villein himself paid a subsitute, who did the ordained work for him on the land of the domain, or he paid his lord a sum of money with which the bailiff hired agricultural workers. It was almost the "farming" system of later centuries, except that the peasant's payment represented, not the rent of a piece of land, but the buying-out of an old servitude.

The real farmer soon appeared. Certain lords, instead of exploiting a portion of land and intrusting the management to a more or less honest steward, who feathered his own nest at their expense, found it simpler to divide up the domain and rent out the land. The peasant, for his part, found it advantageous to cultivate one continuous piece of inclosed land, rather than the scattered strips hitherto allotted to him in the common fields. The rent paid was called in Latin the *"firma,"* a firm sum, whence the words "farm" and "farmer." Thereupon two classes soon developed in English rural life: one, the farmers, almost landowners, free on the land they rented, halfway between the knight and the villein; the other, the agricultural laborers, who had freed themselves from serfage, either by purchase, or by taking sanctuary for a year and a day in a town protected by a charter. For a long time yet attempts were to be made by lords and Parliament to fasten the laborer to the soil; but they failed. The truth was that, in the long run, the lord got better value from a money rent than from services. The battle of Crécy was followed by a scourge which depopulated England and made the restoration of serfage less possible than ever.

What exactly these epidemic plagues were which so long ravaged the world is unknown. The name may have covered widely different maladies, from cholera and bubonic plague to a virulent influenza. Hygiene was poor, contagion swift, terror universal. The plague of the fourteenth century was called the Black Death because the body of the victim became covered with black patches. Coming from Asia, it attacked the island of Cyprus about 1347. In January, 1348, it was raging in Avignon, and by August was moving from the coast of Dorset into Devon and Somerset. The mortality, though exaggerated by terrified recorders, was enormous. There were villages where the living were too few to bury the dead, and the dying dug their own graves; fields lay waste and the unherded sheep wandered over the countryside. Probably one-third of the population of Europe perished, and about twenty-five million human beings. In England the pestilence was particularly long drawn out. Checked in 1349, it fastened its grip again in the following year and reduced the population of the kingdom to about two and a half million.

Such rapid depopulation was bound to have profound economic consequences. The peasantry found themselves suddenly richer, the communal fields being shared amongst fewer numbers. Scarcity of labor made workmen grasping and recalcitrant. The landlords, unable to find laborers to work their land, tried hard to let it off for rent. The number of independent farmers increased, and in the confusion of the landlords they obtained advantageous leases. Some barons granted exemption from rent through fear of seeing their farmers abandon them, and others sold for a song land which became the property of the peasants. Many gave up agriculture and turned to sheep-breeding. This change seemed unimportant, but it was the first remote cause of the birth of the British Empire, because the growth of the wool trade, the need for outlets for this trade, and the need for preserving the mastery of the seas, were all in time to transform an insular policy into an imperial and naval policy.

The Black Death and Its Consequences

Lords and Parliament strove vainly during the fourteenth century to combat the natural workings of the economic mechanism by rules and regulations. A Statute of Laborers was passed in 1349, obliging all men under sixty to agree to work on the land at the wages paid before 1347 (pre-plague rates of pay). Only merchants and those who were reputed to live by some handicraft were exempted. A lord had the first call on his former serfs, and could send recusants to prison. Any lord paying more than the old wages was himself liable to fine. As compensation, foodstuffs had to be sold to laborers at reasonable prices. The fate of this law was that of all which seek arbitrarily to fix wages and prices—it was never properly observed. The Statute of Laborers remained on the statute-book until the reign of Elizabeth; for two centuries every Parliament complained of its violation; employers and employed resolutely dodged its provisions. The charter-rooms of old houses show how the bailiff, after entering the wages paid for harvesting and threshing, would obliterate the entry and substitute a lower figure. The first is doubtless the real figure, the second intended to conform with the law. Or a landlord would say to a peasant: "Your wage will be that of 1347, as any better terms would get us into trouble; but you may graze your sheep on the domain for nothing." Another would grant other advantages, and this competition caused a general rise. Throughout the country, a few years after the pestilence, agricultural wages rose by 50 per cent for men and 100 per cent for women. In 1332 land brought its owner 20 per cent of its capital value; in 1350, the return was only 4 or 5 per cent.

The plague which ruined the landlord enriched the small farmer. Not only could he buy or lease land cheaply, but, whereas the lord paid dearer for labor, the farmer with a working family was unaffected by the rise of wages. He could sell his vegetables and corn at market or fair below the prices of the domain, and still make an honest profit. The day laborer too was better off than formerly; if a strict landlord tried to enforce the Statute of Laborers, he fled into the woods, and headed for another county where the demand for workers was too great for awkward questions to be asked of a willing stranger. Thus, whilst the bowman was becoming the indispensable auxiliary of the knight on the battlefield, the peasant in the cornfield was becoming a factor to be reckoned with. Many complaints were in the air. "The world goeth fast from bad to worse," wrote John Gower about 1385, "when shepherd and cowherd for their part demand more for their labor than the master-bailiff was wont to take in days gone by. . . . Laborers of old were not wont to eat of wheaten bread; their meat was of beans or coarser corn, and their drink of water alone. Cheese and milk were a feast to them . . . then was the world ordered aright for folk of this sort. . . . Three things, all of the same sort, are merciless when they get the upper hand; a water-flood, a wasting fire, and the common multitude of small folk. . . . Ha! age of ours, whither turnest thou? for the poor and small folk, who should cleave to their labor, demand to be better fed than their masters." These are sempiternal plaints, and forever vain. For better or worse the feudal system, sapped on every side, was tottering. The microbe of the Black Death, in the space of a few years, had brought to pass an emancipation which the boldest spirits of the twelfth century could not have conceived.

But before it vanished, the feudal nobility for a century longer was to be incarnate in certain formidable figures. While the ordinary landlord was growing poorer and thereby weaker, a few of the greater barons became virtually petty princes. Intermarriage made them a close caste, linked with the royal family. The kings of England then began to accumulate for their sons, by appanage and marriage, very extensive domains. The Black Prince married the daughter of the Earl of Kent; Lionel, another son of Edward III, became Earl of Ulster; another, John of Gaunt, married the heiress of the premier ducal house of Lancaster and owned ten fortified castles, the most famous of which was Kenilworth, seized from the family of Montfort. The Earl of March likewise had fully ten strongholds, and the Earls of Warwick and Stafford two or three apiece. Lord Percy, Earl of Northumberland, held the northern borders for the King, but also for himself. These great lords all maintained their own companies of soldiery, no longer as vassals, but as mercenaries whose services they hired to the King for his wars in France. In the intervals of these campaigns these restless veterans would pillage farms, steal the horses, and rape the women, and even seize manors. Parliament vainly ordered the magistrates to disarm them. But it needed a very bold sheriff to do that to these brigands, especially as the sheriffdom was a weakened office. The fourteenth-century sheriff was no longer a great lord, but more often a petty knight appointed against his own will, in a hurry to complete his year's term and hand over the duties to another. Gradually he was supplanted by a justice of the peace, a knight of the lesser nobility, an amateur magistrate who later came to play a great and admirable part in the national history. But at the end of the fourteenth century the justice of the peace was hardly in being, the sheriff was losing his grip, and the noble bandits, "proud children of Lucifer," were making their houses dens of thieves and harassing the poor round about them.

CHAPTER VI

The First Capitalists

WAR and pestilence were bursting asunder the feudal framework; but that of guild and corporation was likewise becoming too constricted. Until the fourteenth century wool, the country's chief product, had been shipped to Flanders for cloth-making. A few crude cloths were manufactured in England for common use, but the finer secrets of the craft were confined to the weavers of Bruges and Ghent. Then a chance turned up of transferring this industry to England. The Flemish burghers quarreled with their overlord. The King of France supported him, and many of the craftsmen of Flanders, in defeat, had to leave their own country. Crossing to England, they brought with them their traditions and manufacturing processes. Edward III sought to shelter this budding industry; in 1337 he forbade both the importation of foreign cloth and the export of wool. This brought ruin to Flanders, as it was impossible to procure large quantities of wool except from England. When war with France began, Edward could not maintain the embargo in its full rigor, because he had political reasons for placating his Flemish allies, but he imposed a protective tariff. The duties payable for export were only 2 per cent on woven materials, but rose to 33 per cent on wool. This put a premium upon fraud. Some merchants slipped through the law by exporting unshorn sheep, but this traffic was forbidden by Parliament. Edward III's project succeeded, and cloth-weaving became England's leading industry.

The coming of the Flemish weavers furthered the establishment in England of real capitalist enterprises, notwithstanding the guilds. The textile industry, of course, is a highly complex one, and the number of processes necessary to produce the finished article from the crude wool is high. The wool had to be picked, carded, spun, woven, and dyed; the fabric had to be scoured, fulled, napped, cropped, burled, and finally given luster by pressing. Mediæval ideas required that each of these stages should be carried out by a separate corporation, so that a very complex process of selling and buying had to take place alongside the process of production. To carry out one order, the agreement of fifteen corporations might have to be obtained. It was tempting for a fuller or a merchant-draper to buy wool, to spin and weave it as he chose, and supervise all the operations until it was finally sold. But such concentration of work offended all the guild principles. To escape these trammels, contractors soon began to establish themselves in country districts (much in the same way that, in the twentieth century, certain industries are seen moving away from towns so as to be free of certain trade-union regulations). This new type of employer, buying the raw material and selling the finished product, was soon building his manufactory. In the fourteenth century there were two manufacturers at Barnstaple, each paying tax on an output of a thousand rolls a year. Under Henry VIII, Jack of Newbury came to have a couple of hundred crafts carried on in one building, with six hundred workmen in his employ.

The day was coming when large-scale commerce proved more tempting to the adventurous young Englishman than the wars of chivalry. Within the fences of a thirteenth-century corporation the future of a master-craftsman was assured but circumscribed. His prices for buying and selling were controlled, and he could not make a fortune quickly. The great merchants at the close of the Middle Ages no longer submitted to these over-prudent rules. Their astonishing lives impressed the popular imagination, and they supplanted the knight-errant in ballads. Sir Richard Whittington, thrice Lord Mayor of London, became a hero of legend and song, Dick, the poor orphan boy employed in a rich merchant's kitchen whose cat made him fabulously rich. Actually, the real Whittington was a wealthy merchant who lent money to the King, and amply repaid himself by handling customs duties.

William Canynges, a Bristol cloth-merchant, is another example of these new capitalists carrying on business all over the known world. The King of England himself wrote to the grand-master of the teutonic knights and to the King of Denmark, recommending to their protection his faithful subject William Canynges. At Bristol he entertained Edward IV in his house. Eight hundred sailors were in his employ, and he hired a hundred carpenters and masons at his own expense to build a church which he presented to his native town. In old age he entered a religious Order and died as dean of the College of Westbury. Gradually these great English merchants supplanted the Hanseatic League in European commerce. The Lombard and Florentine bankers, who had replaced the Jews, had themselves to give way to English bankers. The Bardi of Florence had ruined themselves in the service of Edward III, who borrowed heavily from them for his French wars and refused point-blank to repay them on the due date, so that the Hundred Years' War impoverished many Florentine families. Neutrals were already discovering how dangerous and fruitless it is to lend money to belligerents.

Influenced by this trend, the wealthier guilds assumed a new shape. Equality foundered. Luxury in dress and festivity became such that only the richest could live up to it. The Vintners Company of London once entertained five kings at one banquet. Craftsmen who might formerly have aspired to mastery found themselves pushed aside. They tried in self-defense to set up workers' guilds, which were to boycott bad masters, and two distinct classes tended to take form. And at this time also came a series of financial scandals. The merchants of the twelfth century had certainly not been above reproach, and the pillory had held more than one; but their frauds were small because business was simple and easy to control. With large-scale capitalism came the inevitable collusion between wealth and political power. During the old age of Edward III, his fourth son, John of Gaunt, Duke of Lancaster, was surrounded by unscrupulous financiers. Richard Lyon, a wealthy London merchant, was through him introduced to the Privy Council, and became the head of a real "gang." When all English wool had to pass through the "staple port," which at that time was Calais, and be cleared through the customs, Richard Lyon contrived to ship his bales to other ports where no duty was paid. He thus made a vast fortune. With Lord Latimer, the Duke of Lancaster's close friend, he "cornered" certain forms of merchandise arriving in England and fixed prices to suit himself, making some foodstuffs so scarce that the poor could hardly live. Such behavior was in total opposition to the mediæval spirit, which had believed in fixed prices with moderate profits, and viewed as criminal any agreement tending to raise the price of foodstuffs. But this spirit was dying; the King was now in the grip of merchants; they were entering his Parliaments and becoming the sole replenishers of his Exchequer, and henceforth it would be for them that England's foreign policy was shaped.

CHAPTER VII

Disorders in the Church. Superstition and Heresy. Wycliffe and His Followers

IT WAS the Roman Church which civilized England after the invasions. It taught the strong a little moderation, and the rich a little charity, and then was itself vitiated by strength and riches. Saintly men had more than once tried to reform the Church and lead it back to the virtues of its founders. But reform was always followed by relapse. The monks of Citeaux, like those of Cluny, and the mendicant friars like the monks, had succumbed to the temptations of the time. And now, at the close of the fourteenth century, when a whole world, once great, was in disintegration, the Church seemed to be one of the most stricken organs of the body politic. In England it was still producing a few great men, but they were administrators rather than priests. A bishop who owned thirty or forty manors was adept at checking the accounts of his stewards, and at serving the King at the head of the Chancellory or Exchequer. With souls he was hardly now concerned. John Langland, the great poet of this period, whose fervent faith made him the more biting in his criticism of Mother Church, deplored the swarm of bishops *in partibus* then in England, nominal prelates of Nineveh or Babylon, who never visited their dioceses and lined their own pockets by consecrating altars, or hearing confessions which ought to have been made to the parish clergy. Amongst the better clerks, a few uneasy consciences felt that the Church was moving away from the doctrines of early Christianity, that a priest's duty was to imitate evangelic poverty, and that even if he had to render unto Cæsar the things that were Cæsar's, this was no reason for forgetting that God is above Cæsar. In fact, two conceptions of the Church were in opposition—that of Gregory VII and that of St. Francis of Assisi, an evangelical Church and a Cæsarean clergy.

In England at this time the parish priests were as poverty-stricken as the bishops and monks were rich. In principle the priests had to live on their tithe and raise from that both alms and the upkeep charges of their churches. But a custom had grown up amongst lords holding a living of "appropriating" its revenue, that is to say allotting it to a bishop or an abbey, with the result that the vicar received only a minute sum. After the Black Death it became impossible to find priests for the poorest parishes. A statute analogous to the Statute of Laborers sought to avoid competition by forbidding the payment of more than £6 per annum; it was not observed, and they obtained sometimes as much as £12 yearly, but their poverty was still extreme. Furthermore, many of them were ignorant men, more interested in coursing hares in a neighbor's field than in the edification of their flocks. Some let their rectories to farmers and did not even live in the parish. Their meager perquisites were taken from them by the mendicant Orders, whose friars traversed the countryside charged with the duty of saying Masses in the convents. Chaucer drew a cruel picture of the friar going from village to village, entering every house, familiar with every housewife on his round, asking meal, cheese, beef, or "any other thing as we have not the right to choose," and then, for remembrance in his prayers, noting the name of his benefactress in his ivory tablets, cheerfully effacing all the names when he left the village. And it was not only the friar who thus competed with the priest; the country was also overrun with "pardoners," who came from Rome bearing a letter sealed with the pontifical seal, entitling them to grant remission of sins and indulgences to those who bought relics. Chaucer, whose anger was always roused by false religion, describes the pardoner preaching a sermon on the text that greed is the root of all evils—*radix malorum cupiditas*—and then selling to the villagers permission to kiss a morsel of crystal containing a bone and some scraps of cloth.

It was also the mixture of greed and religion which angered Chaucer and Langland in their pictures of the ecclesiastical courts. An archdeacon was at this time entitled to summon before the court any person in the diocese guilty of a moral delinquity, and of adultery in particular. The abuses of such a power may be imagined. Sometimes the tribunal was so venal that the most regular sinners of the diocese had only to pay an annual subscription to avoid being troubled! sometimes the archdeacon himself was honest, but his "summoner," excellently informed regarding the vices of his neighbors, practiced a regular blackmail on the faithful by threatening to cite them unless his silence were purchased. To start with, these courts had been used to condemning the guilty to penitence or pilgrimages. "Penitence was salutary for the penitent and the pilgrimage was a great social force." On the road to Canterbury the knight, the merchant, the weaver, the nun, and the doctor all met, conversing fraternally, and by their contact molding the English tongue and the English soul. It was likewise the pilgrimage which revealed foreign lands to many Englishmen. In Chaucer we find that the Wife of Bath had been to Jerusalem and Rome, to St. James of Campostella and Cologne, and she had countless tales to tell of her travels. But it had become usual to redeem penitences and pilgrimages by a money fine. The skeptical Chaucer, the pious Langland, and the theological Wycliffe are agreed in condemning these scandalous sales of pardons. The monarchy itself was hostile towards the Church tribunals, which were always suspect of being in collusion with Rome. In 1353 Edward III proclaimed the famous Statute of Præmunire, which made it treasonable for an English subject to seek or accept a foreign jurisdiction.

John Wycliffe (*c.* 1320-1384), a bold spirit, a reformer long in advance of the Reformation, teacher of the Bohemian Hussites, a Puritan before the word was thought of, had started his career as an adherent of the "Cæsarean" Church. In Crown employment he had been sent as ambassador to Bruges, and then became one of the most famous theologians in the University of Oxford. Startled by the immorality of the times, he reached the conclusion that the Church's virtues could only be recovered if her wealth were removed and her primitive poverty restored. His ideas became bolder. In his book, *De Dominio Divino,* he expounded the view that God is the sovereign of the universe, and grants power in fief to the temporal heads. His power is thus delegated to fallible beings, be they Popes or kings; to all of these the Christian owes obedience. "On earth God owes obedience to the devil." But every individual Christian holds from God Himself a fraction of *dominium,* and to the tribunal of God he must make direct appeal if God's vicegerents on earth do him a wrong. Man can be saved, not by ceremonies, indulgences, penitences, but by his merits, that is to say by his works. Wycliffe quoted approv-

[157]

ingly a text of St. Augustine: "Whensoever the song delights me more than what is sung, I recognize that I commit a grave wrong." The sermon, in his view, was the essential part of any divine service; it was by serious preaching (not by the mere diversion of the sermons presented by the friars) that the faithful could be brought to repentance and the Christian life.

Up to this point Wycliffe had been simply a rather bold teacher, tolerated by the Church because he was supported by the Duke of Lancaster and the University of Oxford. He became indisputably a heretic when he denied transubstantiation, the dogma of the Real Presence. This was an attack on the miracle of the Mass, and a doctrine which the Pope could not admit without imperiling the whole edifice of the Church. Wycliffe was condemned, and repudiated the Papal authority, teaching in his later years that the Bible is the sole source of the Christian verities. To spread the Scriptures more widely, he had the Bible translated into English, to replace the Latin and French versions which were not understood by the common people. He then formed a group of disciples, who were to live as humbly as the first Franciscan friars. Wycliffe's "poor priests" were at first men from the university resolved to devote their lives to the salvation of the Church; later on this hard life seemed too exacting for young men of wealth and education. Wycliffe did not allow them to own any money, nor could they carry, as the friars did, a bag in which to put gifts—they could accept only food, and that only when they needed it. Wearing long robes of undressed wool, tramping barefoot, they went from village to village tirelessly preaching the doctrines of Wycliffe. Soon they were recruited only from amongst the poor. It is easy to imagine the force exerted in the countryside by ardent young men preaching poverty and equality. It was the time when the peasants, in the taverns, began to discuss Holy Writ. In this newly-revealed Bible they found the picture of a paradisal, ancestral garden, with neither nobles nor villeins:

> When Adam delved and Eve span,
> Who was then the gentleman?

And after the Black Death this seed fell upon fruitful ground.

Nothing makes it easier to gauge the difference between the severity of the Church towards heretics after the fifteenth century, and its relative tolerance in the days when it was still sure of its strength, than the fact that Wycliffe, although condemned as heretical in 1382, remained until his death in 1384 Rector of Lutterworth, and was not personally disturbed. Archbishop Courtenay even had difficulty in preventing the Wycliffites from continuing their teaching at Oxford. Proud of its traditional independence and strong in the support of its students, the university stood out. Its masters inclined to regard themselves as professors rather than ecclesiastics. The university, indeed, was not an instrument used by the Church to impose a certain doctrine on the national spirit, as it subsequently became; nor was it, as in Stuart times, a body of officials in Crown service. Secular and clerical influences were at war there, and the former, friendly to Wycliffe, were the dominant force. To make them yield, the King himself had to summon the chancellor and threaten to deprive the university of its privileges. The Wycliffites thereupon submitted, and for a long time Oxford ceased to be a center of free thought.

In the country at large the "poor priests," the Lollards (or mumblers), as the orthodox Catholics styled them, proved to be more stanch disciples of Wycliffe than the Oxford masters. They were favorably received, and shielded from the bishops, not only by the common people, but by many knights who were annoyed by the wealth of the Church. The bishops, indeed, had difficulty in obtaining the support of the sheriffs and of civil justice against the heresy. When the King promised this support, the Commons at first protested. They yielded when the ruling classes began to think that Lollardry was a social danger, threatening property as well as orthodoxy. In 1401 the statute *De heretico comburendo* was passed, confirming the Church's right to have heretics burnt by the common hangman. Persecutions began, the victims at first being chiefly poor people, tailors, and tanners, whose crime was sometimes the denial of the Eucharist, sometimes the mustering of friends by night to read the Gospels in English, sometimes refusal to observe such ecclesiastical ordinances as were not in the Scriptures. Through these testimonies we catch glimpses of a fervent spiritual life, of secret arguments on the mysteries of the faith among merchants, their wives, and their servants, and sometimes of the Lollardry of a gentleman. Threats of torture caused many to retract. Others stood fast. In 1410 one extraordinary scene was witnessed: a hapless workman, condemned to the stake, found not only fagots, but the heir to the throne at Smithfield Market, where these executions took place. The young Prince Henry, later to be Henry V, argued long and seriously with the tailor Badby, promising him life and money for a recantation. But in vain. Twice the fagots were lighted, and then the prince left the victim to his fate. There, already, was the spirit of St. Joan's judges, a heartfelt desire to save the heretic from himself, and a pitiless antagonism to the heresy.

CHAPTER VIII

The Peasant Revolt

A LONG series of victories on land and sea marked the opening of Edward III's reign, and his personal courage, with that of his eldest son, the Black Prince, had made them national heroes. Fifteen years after the Treaty of Brétigny, humiliation and discontent were rife in the land. The old King was going to pieces in the arms of the fair Alice Perrers, one of his Queen's women of the bedchamber, on whom he lavished crown jewels. The Black Prince was striken with illness, and after prolonged struggles had been forced to leave his post in Aquitaine, borne on a litter, slowly dying. The King's fourth son, John of Gaunt, the formidable Duke of Lancaster, had joined hands with Alice Perrers and was ruling the country with the support of a band of double-dealers. Nearly all conquests were lost again. France had found a great king in Charles V, who had refashioned a navy, and whose generals, men like Du Guesclin and Clisson, realized that in this war the only way to success was never to give battle except when sure of victory. They accordingly allowed the English to march to and fro in the land, burning towns and massacring unarmed peasants. "The storm will pass," said Charles V; and indeed it became clearer that the English successes at Crécy and Poitiers did not represent the true measure of strength between the two countries. The winning and holding of a Continental empire was beyond England's strength, for she "was not strong enough in men or money to occupy permanently the first place in Europe." Finally, and most important, England no longer held that mastery of the sea which made her invulnerable so long as it was hers. The clumsiness of the Black Prince, a better soldier than diplomat, had brought together the King of Castile and the King of France. Their fleets controlled the Gulf of Gascony and the Channel. Not only was an English fleet destroyed at La Rochelle, but French vessels sailed scatheless up the Thames and French flotillas sacked the coastal towns and burned the fishing-villages. England's sole defensive measure was the summoning of the coastal population to arms by beacons kindled on the hilltops—a method which gave the invaders ample time to land, act, and take to flight.

In the general confusion and dismay only one body showed courage— the House of Commons. The division of Parliament into two Houses was now an established practice. The cavalcades of country gentlemen coming to London for the session became a familiar sight to the City burgesses. The House of Commons contained regularly two hundred burgesses, representing a hundred boroughs, and seventy-four knights, representing thirty-seven counties. The latter, though fewer, were dominant and deci- sive, because they represented a real force. It was they who, in the so-called "Good Parliament" of 1376, boldly called Lancaster and his faction to account, insisted on the dismissal of Alice Perrers, and invited the King to insure the maritime defense of the country. Perhaps they would have been less bold if they had not felt behind them the people of London, who were violently hostile to the Duke, or had they not bolstered up their own courage by deliberations with certain lords whom they believed to be on their side. They obtained some promises, as regards replenishing the Exchequer. But once the session was over, the member of Parliament became a plain knight again. The Duke cast the Speaker into prison; Alice Perrers, who had sworn to see the King no more, returned to his side; the bishops, who had sworn to excommunicate this woman, did not raise a finger. When Edward III died in 1377, all the work of the Good Parliament had been undone. The King passed away unmourned: a pitiable old age had effaced the exploits of his youth. The King of France, however, wishing to honor a great adversary, had a Mass cele- brated in the Sainte-Chapelle for the repose of Edward's soul.

As the Black Prince had died before his father, the lawful heir was Edward's grandson, Richard II, called Richard of Bordeaux: a handsome, intelligent lad, who could not reign in person for some years yet. His dangerous uncles, the Dukes of Clarence and Lancaster, were to become his counselors, perhaps his rivals. Standing beside the body of his grand- father, he showed his dignity when he induced the envoys of the City of London and his uncle, John of Gaunt, to exchange a kiss of peace. From the first years of his reign (1377) Richard II had opportunities of showing a surprising courage and presence of mind; within four years came a rising which might well have turned into revolution. Ever since the Black Death, a latent agitation had been hatching in the rural districts. Not that the peasants were more wretched than before: on the contrary, for a full decade wages had risen while prices sank. But men had ceased to believe in the system which held them as serfs. They had seen the shame of the old King, their lords defeated in France, the raids of French flotillas. The Wycliffites had preached to them of the scandalous riches of the abbots. A poem in the vernacular, Langland's *Piers Plowman*, had become known all up and down the land. Langland was no revolutionary; he was devout and an admirer of monastic life. But he depicted the people's lot with such somber realism and the luxury of the great with such scornful hostility, that thousands of men like Piers Plowman were stirred as they heard his lines. The villages in 1381 saw numerous secret meetings, and there were mysterious messages circulated from county to county, through the lay and clerical agitators who preached the reform of the Church and the revolt of the peasants. Bitterness was heightened by the Statute of Laborers. Daily in one manor or another the peasants came into conflict with a lord or his bailiff, who tried to force them to do harvesting for two or three pence a day. The penalties provided against the recalcitrant by this absurd law drove from their fields men who had hitherto been peaceable laborers and now became vagabonds, wandering in the woods, demoralized by their uprooting. "The fugitive serf was as common in England in the fourteenth century as the escaped slave in America in the nineteenth; in both cases an increasing recalcitrance was symptomatic of a whole class being determined on its liberation."

Froissant preserves for us the speech of the best known of these agitators of 1381, the chaplain John Ball: "This priest used oftentimes on the Sundays after Mass, when the people were going out of the minster, to go into the cloister and preach, and make the people to assemble about him, and would say thus: 'Ah! ye good people, the matters goeth not well to pass in England, nor shall not do till everything be common, and that there be no villeins nor gentlemen, but that we may be all made one together, and that the lords be no greater masters than we be. What have we deserved, or why should we be kept thus in bondage? We be all come from one father and one mother, Adam and Eve: whereby can they say or shew that they be greater lords than we? saving by that which they cause us to win and labour, for that they spend; they are clothed in velvet and camlet furred with grise, and we be vestured with poor cloth; they have their wines, spices, and good bread, and we have the drawing out of the chaff, and drink water; they dwell in fair houses, and we have the pain and travail, rain and wind, in the fields, and by that that cometh of our labours they keep and maintain their estates. . . . Let us go to the King, he is young, and shew him what bondage we be in, and shew him how we will have it otherwise, or else we will provide us of some remedy. . . .'"

Thus was John Ball wont to speak on Sundays, after the village Masses, and many went off murmuring, "True words." But the claims of the peasants were really less communistic than John Ball's preaching. They asked only their personal freedom, and that a due of fourpence an acre should replace all forced labor. The immediate cause of the revolt was a tax which the Crown very clumsily sought to levy a second time because the first round of the collectors had not produced enough money. When the peasants saw the King's men again, and when the latter tried to arrest defaulters, a whole village blazed with anger and chased them off. Then, alarmed by their own action, the peasants made off into the woods, which were peopled with numerous outlaws created by the foolish application of the Statute of Laborers. Here was a rebel army already recruited. From steeple to steeple ran the long-awaited signal: "John Ball greeteth you well all, and doth you to understand that he has rungen your bell." In a few days Kent and Essex were ablaze. The rebels sacked houses, killed the Duke's partisans and the lawyers. Their fixed idea was to destroy the written records of their servitude. In the manors which they seized they burned registers and deeds. The nobles, strangely powerless in organizing a stand, fled before them, and soon the outlaws and peasants were entering the towns. It was the turn of the landlords to hide in the woods. The townspeople received the insurgents fairly well. At Canterbury the citizens and rustics joined hands in paying off some old scores and beheading certain much-hated men. Then the shapeless army marched on London. The young King was there, said by the rebel leaders to be sympathetic, of whom the worthy people knew nothing beyond that he was a boy and had to be protected against his uncle, John of Gaunt, the most hated lord of all. Along the footpaths they trudged, grouped by towns or villages, bearing staves, rusty swords, axes, outmoded bows and featherless arrows. On the way they continued to destroy the houses of lawyers and the creatures of Lancaster, and they slew Simon, Archbishop of Canterbury and Lord Chancellor, who fell into their hands, and also the Grand Prior of St. John's. One rebel set the two heads together and forced their dead lips into a kiss.

The King and his followers took refuge in the Tower of London. The town itself would have been easy to defend; the bridge could have been opened in its middle. But one alderman sympathetic with the rebels let them enter, despite the determination of the mayor to stand fast for order. Instantly the streets were a scene of horror. The peasants had thrown open the jails, and, as always happens in revolutions, a swarm of rogues emerged from the shadows to pillage and kill. A block was set up in Cheapside and heads fell fast. A whole settlement of Flemings was needlessly slain, merely for being foreigners. John of Gaunt's Palace of the Savoy was burned. Only the young King was spared by the populace. On the first day he had gone to harangue the crowd from a boat, without landing, and was acclaimed. Nobody knew why, but he was the idol of all these hapless men, and stood to gain by the fact. He arranged a meeting with the rebels at Mile End, in a field outside the town, and there made a feint of granting all their demands. Thirty clerks set about drawing up charters of liberation and sealing them with the royal seal. The peasants believed in parchments, and as each group received its charter it left the field in triumph and returned to London, bearing royal banners which had also been distributed. But Richard's councilors had never intended to uphold the validity of concessions forced by pillage and murder. They were playing for time. And fresh crimes obliged them to take up the offensive rapidly.

The rebels had entered the Tower during the King's absence; the head of the Archbishop of Canterbury and that of the Treasurer were stuck on spikes over London Bridge. At any cost this sanguinary mob had to be kept at a distance. Many bands of peasants, satisfied by their charter, had left the town. A few thousands remained, doubtless the worst elements, anxious to continue the pillage. But from all sides knights and burgesses were arriving to rally round the King. A new meeting-place was fixed for the next day, the horse-market at Smithfield. The boy King rode into it on horseback, followed by the Lord Mayor and a full escort; at the other

end were the malcontents, armed with their bows. Their leader, Wat
Tyler, on horseback, came up to the royal procession. The chroniclers
differ as to what happened. The man was certainly insolent, and suddenly
the Lord Mayor, who carried weapons under his robe, lost his temper
and felled Tyler with a blow on the head. When he dropped the King's
men clustered round him, so that the bands at the other end of the open
space should not see him. But they had seen already, and at once lined
up for battle, stretching their bows, when the young King made an
unexpected and heroic gesture which turned out well. Quite alone, he
left his followers, saying: "Stay here: let no one follow me." Then he
crossed towards the rebels, saying to them: "I will be your captain. Come
with me into the fields and you shall have all you ask." The sight of
the handsome lad coming over to them so confidently disarmed the insurgents, who had neither chief nor plan. Richard placed himself at their
head and led them out of the City.

Murderers and robbers deserve little pity. But amongst those peasants
of 1381 there were many worthy men who believed they were aiding a
just cause; and it is with emotion that we watch the pathetic, trusting
procession of these men as they followed the handsome young King who
was leading them to a cruel end. For the repression was to be as bloody as
the rising. When the peasants' army was dismembered and the laborers
back in their villages, the judges went from county to county, holding
assizes of death. In London, on the block which they had themselves set
up in Cheapside, during the days of butchery, the guilty, and many innocent men, too, were beheaded. The relatives of victims, even women,
craved leave to make vengeance sweeter by themselves executing the
executioners of yesterday. The ruling classes became permanently fearful: their dread even reached the point of forbidding the sons of villeins
admission to the universities. The knights and the liberal burgesses lost
all authority in Parliament. But the spirit of independence in the English
people did not die. In the end it triumphed. By the close of the century
the Statute of Laborers had fallen into desuetude, and the justices of the
peace were commissioned to cope with the wage question in a non-
coercive spirit. Finally, under the Tudors, the serf system was abolished,
and then, "under James I, it became a legal maxim that every Englishman
was free."

CHAPTER IX

The Hundred Years' War (II)

THE boy King whose courage the nobles and burgesses had admired on Smithfield market, whom the peasant bands had followed with veneration, became a fanciful adolescent, and in the end died in prison, scorned by the great and forgotten by his people. Yet Richard II had qualities of bravery and intelligence; he could face his alarming uncles and tell them: "I thank you for your past services, my lords, but I stand in need of them no longer." He tried loyally to make peace with France. He understood the danger to the monarchy of ducal appanages with excessive power in their hands, and tried to be a strong king in the style later achieved by the Tudors; but his subjects had not yet suffered enough to uphold him against the great lords, and after the repression of 1381 the peasants trusted him no more. The Church was apprehensive of heresy, and would have placed herself in the hands of whosoever might give her a sword to smite it. But here again Richard's prudence and tolerance served him ill. His good intentions were spasmodic, his spells of resolution violent and short lived, his favorites badly chosen.

Richard married twice. His first consort was the Princess Anne of Bohemia, through whose connections the Wycliffite heresy was spread in Prague and gave rise to the Protestant movement of the Hussites; his second, a French princess, Isabella, daughter of King Charles VI. This second marriage was distasteful to the English, who disapproved the francophile policy of Richard II and sighed for the days when the bowmen of Crécy or Poitiers came home to the villages laden with booty. Richard had already had trouble with his nobles. A powerful group had striven to monopolize the power and sweets of government in the years of his minority. At the end of a stable period of tolerant rule, the death of Anne coincided, and may well have been connected, with a return of the sense of injury which Richard had once nourished. He took swift steps to discredit and remove the foremost of his old enemies, seized a favorable moment to pack a Parliament with his own men, secured an independent income from customs for the rest of his life, and had his own supporters confirmed in the control of affairs. Success turned the head of this able but somewhat unbalanced king. He became openly despotic, and his opponents were able to recruit fresh strength among those hitherto friendly or neutral. He exiled his cousin Hereford, John of Gaunt's son, and, on the old Duke of Lancaster's death, confiscated the son's inheritance. This was a direct provocation to revolt. Lancaster spent some time in Paris, preparing a *coup d'état*, and when he set foot in England, Richard found himself quickly deserted on every hand, and finally thrown into prison. Parliament, as heir to the Great Council, elected Lancaster to be King, and he was forthwith crowned by both archbishops under the style of Henry IV.

Henry was not a king of pure legitimacy. He owed his crown to Parliament, to the nobility, and to the Church. He therefore had to handle these three powers more carefully than the Norman or Angevin sovereigns had done. It was he who granted the Church the right to burn heretics, by the Statute *De Heretico Comburendo*, in 1401. Through the sixty years of this Lancastrian dynasty the power of Parliament, so much threatened by Richard II, continually increased. The first of the Lancastrian kings, Henry IV, knew that he was a usurper, and never ventured to thwart the Commons. The second, Henry V, spent much of his reign abroad and bequeathed the crown prematurely to a young child, Henry VI, who on reaching adolescence was to become a feeble, simple-minded sovereign. Thus, over a long period, the weakness of the sovereign, his absence, or his fears, made Parliament the real controller of events. "Confronted by factions and unstable powers," comments Boutmy, "the House of Commons, the only permanent and widely national power, acquired from circumstance a kind of arbitrating rôle. These bearers of disputable title-deeds could ask of it only a precarious credit. Still timid and tentative, astonished at its unsought inheritance, it wielded a preponderant authority for a century and more. Its records were filled with precedents, its archives with valuable claims, its standing orders with liberal practices: purely forms, no doubt, not in themselves preserving the substance of political

the French throne after Charles VI, and as regent during the latter's lifetime. He was to rule with a French Council, and to preserve all the ancient customs. His title, while Charles VI still lived, was to be Henry V, King of England and Heir of France; but a few years later, in 1422, he died in the forest of Vincennes, probably of dysentery, leaving a son one year old. In English eyes Henry remains a great king. He led them to fresh victories, and his private virtues were genuine. He was generous, courteous, sincerely religious, chaste, and loyal. A man of few words, he replied only, "It is impossible," or, "It will be done." His moderation, conspicuous in a stern age, did not prevent him from being ruthlessly cruel when the interests of country and Crown seemed to require it. His good side and his bad had appealed equally to his people. But he would certainly have been a greater statesman had he withstood the temptation to plunge into this French campaign, which after such great successes ended in disaster.

The symmetry between the two parts of the Hundred Years' War is complete. After Crécy, where feudal routine was defeated, France had produced a realist soldier in Du Guesclin. After Agincourt, France was saved by the sound sense and the faith of Joan of Arc. When the infant Henry VI, still in the cradle, became King of England in 1422, the game seemed to be lost for the French Dauphin. Charles VI died two months after his foe; Henry's uncles, the Duke of Bedford, regent in France, and the Duke of Gloucester, planned to have the child consecrated as King of France at Rheims, as soon as he was old enough to speak the sacred formulas; and there seemed to be none to prevent this. From 1422 until 1429 the Dauphin Charles wandered through his few surviving provinces, without a kingdom or capital, without money or soldiers: "The King of Bourges," he was called, derisively. Was he even the Dauphin? There were many doubts as to his birth. He himself was uncertain. Bedford, master of the north of France, undertook the conquest of the center and laid siege to Orléans. Charles had thoughts of withdrawing right into Dauphiné. It seemed to be the end.

And yet the English domination in France was frail and artificial. It rested, not on real strength, but on the divisions of Frenchmen, and the first blow made it collapse. The story of Joan of Arc is at once the most amazing miracle in history and the most logical sequence of political acts. The plans dictated to Joan by her voices were simple to the point of genius: "Give the Dauphin self-confidence; set Orléans free; have Charles crowned at Rheims." St. Joan's life (1412-1431) was too short to let her accomplish more than these three acts; but they sufficed. With Charles crowned, Henry VI could never be the lawful King of France. Once started, the people followed. The feelings roused by the victories of Joan and Dunois, the pity and horror provoked by her trial and martyrdom, filled France with hatred of the invader. In vain did Bedford have Henry crowned at Notre Dame in Paris, in vain the Burgundian faction and the Sorbonne (whose consultations had sanctioned the burning of the Maid) welcomed the young English King with lavish pomp. The Dauphin gained ground. The House of Burgundy quarreled with England. Even Paris, at last, expelled the English garrison. Normandy was set free. When Charles VII died in 1461 the English held not a yard of France except the town of Calais, which they were to hold for a century longer, a Gibraltar of the Channel.

It is remarkable that modern English historians, just as they regard Bouvines, a French victory, as a fortunate battle, now agree in admiration of Joan of Arc and in believing that she saved England from despotism. Had it not been for her, the King of England would have lived in Paris; and there, supported by a French army and enriched by taxes levied in France, he would have refused to submit to the control of his own subjects. Thanks to her, an end was made of the parlous dream of Continental empire which so long enticed the English sovereigns. These long years of struggle had given other lasting results. In both countries the sense of nationality, a new and powerful emotion, was born of contact with strangers. The people of Rouen and Orléans, Bourges and Bordeaux, with all their differences and old enmities, nevertheless felt that between them was something which marked them off from the "goddams," as the English were termed. And the English, on their side, notwithstanding their ultimate defeat, had now the memory of great deeds done in common. But meanwhile, between England and France, there was born a hatred which endured almost uninterruptedly until the end of the nineteenth century, and left the common people of both countries with the heritage of an insuperable distrust.

CHAPTER X

The Wars of the Roses

THE French wars over, England was flooded by troops of soldiery used to profitable pillaging, and quite ready to espouse any cause, good or bad. The letters of the time are full of murder, riot, lawless executions, recounted in the most natural tone, as of inevitable incidents. The first Duke of Suffolk, crossing to Calais, found his boat hailed and stopped by an unknown vessel. He was taken aboard and greeted with the words "Welcome, traitor!" After a day and a night for shriving he was put into a small boat and, without trial, his head was cut off by one of the crew, with five or six strokes of a rusty sword. In 1450 the men of Kent rose under the leadership of an adventurer named Jack Cade, who styled himself Mortimer and claimed descent from Edward III. This leader reached London, and was arrested only through his quarreling with the burgesses; before being killed himself, he beheaded the King's Treasurer and a sheriff of Kent. The nobles were at this time ready enough to follow such usurpers because the King himself was merely the son or grandson of a usurper. These Lancastrian kings knew this well enough. When Henry V, at his father's death-bed, thought him gone and laid his hand on the crown, Henry IV raised himself from lethargy to murmur: "It is not yet yours, nor was it ever mine. . . ." Against the weak Henry VI there rose Edward, Duke of York, a nearer heir of Edward III through his maternal descent from the Duke of Clarence, whereas the Lancastrians sprang only from the younger son, John of Gaunt. And round the Red Rose of Lancaster and the White Rose of York there gathered groups of warrior lords whose sole political aim was to win fortune by the triumph of their faction.

These struggles of private ambition and greed roused scant interest in the country at large. Life went on, tilth and harvest. London's trade developed. The Hanseatic League met a formidable rival. These battles were waged only by a score or so of great barons, their friends and vassals, and above all by their mercenaries. They had to be prudent and respect the neutrality of towns and villages in their conflicts, as armed men were numerous and if vexed would rally against one Rose or the other. The battles which determined the possession of the throne were fought out by a few thousands of men. They confirmed the decline of cavalry. Bowmen were dominant in battle on both sides, but gradually man, that courageous animal, grew used to facing the arrows. The barons charged the bowmen, and in hand-to-hand fighting victory was decided by ax and sword. But despite the small numbers of combatants, these battles drew vast quantities of blood from the one class involved in them, and after the Wars of the Roses the English noble families were gravely reduced in number.

The hapless Henry VI was born out of time. He was no fool, but certainly no king: a saint, rather, and in worldly matters a child. A man more gentle, more estimable, more weak, could hardly be imagined. In the great wars in his reign he was only an onlooker, leaving Somerset or Warwick to act, and himself appearing on the stage only to take his place in a procession or ceremony. He lived amongst men and women who hated one another, and thought only of reconciling them. Married to a fury, Margaret of Anjou, he showed her nothing but patient affection. His only pleasures were in hearing daily Mass, and the study of history and theology. Hating pomp, he dressed as an ordinary burgess, and wore the round shoes of the peasant instead of the fashionable pointed ones. When he donned his royal robe, it was over a hair shirt. He said his prayers like a monk at every meal, and on the table before him there always stood an image showing the five wounds of Christ. These pious, weakling monarchs, as Chesterton remarked, were those who left the noblest and most enduring memorials. Edward the Confessor had built Westminster Abbey; Henry VI founded Eton College (1440), and built the wonderful chapel of King's College, Cambridge. These great foundations ruined him. At a time when everybody, nobles and merchants alike, grew richer, the King alone was overwhelmed with debts. In 1451 he had to borrow money to keep Christmas, and on Twelfth Night, having no more credit, the King and Queen could not dine. This naïve,

unsubstantial sovereign was to become an easy prey to brutal and unscrupulous knights.

In 1453 Henry VI, who was a grandson of the mad King Charles VI
of France, showed unmistakable signs of insanity. He had lost his memory
and reasoning power, and now could not walk or stand upright. He did
not even understand that a son had been born to him. His cousin, the
Duke of York, supported by Warwick, a powerful lord who won the
twofold designation of the Last of the Barons and the Kingmaker, had
himself crowned at Westminster under the title of Edward IV. After
years of fugitive existence, the gentle Henry was shut up in the Tower,
where, according to the Yorkist chroniclers, he was humanely tended,
and according to the Lancastrians was abandoned in horrible neglect.
"Forsooth and forsooth," he said, mildly, to his warders, "ye do foully
to smite a king anointed thus." Then a quarrel between Edward IV and
the Kingmaker suddenly restored the throne to Henry and the Red
Rose. Finally, Edward of York defeated Warwick, who was killed at
Barnet in 1471; he also slew the Prince of Wales and caused the King
himself to be murdered in the Tower. After which systematic massacre
Edward IV reigned almost unopposed until 1483. He was the very counterpart of his pious cousin, a true Renaissance prince, brilliant and cynical. He enjoyed fondling City merchants' wives, and his good looks made
them not unwilling victims. Thanks to the liberality of these ladies and
their husbands, Edward lived from day to day by the largesse of his
subjects. Naturally, the givers were not losers; the privileges and monopolies granted to them allowed them to reimburse themselves from the
general buying public, and it was all an ingenious form of indirect taxation.

The accession of the House of York dealt a rather heavy blow to the
prestige of Parliament. Whereas the usurping Lancastrian kings had
requested their investiture at the hands of Parliament, the Yorkists claimed
to rule by sole right of inheritance. Besides, the House of Commons
about this time was no longer really representative of the commons of
England. At first any burgess paying taxes had been entitled to vote. But
just as the enrichment of the great merchants had changed the guilds
into closed rings, so many boroughs had bought Crown charters which
excluded newcomers. The right of choosing borough representatives was
confined sometimes to the mayor and his councilors, sometimes to a

council consisting of the richest townsmen. Thus began the steady process whereby, through several centuries, so many English constituencies were transformed into "rotten boroughs," in which the body of electors was so small that it could easily be corrupted. Similarly, after 1430, the shire knights were elected only by freeholders of land having an annual value of forty shillings (or about £20 today). Many men previously voters were thus disfranchised. This regime was to last until the electoral reforms of 1832, and insured the legal predominance of a numerically small class, because of the strong pressure exercised at elections by the most powerful lords on their tenants and friends. In 1455 the Duchess of Norfolk wrote to John Paston, greeting her "right trusti and welbelovid," and pointing out that since it was "thought right necessarie for divers causes that my Lord have at this tyme in the Parlement such persons as longe unto him and be of his menyall servaunts . . . ye wil geve and applie your voice unto our right welbelovid coson and servaunts, John Howard and Syr Roger Chambirlayn, to be Knyghts of the shire. . . ." These recommendations belong to all ages, but in the fifteenth century the House of Commons was peculiarly the creature of the noble factions.

Edward IV left two young sons, the elder of whom ought to have been his successor; but his brother Richard, Duke of Gloucester, had his nephews murdered whilst confined in the Tower, and so became king himself as Richard III. Shakespeare painted a horrifying portrait of this cruel, brave, brilliant hunchback, and despite the attempts of some historians to rehabilitate Richard III, it is probably best to accept that picture. When the twofold murder in the Tower became generally known, a definite outlet was given to the sense of revolt which had long been fermenting in the hearts of Englishmen weary of civil wars and the snatching of crowns. There seemed to be a chance of reconciling the two Roses. There remained one Lancaster, Henry Tudor, Duke of Richmond, a faintheart stripling who had cautiously fled into Brittany, and was directly descended through his mother, Margaret, from John of Gaunt. If this Henry could marry Elizabeth of York, the daughter of Edward IV, the two houses would be merged. Richard saw the danger, and tried to conciliate the burgesses by summoning a Parliament. He thought of marrying his niece himself. But Henry Tudor, having speedily left Harfleur, landed in Milford Haven with two thousand soldiers, English refugees and Breton adventurers. Wales rallied to him because the Tudors were Welsh. In 1485 he met Richard on Bosworth Field, the battle's outcome being decided by the Stanleys, great lords in Lancashire, who sided with Henry because Lord Stanley had been the second husband of Henry's mother. Richard bravely rushed into the swirl of the fight, laid low several warriors, but was himself slain. The crown which he wore during the battle fell into a bush, and was recovered afterwards, to be placed by Stanley on the head of his stepson, who thus became Henry VII.

> O, now let Richmond and Elizabeth,
> The true succeeders of each royal house,
> By God's fair ordinance conjoin together!
> And let their heirs, God, if thy will be so,
> Enrich the time to come with smooth-faced peace. . . .

And in the following year this marriage took place. The Wars of the Roses were over.

CHAPTER XI

The End of the Middle Ages

WHAT traits in England's national character had taken shape by the close of the fifteenth century? The Hundred Years' War had ended in an English failure, but its memory lingered as a thing of glory. All its battles had been fought on foreign soil. Only a few coastal towns had seen the enemy, on furtive raids. The English people had come to regard themselves as invulnerable in their island, and were disdainful of other nations. "The English," said Froissart, are proud, and cannot force themselves naturally into friendships or alliance with foreign countries, and in particular there are not under the sun a people more dangerous. . . ." This pride was enhanced by the wealth of the country, which then impressed every visitor. "It is greater than that of any land in Europe," said the Venetian envoy. Reading Chaucer's description of the Canterbury Pilgrims, one can picture the easy circumstances of every class in fourteenth-century England. Men and women wear good cloth, often hemmed with fur. Chaucer's Franklin, the small country landowner, is a bluff epicurean, zestful of living, whose cellar equals the best and whose table never lacks its plump partridges or pike, and

> Woo was his cook, but—if his sauce were
> Poynant and scharp, and redy al his gere.

The arms of the spinner and dyer are mounted in massive silver, and these craftsmen are fully worthy to take their seats as councilors in Guildhall, burgesses whose wives are styled "madam" and wear for their churchgoing gowns fit for a queen. When Sir John Fortescue was banished to France during the Wars of the Roses, he exclaimed upon the misery of the French peasants: they drank water and ate apples with rye bread,

[178]

had no meat, except occasionally a little lard, or the entrails or heads of beasts killed for the nobles or merchants. Such, concluded Fortescue, an ardent admirer of Parliaments, were the fruits of absolute power.

But the Englishman prided himself still more on his comparative liberty. The complacent Fortescue, in 1470, was extolling the English laws: "How should they not be good laws, being the work not of one man only, nor even of a hundred councilors, but of more than three hundred picked men? Besides, even did they happen to be faulty, they can be amended with the consent of all the Estates of the realm. . . . In England the will of the people is the prime living force, which sends the blood into the head and into all the members of the body politic." Triumphantly he contrasts the liberty of the Englishman, who pays only agreed taxes and can be tried only in regular form, with the constraints to which the Frenchman is subject, being obliged to buy the monopolized salt and pay arbitrary levies, and who is "flung in a sack into the Seine," without trial, if his prince deems him guilty. Fortescue, of course, exaggerated. The victims of Richard III had obviously not been shielded by legal forms. But certainly Richard would not have dared to levy a tax unsanctioned by Parliament, whereas in France, having obtained in 1439 a direct tax from the Estates for paying the army, Charles VII contrived to make this a perpetual levy, and his successors fixed its total without summoning the body which granted it.

Whence came these differences between the two peoples? It should first be remembered that the French kings had a far harder task than the English, who ruled the whole of their land from the Conquest onwards, and from the twelfth century were able to impose on the local lords the Common Law and the itinerant judges. The French people, suffering cruelly from the independence of the great feudal magnates and from foreign invasion, were ready to grant their king a large credit of power, provided that he maintained order and guarded the frontiers. In Continental France the enemy was near, a standing army essential. In England the people's liberty weakened the king, but the dividing sea shielded the weak points. Secondly, there was the fact that in England every man was his own soldier and the guardian of his own peace. The yeoman, the archer or fighting man in time of war, was, in peace, simply the small landowner. To impose his will on such men the king had no troops. This was shocking to Froissart: "It comes about," he said, "that the king their Lord must range himself with them and bow to their will, for if he does otherwise and ill ensues, ill will befall him." Since Charles VII, the kings of France had possessed a small army (fifteen companies of foot soldiers and light horse), and the most powerful artillery of the time. The French villages had no militia. In France, from the *francs-archers* of Charles VII right down to the National Guard of Revolutionary times, the citizen-soldier was a failure. Thus, in France, a permanent *taille* insured the pay of the army, and the permanent army insured the payment of the *taille*. The king of France did not often need a parliamentary body, and took good care not to convoke it more than was necessary. Even if he did, the three Estates—nobles, clergy, and the third estate—would be at one another's throats, devouring each other. The combination of rich merchants and petty nobility which made up the strength of the English Commons would have been inconceivable in fifteenth-century France. Furthermore, in England, a more vigorous monarchy was to become a necessity if violence and lawlessness were to be ended. The English people, likewise suffering from the anarchy of the Wars of the Roses, called for something approaching despotism as the century came to its close, but their king had always to observe the due forms. The idea of a limited monarchy was firmly fixed in English minds from the end of the Middle Ages.

Violence, in England, was not a necessary adjunct of the feudal chiefs. Brutality always marked these Angles and Saxons. Custom and courtesy later held this violence in check, but underneath outward show it was to survive into times within living memory. Sir John Fortescue held it to be meritorious, even when it led to crime: "There are more men hanged in England," he said, proudly, "for robbery under arms and for murder, than there are in France for such crimes in seven years. If an Englishman is poor, and sees another man having riches that can be taken from him by force, he fails not to do so, unless he be himself entirely honest." Chaucer's picture of the miller is typical:

> The mellere was a stout carl for the nones
> Ful big he was of braun, and eek of boones; . . .
> He was schort schuldred, brood, a thikke knarre,
> Ther nas no dore that he nolde heve of harre,
> Or breke it at a rennyng with his heed. . . .

Violence had been restrained in mediæval times by the twin forces of chivalrous courtesy and religious charity. But in the fifteenth century the very men who read the romances of chivalry and set up religious foundations, did not scruple to filch from the weak or beat their wives. Family morality was stern, marriage was regarded as a business arrangement; a father might sell his daughter before she was old enough to protest. After marriage, women took their revenge. The Wife of Bath, in Chaucer, tells how they treated their husbands, with a sempiternal mixture of coquetry, immorality, and cruelty. In various respects the condition of women, and of widows especially, was then better than it is in certain countries today. Although the laws of property weighed heavily on women, they could carry on any trade, form part of a guild, and become sheriffs or high constables. They could travel unaccompanied, and joined in the common life of a pilgrimage. Margaret Paston managed her husband's most weighty business, and won his praise for her prudence.

The famous Paston Letters show that in both sexes education was fairly extensive. When a husband and wife were separated, they wrote to each other. For a long time girls and boys were brought up together. Later the kings founded special schools for boys, such as Winchester and Eton. The conversations of the Canterbury Pilgrims give a favorable impression of the average culture of the men and women of the fourteenth century. Even those who did not know Latin can aptly cite the names of Cicero and Seneca, or those of Virgil and Dante. Emancipated from many superstitions, they smile, for instance, at those who are alarmed by dreams, which they readily attribute to the harmful secretions of the body and a superfluity of bile. With Chaucer (1340-1400) the literature of the Saxon speech early reached a perfection which would be equaled but never excelled. One result of the Hundred Years' War had been the birth of a prejudice against French literature, as that of an enemy country. Even amongst the elect there was a desire for a great native writer; and in Chaucer he was found. This poet, like Shakespeare in a later age, had known humanity in all its kinds; he lived at the court of Edward III, was an ambassador in Florence and Rome, and sat in Parliament at Westminster. He was, therefore, admirably equipped to present a full and living picture of the England of his time. Like Shakespeare, he discloses human beings very near to ourselves. It is the great artists who help us to realize that, although scenes and manners may change, the passions of mankind change very little.

By this time the background of life itself begins to come nearer to what is familiar to ourselves. During the whole of the Middle Ages the rich had lived in a fortified house, built to withstand siege or shelter soldiers. But from the fifteenth century the desire of knights and great merchants is to own country houses agreeable rather than defensive. Rooms are more numerous; masters and servants cease to eat in the same hall. A new room, a sort of parlor, enables visitors to be received elsewhere than in the bedchamber, and it has a fireplace to take a coal fire, and deep windows fitted with small panes of glass, underneath which are hewn stone seats covered with cushions. On the walls hang tapestries and paintings, and a Spanish carpet covers the floor. The feather bed has been imported from France, a valuable property bequeathed by will to a favorite child or the surviving spouse. Every such house has its methodically designed garden, marked out with walls or clipped hedges, planted with flowers, medicinal or scented herbs, and salad vegetables. Along the graveled footpaths, with their edges of thick turf as soft as velvet, move the ladies with their enormous head-dress. Luxury in dress was at this time so extreme that sumptuary laws were called for. And another sign of wealth was the crop of churches throughout the country; every village took pride in embellishing its own church with tapestries or statuary. But the houses of the poor, and even of the middle class, remained primitive. Chaucer's miller was content with one room for his wife, his daughter, a baby, and two Cambridge students come to visit them.

Towards the end of the fifteenth century the first printed books began to appear in these houses. The printing-press satisfied, rather than created, a need. This period resembles our own in its characteristic accession of a whole new class of readers to culture. Such periods produce a steady demand for books of popularized knowledge. Our own demands works of science and encyclopædias; the fifteenth-century reader wanted books of devotion, grammars, rhymed chronicles, translations of the great Latin authors. Every squire then had his library of manuscripts: the inventory of those owned by John Paston in the reign of Edward IV is extant and contains only one printed book. The first printing-press in England was set up by William Caxton (1422-1491), who learned the craft at Cologne. Near Westminster he started what was virtually a publishing business, producing handsome books which he sold readily. He was patronized by Edward IV, a man of culture. The invention of printing, by popularizing theology, fomented the wars of religion, rather as in our own day the invention of wireless facilitates the diffusion of political passions.

To draw too precisely the frontiers between the Middle Ages and the Renaissance would be to artificialize a natural process. Like the Roman Empire before it, mediæval civilization died a slow death. But there is no mistaking an age of transition in these closing years of the fifteenth century, when Caxton's press was supplanting the monastic copyist, when the English tongue was rivaling the Latin, when the burgess grew rich as the knights dropped lower, when the cannon made a breach in the walls of the keep, when the merchant was escaping from the guild, the faithful from the clerk, the serf from the lord. A society with centuries of greatness behind it was in decline. Another was rising, and none could yet say what it would be. The England of 1485 was ready for the smile of fortune; all observers were struck by the wealth of her farmers and craftsmen, and by the maturity of their spirit. She lacked nothing but strong governance. And this, contrary to all expectations, was to be given to her by young Henry Tudor and his heirs.

Book IV

THE TUDORS, OR THE TRIUMPH OF MONARCHY

stronger than England—still only a small country—and this left the warrior nobles no opportunities for Continental adventuring. They could only fight amongst themselves, and the Wars of the Roses had the two-fold result of making citizens and peasantry weary of all feudal anarchy, and of enfeebling the relics of the Anglo-Norman baronage. Who could inherit their power? There was the Parliament, but after a brilliant start Parliament also had lost much of its prestige during the troublous times. The House of Commons made itself felt only by joining hands with one faction or the other. In any case, it could be freely elected only if a strong central power protected the electors against interference from local magnates. Only the King could bridge the gap between feudal and parliamentary rule. With nobility and the Commons in abeyance, the path lay open to monarchy.

In disarming the surviving nobles and their partisan bands, the Tudor kings made use of three newer classes—the gentry, the yeomen, and the merchants. The gentry consisted of the mass of country gentlemen. The word "gentleman," which began to be used in Elizabethan times, had acquired a meaning far removed from that of the French *"gentilhomme."* A "gentleman" need not be of noble rank, need not even own feudal lands. The gentry comprised the descendants of the knight as well as the rich merchant, the former mayor of his borough, who had bought an estate to retire to, and likewise the successful lawyer who had become a landed proprietor. Then as now, doubtless, there was a probationary period before the county families proper accepted the new squire. The gentry's minimum line in property qualification was the twenty pounds of revenue which in the old days constituted the knight, and by now entitled a landowner to be a justice of the peace. In fact, wealth succeeded birth as the basis of a small aristocracy, whose rôle in the State might be compared with that played in the France of Louis-Philippe by the middle classes, although it remained essentially a rural aristocracy. Between the squires and the peers of the realm there was no watertight partition. The heirs of peers entered the House of Commons on an equal footing with the country gentlemen.

The yeomen also were a rural class, coming below the gentry and above the old-time villein. Roughly speaking, the yeomanry included persons having at least forty shillings of revenue requisite for jury service or a county electoral qualification, but not attaining the twenty pounds which would make them, in this sense, gentlemen. Outright ownership of land was not necessary to become a yeoman. Copyholders, and even those with a less certain tenure, could be yeomen. Bacon defined the yeomanry as the intermediate class between gentlemen and peasantry; Blackstone, as the class of the country electors (the gentry being the class of eligible representatives). In the seventeenth century the yeoman class was to number about 160,000, and formed the backbone of England and the English armies. There is thus a clear difference between the structure of England and the States of the Continent, where land was owned by so few persons outside the nobility. These yeomen were the famous bowmen of the Hundred Years' War. They feared neither fighting nor manual toil; they formed a stanch and solid body, economically, politically, and socially; and having everything to lose by public disorder, they sided with the King.

In the early sixteenth century the English merchants did not yet hold their later pre-eminence in the wider world. A few, half-pirates, half-shipowners, pushed as far as Russia to sell their cloth, or competed with Venetians or Genoese in the Mediterranean; but in the conquest of new worlds which was then beginning, England took no part. When the military successes of Islam barred the Mediterranean route to the Indies and forced Europeans to embark on great maritime adventures to find a new route to the riches of the East, the Portuguese and Spaniards were alone in sharing the lands of their discovery. Who would have thought that England, this small, agricultural, pastoral island, would acquire a colonial empire? But there was one man in those days who caught a glimpse of his country's future lying on the seas, and that man was Henry VII. He encouraged navigation as far as lay in his power. He built great ships, like the *Mary Fortune* and the *Sweepstake*, which he hired out to merchants. In the Mediterranean, about the year 1500, the galley was still the man-of-war, although the merchantman was a sailing-ship; but the English merchantman and vessel of the line were sister ships. This was partly because the Atlantic and the North Sea had never been safe for galleys, and partly because the English, a practical race, wished in time of peace to devote their whole fleet to commerce. When war came, carpenters were set to work by royal requisition to build "castles" for troops, fore and aft. During the fifteenth century these "castles" became permanent, and Henry VII was one of the first to place cannon on board his vessels. To repair his ships he set up an arsenal at Portsmouth. He fitted out expeditions such as Cabot's, which, seeking the spices of the Orient, discovered the cod of Newfoundland. His Navigation Act (1489) forbade the importation of Bordeaux wines in foreign ships (and the fact that the displacement of British ships is today measured in "tons" is a relic of the reckoning of so many "tuns" of claret). In a word, Henry VII apparently realized that the struggle for external markets would become a dominating political issue; his fostering of the fleet and of sea-borne trade won him the loyalty of the large towns, and of London in particular.

Supported by this triple power of gentry, yeomen, and merchants, the King could checkmate the surviving power of the baronage. Knowing how provincial juries could be intimidated by the prestige of their former masters, he brought any dangerous charges before a prerogative court, formed from his own Council, which was called the Court of Star Chamber from the decoration of the room where it sat. Sentence of death was rare under Henry VII. "He drew more gold than blood," being rightly persuaded that an extraction of money would be quite soon forgotten by the victim, whilst it would certainly fill the royal coffers. But he compelled respect for his will. Once, when visiting the Earl of Oxford, he was received by a whole company of uniformed servants. A recent law strictly forbade noblemen to maintain such bodyguards, who could too readily be transformed into soldiers. As he left, King Henry said to his host: "I thank you for your good cheer, my lord, but I may not endure to have my laws broken in my sight. My attorney must speak with you." And the earl was glad to be free of the matter with a fine of £10,000. These methods of combating the old feudal machine were harsh but salutary, and the Star Chamber itself performed much useful work. But the principle of the prerogative courts, inasmuch as they deprived the accused of the benefit of jury trial, was reprehensible, and contrary to the liberties of the realm. This was clearly seen when, under the Stuarts, they became instruments of tyranny.

In politics as in justice, Henry VII gave legality a holiday. He summoned Parliament only seven times during his reign. But who could grumble? The confusion of the civil wars had resolved any political conflict in favor of the Crown. True, the king ruled only with the help of his Council, but the Council did not, like that of the Norman kings, represent only magnates and prelates. The new councilors were the sons of burgesses, trained in the universities. Many of the families destined in future centuries to take a great part in the governance of England— the Cavendishes, Cecils, Seymours and Russells—started in this Tudor administration. Noble lines were founded, not now by the warrior, but by the high functionary. The personal servant of the king is succeeded by the Secretary of State. The Acts of the Privy Council show us how detailed this administration was becoming: it is often like some family business. In June, 1592, for instance, the Council was concerned with one Thomas Prince, a schoolmaster, who had spoken against religion and the State. It was decided to write to the assize judge of his county to ask whether there were grounds for a prosecution. The Council ordered the owner of a meadow to repair the tow-path running across it, and authorized a butcher to slaughter beasts during Lent for the kitchens of the French embassy. Provision was made for everything: if troops were arriving at Portsmouth, the Council would write to the mayor requesting him to take steps that they be provided with foodstuffs. For as yet there was no national bureaucracy. Court and king could govern only by utilizing the close network of local institutions in shire and borough.

CHAPTER II

Local Institutions in Tudor Times

AN IMPORTANT contrast between French and English history is found in the development in France of a hierarchy of officials dependent on, and paid by, the central government, as against the growth in England of local institutions voluntarily administered. The natural tendency of the Tudor sovereign was to use whatever was ready to hand, and to solve new problems by referring them to the established mechanism. What survived of the old Saxon *folkmoot* in the countryside, after several centuries of feudalism? The parish meeting seemed to bear the nearest resemblance. In the thirteenth century the priests obtained payment from their parishioners for church repairs and the purchase of books and vestments, the cost of which had previously come out of the tithe; and to administer this modest budget the parishioners probably appointed a few representatives. The churchwarden, the legal guardian of parochial property, bought the pyx and chalice, the sacerdotal wine and ornaments, and a costume for the beadle, who expelled dogs or drunkards from the church, staff or whip in hand. The sexton dug the graves, cleaned the church, and lit the fire. The parish clerk had charge of the registers and rang the bell. The parish revenue came from its land, or from herds belonging to the parish, and from the church rate, as fixed by the vestrymen in proportion to every man's goods.

With the sixteenth century, for reasons which will later be apparent, the problem of the poor assumed new and grave aspects, and the Tudor kings adopted the parish as the basis of a system of relief. Every Eastertide the parish had to appoint four guardians of the poor, who collected alms with the churchwardens. Every parishioner was asked for such charity as he could give weekly to the poor. The amount of alms was at first left to each man's discretion; those who refused to give were summoned before the bishop, and occasionally imprisoned. But with the spread of poverty in the land, the charge had to be made compulsory. In principle every parish had sole responsibility for its poor, and it was strictly forbidden for any person without means of subsistence to wander from village to village. To give alms to a vagabond was an offense. If one such were caught, he was liable to whipping, and if habitually offending branded with a "V" on the shoulder to mark him out. The rogue, or dangerous vagabond, was marked with an "R," although if he could prove that he could read he might claim benefit of clergy, in which case a mark on the thumb sufficed. Thereafter, duly whipped and branded, these wretches were sent back to their native parishes, being given a limit of so many days for the journey. Custom being thus, no parish could tolerate the settlement within its bounds of an indigent family whose children might one day be a charge upon its resources. A child put out to nurse in a village other than that of its parents was often sent back by the authorities of the foster-parish to the parent-parish, to avoid any subsequent trouble. A man might become, in fact, a prisoner in his parish.

But in the sixteenth century it was coming to be recognized that society has a duty to keep alive, after a fashion at least, its aged and infirm, its blind and crazed. A law of 1597 ordered the building of hospitals for the infirm on waste lands, and the provision by the guardians of stocks of raw material (iron, wood, wool, and flax) to enable them to give work to the workless, and also that poor children should be put out as apprentices. This led to the building by wealthy men of free houses for the poor, almshouses, buildings which often strike us nowadays as full of charm, for it was an age of many graces. The law required that every cottage be surrounded by about four acres, to enable the occupant, by cultivating his plot of land, to produce his own livelihood. To the penniless aged the parish had to pay a weekly pittance of a groat or a shilling. If the burden of the poor of one parish became excessive, a richer parish might be ordered to help its neighbor. But the principle of local help was maintained, and the central government never took part in such relief.

In every parish one man was charged with arresting and whipping vagabonds, pacifying brawlers, stopping illegal games, and in general compelling respect for the King's Peace. This non-professional police officer was elected for one year and was called the petty constable. The office had been created by Edward I, to inspect weapons, insure the protection of villages, and pursue malefactors. This unfortunate citizen had a troublesome year before him, as he was entirely responsible for the tranquillity of his parish. If a vagabond was arrested by some one else, the constable instantly found himself sentenced to a fine for neglect of his duties. If he himself made an arrest, he must keep the malefactor in his own house (there being frequently no prison), and then conduct him to the county court. It was he, too, who had to place petty offenders in the village stocks. If a vagabond was being sent back to his native parish, the constables of all the parishes lying between had to pass him on from one to the next. To ourselves, accustomed to seeing such duties intrusted to professional police, it is hard to believe that they could be fulfilled, year after year, by elected villagers; but it must be remembered that this was an old English tradition, that in every village the ex-constables, a numerous class, were ready to guide the novice and lend him a hand if need be, and also that in the quarter-sessions of the county court the constable could find instruction in the example and converse of his colleagues. Abuses and local tyrannies there certainly were. Shakespeare depicted some such. But it is comprehensible how great a measure of stability was given to the country at large, by this age-old habit of its citizens' maintaining law and order by their own exertions.

Just as the yeoman was called upon to act as constable or sit on the jury, so it was the squire's duty to accept the function of justice of the peace. This post was not an elected one; he was chosen by the king, and the commission could be revoked at the royal pleasure. He was the link between parish and county. In the parish wherein he was the big landowner, living in the manor-house, he was respected as the leading personality in the community. Four times a year he sat with his colleagues in a county town at the quarter-sessions, where he dealt with the most diverse business, some judicial, some administrative. It has been said of the justice of the peace that he was the Tudors' maid-of-all-work, and in point of fact his rôle was so great that, from the sixteenth century onwards, even in times of upheaval, the English countryside was nearly always free from lawlessness. Even if the brain centers momentarily failed, the local ganglia insured the reflexes. The justice of the peace was a figure at once complex and admirable. He was not only an agent of the central power, but also a local power independent of the government.

He exercised sundry functions which today would be those of civil servants, but had a practical knowledge of the administration of estates which an ordinary official could not have possessed. Between moribund feudalism and the new growth of a bureaucracy, he stood for the enduring forces within England. At first there were only six judges to each county; later, their number rose (in 1635 the North Riding of Yorkshire had thirty-nine). During their stay in the district, justices of the peace received four shillings a day; when a case called for local investigation, the court intrusted it to two justices of the peace, one as a check on the other. As their chief executive officer, there was the high sheriff of the county, appointed for one year. Minor offenses were dealt with by the petty sessions, attended only by justices of the immediate neighborhood. Thus all the parish life passed under the eye of a justice of the peace, before whom delinquents were brought by the constable. But in spite of the considerable volume of work thus imposed, the office was a coveted one, as being both honorable and the sign of a man's importance in his locality. Like any human office, its efficiency depended on the qualities of its holder, but most justices seem to have been salutary tyrants and quite reasonable administrators.

Village life in Tudor times may be imagined moving round the pleasant manor-house of gray stone, with its brick-walled gardens—the house of the squire-justice. The communal fields still survived, in regions where they had been customary, providing plenty of trouble for the constable as they facilitated theft and bickering. On weekdays everybody worked, not to work being an offense. On Sundays men had to practice at the archery butts and teach their children the use of the bow; but this was now only a tiresome survival. The villagers preferred other games, which the constables had to suppress. They also crowded into the ale-houses, where they drank and played except during church hours. Church attendance on Sunday was obligatory, and those who failed to go were fined for the benefit of the poor. All activities were under surveillance. It was a grave offense to accuse a woman of witchcraft, as the consequences for her might be terrible. Sometimes old women were suspected of casting spells on cattle or men, but fortunately the justices shrugged their shoulders and refrained from burning all the witches brought before them.

The village horizon was narrow. No man dared leave his village without valid and lawful reason. Strolling players could move about only with a warrant granted by a justice of the peace, in default of which they were treated as rogues and vagabonds, and whipped and branded accordingly. University students wishing to travel had to carry passes from their colleges. Tilling the fields and performing the numerous public duties of the village left men little leisure to think of other matters. But they could catch glimpses of the function of a central government. New edicts were proclaimed in the king's name, from the pulpit or at the market cross. The yeomen went to the town for the quarter-sessions; the justices received their commissions from the king himself; the lord lieutenant occasionally went to London and was acquainted with the king's Ministers. Slowly, in every village, there was forming the living cell of a great body, the State.

Chapter III

The English Reformers

Side by side with the transformation of the mediæval political structure, there came about in Tudor times a corresponding change in the spiritual and intellectual structure of England. The consequences there of the Italian Renaissance and the German Reformation were very remarkable. National traits were by now well defined. The sensuousness of the great Italians, their passionate love of statues and pictures, their awakening to pagan antiquity, the sermons exalting the Christian virtues by lines from Horace or apothegm of Seneca, the humanist and all-too-human Popes, were all very disturbing to many young Englishmen who came to sit at the feet of Savonarola or Marsilio Ficino. In Henry VII's England, as elsewhere in Europe, Plato was set above Aristotle; the scholastic subtleties of the Middle Ages were by now so scorned that the name of the *"Doctor Subtilis,"* Duns Scotus, so long the very synonym of wisdom, engendered the word "dunce." But in the English universities men of learning used their knowledge of Greek to prepare commentaries on the Gospels rather than to imitate the Anacreontic poets. Italy filled them with "amazement and repulsion." Throughout their history the English have been attracted towards the Mediterranean civilizations, but in their lure they recognize a Satanic snare. Italy welcomed rebels or artists, and inspired Chaucer; but she startled the average Englishman. "Englishman italianate, devil incarnate," said a sixteenth-century proverb. And yet the Englishman felt himself as remote from Germanic violence as from Italian sensuality. The brutality of Luther's genius alarmed the scholars of Oxford, and at first attracted only the Cambridge youth or the Lollard "poor priests." The early Oxford reformers desired to rectify the errors of the Roman Church, but did not imagine that a Christian could leave its fold. Some of those who first spread the new learning, men like Thomas More and John Fisher, were later to die for the old Church.

John Colet, at once a great Latinist and a rich burgess, is the most representative figure of this generation. He was the son of a lord mayor of London, Sir Henry Colet, who from the day of his son's ordination obtained rich livings for him. John Colet pursued his studies at Oxford, read Plato and Plotinus, and about 1493 traveled in France and Italy. There he acquired a deeper knowledge of the Church Fathers, whose philosophy he preferred to the scholastic doctrines still taught at Oxford. On returning to his own university, this young man of thirty began a course on the Epistles of St. Paul which drew crowds of enthusiastic students. Colet expounded the original text of the Epistles to the Corinthians and Romans with a stimulating intimacy of understanding. He spoke of the personal character of St. Paul, compared the Roman society depicted by the apostle with that revealed by the writings of Suetonius, and made use of Greek texts contemporaneous with St. Paul, to the natural amazement of a public unaware of such historical aspects of religion, and for the most part living in the belief that the Scriptures had originally been penned in Vulgate Latin. The young professor sprang into sudden fame. Priests came to consult him, and were reassured; he made commentaries for them on his pronouncements, and cannot have been regarded as dangerous, since he was appointed dean of St. Paul's at an early age. When his father left him a large fortune, he devoted it to founding St. Paul's School in London, where Greek and Latin should be taught to one hundred and fifty-three boys—this number being that of the miraculous draught of fishes, still commemorated by the boys of the school wearing a silver fish as an emblem. A curious fact, typical of the man and his time, was that Colet intrusted the administration of his gift, not to the dean and chapter of St. Paul's Cathedral, nor to the University of Oxford, but to the Honorable Company of Mercers. Church scholarship, like the royal administration, was pleased to have the support of the English merchants. The school's syllabus was carefully planned by its founder, to include the teaching not only of the mediæval *trivium*—dialectic, grammar, rhetoric—but also Greek, Latin, and English. "No wonder," wrote his friend, Thomas More, "that your school raises a storm, for it is like the wooden horse in which armed Greeks were hidden for the ruin of barbarous Troy." The strange thing, however, was that the builders of the wooden horse did not desire the ruin of Troy.

Of Colet's friends and followers, the most remarkable was Thomas More, who was at once a great administrator and a great writer, his *Utopia* being the best book of its age. Hostile towards warlike glory, More desired the death of the old chivalrous conceptions, and proclaimed a communistic mode of society, disdainful of gold, making work obligatory upon all, although limited to nine hours a day. Monkish asceticism he condemned, and believed in the excellence of human nature. And in his pictured utopia all religions were permitted, Christianity being given no peculiar privilege. These theoretic ideas of More have often been contrasted with his actual practice, and surprise caused by this prophet of tolerance having himself been an intolerant Chancellor, and at the last a martyr for Catholicism. But to create an imaginary country and to govern a real one are totally distinct activities, and the necessities of action are not those of untrammeled thought.

The true aim of John Colet, of Thomas More, and of their friend Erasmus was the reformation of the Church, not by violence or persecution, but by reason and enlightenment. The movement is best typified in Erasmus. Although born in Holland, he was far more European than Dutch. He scarcely knew his native tongue, but spoke and wrote in Latin. His books, translated into many languages, gave him an intellectual renown which so far impressed the Emperor Charles V, King Francis I of France, and King Henry VIII, that all three were rivals for his presence on their soil. His authority in Europe was greater even than that later enjoyed by Voltaire, or by any man of our own times. Twenty-four thousand copies of his *Colloquies* were sold, a prodigious figure for a Latin book in a sparsely peopled Europe where few could be counted as educated. The common tongue, Latin, facilitated friendships between the humanists of all nations. It was in Thomas More's house that Erasmus wrote his *Praise of Folly*, and at Cambridge that he completed his great edition of the New Testament from the Latin and Greek texts. Nowhere did Erasmus find a more congenial air to breathe than in England. "When I listen to my friend Colet," he said, "I fancy I hear Plato himself. . . . Whose nature is so humane and charming as that of Thomas More?" If anything, it seems, these Englishmen were a little too saintly for him. Thomas More had banished austerity from his utopia, but in this world wore a hair shirt; and when Erasmus stayed with Bishop John Fisher he admired his library but deplored the chilly draughts.

Regarding these early English reformers, no error could be greater than to view them as precursors of an anti-Catholic movement. They simply wished to improve the spirit and morality of the clergy. But they encountered strong currents of opinion which carried their disciples infinitely farther away than they would themselves have desired. Sixteenth-century England was not anti-religious, but anti-clerical. A bishop in those days declared that, if Abel had been a priest, any London jury would have acquitted Cain. All the old grievances were still alive—ecclesiastical courts, monastic wealth, episcopal luxury. The Papacy, too remote, sacrificed English interests to those of Continental princes whose proximity could exert a more direct force on Roman policy. English monarchs and statesmen were pained to see their sovereignty partially delegated to a foreign power which knew so little about their country. And since the days of Wycliffe, Lollardry was an underground force. In merchants' lofts, in the taverns of Oxford and Cambridge, the English version of the Bible was read and commented upon by fervent voices. In the middle classes, under Wycliffite influence, centers of ascetic, individualist morality had come into being, which in years to come would be rekindled and fanned into living flames. Here the doctrines of Luther would find a ready welcome, the ascetic teachings of Calvin still more.

The reign of Henry VII (1485-1509) favored the development of the studies and ponderings of such reformers, as it was a reign of comparative peacefulness. These four-and-twenty years show few events of importance. But great sovereigns, like great statesmen, are often those who, like this first of the Tudors, are able to invest their names with a zone of silence. It is not by chance that under the rule of such men no grave incident arises. Especially in the early years of a dynasty or a regime does wisdom ordain quietude. If the Tudors contrived to strike solid roots, if local institutions became strong enough to supplant the machinery of feudalism, this was due to the twenty-five years of peace at home and abroad which this cautious, mysterious progenitor gave to his country before the dramatic reigns of his son and grandchildren.

Chapter IV

Henry VIII

Fashion molds kings just as it imposes costume and custom. A great mediæval king had to be courteous, chivalrous, stern, and devout; a great prince of the Renaissance was a cultured libertine, spectacular, and often cruel. Henry VIII had all those qualities, but they were translated into English: that is, his libertine life was conjugal, his culture was theological and sporting, his splendor was in good taste, his cruelty was legally correct. So he remained in his subjects' eyes, despite his crimes, a popular sovereign. Even today he is defended by English historians. The grave Bishop Stubbs opines that the portraits of his wives explain, if they do not perhaps justify, his haste to eliminate them. Professor Pollard wonders why it is particularly blameworthy to have had six wives, when Catherine Parr had had four husbands and her brother-in-law, the Duke of Suffolk, four wives without anyone blaming them. Henry, he says, might have had many more than six mistresses without damaging his reputation. True enough; but Henry IV of France never had the necks of the fair Corisande or Gabrielle d'Estrées laid on the block.

When Henry VIII succeeded his father in 1509, he was eighteen years of age, a fine athlete, proud of his person (immensely gratified when the Venetian ambassador told him that his calf was more shapely than Francis I's), a capital bowman and tennis-player, a great horseman who could wear out ten horses in a day's hunting. He had literary tastes, being well grounded at once in theology and the romances, composed poems, set his own hymns to music, and played the lute "divinely." Erasmus knew him as a child, and was struck by his precocious intelligence. The new humanists found in him a friend. He brought Colet to London and appointed him a court preacher; he made the reluctant

Thomas More a courtier, and then his Chancellor; he asked Erasmus to accept a pulpit at Cambridge. It should be added that he was very devout, and that his Oxford friends, reformers though they were, had strengthened his respect for the Catholic faith. Surprising as it may seem, he sought throughout his life to satisfy the scruples and fears of "a completely mediæval conscience."

Shortly after his accession the King married Catherine of Aragon, widow of his brother Arthur and a daughter of Ferdinand of Spain. She was neither his choice nor his love: it was a political marriage. To contemporary England, a secondary power, this Spanish alliance was both an honor and a safeguard, and when it was broken by the early death of Prince Arthur, the Council, in their anxiety to have Catherine as Queen, begged Henry to take her as his wife. But a text in Leviticus forbade the union of brother-in-law with sister-in-law, and a Papal bull had to be obtained in 1503; it had to be proved that Catherine's first marriage had not been consummated. Witnesses were found to swear this, and on the day of the wedding with Henry she wore the hanging tresses of maidenhood. These facts assumed significance later, when the King sought to repudiate her. At the beginning of his reign Henry took little part in governing, and left all authority to the Minister of his choice—Thomas Wolsey, the son of a wealthy butcher in Ipswich, whom the Pope at Henry's request appointed as a Cardinal. Vanity and ambition ruled Wolsey's character. *"Ego et rex meus,"* he wrote to foreign sovereigns, which, it has been said, was sound Latinity but bad theory. His household was regal, with its four hundred servants, its sixteen chaplains, its own choirboys. To found the great college at Oxford, now known as Christ Church, and to compel admiration of his liberality, this archbishop did not scruple to rob the monasteries. When Pope Leo X made him not only Cardinal, but Papal Legate in England as well, Wolsey held in his own hands the whole civil and ecclesiastical power in England. Even the monks and friars, independent of the secular clergy, had to obey this Legate of Rome. He thus inured the English to the new idea of spiritual and temporal authority being both in one man's hands. Intoxicated with power, Wolsey treated Rome with scorn; he had schemes for bribing the Sacred College and having himself elected Pope, threatening the Church with schism if he were not chosen. Such gestures of violence prepared the English Catholics for rupture with Rome, but neither the

Cardinal nor his royal master then supposed the break to be near. When Luther's declaration was made public, the King himself wrote a refutation which earned him the Papal title of Defender of the Faith (1521).

Foreign affairs were Wolsey's favorite concern. Abroad as in England, strong monarchies were then emerging from the feudal struggles. The Kings of France and Spain were by now the heads of great States: if one gained mastery and dominated Europe, where would England stand? The natural rôle of England was to maintain the balance of power on the Continent. This involved a shifting and apparently treacherous policy, which at first succeeded: Francis I and Charles V of Austria were rivals for the alliance of Henry VIII. On the Field of the Cloth of Gold, in 1520, the Kings of France and England staged a contest in magnificence which was never to be equaled again. But to follow that meeting speedily, Wolsey had already prepared another—between his master and the Emperor Charles. His duplicity even went so far as to cause his own dispatches to be seized, so that he himself could countermand them in the name of the King. To one international conference he sent an ambassador provided with two contradictory sets of instructions, to be shown to the Spaniards and French, respectively. After a long show of favor for the French alliance, Wolsey at last chose that of the Emperor, because the English merchants so insisted. An interruption of trade with Spain and the Low Countries would have ruined the wool merchants and drapers. But trade is a bad counselor in diplomacy. By sacrificing Francis I, England upset the balance of power in favor of Charles V. After the battle of Pavia in 1525, the Emperor, sovereign of Spain, Italy, Germany, and the Low Countries, was the master of all Europe. In particular, he had the Pope within his grip; and this, by indirect ways, was to prove the undoing of Cardinal Wolsey.

It is unjust towards Henry VIII to explain his divorce and the breach with Rome by his passion for the dark eyes of Anne Boleyn. He could easily have had Anne Boleyn without promising her marriage; but the problem before him was more complex. If England was to be spared a new War of the Roses (and dire memories of anarchy were still fresh in many minds), it seemed essential that the royal spouses should have a son. But Catherine, after frequent miscarriages, had produced only one daughter, Mary, born in 1516, and her health left small hope of her bearing other children. Could Mary Tudor be regarded as heiress to the throne? The English Crown had been transmitted through the female line; Henry VII himself received it only through his mother. But since the Conquest the only woman who ruled had been Matilda, and two decades of disorder were a disheartening precedent. Dynastic and general interests demanded a son, and the King, eager to have this heir, began to wonder whether some evil star did not overhang his marriage. Had the Papal dispensation been valid? Henry was superstitiously ready to doubt it, after so many disappointments. But he still hesitated to divorce. Catherine was the aunt of Charles V, who would certainly side with her, and it was Henry's cherished hope that the Emperor would marry Mary, to crown a great alliance. When Charles went back on his promises and chose as his consort an Infanta of Portugal, the King of England felt that he need not trouble further about the Emperor's feelings.

In love with the charming, merry, young Anne Boleyn, Henry VIII wished to marry her in order to have a lawful heir, and sought means of getting rid of Catherine of Aragon. Civil divorce was unknown, and in any case would not have helped the King. He had to petition Rome for the annulment of his marriage. This seemed easy enough, as the Pope had previously showed extreme latitude in such matters where crowned heads were concerned. Besides, if necessary, there was a plausible case for annulment, although it was precisely this which had been set aside to enable the marriage to take place: Catherine had been her husband's sister-in-law. True, a Papal bull had declared her second marriage valid; but might not a second bull sever those whom a bull had united, and could not fresh investigation plead that the marriage of Catherine and Arthur had after all been consummated? The rumor spread that Henry doubted the lawfulness of his marriage, and had grave scruples of conscience about remaining illegally wedded. Wolsey was instructed to negotiate with the Papal court, and immediately met with an opposition of a quite secular kind: Charles V, with Rome in his grasp, refused to let his aunt Catherine and his cousin Mary be sacrificed. The Pope, for his part, would have been ready enough to satisfy Henry, and send as Legate to England the Cardinal Campeggio, who was to hear the case along with Wolsey. The King supposed that the matter was settled, but Catherine appealed to Rome and induced the Pope to have the case heard in his own court. Henry's annoyance this time was extreme, and Wolsey's position became dangerous. Like all men with ambition, the Cardinal had enemies. A charge of *præmunire*, tantamount to treason, was made against him because, being an English subject, he had consented to be a Papal Legate and deal with matters pertaining to the King's court before a foreign tribunal. The charge was absurd, as the King himself had authorized and favored the nomination. But the Cardinal found no defenders; he had to give up all his wealth, and only mortal illness saved him from the scaffold. Human character always holds surprises: when this man of vaulting ambition died, it was found that under his robes he wore a hair shirt.

With anxiety in his heart, Sir Thomas More took Wolsey's place as Lord Chancellor. But the two men who at the moment had most authority with the King himself were chosen because, in this matter of the divorce, they brought a gleam of hope. The first was Thomas Cranmer, an ecclesiastic with whom Henry's secretary, Gardiner, had once had conversation, in the course of which he had said that the King need not pursue his case at Rome: all he needed was that some eminent theologians should certify the nullity of his first marriage, and he could then take the moral responsibility of a fresh marriage with neither scruples nor danger. The King was delighted, had this ingenious ecclesiastic invited to the home of Anne Boleyn's father, and began to follow his advice by consulting the universities. Theologians, like lawyers, can make texts square with facts. From Oxford and Cambridge the desired opinions were produced by a little cajoling and intimidation; the University of Paris was favorable because it hated Charles V; and the universities of northern Italy followed Paris. Before long the King was able to lay before Parliament the opinions of eight learned societies, agreeing that a marriage with a deceased brother's widow was null and void, and that not even the Pope could in such a case grant dispensation. Members of Parliament were requested to report these facts to their constituencies and to describe generally the scruples of the King. Henry, indeed, felt that the country was opposed to the divorce. As he went through the streets men called out to him to keep Catherine, and the women referred insolently to Anne Boleyn. But time was going by. Anne was expecting a child, who ought to be the desired heir and must therefore be born in wedlock. The gentle, malleable Cranmer was appointed Archbishop of Canterbury, and secretly married the King and Anne in January, 1533. At Easter the marriage was made public; Anne was crowned, Henry excommunicated. The breach with Rome had come.

CHAPTER V

Schism and Persecution

THE rupture would have been less crude if Henry VIII had not had other counselors besides More and Cranmer. The former, a man of fine conscience, would have accepted only wise and temperate reform; Cranmer, too weak to be harmful, would have talked and temporized. It was Thomas Cromwell who played the Narcissus to this Nero, the Iago to this Othello. A small, squat man, ugly and hard, with a porcine face, narrow eyes, a mischievous mouth, he began life at Putney as a wool merchant and fuller; travel in Flanders and Italy taught him the arts of trading, the new political ideas, and made him a fervent reader of Italian books on statecraft. On his return he became a moneylender, and a favored servant of Cardinal Wolsey. Cromwell was highly intelligent, vulgar but witty, and had in him neither scruples nor religion. Rival theologies were of no account to him, but he was conquered by the theory of State supremacy. When he met the King he advised him to follow the example of the German princes who had broken with Rome. England should no longer have two masters or twofold systems of justice and taxation. As the Pope refused to confirm the repudiation of Catherine, the King should not bow, but must make the Church his servant. Henry VIII despised Cromwell; he always called him "the wool-carder," and ill-treated him. But he made use of his skill, his servility, and his strength. The wool-carder became within a few years Master of the Rolls, Lord Privy Seal, Vicar-General of the Church, Lord Great Chamberlain, a Knight of the Garter, and Earl of Essex.

The spoliation of the Church was according to law, and Henry VIII respected parliamentary forms. The Parliament of 1529, which sat for seven years, voted all the special measures put before it by the Crown.

To begin with, the clergy were informed that, like Wolsey, they had violated the Statute of Præmunire, in agreeing to recognize the authority of the Cardinal as Legate. As amends for this offense they had to pay a fine of two million pounds, grant the King the title of Protector and Supreme Head of the Church, and abolish the annates, or first fruits of ecclesiastical benefices and posts, which had previously been paid to the Pope. (They were, in fact, appropriated to Henry's use.) The Parliament then voted successively the Statute of Appeals, forbidding appeals to Rome, the Act of Supremacy, making the King the sole and supreme head of the Church of England, giving him spiritual as well as lay jurisdiction, as also the right to reform and suppress error and heresy; and lastly the Act of Succession, which annulled the first marriage, deprived children born thereof of their rights to the throne in favor of the offspring of Anne Boleyn, and obliged all the King's subjects to swear that they accepted the religious validity of the divorce. It may be wondered how a Catholic Parliament voted these measures confirming the schism, in which the Pope was referred to merely as "Bishop of Rome." But it should be borne in mind that there was the deepest respect for the King's person and will; that the nascent nationalism of England had long been intolerant of foreign jurisdiction; that the Papacy was regarded as an ally of Spain and France; that, apart from the national sentiment, a strong anti-clerical prejudice demanded, not the ruination of the Church, but the abolition of Church tribunals and the seizure of monastic wealth; and lastly, that new social classes ignorant of Latin, the quickening strength of the nation, had learned to read printed books, that lay clerks had become as numerous as those in holy orders, and that many men desired an English Prayer Book and an English Bible, much in the way that they had replaced the *Roman de la Rose* by *The Canterbury Tales*. The Reformation in England was not only a sovereign's caprice, but also the religious manifestation of an insular and linguistic nationalism which had long been germinating.

A Church with ten or twelve centuries behind it has deep roots, and the most powerful of monarchs could not wrench them up without a struggle. With a few exceptions, bishops and priests showed remarkable pliability. They had long been affected by the growing strength of national sentiment, and the English prelates were on the whole statesmen rather than churchmen. The House of Lords, where they sat, voted all

· ANNO · ETATIS ·   · SVÆ · XLIX ·

HENRY VIII

Copy of a portrait by Hans Holbein the younger
in the Palazzo Corsini Gallery, Rome.

WILLIAM SHAKESPEARE

The Droeshout portrait
from the title page of the First Folio.

the reforms without protest. The higher clergy, it has been remarked, were pervaded by a sort of pre-Anglicanism. The lesser clergy were poor and felt some measure of security in becoming a body of State officials; they had been influenced by Lollard teachings, and had never gladly accepted the celibacy of their order. When the oath was submitted to all, and it became treasonable to deny the chastity and sanctity of the marriage between Henry and Anne, and to acknowledge the supremacy of "the Bishop of Rome who usurps the title of Pope," nearly all the priesthood swore to it. But the Lord Chancellor, Sir Thomas More, and Bishop John Fisher refused to recant the articles of Catholic faith. Both were beheaded, the Bishop reading from St. John's Gospel before his death, and More declaring at the scaffold's foot that he died "the King's good servant, but God's first." The severed heads of these two great men, now sanctified by their Church, rotted on spikes at the end of London Bridge. This divorce comedy was becoming a hideous tragedy, and a reign of terror set in. Numerous monks were hanged, drawn, and quartered. In some counties the Catholics were inflamed with just horror when they heard of these human butcheries, and rose in revolt. But they were crushed. Rome had excommunicated Henry VIII; but what mattered that sentence to a monarch who had deliberately set himself outside the pale of the Church? Sanctions would have been necessary, and the Pope tried to induce the Catholic sovereigns, Francis I and Charles V, to apply them. But both declined, reluctant to quarrel with England, whom they required for their diplomatic chess-board. Thus shielded from the Pope by the dissensions of the Catholic sovereigns, and at the same time respected by his Parliament and flattered by his national Church, Henry VIII was able to continue his outrages with impunity.

The refusal of the monks to accept the oath rejoiced the heart of Thomas Cromwell, who had long been pondering their undoing. England contained about twelve hundred monastic houses, owning vast domains. Confiscation of their property would enrich the King and the liquidators. The popular wave of feeling against the monks, and widespread legends of their vices, would silence their defenders. These legends were exaggerated, and to a great extent completely untrue; the day was to come when, after the dissolution of the monasteries, their old tenants who so often had maligned them regretted their passing. But Cromwell, appointed as Vicar-General with the right of visitation, compiled huge records of the monks' misdeeds, and by revealing these "atrocities" to Parliament procured the dissolution, first, of the smaller monasteries, and then of all religious houses. Religious and fiscal functionaries began the visitation of the monasteries. Formalities of law required the monks to make a "voluntary renunciation," and a Dr. John London especially became famous for his skill in speedily inducing a "voluntary" spirit. When the deed was signed the King took possession of the abbey, sold its contents, and gave, or more often sold or rented, the domain to some great lord, whose loyalty to the new Church thus became assured. The sales ruined the monks. Manuscripts were sometimes bought by grocers to parcel their wares: "old books in the choir: 6 pence," ran the inventory of one library. Some of the despoiled clerks were granted leave to exercise the functions of the secular priesthood; others received a pension of a few shillings; large numbers left England for Ireland, Scotland, or the Low Countries. In five years' time the liquidation of monastic property was completed, bringing much to the royal treasury, and enriching those to whom the King handed over the abbeys or those who bought them cheap. The political outcome of these measures was analogous with those seen in France when the national properties were sold after the Revolution of 1789. The purchasers became accomplices. Fear of a return of the former owners gave the new religious regime the support of a rich and powerful class. Henceforward self-interest and doctrine would conspire against a counter-attack from Roman Catholicism.

The Credo of this new Church was for a long time vague. If the hands of Cromwell, Cranmer, and Latimer had been free, they would have linked it to the Lutheran body. After his war on convents, Cromwell began one against images. Latimer burned statues of the Blessed Virgin, while Cranmer scrutinized relics, in particular the blood of St. Thomas Becket, which he suspected of being red ocher. St. Thomas, a manifest traitor to his king, was struck from the calendar of saints, and Cromwell's emissaries despoiled his shrine at Canterbury. But Henry VIII, like his people, had instinct, and knew that although Englishmen had often been hostile to the monks and the ecclesiastical courts, they were in general unlikely to welcome the innovations of the Protestants. Henry himself clung to his title of Defender of the Faith, and to his claim to be the head of a "Catholic" Church; but he wanted this, contradictory though it seemed, to be a national Catholicism. His persecution of the loyalists of the ancient faith was followed by one, no less vigorous, of the Protestants. The first printer of an English Bible, Tyndale, was sent to the stake, and others perished likewise for denying Transubstantiation. After several attempts at formulating an Anglican creed, Henry brought the House of Lords to pass the Six Articles, which affirmed the truth of Transubstantiation, the needlessness of communion in both kinds, the validity of vows of chastity, the excellence of clerical celibacy, and approved confession and private Masses. Flagrant contravention was punishable by the stake, and not even recantation would save the guilty. The Protestant bishops, such as Latimer, had to resign. Cranmer, who had been secretly married since before the Reformation, and was reputed to take his wife about in a perforated trunk, had to send her to Germany. It may seem surprising that the English people accepted the idea of granting religious infallibility to an elected Parliament. But the craving for stability, as well as indifference and terror, account for a strange degree of compliance.

It had required a schism to rupture Henry's first marriage; an ax sufficed to sunder the second. Poor Anne Boleyn made two mistakes; instead of the expected heir, she produced a daughter, Elizabeth, then a stillborn son; and she deceived the King. For these crimes her pretty head was slashed off. Within a few days, clad in white, Henry married Jane Seymour. The obsequious Cranmer, on the faith of certain confidences of the dead woman, had annulled the second marriage, and the Princess Elizabeth, like Mary before her, became a bastard. Jane Seymour had a son, who was to reign as Edward VI, but she died in childbed. Cromwell, ever anxious to bring the King closer to the Lutherans, suggested a fresh matrimonial alliance, this time with a German princess, Anne of Cleves. The man of affairs sought to play the rôle of matchmaker; but the wife proved distasteful and the experiment cost Cromwell his life. Henry's fifth wife, Catherine Howard, also went to the block for infidelity to her lord. His sixth, Catherine Parr, survived him. The reign ended in blood. Absolute power releases a man's worst instincts. Henry VIII brought judicial murder upon Protestants and Catholics, upon the aged Countess of Salisbury. Even Cranmer felt his head endangered; but Henry seems to have felt genuine affection for this man who placed an almost naïve confidence in his terrifying king. Cranmer it was who knelt at Henry's deathbed (1547), bidding him at the last put his trust in God and Jesus

Christ. Whereupon the King clasped the archbishop's hand and breathed his last.

It is hard to avoid a sense of horror in contemplating the reign of Henry VIII. In vain are we assured that he reorganized the fleet, built great arsenals, established a school of pilots, annexed Wales and pacified Ireland. No temporal successes can obliterate those scaffolds on Tower Hill or darken the flames of Smithfield. The excuse is proffered that these dire penalties struck at only a minority. What matter? So much cruelty could not be necessary. It may seem true that the separation of an insular State from a universal Church had become almost inevitable. The Papacy had been able to exercise a vast political and juridical power in Europe for ten centuries, because the collapse of the Roman Empire had left the various countries with weak civil power and divided sovereignty. As soon as strong States came into being, the collision became fatal. When France, in her turn, came at a much later date to experience these conflicts, an age of milder manners had arrived, and the divorce of Church and State could be effected without bloodshed and without a religious rupture with Rome. The Church of England owed one advantage to the premature loss of prerogatives which the Churches of the Continent retained for three or four centuries longer—namely, the almost complete absence of an anti-clerical movement in England. The rival Churches in England were to engage in mutual struggles during the seventeenth and eighteenth centuries, but no political party dared to call itself anti-religious.

CHAPTER VI

Edward VI: the Protestant Reaction

A STRANGE trio, the children of Henry VIII. The heir to the throne, Edward VI, son of Jane Seymour, was a solemn, precocious little boy who read ten chapters of the Bible every day and was styled by the reformers "a new Josiah." Mary, daughter of Catherine of Aragon, was already thirty-one. She was beginning to look faded, with the pallor of her round face accentuated by the red hair, and she seemed sickly and gloomy. More proud of being a descendant of the kings of Spain than of being the King of England's daughter, she remained a fervent Catholic, surrounded by priests and spending her life in the chapel. Anne Boleyn's daughter, Elizabeth, was a slight girl of fourteen, quite pretty, well built, very vivacious, and showing the traditional Tudor fondness for classical culture. Latin she wrote as well as English, spoke French and Italian, and, according to one of her tutors, read more Greek in one day than a canon read Latin in a week. Being a Protestant like her half-brother Edward, though with less conviction, she was on terms of real understanding with the boy King, and they both stood together in opposition to Mary, on whose Masses he soon laid a ban. Mary retorted that she would lay her head on the block rather than submit to such an order. The Council recalled that she was a cousin of Charles V and deemed it imprudent to press the matter.

The religious problem had not been solved by the schism. Whilst some counties were regretting Catholicism, London was stirred up by Protestant preachers like Latimer and desired a more complete reformation. Most Englishmen were ready to accept a compromise which, while maintaining the essential rites familiar to them, would have loosed all ties with Rome. The Archbishop of Canterbury, Cranmer, continued to waver nervously between Lutheran and Roman views. But it was he who gave the Church of England its Book of Common Prayer, written in truly admirable prose, to which he himself contributed litanies and collects, and so enabled that Church to acquire in succession to the Church of Rome that æsthetic potency without which a religion has little hold over the souls of men. Anti-Catholic persecutions continued. In the churches walls were white-washed, stained glass broken, the crucifix replaced by the royal 'scutcheon. All symbolic ceremonies were abolished: the consecrated bread, the holy water, the adoration on Good Friday, all vanished. Lent, however, was to be observed, in order to help the sale of fish. In 1547 the marriage of the clergy was authorized and Cranmer was able to recall his wife. The Act of Uniformity, voted by Parliament, obliged all churches to use the Book of Common Prayer and observe the same ritual. But even this uniformity had a variety of forms. The Privy Council, laymen more Protestant than the Archbishop, touched up the Prayer Book. Kneeling, prescribed by Cranmer in the first edition, was attacked by zealots as a superstitious practice, and in the second was proscribed. How were men to grow used to this rigorous yet shifting orthodoxy?

These far-reaching changes were painful to simple souls, who clung to the rites which for a thousand years had been woven into the pattern of their ancestors' and their own lives. The Cornish peasants, who spoke a language of their own, rose in revolt because London sought to impose on them a Prayer Book written in a tongue unknown to them. Cranmer retorted that they did not know Latin, either; but Cranmer, the professor and theologian, did not know the peasantry. These people knew the sense, if not the literal meaning, of their traditional prayers. Besides, the revolt was then agrarian as well as religious. It was a time of deep popular discontent. Unemployment, almost unknown in the mediæval economy, was becoming a grave evil. Its causes were manifold. The enforced disbanding of the lords' armed men in the opening years of the century had sent thousands of soldiers tramping the roads with no craft or trade. Agricultural laborers found work scarce. At the time of the Black Death some of the great landowners began to breed and graze sheep instead of growing grain, and this needed fewer hands. During the sixteenth century many squires made bold to inclose parts of the common meadows and heaths, in order to keep their flocks. This process of "inclosures" deprived peasants of their land, workers of their work. Everywhere hedges rose up—"the new gyse."

Naturally, it pleased the big landowners. Ever since Spain's discovery of the silver mines in South America prices in Europe had been rising. The squire, who paid dearly for any purchases, still received fixed rents from his farmers. But the demand for wool was limitless and its prices were high. The temptation was strong, and by 1550 the landowners were yielding to it all the more readily because the dissolution of the monasteries and the sale of their property had created a whole new regiment of country gentlemen. The mental attitude of these new owners of the soil was very different from that of a thirteenth-century lord. The latter only asked that the land should provide him with a certain number of knights, but the new capitalist demanded interest on his capital. He made agriculture a business, and, as it has been said, the ewes turned the sand into gold. What mattered these peasants whom he scarcely knew by sight? His son, and his grandson in particular, would one day become squires with a sense of duty; but every first generation is merciless. By the time of King Henry's death the peasants were murmuring.

The Privy Council saw danger ahead, and tried in vain to intervene. Some laws ordered the restoration of destroyed farms and the renewed cultivation of arable land; others forbade any single man to own more than 2,000 head of sheep. (Some landowners had flocks of 24,000.) But the law was lamed by trickery. The owner kept his sheep in the names of his wife, or children, or servants; instead of rebuilding a farm, a symbolic room was newly plastered in the ruins; a symbolic furrow was plowed and the commissioners were assured that the fields were tilled. In any case, these commissioners were justices of the peace, themselves landowners, and often delinquent ones. They closed their eyes. In some counties the villagers waxed wroth and tore down the gentry's hedges. In Norfolk Robert Kett, a small landowner who was also a tanner and a man of advanced ideas, put himself at the head of the peasants to sally out and destroy the hedges of a hated neighbor. Immediately rebellion swept across the discontented countryside. Leading 16,000 men, Kett occupied the city of Norwich. But the revolt was in vain, as neither the peasants nor their leaders knew clearly what they wanted. It ended as all risings then ended, in a bloody butchery and in Kett's execution. But it was one of many other symptoms of disease.

During the minority of Edward VI the regency was in the hands of his uncle, Edward Seymour, Duke of Somerset, the brother of Jane Seymour.

The most conspicuous of his qualities was his tolerance. But he was held responsible for these agrarian disturbances. His pride offended the courtiers; his demagogy perturbed the landlords; the merchant class was shocked by his swelling coffers; the zealots disliked his comparative forbearance. The landed aristocracy, led by the Earl of Warwick, took forfeit of his head. The strange boy King, his impassivity matching his piety, noted in his journal his uncle's execution in the Tower between eight and nine o'clock in the morning of January 22, 1552, and set down his faults: "ambition, vainglory, entering into rash wars in my youth . . . enriching himself of my treasure, following his own opinion, and doing all by his own authority." Warwick, later Duke of Northumberland, became chief of the council of regency, and pursued the persecution of the Catholics more vigorously than Somerset. Edward VI then fell ill, and when it was clear that his sickness was mortal, Northumberland, in apprehension of the Crown coming to the Spanish and Romanist Mary, put forward the claims of Lady Jane Grey, a great-granddaughter of Henry VII, and married her to his own son. He made the dying King sign a testament in favor of Lady Jane.

This hapless young woman, an unwilling usurper, was proclaimed Queen by Northumberland, who marched on London. But Mary was not the woman to be brushed aside unprotesting. The Spanish ambassador wrote to Charles V that she was so ardent and resolute that if he bade her cross the Channel in a washtub, she would make the venture. A true Spaniard, she had a soldier's courage and a fanatical devoutness. She had only to show herself to conquer, and the glamour of her father's name was as a shield. The Catholics, still vigorous, welcomed their deliverance at her hands; she promised impartiality to the Protestants; and the numerous masses of indifferent men were weary of a regime which confiscated their property for the benefit of private exploiters on the pretext of reforming Church ritual. Bonfires blazed when Mary appeared in London, and the counties sent troops to her. The Council, startled by what it had done, sent a herald and four trumpeters to proclaim her Queen in the City. She made a triumphal entry, her sister Elizabeth riding alongside her. Even Northumberland, hearing of these events, waved his hat in the air and cried "Long live Queen Mary!" But he acclaimed her a few days too late. He was imprisoned in the Tower and beheaded. The girl who had been his toy, poor Lady Jane Grey, had to wait six months before the same ax fell.

CHAPTER VII

Mary Tudor and the Catholic Reaction

MARY TUDOR is a lamentable example of the ravages that may be wrought in a woman's soul by the conjunction of love, bigotry, and absolute power. She protested that she would sooner lose ten crowns than imperil her soul. But she was a Catholic in a country where the generation now attaining manhood had been born out of the Roman allegiance, and where the capital city, the center of gravity, had very strong Protestant leanings. It has been said that, if Paris was worth a Mass, London was worth a sermon. But Henry IV of France was a statesman, and Mary Tudor a believer. Now although the majority of the nation still hankered after the old ceremonial and desired a return to the "national" Catholicism of Henry VIII, the same majority retained its hatred of Rome. In particular, those who had acquired Church property, a rich and powerful clan, dreaded an act of submission to the Pope, which would cost them dear, and the married priests feared a return to the old faith, which would have compelled them to choose between their cures and their wives. A dexterous sovereign might have turned these conflicting desires to good account in coming to terms. The English had already received so many dogmas from the Tudors that they might easily have accepted a few supplementary clauses to please a daughter of King Henry; but in her uncompromising zeal Mary wished to impose, not to negotiate. During the long and painful years of her youth religion had been her one consolation. She was ready to undergo martyrdom to bring her people back to Rome. Through her first Parliament she re-established the Latin Mass and expelled married priests from the Church. Her sister Elizabeth, the crowning hope of the Protestants, felt herself threatened, and came tearfully to ask the Queen to have her instructed in the true religion. To Mary this conversion was affecting and delectable; but the

[217]

Spanish ambassador took a sceptical view, as he viewed this adroit and reserved princess with more perspicacity.

The abrupt return to Papacy was the Queen's first rash step; her marriage completed her alienation from the people. Parliament had good reason for dreading the influence of a foreign king, and respectfully prayed Mary to marry an Englishman. The Council and the nation had chosen for her young Edward Courtenay, a great-grandson of Edward IV. She denied their right to limit her matrimonial choice. In her earlier years she had shown some affection for an Englishman, Reginald Pole, like herself of royal blood. But Pole quarreled with her father over the divorce, went into exile at Rome, and had there become a Cardinal. He was now to return to be Archbishop of Canterbury. Mary's only willing choice in England was accordingly ruled out. The Spanish ambassador, Renard, who had great influence with her, thereupon broached a plan of Charles V, who offered Mary the hand of his son Philip. When Renard put forward the idea of this match, she laughed not once, but several times, with a glance showing him that the project was pleasing to her. And in subsequent conversation she swore that she had never felt the pricks of love, and had never considered marriage except since it had pleased God to set her on the throne, and that her marriage, when it took place, would be against her own affection and out of respect for the common weal. But she begged Renard to assure the Emperor Charles of her desire to obey him in all matters, as if he were her own father. Although these negotiations were kept secret, their purpose was guessed by the Queen's Ministers, to their perturbation. If an alliance were made between England, a weak and lately schismatic nation, and Spain, orthodox and all-powerful, what would be the fate of England? The kingdom would become subject to a formidable monarch. The English heretics already feared the courts of the Inquisition and the *auto-da-fé*, as frequent in Madrid as bull-fights. But, alas, as soon as this virgin of thirty-six beheld a portrait of the handsome Spanish prince, she fell passionately in love. Everything conspired to heighten her passion for him; by marrying Philip she would satisfy at once her pride in being a Spanish princess, her Catholic beliefs, and her strong and unsatisfied desires. One night in her oratory, after several times reciting the *Veni Creator*, she vowed to marry Philip and no one else.

The Spanish ambassador melted down four thousand gold coins, and had chains forged of this gold for distribution to members of the Council. Was his action symbolic? The Councilors were converted to the idea of the marriage by gifts, arguments, and promises, but nevertheless they advised prudence in action. Philip must respect the laws of England; if Mary died, he could have no claim to the Crown; a son born of the marriage would inherit the thrones of England, Burgundy, and the Low Countries; and Philip must pledge himself never to draw England into his wars against France. It was a sound treaty, but what real safeguards did it offer against a woman in love? The English people, hostile to foreigners and very hostile to Spaniards, showed their displeasure at once. The envoys sent by Charles V to negotiate the marriage were pelted with snowballs by London urchins, who played games of "the Queen's marriage" in the streets, the boy who played the Spanish prince being hanged. And in several counties revolt broke out. Sir Thomas Wyatt marched on London, but her faith and her love seemed to make Mary invincible. Her Ministers sought to make her take refuge in the Tower; but she remained at Whitehall, smiling, and, thanks to the spell of the Tudors, gained so ample a victory that nobody again ventured to raise a voice against the Spanish marriage. Rebels were hanged by the dozen. After which came the arrival of the Spanish prince. His father had described the pride of Englishmen, and bade him doff his Castilian arrogance. Philip did his best to be ingratiating, not without success. The London merchants were impressed by the procession through the city of twenty carts of bullion from the gold-mines of America; seeing which deposited in the Tower, the merchants felt convinced that at any rate Philip had not come to rob them. On one point Philip remained intractable: there must be a reconciliation with Rome. He would rather not reign at all than reign over heretics. The Pope was advised of this, and sent over Cardinal Pole as his Legate to receive the submission of England. The gold bars in the Tower helped to prepare the minds of the noble families for this great event.

The Papal Legate landed. Philip and Mary declared that he had been created by Providence for this mission, which he certainly accomplished with the utmost tact. Pole combined the subtlety of a Roman prelate with the aloof shyness of a great English lord. His modesty, notwithstanding his high reputation, had led him to live at Rome a life of self-effacement from which he was now emerging for the first time. It pleased him that the password of the guard at Calais was "Long lost, and found again. . . ." At Dover he was enthusiastically welcomed. It was known that the Pope had undertaken that the holders of ecclesiastical property should remain in possession. "What could not be sold," he said, "can be *given*, to save so many souls." Parliament assembled at Whitehall to receive the Legate, and there in a lengthy speech he reviewed the history of the schism, and a few days later granted plenary absolution for the past. Both Houses received this kneeling. England was made whole.

The Queen believed herself pregnant. When the day of confinement came and the bells were already pealing, the doctors realized that the pregnancy had been a manifestation of nervous imagination. This was a painful blow to Mary. Her mental state caused anxiety. Philip had left for Spain, declaring that his absence would be brief; but she had felt his vexation at this ridiculous fiasco of the confinement, and also at the attitude of Parliament, who refused to let him participate in power. This Queen who had astonished people in her unwedded days by her courage, had become feeble and disheartened since being in love. The cruelty of her persecution of the Protestants, which gave her the name of "Bloody" Mary, is doubtless partly explicable by a mental disorder which came very near to madness. Such rigorous action did not come from Philip's counsel. The burning of heretics, he thought, was excellent in Spain and the Netherlands; but in England prudence called for patience. Mary had none. On January 20, 1555, the law against heresy was restored; two days later the commissions began their sessions; on February 3rd the first married priest was burned at Smithfield. About three hundred Protestants were martyred at the stake. So hideous was the torture that the bystanders sought to shorten it by attaching bags of gunpowder to the necks of victims. And on this even the executioners, in their distress, turned a blind eye.

Some of these men died sublimely. The aged Latimer, who had been a great Protestant preacher, was burned at Oxford at the same time as Dr. Ridley. Recantation might easily have saved his life, but when the doctrinal debate which always preceded the punishment was opened, he replied that he had sought in vain in the Gospels for the Mass. "Play the man, Master Ridley," he said to his companion in the ordeal when the chains tied them both to the stake, "we shall this day light such a candle, by God's grace, in England as I trust shall never be put out." At the moment of paying the forfeit, Cranmer, who during his life had so often been weak and vacillating, and had even renounced his beliefs in prison, recovered all his courage and abjured his recantation.

The accounts of these sacrifices were collected by a Protestant writer, John Foxe, in his *Book of Martyrs*, which long held a place beside the Bible in English homes. Mary's persecution gave the Protestants something which hitherto they had lacked—a sentimental and heroic tradition. The Catholic victims of Henry VIII had moved the mass of English people less, because so many of them had been monks or friars, and therefore exceptional beings. But Mary's victims, save for a few ecclesiastics, were ordinary men and women, and in a country where diversity of opinion had become so great, every man felt himself threatened. Hatred of the Queen and the Spaniards rose higher. Despite his pledges, Philip drew his Queen into a war against France, and the campaign cost England the stronghold of Calais. "May God preserve Mistress Elizabeth!" murmured the subjects of Mary Tudor. And Mary meanwhile was a dying woman, abandoned by all. Even Pope Paul IV had sided against her and against Spain. Once more she believed herself to be with child, but it was only the dropsy. On November 17, 1558, within a few hours of each other, Queen Mary and her cousin, Cardinal Pole, left this world. For a whole month she had been almost alone. The whole court had gathered round Princess Elizabeth.

CHAPTER VIII

Elizabeth and the Anglican Compromise

THE accession of Elizabeth was greeted by the English people with almost unanimous joy. After their dread of Spanish tyranny, it was a relief to hail a Queen free of any foreign link. Not since the Norman Conquest had England had a sovereign so purely English in blood. Through her father Elizabeth was descended from the traditional kings; through her mother, from native gentry. Throughout her reign she flirted with her people. It has been said that the Tudor monarchy was as fully absolute as that of Louis XIV or the Empire of the Cæsars; it has been recalled that Elizabeth led her Parliaments on a halter, that her warrants were like *lettres de cachet,* that her judges tortured accused parties in defiance of the law of the land. But Louis XIV and Tiberius had armies at their bidding to compel their will. Elizabeth, like her father and grandfather before her, had only a guard which the City militia could easily have put to route. She was strong only because she was loved, or at least was preferred to others. Threatened by a Spanish invasion, she summoned "not a high Constable, nor the head of her army (which she did not possess), but the lord mayor of London." She asked him for fifteen ships and five thousand men, and was informed that the City would be happy to offer Her Majesty ten thousand men and thirty ships. Nearly all the kingdom showed equal loyalty. The few risings were easily repressed, and deemed criminal by the people at large. At a time when nearly every kingdom in Europe was torn by religious strife, or stifled by terrors, she enjoyed showing the foreign ambassadors how she trusted her subjects. She forced her coach into the heart of the crowd, stood up, and talked with those surrounding it. "God save Your Majesty!" they cried. And "God save my people!" she answered. Whether in London, or on her yearly journeys from town to town, she was continually on display, alert, quick-tongued, erudite, with compliments for a mayor on his Latin, for a housewife on her cooking. "She swore, she spat," writes Lytton Strachey, "she struck with her fist when she was angry; she roared with laughter when she was amused. . . . Her response to every stimulus was immediate and rich: to the folly of the moment, to the clash and horror of great events, her soul leaped out with a vivacity, an abandonment, a complete awareness of the situation, which made her, which makes her still, a fascinating spectacle."

Her strength had many secrets; the most effective was a swift intuition of what could please her people. There was also a sense of economy worthy of King Henry VII. Avarice, a vice in subjects, is a virtue in princes. The people asked few liberties of Elizabeth, because she asked them for little money. Her annual budget did not reach £500,000. Being poor, and also because she was a woman, and not cruel, she disliked war. Occasionally she engaged in war, successfully, but she never ran to meet danger. To avoid it she was ready to lie, to swear to an ambassador that she was totally ignorant of a matter which had really been engaging all her attention, or, in the last resort, to shift the discussion on to a sentimental plane where her sex helped her to win her way. "This country," wrote the Spanish ambassador, "has fallen into the hands of a woman who is a daughter of the devil and the greatest scoundrels and heretics in the land." For vast schemes she had little liking, and shared the view of her subjects that life should be lived from day to day. Englishmen, even in the Middle Ages, had never liked the Crusades; they preferred to provide subsidies for others to engage in them. Certain of Elizabeth's counselors would have liked to thrust her into a league of Protestant nations. She tacked sharply, and slipped out of it at the last by lending money and a few regiments. Her strength lay in withholding herself from force. "She found herself" (to quote Strachey again) "a sane woman in a universe of violent maniacs, between contending forces of terrific intensity —the rival nationalisms of France and Spain, the rival religions of Rome and Calvin; for years it had seemed inevitable that she should be crushed by one or other of them, and she had survived because she had been able to meet the extremes around her with her own extremes of cunning and prevarication." Expedition or conquest, whichever it might be, she preferred to leave the responsibility for any bloodshed to others, and if in doubt, to stand aside. Her reign was far from being unstained by injustice; but probably she did as little harm as possible in a difficult time.

On one point, and one only, she always opposed her people's will. The Commons pressed her to marry. It seemed urgent to insure the succession. So long as the Queen had no heir, her life and the national religion were imperiled. The murder of Elizabeth would suffice to give the throne to the Catholic Mary Stuart, Queen of Scots, the great-granddaughter of Henry VII and wife of the French Dauphin. It was a temptation to fanatics. But Elizabeth refused to consider marriage. Kings and princes paid their court in vain. With one and all she played the same game of coquetry, agreeable messages, poetic and sometimes bold flirtation, but every time she ended matters by slipping out of the long-drawn game. In this way she tantalized Philip II, Prince Eric of Sweden, the Archdukes Ferdinand and Charles of Austria, the Duke of Alençon, not to mention those handsome Englishmen whom she liked so well—Leicester, Essex, and Raleigh, courtiers, soldiers, and poets, to whom she granted great freedom and incomplete caresses, until the moment came when the woman became again the Queen, and sent them to the Tower. What did she want? To die a virgin? Or was she a virgin? Ever since her youthful days, when her stepmother's husband, Thomas Seymour, used to sit on her bed and amuse himself with her in ribald fashion, she had compromised herself with many men. She enjoyed their flatteries; it delighted her to be called the Faery Queen, or Gloriana. But the best-informed incline to think that she was never fully the mistress of any man, that she had a physical horror of marriage, and that a definite incapacity for motherhood made her decision final. A childless marriage would have subjected her to a husband and deprived her of her exceptional prestige as the Virgin Queen.

Some of the handsome youths who courted her certainly touched her heart; but she was always able to keep her mind free from the bewilderments of her senses. Her chosen counselors were men of different stamp. Like her grandfather, she chose them from the "new" men, sons of yeomen or merchants, conspicuous for intelligence rather than high birth. In the Middle Ages, chivalrous virtues or ecclesiastical dignities had made men Ministers; but Elizabeth required that hers should be men with administrative talents and gifted with two newer sentiments—patriotism and a feeling for State interests. Her chief counselor, William Cecil (later

Lord Burleigh), came of a yeoman family enriched by the distribution of monastic property, and was the founder of a family which, like the Russells and Cavendishes, was to be closely linked with the governance of the country until the present day. Although all witnesses concur on the intelligence of William Cecil, Macaulay reproaches him for paying undue attention to the enrichment of his family, for deserting his friends, for calculation in his Protestantism. This is a stern, and probably unfair, verdict. It is true that Cecil did not choose the stake under Mary, that he believed William Cecil's life was worth a Mass; true also that later he sent to the scaffold men whose only crime had been their devout and loyal observance of rites which he himself had formerly been cautious enough to observe. But in matters of State he proved his courage. He often resisted Elizabeth, and to some extent imposed his views on her. A middle-class man, he knew the middle classes accurately, and his ideas were congenial to them. On Elizabeth's accession he showed himself distrustful, having little fancy for the rule of women. He ventured to reproach the ambassadors who addressed themselves to the Queen. Gradually he came to realize her strange, profound wisdom, and in the end they formed a wonderfully matched team, in conjunction with men like the grave Secretary of State Walsingham, more rigorously Protestant than Cecil, who desired "first the glory of God, and then the safety of the Queen." To Cecil Elizabeth remarked: "This judgement I have of you, that you will not be corrupted with any manner of gift, and that you will be faithful to the State, and that, without respect of my private will, you will give me that counsel that you think best." Wherein she showed her feminine quality as a good judge of men. So close did the union of Queen and Minister become, that it might be said of Elizabeth that she was at once female and male—herself and Cecil.

Was she Catholic or Protestant at heart? Many think she was pagan, or at least a sceptic. After a Protestant upbringing she had not hesitated, like Cecil, to save her life in the Marian persecution by a simulated conversion. She was perhaps philosophically religious, in the manner of Erasmus. On her accession she prayed God to grant her grace to rule without shedding blood. In that she failed, but she did her best. She was always proud of the loyalty of her Catholic subjects. Noticing an old man one day in the crowd who cried out: *"Vivat Regina. Honi soit qui mal y pense!"* she pointed him out delightedly to the Spanish ambassador as a priest of the old religion. She prudently rebuffed certain monks who came to meet her bearing candles: "Take away these torches," she said; "we can see well enough." But in her own chapel she always kept a crucifix, and sharply silenced a preacher who ventured to criticize this habit. In religion as in politics she temporized, seeking an average in belief and cultivating compromise. Early in her reign Cecil obliged her to revert to the religious position of Henry VIII. In 1559 Parliament voted for a second time an Act of Supremacy, which abolished the Papal power in England, and the Act of Uniformity, which made the Book of Common Prayer obligatory in all parishes, as also the holding of services in the common tongue. By virtue of these Acts anyone upholding the spiritual power of the Pope was liable to confiscation of property. A refractory offender was guilty of high treason.

In 1563 came the adoption of the Thirty-Nine Articles, which were to remain the basis of Anglican belief. Their moderate Protestantism approximated to the feelings of the nation. Cardinal Bentivoglio estimated that about one-thirtieth of the people were zealous Catholics, but that four-fifths would readily return to the Catholic faith if it were re-established by law, although being incapable of revolting if it were not. Actually, when Anglicanism was reintroduced by Crown and Parliament, 7,000 out of 8,000 priests accepted the change, although 2,000 of the most Protestant had been driven out under the rule of Mary. This submission was proof, not that the English were irreligious, but that many of them desired to retain Catholic rites while suppressing the use of Latin and refusing obedience to the Pope. Except in a few families, devotion to the sovereign was stronger than religious feeling. In the early years of the reign the crypto-Catholics were hardly disturbed. They were asked only to attend the Anglican service, and if they failed to do so had to pay a fine of twelve pence. In many manor-houses a priest was kept hidden, living in a small room hollowed out in the thickness of the walls, and saying Mass in secret for all the neighboring Catholics. The servants and country folk were privy to this, having their own regrets for the days of the good friars, "when forty eggs were sold for a penny and a bushel of the best grain for fourteen pence." If Elizabeth had been all-powerful, some degree of toleration would have been established. She had crypto-Catholics in her own court, and required of them only a semblance of submission. She wanted neither a Protestant inquisition nor a torture-chamber to test consciences. But her Ministers, many more sectarian than herself, sent the refractory to prison. Still, during the first ten years of the reign there were no death sentences. In some churches the priests continued to wear their surplices, play the organ, and use wedding rings. Nearly everywhere the pre-Reformation windows were respected to avoid expense, but they were replaced with plain glass when broken. Thrift and indifference combined to make such compromises acceptable.

But three factors enabled Cecil, and Walsingham more particularly, to show more severity and force Elizabeth's hand. The first was the Massacre of St. Bartholomew in Paris; the second, a Bull of excommunication against the Queen, delivered at a very inopportune moment by Pope Pius V; and the third, the establishment of seminaries abroad, as at Douai, with the intention of preparing the Catholic reconquest of England. Excommunication of the sovereign implied the freeing of the Catholic subjects from their bonds of loyalty, and it was even alleged that the Pope would willingly grant absolution for the murder of Elizabeth. In December, 1580, the Papal Secretary of State made a suspiciously equivocal reply to a question put forward in the name of certain English Jesuits: "Considering that this woman has caused the loss of so many millions of souls to the Faith, it is beyond doubt that whoever may dispatch her from this world with the pious intention of serving God, not only will not sin, but will acquire merit." After 1570, Catholic priests and laymen were executed in England, not for heresy, but for high treason. Many of the men thus hanged, with hideous ceremonial and mutilation, were actually innocent, or saints. This was so in the case of the noble Jesuit, Edmund Campion, of whom even Burghley had to admit that he was "one of the jewels of England," whose only crime had been that of going from house to house in disguise, preaching and celebrating the Mass. As he died, he said that he prayed for the Queen. Thus, although Elizabeth inclined to clemency, the victims of fanaticism during her reign were as numerous as under Mary. Her Council sent to their deaths one hundred and forty-seven priests, forty-seven gentlemen, and a large number of humble men, and even women. Those who did not perish did not escape persecution. John Shakespeare, father of the poet, is an example, for he was a Catholic, and the text of his will is simply the translation of a formula brought from Rome by Campion and recommended to the Jesuit Fathers by the Cardinal-Archbishop of Milan.

Geneva suffered as well as Rome, and Calvinism, then spreading in England, was equally suspect with Catholicism. The Puritans would gladly have obliterated the last traces of Roman ceremonial and suppressed every hierarchy smacking of the "Scarlet Woman." They had little respect for the Anglican bishops, parading their detestation of vice and their wondrous zeal for religion. They desired to reorganize the State on biblically inspired lines, and to administer England through the Church elders. They would, if they could, have restored the Mosaic laws, and the penalty of death for blasphemy, perjury, desecration of the Sabbath, adultery, and fornication. Such fanatic Puritanism was disquieting to the Queen, the bishops, and the most reasonable among the faithful; but the moderate Puritanism gained adherents. In the Parliament of 1593 the bishops put forward stern measures against Puritanism; but in vain: the bill was rejected. The Puritans were deemed to be truly men of God, His true and wholehearted prophets. And the prestige of Elizabeth was such that not even these prophets could prevail against her. But this pious demagogy was to prove more dangerous to her successors.

CHAPTER IX

Elizabeth and the Sea

WHEN the European navigators, striving to reach the spices and perfumes
and jewels of the East in spite of the barrier of Islam, discovered the
lands beyond the Atlantic, few nations seemed in a position to share in
these conquests. Italy had to defend the Mediterranean against the Turks;
France was torn by the wars of religion; England was in sore need of her
ships for her own coasts. Spain and Portugal were the only claimants to
the new continents, and these two Catholic powers accepted the arbitration
of Pope Alexander VI. What should be the just frontier between these
unknown lands? The Pope simply drew a line from one pole to the other
on the map of the world: a straight line if the earth were flat, a great
circle if it were a sphere. But in either case, all lands discovered to the
west of this line would be Spain's, and to its east, Portugal's. This gave
Africa and India to Portugal; and to Spain, all of South America except
Brazil. Thus Portugal built an empire from the Persian Gulf to the Malay
Archipelago, and the incense-laden barques perfumed the quays of Lisbon. The Spaniards, too, discovered that between Europe and India lay
a continent devoid of mosques or bazaars, with neither Arabs nor Hindus,
but where amazing civilizations had flowered in the past, where floods of
riches poured from gold-mines, silver-mines, ruby-mines, and where empires like those of Montezuma in Mexico or the Incas in Peru held
accumulated treasures in the keeping of poorly armed people. And before
long the gold-laden galleons were crossing the Atlantic, and the wealth
of the kings of Spain became fabulous.

Mary Tudor's government could not but respect the possessions of
Philip II. They covered the world. His Italian provinces made the King
of Spain master of the Mediterranean; through Burgundy he controlled

[229]

the trade of Flanders and the mouth of the Rhine; in his American colonies he had the richest mines of gold and silver in the world. His financial and commercial power seemed invincible. The English merchants, doomed to sniff from afar the prodigious banquet of the Catholic kings, had one last hope. If Spain had found a southwest passage, and Portugal a southeast passage to the Indies, perhaps there might be a northeast or a northwest passage. For years the English seamen sought them. Chancellor went northeast, and found only the route to Muscovy; Frobisher, heading northwest, was stopped by the polar ice.

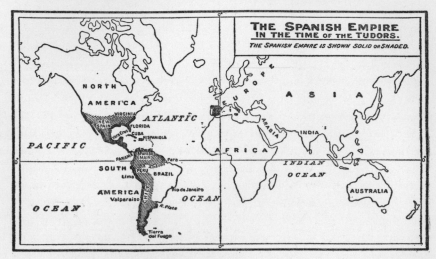

THE SPANISH EMPIRE
IN THE TIME of the TUDORS.
THE SPANISH EMPIRE IS SHOWN SOLID OR SHADED.

But although the English sovereigns did not dare a breach with the formidable Spaniards, and even if Elizabeth insisted that there must be no official act of hostility to the Spanish colonies, the English merchants had no grounds for respecting agreements which closed the richest regions in the world against them. "English piracy in the Channel was notorious in the fifteenth century, and in the sixteenth it attained patriotic proportions." Only a vague line separated commerce from piracy. Certain forms of the latter, indeed, were lawful. A captain who had been robbed by a foreign ship was given "letters of marque," which entitled him to reimburse himself at the cost of any other vessel of the same nationality as his aggressor. Even foreign courts of law recognized these "letters of marque," and treated the pirates bearing them on the footing of traders, instead of hanging them out of hand. English seamen, owners of a ship armed with a few guns, would openly ply a trade of robbing Portuguese vessels returning from the Indies. Others would organize profitable raids on the Spanish settlements, where they found themselves in competition with the French corsairs, men of great experience in such enterprises.

John Hawkins, son of a Plymouth shipbuilder, was the first to substitute for piracy a regular commerce with the Spanish colonies. Trader as well as seaman, he had taken part in youth in expeditions to the Guinea coast, where he learned the arts of abducting negroes to be sold later at a good price to the Canary Islands. In 1562, now on his own account, he carried off a number of slaves and bartered them in the Spanish colonies for ginger and sugar. These voyages were immensely profitable, and on one such he anchored to take in supplies in the Spanish haven of San Juan de Ulloa. Whilst he lay there the Spanish fleet sailed in. Hawkins was not strong enough to offer fight; he tried to come to terms, but was treated as an enemy by the Spanish viceroy. Returning home, he laid a plaint before the Queen. Elizabeth, in Council, solemnly declared that Hawkins was in the wrong, that the Spanish possessions must be respected, and that mariners who violated the treaties would do so at their own peril. After which she took the offender into her service, and made him Treasurer of the Navy. To this he contributed his experience. But Spain would doubtless have long held the mastery of the sea if Francis Drake had not now challenged it.

Francis Drake was a story-book sailor, bold to the pitch of temerity, capable of sentencing one of his lieutenants to death if discipline on board seemed to require it, and engaging the condemned man in friendly converse during the last hours before hanging him. Worshiped by his crews despite his severity, he was soon the idol of England. Hawkins had tried unavailingly to carry on legal trade with the Spanish colonies; Drake jumped headlong into illegality. With two ships and fifty men he attacked the strongest Spanish fortresses, bringing back his small vessel to Plymouth, laden with gold, one Sunday at the church hour. The Plymouth seamen could not restrain themselves and came out of church to hear the tidings. Drake had landed on the isthmus of Darien, attacked the mule convoy bringing gold from Peru, routed the escort, captured the treasure. The venture delighted Elizabeth's secret heart. In 1577 Drake set off again in the *Golden Hind* for a long voyage, in the course of which he proposed to circumnavigate the globe, by the Magellan Straits and the East Indies. The expedition was backed by several associates; one of them was the Queen, who still officially castigated these peaceful attacks on a friendly power, but was as eager as any in claiming her share of the booty on its reaching England.

This time Drake's little fleet carried cannon and some hundreds of men. He reckoned it large enough to attack islands and ports where Spain had only one stronghold. The arrival of Drake's flotilla took the Spanish governors by surprise. The English demanded ransom-money, or the town was burned down. But these were only accessory profits; Drake's real aim was to find the fleet which brought the gold and silver every year from Eldorado. Between Lima and Panama, an Indian paddling across a bay, quite incapable of distinguishing between Spaniards and English, mistook Drake for one of his masters and piloted him to a creek where the leading galley lay at anchor with her cargo of gold. Drake had only to transfer the cases. Then, crossing the Indian Ocean and rounding the Cape of Good Hope, he returned to England in 1580 with a cargo valued at £326,580, or, as some say, £600,000. Of this booty Elizabeth had a large proportion, the other partners receiving a percentage on their capital which ran into thousands. Laden with Spanish booty, he had hoisted the St. George's flag as he sailed past Cartagena.

When the exploit became known in Spain, fury rose high against the seamen of the "Jezebel of the North." To the Spanish ambassador's protest Elizabeth replied that she knew nothing of the matter, and would certainly be the last to tolerate shameless attacks on the possessions of her well-beloved brother. Meanwhile Hawkins was putting the fleet on a fighting basis, and the Queen was intrusting her best financier, Sir Thomas Gresham, with the purchase of arms in Antwerp and cannon at Malines. She felt, no doubt, fully prepared when she took the Spanish ambassador on board the *Golden Hind* at Deptford, and there told Drake sternly that the Spaniards regarded him as a pirate; then, bidding him kneel on the deck, she gave him the accolade with majestic calm, saying, "Arise, Sir Francis." War between England and Spain was becoming inevitable. In Spain the Inquisition was ordered to deal with captured English seamen as heretics. Sir Francis Drake, at the head of a royal fleet, harried the Spanish colonies, affirming the right of English seamen to the freedom of the seas, and of worship. Philip ordered a great Armada to be fitted out at Cadiz to attack England. With unmatched boldness

Drake sailed round the Spanish coast, entered this fortified harbor, and there destroyed by gunfire the finest fighting-galleys. Within a few minutes the galley—an oared cruiser, the type of craft which had dominated the Mediterranean for thousands of years—was seen to be doomed, to make way for the sailing-ship.

Philip II was tenacious, and despite the damage wrought by Drake at Cadiz, his Armada was ready in 1588. The Spanish plan was grandiose and ingenious. The Duke of Parma, commanding the Spanish troops in the Netherlands, was to prepare a landing by 30,000 men, and barges for their transport to England. But infantry loaded into barges would be defenseless, and the warships from Spain were to line the course of their crossing, ready to stop any enemy vessel. At the head of the Armada, bringing another 30,000 soldiers, was placed the Duke of Medina-Sidonia, a great gentleman and soldier, but ignorant of maritime matters. The English fleet was commanded by Lord Howard of Effingham, who had Hawkins, Drake, and Frobisher under his orders, and consisted of thirty-four warships built for Elizabeth by Hawkins, as powerfully armed as those of Henry VIII, but longer and lower in build, and one hundred and fifty merchant vessels furnished by the ports. The great Spanish fleet arrived off Plymouth in a formation like that of a land army. The Duke of Medina-Sidonia, as was then customary, counted on transforming the naval battle into a contest of foot soldiers. The grappling-irons were already prepared for boarding, the invincible Spanish infantry were massed on the raised decks, when the English fleet was seen to be assuming an unexpected formation. The vessels of Drake and Hawkins came on in Indian file, out of range of any armament. Then the tragedy began. The English opened fire, and Medina-Sidonia, in impotent despair, saw that the English guns outranged his own. He could do nothing but break off the action, which he did as best he could by laying a course for the Low Countries and the Duke of Parma. He succeeded in making off without excessive losses, after a battle which was indecisive because the English fleet was short of munitions.

Parma was not ready and asked Medina-Sidonia for another fortnight. But the English admirals espied the Spanish fleet at anchor off Calais and attacked it with fireships filled with powder and tar. The Spaniards had to cut their cables to escape this new danger and headed towards the North Sea, where the English cannon accounted for numerous vessels.

A storm joined in the battle. Where could they head for? Sweden, or Scotland, or Ireland? The Duke chose Ireland, a Catholic country, where he hoped to be able to land if need be, and accordingly tried to round the north of Scotland. If he had been a sailor, he would have realized that his vessels were unfit to attempt this difficult passage. Many of them had no drinking-water left. Disorder soon became disaster. Scattered by gales, pillaged by coastal dwellers, the fleet which a week before had been the glorious Armada found itself at the mercy of waves and rocks. Out of a hundred and fifty ships about fifty returned to Spain. Out of 30,000 soldiers, 10,000 were drowned, without counting the victims of cannon-balls or sickness. Spain had lost the mastery of the seas.

This naval victory appears to us now as the first signal of English power; but to the Elizabethans it was far from seeming a decisive victory. Despite the shattering of her Armada, Spain was still the strongest country in Europe, and England was a small island with no army. France, harassed by religious warfare, became the battlefield of their unequal struggle, Elizabeth going to the defense of the French Huguenots, Philip siding with the Catholic League. The Spanish foot soldiers occupied Calais. The Protestant armies were beaten. The English tried another expedition to Cadiz, and continued to harass Spanish trade from the Azores to the Antilles. But Philip, on his side, built a new Armada and successfully invaded Ireland. The England of 1588 had been exalted by a sense of triumph and patriotism, which is easily felt in the historical plays of Shakespeare; but in the last years of the reign, when an English army had been defeated by the Irish rebels and when Spain was holding the Channel ports, a wave of pessimism crossed the country. Hamlet's melancholy was then a common enough mood, and Shakespeare's plays mirrored the passions of the onlookers.

It can hardly be said that Elizabeth's reign saw the first foundations of the British Empire laid. Newfoundland, where English fishermen had long been going, was occupied, though precariously, in 1583. One of Elizabeth's favorites, who was also one of her most cultivated subjects, Sir Walter Raleigh spent a great part of his fortune in trying to establish a colony on the coast of North America, to which the Queen herself gave the name of Virginia. But the colonists whom he left there in the course of his expedition of 1587, numbering eighty-nine men and seventeen women, were not to be found when an expedition with fresh stores was sent there two years later. One of Raleigh's followers is credited with introducing the potato and tobacco into England. Raleigh was one of the first Europeans to smoke, starting the fashion by offering his friends small pipes with silver bowls. During the following reign, the tax on tobacco produced £5,000 in 1619, and £8,340 in 1623, at the rate of 6s. 8d per pound of imported tobacco. The great companies, owned by shareholders and holding monopolies of trading in specified countries, developed during the sixteenth century. The Merchant Adventurers controlled in particular the trade with the German rivers, the Rhine and Elbe. Another company was concerned with the Baltic trade. The Muscovy Company held a monopoly for Russia, Armenia, Persia, and the Caspian. The Levant Company dealt with Turkey and the Adriatic ports. And at the very close of the reign, in 1600, the East India Company was founded, having the sole right of trading with the islands and ports of Asia, Africa, and America, from the Cape of Good Hope to the Magellan Straits. This company in time entered into rivalry with the Portuguese and Dutch. More blood was shed over the clove, said Thorold Rogers, than over the dynastic struggles. This system of companies, which incited at once to aggression and to commercial greed, was the most dangerous of all colonizing methods to the natives of the lands concerned, and the most difficult for the national government to control.

CHAPTER X

Elizabeth and Mary Stuart

EVER since the repulse of Edward I, Scotland had succeeded in maintaining independence from the English kings. The rude, undisciplined Scottish nobility remained quite feudal. The ruling dynasty was that of the Stuarts, who were descended from a daughter of Robert the Bruce. This dynasty had the twofold support of the Catholic Church and the Franco-Scottish alliance, a circumstance which was disturbing to England. The Stuarts, a family as cultivated as the Tudors, interested in theology, poetry, architecture, and even pharmaceutics, did not, as their English cousins did, hide a sound sense of reality under this brilliant surface. James IV of Scotland had married Margaret, the daughter of Henry VII of England. Henry's counselors had expressed a fear that this union might let the English crown fall into Scottish hands. But he replied that in such an event it would be Scotland that would be annexed by England. The son of Margaret Tudor was James V; and from his marriage with the French princess, Mary of Guise, was born Mary Stuart, whose birth took place only a short time before her father died, so that from her cradle she was queen of a wild, restless people. Her mother, Mary of Guise, acted as Regent of Scotland, and had her brought up in France. She grew up a pale, long-faced girl, whose loveliness captivated the Dauphin Francis. Scarcely had she married him when her father-in-law, Henry II of France, died, and the Queen of Scots found herself also Queen of France. Her Tudor descent made her the nearest heir to the throne of England, and perhaps even Queen of England already, if Elizabeth were regarded as of illegitimate birth. It is easy, therefore, to imagine the importance with which Europe regarded the actions and feelings of the young woman, the mistress of two, if not three, countries. In 1560 her tuberculous husband died of an aural infection; the Guise faction lost its power in France; Mary Stuart had to return to Scotland.

She came back to rule a country little suited to her. The new Reformed religion had instantly attracted a thoughtful and poverty-stricken people, who had cared little for the feudal splendor of the Catholic bishops; and the Scottish nobles, their appetite whetted by the example of England, coveted the spoils of the monasteries. A series of religious revolutions and counter-revolutions ended, thanks to Elizabeth's support, in favor of the Protestant party, the "Congregation," a semi-political, semi-religious assembly, representative of the people, the Church, and the nobility, the last taking the lead as "Lords of the Congregation." Cardinal Beaton had previously been cruelly murdered in his palace at St. Andrews. The real master of Scotland at the time of Queen Mary's return in 1561 was John Knox, a man formidable in the strength and narrowness of his faith, and whose rugged biblical eloquence delighted his compatriots. Knox had been a Catholic priest, then an Anglican. It was he who induced Cranmer to suppress kneeling in the second version of the Book of Common Prayer. Imprisoned at St. Andrews, after the murder of Beaton, by French troops sent to the Cardinal's assistance, he spent nineteen months in the galleys of the King of France. In the time of Mary Tudor he lived at Geneva, where he was completely won over to the Calvinist doctrines. Like Calvin, Knox believed in predestination; he held that religious truth must be sought only in the Scriptures, without recourse to any dogma introduced by men; that worship should be austere, with neither pomp nor images; that the Calvinistic institution of the Elders of the Church should supplant bishops and archbishops; and that John Knox himself was one of the elect and directly inspired by God. Having convinced the Scots of all this, he made the Scottish Kirk into a Presbyterian body, completely democratic, with no heirarchy. The church members of every parish appointed their ministers, and in the General Assemblies of the Church these ministers and the leading laymen sat side by side. The union of squires and burgesses to control the Crown, which in England took a parliamentary form, appeared in Scotland as an ecclesiastic assembly. There, the Church was the State.

John Knox had several powerful reasons for hating Mary Stuart. She was a Catholic, and Knox bombarded the "Scarlet Woman" with his pious thunderbolts; she was a woman, and in the time of Mary Tudor and Mary of Guise he had written a pamphlet attacking queens and queens-regent—*The First Blast of the Trumpet Against the Monstrous Regiment of Women;* and she had been Queen of France, a country in which Knox had known chiefly the dungeons. Mary Stuart returned to Scotland and landed at Leith in a dense wet fog. "The very face of Heaven," said Knox, "did manifestly speak what comfort was brought into this country with her—to wit, sorrow, dolor, darkness and all impiety." She came with youth and grace and poetry about her; and she met violence, fanaticism, hate. Her subjects welcomed her at first with great demonstrations, but their uncouthness startled the young woman. They sang psalms under her windows at Holyrood all night. On the route of her procession platforms had been put up, on which there were cheerful pictures of idolaters burned for their sins. The denizens of one district proposed to display also the effigy of a priest slain at the altar at the Elevation of the Host, but were persuaded that this was tactless. But, with patience surprising in a girl of eighteen, Mary slowly gained a foothold. She spoke little, plied her embroidery needle at meetings of her Council, and even won over some of the Protestant nobles by her charm. Even Knox she received amiably. In return, he expounded the duty of a subject to rise up against an impious ruler, as might be shown in the Bible by Isaiah and Hezekiah, Daniel and Nebuchadnezzar, and many other treasured instances. She had never before encountered a prophet; this one dazed and even prostrated her. "I see," she said, "that my subjects obey you and not me." He retorted that all he asked of prince and people was that both be obedient to God. He then preached to her about the Mass, a ceremony which he argued had no Scriptural justification. She was no theologian, but there was charm in her answer: "Ye are over-sair for me, but if they were here that I have heard, they would answer you." Knox went off expressing his wish that she might have the success in Scotland that Deborah had amongst the children of Israel.

The relationships between Mary and Elizabeth were complex. Political conflicts were crossed by feminine jealousies. When Mary's ambassador, Sir James Melville, came to London, Elizabeth tried hard to charm him. She spoke all the languages she knew, played on the lute and asked whether Mary played so well, danced before the Scotsman, who had to own that "Mary danced not so high and disposedly as she did." From a direct comparison of beauties Melville escaped, by averring that Elizabeth was the fairest Queen in England and Mary the fairest in Scotland. Which was the taller? Queen Mary? Then, said Elizabeth, "she is too tall." In these comments of a sovereign John Knox would have found fresh arguments against the "monstrous regiment of women." But in Elizabeth this frivolity was only a useful mask. On the question of the succession she never wavered. She could not allow Mary to style herself Queen of England, nor to unite the two kingdoms in her coat of arms, even although the Queen of Scots took no steps to claim her rights. Any such claim might have dangerously undermined the loyalty of the English Catholics, specially as so many of them lived in the northern counties, near the Scottish border. If Mary married a Catholic prince, French or Spanish, England might be threatened with a new Marian persecution. On the other hand, if Mary Stuart would consent to marriage with an English Protestant of Elizabeth's choosing, the English Queen would be willing to name the Queen of Scots as her successor and guide her with her counsels.

A friendly correspondence began between the two Queens, in which Elizabeth, playing the elder sister, pelted her cousin with sharp-edged proverbs: "Remove bushes, lest a thorn prick your heel," or, "The stone falls often on the head of the thrower." Dull counsel, but perhaps useful, as Mary, after her early show of patience, was now yielding under the nervous strain. When Knox denounced her possible marriage to a Papist "infidel," she summoned him to her presence and addressed him in a rage. "I have borne with you," she cried, "in all your rigorous manner of speaking . . . yea, I have sought your favors by all possible means. I offered unto you presence and audience whensoever it pleased you to admonish me, and yet I cannot be quit of you. I vow to God I shall be once revenged." Sobs cut her short, and her page—according to Knox— could hardly find napkins enough to keep her eyes dry.

Few women have better claim to indulgence than Mary Stuart, thrown so young and uncounseled among the unscrupulous nobles and inhuman preachers of a fierce and troublous age. Her courage won the first game. But when she allowed her womanhood to come before her sovereignty, troubles came thick and fast. It was natural that she should refuse the handsome Leicester, recommended by Elizabeth, as husband; she had no mind to take her cousin's leavings, and in any case Leicester would have made a poor king. But Lord Darnley, her own choice, was worse. He could claim Tudor descent, as she could, and his youthful body certainly had grace; but he was a poor-souled man, a coward at heart, with sudden furies, and Mary tired of him as quickly as she had fallen in love with him. She was then foolish enough to make a favored counselor of a young Italian musician, David Rizzio, who had come to Scotland in the train of the Duke of Savoy. The court lords, outraged at an upstart's eminence, swore revenge, and plotted with Darnley to get rid of Rizzio. They killed him clinging to Mary's skirts when he was at supper with her. Three months later she gave birth to a son, who was to become James VI of Scotland and James I of England, and was at the time reputed to be the son of Rizzio. Mary's position became untenable. She hated her husband, Darnley, and was wildly in love with the most redoubtable of the Scottish lords, the Earl of Bothwell, who had first violated, then conquered her, and was distrusted by all Scotland. Bothwell prepared the murder of Darnley. Was Mary Stuart privy to the plot? It is certain that the Queen installed him, when he was ill, in an isolated house outside the city walls of Edinburgh; there, in Kirk o' Field, she left him one evening; during the night the house blew up and Darnley was found dead in the garden. No one doubted Bothwell's guilt. But three months later the Queen married the murderer, and this was more than public opinion, even in the sixteenth century, could stand. Mary was abandoned by the Pope, by Spain and France, by all her friends. There was a rising in Scotland. After a short struggle Bothwell fled, in rather cowardly style, and Mary was brought captive to Edinburgh by soldiers who cried out, "Burn the whore!" She was deposed in favor of her son, James VI, her history having shown, as the Venetian ambassador said, that affairs of State are no business for a woman.

She would certainly have been executed if Elizabeth had not shielded her, greatly to the distress of Cecil and Walsingham, who could explain their mistress's policy only by her horror of the Scottish rebels and her wish not to offer her own subjects the spectacle and example of a queen's head on the block. At last, after ten months in captivity on Loch Leven, Mary escaped on horseback and reached England in May, 1568. What was Elizabeth to do? Must she tolerate the presence within her realm of so dangerous a claimant? Never did she display more virtuosity in hesitation. Her counselors would have treated Mary ruthlessly, as reasons of State demanded. "If ye strike not at the root," wrote John Knox, "the branches that appear to be broken will bud again, and that more quickly than men can believe." Mary asked for an investigation to be made by Elizabeth into the actions of the Scottish rebels; Elizabeth agreed to this, but ordered the inquiry to be extended to the murder of Darnley, in order, she said that "her sister" might be cleared of any suspicion. Certain letters in proof of Mary's guilt, the famous "Casket Letters," were produced against her. She denounced them as forgeries. The court found the charges not proven. But Elizabeth still held her prisoner—and can hardly be blamed for so doing, as the hapless Queen of Scots had been, and still was, connected with all conspiracies. The number of plots hinging on Mary makes one marvel at Elizabeth's patience. It was for Mary that the Catholic north rose in 1569, and for her that the Duke of Norfolk died. She encouraged Spain as well as France, the Duke of Alençon as well as Don John of Austria. She conspired against Elizabeth with the Pope, through certain Florentine bankers. The Commons demanded her head; Walsingham constantly denounced her as a snake in the bosom. There can be no doubt that Elizabeth might have had a round score of sound reasons for executing her fair cousin. But she refused.

Nineteen years went past for Mary in her English captivity, from 1568 until 1587. The beautiful pale horsewoman became sickly and over-ripe; the chestnut hair turned gray. In her places of captivity she embroidered small objects for Elizabeth, and plotted, plotted incorrigibly. Elizabeth was growing old; it was certain now that she would die childless; the question of the succession became more and more grave. After this prolonged incarceration, the Pope and the Church were forgetting that Mary had been an adulteress, perhaps a murderess, and again built high hopes on her. Good Protestants grew anxious at the day of reckoning drawing near. Walsingham, charged with her supervision, contrived to intercept her correspondence regularly. After all these years of captivity, she still clung to "the Enterprise," which meant the downfall of Elizabeth. Now, in 1587 a war with Spain seemed a likelihood, and Walsingham deemed it essential to stifle any risks of internal danger before engaging in war abroad. A spy was sent to lay a trap for Mary, into which she fell completely. A band of young men had planned to kill Elizabeth, and their leader, Anthony Babington, wrote a letter to Mary, which of course was intercepted, in which he announced the murder and asked her advice. Mary's enemies anxiously awaited her reply. It did not disappoint them. She approved, and even gave advice to the murderers. This time Walsingham had her head in his hands. Mary was tried at Fotheringay, and unanimously found guilty. The Commons demanded immediate execution. Her son, James VI, did not forget that his mother's death would leave him heir to the English throne: his religion, he declared, had always made her conduct hateful to him, although his honor constrained him to defend her life. Elizabeth still hesitated. In obedience to real clemency? To horror of her action? To fear for her safety? At last she signed the death warrant. It needed three strokes of the executioner's sword to sever that head, on the morning of February 8, 1587. The calamities of Mary's youth had been forgotten, and in the eyes of the Catholics she became as a saint.

Elizabeth lived to be seventy, a very advanced age for the time; and almost to the last she shone, she flirted, she danced. Burleigh had died before her, and she had replaced him by his second son, Robert Cecil, a great Minister like his father before him. Leicester had been succeeded in the old woman's favor by the Earl of Essex. He was graceful and charming, but arrogant and easily offended. Emboldened by the Queen's feeling for him, a vague sentiment compounded at once of maternal fondness, tenderness, and sensuality, and having been further encouraged by a successful expedition to Cadiz which made him a popular idol, he became insufferable. He treated the Queen with astounding impertinence and roughness, but she always forgave. But he played his last card when he asked for command of the army sent by Elizabeth to crush the Irish revolt instigated by the Spaniards in 1594. He behaved like a spoiled child, and, as a traitor, had thoughts of bringing his troops back to London to dethrone his sovereign, and at the same time was writing her angry, passionate letters. Elizabeth now viewed him sanely. He had failed: "You had your asking," she wrote, "you had choice of times, you had power and authority more ample than any ever had, or ever shall have." When he came home after deserting his post, and tried to organize a plot for seizing her instead of slaying her, she handed him over to his fate. "Those who touch the scepters of princes," she said, "deserve no pity." The handsome Essex was beheaded at the Tower, and met his fate with humility and devoutness.

His death cast a shadow of sorrow over the Queen's last years. She still dyed her hair an unnatural hue, still bedecked herself with pearls and diamonds and cloth of silver and gold; she still received the homage of her Parliaments, promised to abolish the monopolies which had enriched too many of her courtiers, and gave her hand to be kissed by all the gentlemen of the Commons because she thought she was taking leave of her last Parliament; sometimes she even still danced a couranto. But soon she fell back on the cushions. The end was near, and she knew it. Only at the last would she name her successor. She knew it must be James VI of Scotland, and that her Ministers were already in correspondence with Edinburgh. She never spoke of it. *"Video et taceo"* had always been her motto. In January, 1603, she felt more stricken, went to bed, refused to see a doctor, and turning her face to the wall sank into a lethargy from which she never emerged.

CHAPTER XI

Elizabethan England

THE bodies of the Elizabethans were made as ours are made. They had the same brains, the same hearts, the same loins, and the passions which they felt were doubtless much the same as those of their descendants. But the swirls and quirks of their clothes distorted so cunningly the lines of these bodies, and the splendor of their metaphors so strangely disguised these inborn passions, that to many historians they have seemed as monsters. In particular men have been astonished at the contrast between the delicacy of their poems and the cruelty of their public shows, between the luxury of their dress and the filth of their living. But every epoch holds such surprises, and historians yet unborn will find it no less hard to reconcile the intelligence of our scientists or the acuteness of our novelists with the stupidity of our economic system or the savagery of our wars. The captains and apprentices who crossed the Thames to see a play of Shakespeare's at the Globe Playhouse were the same who enjoyed seeing a wretched bear baited by a pack of dogs, or watching the bloody butchering of a traitor. Habit had hardened them, just as it made the stench of the London streets tolerable to men as refined as Essex or Carlisle, and just as it makes tolerable to the corresponding æsthetes of our own day the most cruel political philosophy and its deadly consequences.

Because the Queen loved luxury, and as the country was growing richer, fashion exercised a ruthless and capricious tyranny over the Elizabethans. Round their ladies, the French invention of the crinoline was enlarged until it became like a table on which they rested their arms. Above this huge bell, a corset of whalebone or steel compressed the figure into a wasp-like waist. Vast ruffs, a Spanish fancy, were stiffened by starch or by wire, a diabolic invention lately introduced to England by the wife of the Queen's Dutch coachman. The richest materials—velvet, damask, and cloth of gold or silver—were needed for the gowns of ladies or the doublets of men. Great lords, in their mythological diversions, pitted their imagination against the poets, who quite often were themselves great lords. Luxury and comfort pervaded the houses of the gentry and the burgesses. A lady of quality, before rising, required her page to light a fire in her room; before going to bed, her maid had to warm the bed with a warming-pan. All over the countryside rose new mansions, mingling Italian styles with the traditional Gothic. In gardens as in houses men sought symmetrical plans and variegated ornament. Yews and box trees were clipped in spheres and spirals. And the speech of the lords and ladies was no less fantastically turned than the topiary in their gardens. John Lyly's romance of *Euphues* appeared in 1580, and every lady of culture prided herself on her euphuism. The joy of inventing words and phrases, the mental intoxication of a reborn language, engendered a preciosity which was manifested in both poems and speech, and hovered over the uncertain frontier between the lovely and the ludicrous.

The court and its imitators may have read Sir Philip Sydney and Sir Thomas Wyatt, Spenser and Marlowe, the sonnets of William Shakespeare; but under this shot-silk surface there still flowed a compelling Puritan current. The library of Elizabeth, Lady Hoby (1528-1609), the catalogue of which has been preserved, consisted mainly of devotional books, with the Bible and Foxe's *Book of Martyrs* as its core. One of the most widely read authors of Shakespeare's day was the preacher Henry Smith, known as "silver-tongued Smith," whose sermons ran into numerous editions between 1590 and 1630. Next to sermons, the printing-press was kept busiest with rhymed ballads about current events, or with Puritan tracts like those of the pseudonymous "Martin Marprelate." Poems found few readers, but Elizabethan writers lived not so much on the sale of their books as on the gifts of the patrons to whom they dedicated them. A stage play brought its author between six and ten pounds, and a fairly active playwright turned out ten or twelve a year. The London booksellers sold considerable numbers of books translated from the Italian or French, such as the tales of Boccaccio or the essays of Montaigne. From such foreign sources Spenser and Shakespeare, and many others, drew themes which they embroidered with the sad, gentle gravity, the rustic poetry, the homely philosophy of their race, and to which they gave a peculiarly English charm.

It was under Elizabeth that the theater took an outstanding place in the life of London. Since the days of Henry VII there had been troupes of players, but few permanent playhouses. These mummers played in the yards of taverns or in manor halls. When the City authorities turned Puritan and expelled the actors, they took refuge across the river, beyond the lord mayor's jurisdiction. Several playhouses were then built, the most famous being the Globe, a part share in which was owned by Shakespeare. Men are quick to make a permanent characteristic from a chance detail. The builders of these early theaters nearly all tried to reproduce the courtyard of an inn, with its open-air gallery running along the doors of the rooms. This gallery was useful for representing, as it might be, the parapets of a fortress, the balcony of a lady's room, or the summit of a tower. The spectators paid a penny for admission, and from sixpence to a shilling for a seat, either on the stage itself or in the galleries, which, with a reminiscence of the ancestral inn, preserved their separate rooms—whence, probably, the modern boxes. The opening of the play was announced, as may still be seen in country fairs, by a flourish of trumpets. The public, a throng of apprentices, law students, soldiers, and gentlemen, was intelligent and serious. They relished the blood-thirsty melodramas, but could equally well appreciate the most poetic plays of Marlowe, or Ben Jonson, or Shakespeare.

How can a few words suffice for William Shakespeare, the animator of a world? Was he superior to all other dramatists of his day? Remarkable as these were, it yet seems certain. No other played such a full gamut of tones, or touched so immeasurable a range of themes and kinds. None could so happily blend exalted poetry with solid construction, or give expression to such profound thoughts on human nature and human passions in language so compelling. Was his superiority recognized by his contemporaries? Not with the unanimity of modern opinion. When this actor-playwright began about 1590 to offer his manuscripts to the theatrical companies, he excited the jealousy of his competitors, the erudite university poets. But the public applauded him. In a manual of literature and arts published in 1598, *Palladis Tamia,* Francis Meres refers to Shakespeare's mastery of both tragedy and comedy—"among the English the most excellent in both kinds for the stage"—and also to his skill in depicting the sorrows and perplexities of love. He says also: "The Muses would speak with Shakespeare's fine-filed phrase if they would speak English." Friendly with persons at court, and sharing their life in the last years of Queen Elizabeth, he could present the fierceness of ambition and the torments of power as well as he could the passions of love. The wisdom of a race is made up of common truths to which great writers have been able to give unique forms. The debt of the French people to the moralists like Montaigne or La Bruyère corresponds to the debt of the English people, instinctive, poetic, and often inconstant, to Shakespeare.

The England of Shakespeare's time seems to us to be burgeoning with songs and poems, and we are tempted to imagine the humblest apprentice or the simplest villager playing the viol or tossing off a madrigal. But the poetry and blitheness of Elizabethan England need not be exaggerated. Life for the common folk was as hard then as today, and harder. In Shakespeare we can catch glimpses of the hard-pressed farm wench, clattering her pail of frozen milk in the dead of winter, her nose red with the cold, her hands chapped with scrubbing dirty clothes. Although the price of wheat had risen as a result of the falling value of gold, rural unemployment must have been severe, as it proved necessary to frame two important Poor Laws in 1597 and 1601. The squires, whose power was waxing, often proved harsh, and religious persecution was formidable for any who ventured on independent ways of thinking. But there were also Christian landowners who cultivated hospitality and courtesy. The manors, like the villages, were still self-sufficing. A good housewife, be she lady or farmer's wife, did all the work of her house, making everything from jellies to candles. There was grace in the village festivities, and old pagan traditions survived, such as the maypole, with its evocation of spring and the primitive Eastertide. Villagers could play diverting comedies, as Shakespeare showed in "A Midsummer Night's Dream," and foreigners noted that the English were the most musical people in the world. Not only did they produce composers as admirable as Thomas Byrd, but nearly every house had its lute, viol, or virginal, and songbooks in plenty. All visitors and many menials, could read the score of a song at sight and take their part in a glee of three or four voices.

This taste for poetry and music called for a fairly advanced education.

And this the Elizabethans did not lack. After Winchester and Eton, new schools were founded by rich patrons—Rugby in 1567, Harrow in 1590. In principle these schools were free and intended for the children of the neighborhood, the founder paying the masters' salaries and the pupils' board. Only those from other parts paid fees, and these were nearly always sons of the well-to-do in the country. Gradually these outsiders gained a majority and for them the schools came chiefly to exist, Harrow, for instance, retaining only forty free scholars. Elementary education was provided in the "petty schools," often by women who taught the alphabet and the rudiments of writing from a stock of knowledge hardly extending any farther. Later a boy might go to the "grammar school," there to be taught often by a teacher of real learning, even in the country. Even the small towns had their men of culture at this time. Amongst the friends of the Shakespeare family at Stratford-on-Avon, one was a Master of Arts of Oxford, and another read Latin for enjoyment. The literary historians used to be astonished by the wide knowledge that Shakespeare, an actor of humble origins, possessed. But it was a knowledge shared by a wide public, especially in London. The Inns of Court formed a center of culture from which sprang some of the best poets and dramatists of the age. Turning the pages of books which once belonged to the men or women of the time, one may often find the margins sprinkled with Latin notes, conspicuous alike for their sound sense and cogent wording, and one feels that, although scientific methods today may be more efficient than in the Elizabethan era, these people were superior in taste and intelligence to their equivalents in our own times.

CHAPTER XII

The End of an Age

WE SEE, then, that sixteenth-century England produced an art and a literature of her own. From the European Renaissance she extracted whatsoever suited her genius, and then she detached herself from the Continent. In Tudor times everything combined to increase her insularity: the growth of the national language, the building of a powerful fleet, the breach with the Roman Church. In the memoirs of Sully there is an account of an embassy to London in the early years of the seventeenth century, which enables us to gauge the force of English xenophobia at that time: "It is certain that the English detest us, with a hatred so strong and widespread, that one is tempted to regard it as one of the inborn characteristics of that people. More truthfully, it is the outcome of their pride and presumption, there being no people in Europe more haughty, more disdainful, more intoxicated with the notion of their own excellence. If they are to be believed, reason and wit exist only amongst themselves; they worship all their own opinions and scorn those of other nations; nor does it ever occur to them to listen to others or to question their own. Actually this characteristic harms them more than it does us. It places them at the mercy of all their fancies. Ringed by the sea, they might be said to have acquired all its instability." And one secret of the Tudors' popularity was their skill in flattering the pride and insular prejudices of their subjects.

The rule of the Tudor monarchs was a strong one, but its force did not depend on soldiery or police. Based on public opinion, on the yeomen and farmers and merchants, it acquired possession of the spiritual power. The kings of France and Spain made common cause with the Church of Rome to create absolute monarchies; the kings of England made alliance with Parliament to oppose Rome and themselves to head a national Church. Their espousal of the Reformation might have ruined England if the two great Catholic powers had joined forces to crush this lesser kingdom. The Tudors were saved by the rivalries of Hapsburg and Valois. Thanks to a European cleavage, England was able to engage in that policy of the balance of power which is forced upon her by her situation, and which consists of confronting the dominant power on the Continent with coalitions supported by English wealth and an English fleet. In Elizabeth's time she had not as yet an imperial policy, and nobody in the sixteenth century imagined that the overseas territories, then coveted only for their removable riches, might one day become the homes of colonists.

When the seventeenth century opened, the minds of sovereigns were no longer haunted by the dream of a Roman and Christian Empire. The sole aim of their strivings came to be the strength of the national State. In France and Spain the rule of the central power was exercised by officials who were themselves supported by soldiery; in England the local institutions of the Middle Ages retained their authority intact. Parliament, the link between the Crown and the public opinion of shires, towns, and villages, was respected by the Tudor kings. Henry VIII used it to gain acceptance for his religious reforms. Elizabeth humored her Parliaments with a care which indicates how powerful they probably were. In 1583, at the very height of the Queen's authority, Sir Thomas Smith wrote in his *Commonwealth of England*: "The most high and absolute power of the Realm of England consisteth in the Parliament . . . for every Englishman is intended to be there present, either in person or by procuration and attorney, or what pre-eminence, state, dignity, or quality soever he be, from the Prince (be he King or Queen) to the lowest person of England. And the consent of the Parliament is taken to be every man's consent." Thus, in the sixteenth century, an English jurist regarded Parliament as the highest power. By the close of Elizabeth's reign that power had become conscious of its own strength. Criticism of acts of the Crown was vigorous enough to prove the independence and authority of Parliament.

Just as feudalism perished of its own success, so the English monarchy was soon to be weakened by the very services which it rendered. The immense respect which invested the Tudors was born as much from memory of the disasters previous to their advent as from the inherent merits of this family. But proverbially—"the danger past, God forgotten." Encouraged by the internal order restored by the monarchy, and by the external security arising from England's new maritime power and the divided state of Europe, the squires and burgesses were soon seeking to impose their will on the King, as expressed through Parliament. Crown and Commons were to play a great match, the stake being the supreme power; and the rashness of a new dynasty gave Parliament the victory.

Book V

THE TRIUMPH OF PARLIAMENT

was his motto. His clothes were padded to withstand stabbing, and the sight of a sword made him queasy. He was fairly cultured, but intellectual rather than intelligent. In a precocious youth he wrote verses, theological treatises, and works on political doctrine wherein he demonstrated that kings are intended by God to rule, and subjects intended likewise to give obedience. The King, therefore, was above the Law, but, except in exceptional cases of which he alone could be judge, he ought to submit to the Law in order to set an example.

This was proud teaching, but it had served well in Scotland to compel the respect of an overweening and formidable clergy, which arrogated the right of judging the sovereign and coaxing him by calling him "God's silly vassal." James I arrived in England with a dangerous conviction of his intellectual superiority. In all good faith he believed himself a theologian of genius who would bring the truth to the bemused English. He knew virtually nothing of the character of his new subjects, and did not try to understand them. Forthwith he ranted and stammered and slobbered before their assemblies, unconsciously amusing them by his Scots accent. He expected his eloquence and erudition to be praised to the skies. But he was dealing with a race who were in no temper to lend ear to an argumentative intruder.

In spite of a Calvinist upbringing, the new King settled down quite comfortably with the Anglican Church. He had suffered from the democratic freedom of the Presbyterians in Scotland, and was not displeased at finding in England a Church which acknowledged a hierarchy having the King at its summit. Elizabeth had imposed a conformity as rigorous as the old one of the Roman Church. All men had to profess the Thirty-nine Articles; the clergy could use only the Book of Common Prayer; and the ecclesiastical commissions were quite as strict as the Roman courts had been. To the true Anglican the Reformation did not appear as a break with the past; his Church seemed to him "Catholic," that is to say, universal. The average Protestant, it has been observed, abandoned the Roman faith because it was no longer in fashion, but his inner heart kept turning towards it. The Anglican doctrine, which was the State religion, found itself attacked on both flanks, by the Catholics and the Puritans. The Catholics in England, during the latter part of Queen Elizabeth's reign, had suffered persecutions the severity of which was intensified by the war with Spain and the Jesuit conspiracies. Excluded from all local or national official posts, they were not even allowed to leave their own properties without the signed permission of a justice of the peace. They were liable to heavy fines (although in practice these were not often levied) for non-attendance at the Anglican service. A priest who said Mass, and any who harbored him, could be sentenced to a traitor's hideous death, but the threat was comparatively rarely carried out, and in many country houses the Catholic chaplain was still to be found in a hidden loft. By the early years of James I's reign the adherents of the old faith numbered (it has been estimated) barely one in twenty of the population. They cherished high hopes when a son of Mary Stuart ascended the throne. He was known to have corresponded with the Pope and to favor toleration. He did, in fact, offer to abolish fines for religious offenses, but only on condition that the Catholics declared their loyalty to the King and not to the Pope, and that they should refrain from proselytizing. These terms were incompatible with genuine faith, and it was not long before the Catholics became so disappointed that a number of them began plotting against the King.

The most dangerous of these conspiracies was the famous Gunpowder Plot. Its aim was the simultaneous slaying of the King, the Lords, and the Commons, by blowing up the House of Lords when all were there assembled. With the Protestants thus left leaderless, a Catholic rising would have a chance of success, as the plotters counted on the inertia of the masses. The type of the conspirators and the methods employed are reminiscent of the terrorist plots in Russia at the end of the nineteenth century. They were men of good birth. The most famous of them, Guy Fawkes, a Catholic soldier, had learned the arts of sapping and tunneling during the wars in Flanders. He and his friends began by renting a cellar opposite the Houses of Parliament, but soon discovered accidentally a site lying immediately beneath the House of Lords, which would free them from the need for digging a mine themselves. Renting this, they filled the place with barrels of powder concealed under fagots, and their attempt would doubtless have succeeded if the plotters had not deemed it necessary to warn some of their partisans in order to organize the rising which was to follow the explosion. One of their confidants felt it his duty to warn the authorities. Guy Fawkes stayed on alone, with great courage, to light the fuse at the proper moment. He was found and arrested on the night of November 4-5, 1605, and put to a cruel death.

With him died also his accomplices and Henry Garnet, the Provincial of the English Jesuits, accused of instigating the crime. This charge seems to have been untrue: Garnet sinned only by his silence, but the indignation roused by the disclosure of an attempt so grave and so nearly successful, made all Catholics still more suspect. They were deprived of civic rights, banned from the Bar and from the practice of medicine, and even from managing the property of their children under age. The Gunpowder Plot achieved the ruin of Catholicism in England for many years to come. In men's minds it became linked with dark ideas of plotting against the safety of the State, and for a full century any sovereign or statesman suspected of alliance with Rome was condemned by public opinion.

On its other flank the Anglican Church had to suffer the attacks of the Puritans, those who wished to purify the Church, not only from all contact with Rome, but from any Romanist practice as well. It was not so much a doctrine as a mental attitude. On James I's accession a petition was presented to him by the Puritan clergy, who asked that every clergyman should be entitled to decide for himself whether he should wear a surplice, that the sign of the cross be suppressed in baptism, as also the bowing of the head on uttering the name of Jesus, genuflexion before the altar, the ring in the marriage ceremony, and they called for strict Sabbath observance. Others, more radical in temper, wanted to abolish bishops and set up a Presbyterian Church on the Scottish model. A third group, the Independents, claimed for every man the right to choose his beliefs. But all three shared a deep dislike of gayety and an intense love of civic liberties, a fondness for simplicity of living and austerity in worship. The Puritans detested the sensuous, southern poetry of the Elizabethan Renaissance. Was this the Saxon blood? Or the climate? The joyousness of the Mediterranean was a cause of astonishment and scandal to them. To a certain vein of poetry, it is true, they were sensitive, but it was that of the Psalmist or Ecclesiastes rather than of Spenser or Shakespeare. They baptized their children with the names of Hebrew patriarchs or warriors, and regarded themselves as a new people chosen of God, charged with the extermination of the Amalekites of the court. Constant reading of the Bible made them to live in a collective dream, gloomy if often exalted. They hated all who shared not their beliefs, seeing these as the children of darkness and themselves as the children of light. They deplored the theater, were horrified by sin, especially by the sin of the flesh, dressed with willfully outmoded modesty, and cut their hair short to show their scorn for the courtiers with their curled wigs. In short, they were dreary, honest, insufferable, and strong.

At the beginning of James's reign the Puritans formed part of the National Church and hoped to imbue it with their teachings. A conference was held at Hampton Court, under the King's presidency, to consider their petition. James took pleasure in this theological debate until the words "presbytery" and "synod" were introduced. They had painful associations for him. "A Scottish Presbytery," he said, "agreeth as well with a monarchy as God with the devil. . . . Then Jack, Tom, Will, and Dick shall meet and at their pleasure censure me and my Council." And taking up his hat to close the sitting, he exclaimed: ". . . No bishop, no King! . . . I shall make them conform themselves or I will harry them out of the land." With that one sentence he turned the religious quarrel into a political one. The Bible had taught these Puritans that the faith must be militant, and that it is the duty of every man who has seen the truth to make the truth prevail. And they would try to make it prevail against the King himself, since he so constrained them. In 1604 James had to expel from the Church three hundred Puritan clergy who refused to observe the Anglican rite.

From now onwards three parties must be distinguished in the English clergy: a High Church party, the nearest to the Church of Rome and accepting the ritual imposed by the Tudor kings; a Presbyterian, nonconforming party, remaining within the Church but anxious for its reform; and an Independent or Congregationalist party, disapproving equally of Anglican episcopacy and Presbyterian synods. The Independents held that there should be no such thing as a State Church, whether of the English or the Scottish pattern. A Church, in their view, was a group of Christians united only by their own will. Some of them, in their respect for individual liberty, went so far as to suppress the baptism of children, only allowing the baptism of adults in a state of full belief, thus coming to be known as Baptists.

It is important to realize that the Independent Protestants, if they remained in England, could not hope to practice their faith in peace. Within the official Church a clergyman could be more or less ritualistic; outside it, there was no safety. Many chose exile, and after 1608 emigrated to Holland; and even there many of the extremists were perturbed by the heresies in the air. In 1620 some of them returned from Holland to Southampton, but only to embark at once on the ship *Mayflower*, which was to convey them to America. They planned to settle within the northern limits of the Virginia Company's claims, but winds and tides took them to a still more northern landing-place, on the coast of what is now called New England. During the next few years, which were not favorable to the Puritans in England, they were joined over there by thousands of emigrants, and in their new country these men who had preferred exile to heresy established, as the logical outcome, a theocracy.

CHAPTER II

King against Parliament

KING JAMES I and his Parliament had nothing in common. A frivolous and vicious court seethed with scandals, of which adultery was the most trifling. The King, a fond and feeble man, could not dispense with favorites, chosen for pretty looks rather than statesman-like gifts. With these he debated the highest matters of State, not at the council table, but after supper or a hunting-party. On his accession he was wise enough to keep by his side Robert Cecil, whom he created Earl of Salisbury in 1605, and a few others of Elizabeth's ablest counselors. But gradually power slipped into the hands of his favorite, Robert Carr, who became Earl of Somerset, and then to George Villiers, a superbly handsome youth in his early twenties, poor but well-born, who was cynically pushed forward by the Archbishop and his allies to supplant Somerset. Villiers had caught the eye of James at once. Groom of the Chamber, Knight of the Garter, Baron, Viscount, Marquess, Lord High Admiral, Warden of the Cinque Ports, Duke of Buckingham, the favorite Minister of James I, then of his son, Charles I—"never," said Clarendon, "any man in any age, nor, I believe, in any country, rose in so short a time to so much greatness of honor, power, or fortune upon no other advantage or recommendation than of the beauty and graciousness of his person." The letters that passed between Buckingham and James show the astonishing familiarity with which the subject treated his sovereign. And it is easy to picture how this merrymaking and dissolute court horrified the sober knights who represented the English yeomen and burgesses in Parliament. These country members were unspoiled by London life. They were, it has been well said, the heirs of long generations of a healthy, country life, formed by the Elizabethan culture and inspired by the Puritan religion. The court

[262]

had no grip on them. They were not covetous of preferment and they knew that the King's only armed force was the trained bands or country militia, who thought as Parliament thought. Impervious to fear or favor, they proudly exercised the privilege of attacking the royal administration, and after one sitting, when they freely spoke their minds about the Duke, and even the King, they returned on foot fearlessly from Westminster to the City, fully aware of being protected against the angers of the court by the silent but active complicity of the citizens, high and humble, of the capital.

Such was the Parliament, conscious of its duties and its strength, upon which James I ingenuously wished to impose the doctrine of the divine and hereditary right of kings. It was a theory new to England, where heredity, if the safety of the country so demanded, had always been overruled by the choice of the Council and then of Parliament. The logical mind of James I sought to make the monarchy systematic and coherent; and this, in a land blessed by inconsistence, meant certain unpopularity. According to the royal theologian, not only did the King, crowned and anointed, become a sacred personage, but, as God had in advance chosen and consecrated all future kings, Parliament could merely record the divine ordinances. The King was responsible to God, but not to his subjects. He was not subject to Law, because he was the Law. *"Rex est lex"*: this doctrine, with which James I had successfully confronted the claims of the Scottish Church, could only offend the House of Commons.

Against the King's abstract system, Parliament set up English custom. It did not yet claim control of the executive's action. Save for treason, ministers had never been responsible to Parliament, on which their administrative acts were not dependent. But the general principles for the governance of the nation—that is to say, the laws—should be laid down only by "the Crown in Parliament," and such laws were obligatory on the King himself, on his ministers, and on his Council. When the Stuarts came upon the scene, the conflict began between royal absolutism and the legislative power of Parliament. Considering only the theoretic right, a case could be made for both positions, that of absolute monarchy and that of limited monarchy. To Parliament, as to the Crown, the sovereignty of the people had been delegated, and in Tudor times the monarch had often expressed popular feeling better than the Commons. As a matter of practice, however, the conflict had to be settled. A political regime can survive only if it provides a mode of expression for the real forces of the country and, at the same time, consecrates a supreme power in the State which can have the last word at a decisive moment. Sovereignty, as Hobbes was later to say, is indivisible.

A government respects the liberty of the citizens in so far as it needs their assent to the imposition of taxes. The King of France became an absolute sovereign because he was able to establish the *taille* as perpetual. Elizabeth's power was increased in proportion to her economical spending and to the exceptional sums accruing to her from the exploits of Drake and the pillage of the Spanish treasures. James I, with his ostentatious court and favorites to be loaded with gifts, was bound to be an extravagant sovereign. One contemporary commented that although all kings threw money from the window on the coronation days, James was the first to do so every day. His very feminine taste for jewelry cost him sometimes as much as £37,000 a year, whereas he devoted only £27,000 to the army. In 1614 he needed £155,000 for his household, whereas Elizabeth spent on this only £27,000 in 1601. Even had he been thrifty, the rise in prices would in itself have caused him difficulties. (A Star Chamber dinner cost the Treasury, for an equal number of guests, two pounds in 1500, but twenty pounds in 1600.) Although James I avoided wars, he spent £600,000 a year, while his revenues amounted only to about £400,000, of which £150,000 came from the tunnage and poundage, fixed duties on wool and leather which Parliament customarily voted to the King for life. To fill up the gap James tried various expedients: he solicited freewill offerings; he forced landowners who declined knighthood on account of its obligations, to pay a substantial sum to release themselves; he sold peerages; he sold the timber of Crown forests. Finally he proposed to Parliament the Great Compact, whereby the King was to renounce all his former feudal rights in exchange for a life income of £200,000. This compromise was rejected by Parliament which was dissolved by the King. For ten years on end, between 1611 and 1621, it was not again summoned, except for a few weeks in 1614. Could the Crown live without it? The solution of the problem of sovereignty depended on the answer to that question.

If a king is to live without money, he must live without war. And this was the fervent desire of the pacific James. In 1604 he concluded an inglorious but not shameful peace with Spain. The Spaniards gave England her claim to the freedom of the European seas; the English did not renounce the freedom of the ocean. Nothing was settled; there was no real compromise. With the death of Cecil in 1612, Elizabethan prudence vanished from the royal Councils. Attempts were made to arrange for the marriage of the heir to the throne with a Spanish Infanta. No scheme could be more unpopular. An Infanta, the Protestants believed, would bring Jesuits, fagots and plots in her wedding-chest. The Prince himself declared that he would not lay two religions in one bed. After the disgrace of Carr the anti-Spanish party seemed for a few years to have the upper hand. A veteran of the Elizabethan wars, Sir Walter Raleigh, was fetched out of the Tower of London, where James had confined him for supposed conspiracy. Raleigh had always desired an empire for England, and now, after thirteen years of captivity, he passed suddenly from prison to a ship's bridge, and sailed by the King's orders for Guiana, whence, like Drake, he was supposed to bring back fabulous treasure. But he was badly equipped and poorly supported, and was beaten by the Spaniards. Then, after "that sea-whiff between dungeon and death," he was beheaded by his King to placate Spanish feeling. George Villiers, Duke of Buckingham, who had taken Somerset's place in the King's affections, was in his turn beguiled by the ambassadors of the Escorial. Prince Henry had died in 1612, and Charles, the new heir-apparent, seemed less stanchly Protestant.

The religious struggles on the Continent at this time roused those violent passions in the English Puritans which are always kindled in a country by foreign happenings which seem to mirror its own internal struggles. In 1618 there began in Central Europe that great war which was later called the Thirty Years' War, whereby the House of Austria, with Spanish support, strove to renew the unity of the Empire and the hegemony of the Roman Church. The oppressed Hussites of Bohemia had intrusted themselves to the young Elector Palatine, who had married the Princess Elizabeth, the attractive daughter of James I. Attacked by the Catholic princes in both of his kingdoms, the Elector appealed to his father-in-law for aid. Public opinion in England backed him. The Puritans would have hesitated to pledge England to a campaign in Bohemia, a land which appeared to them as Oriental, remote, unknown. But they were ready to defend the frontier of the Rhine. To do so it would have been necessary to prevent the Spaniards from landing in the Low Countries, and this

[265]

meant having a fleet as powerful as England had had in Drake's day. But James had been negligent of his strength. With no Parliament and no money, he had also no ships ready for war. By a too passive love of peace he had played, willy-nilly, right into the hands of less pacific princes. And at last, in 1621, in order to prepare for war against Spain, or at least to give the Spaniards that impression, James had to summon Parliament.

Between a Parliament knowing it was reluctantly summoned, and a king who disbelieved in its rightful claims, a clash was inevitable. Parliament subordinated the voting of subsidies to the redressing of grievances. Abuses were numerous—the sale of monopolies and posts, the corruption of judges. The Lord Chancellor, Francis Bacon, a man of high intellect but weak character, was made a scapegoat, confessed to malpractices, and was condemned to confiscation of property and dismissal. This was the first impeachment of a great public figure since 1459, and a clear sign of the independence of the Commons. They wished also to intervene in foreign affairs. A strongly Protestant House wanted war against Spain and a campaign in the Palatinate. The King's intention had been only to threaten Spain, and it would have horrified him to go on from threats to action. Along with Buckingham, he prepared a new scheme for a Spanish marriage, this time for his son Charles, hoping that the restoral of the Palatinate to his son-in-law would be a clause in the contract. Parliament expressed strong dislike of this compromising policy, and the King informed it that high matters of State were not its concern. To which the Parliament's reply was that the liberties and privileges of Parliament were the ancient and undisputed heritage of English subjects, and that difficult and urgent matters concerning the King, the State, the defense of the realm and of the Church of England, were appropriate subjects for debate by Parliament. So deeply did these assertions shock the King that he tore the page that showed them from the records of the House, expelled the members, and arrested seven of their number, amongst them John Pym, one of those responsible for the offending page and a man of high authority in the House of Commons. Then, in February, 1621, he sent off Prince Charles and the Duke of Buckingham to achieve the conquest of the Infanta in Spain.

The joint letters of Charles and Buckingham during this journey afford astonishing reading. They show how highly personal and rather puerile any policy of favoritism is. These two romantic youths had left in disguise. They addressed the King in their letters as "Dear Dad and Gossip," and signed them "your Baby and your Dog"—Charles being the baby and Buckingham the dog. James I was in correspondence with the Pope, to whom he promised lenient treatment of English Catholics if the Holy See would sanction the Spanish marriage without insisting on excessively strict religious terms. This was a praiseworthy promise, but not within his power to give. The Pope replied by requiring that any children born of the marriage should have Catholic nurses. Meanwhile the Spaniards were being riled by the conceit and behavior of the English mission. Sir Edmund Verney, who accompanied the Prince, struck a Spanish priest, and the King of Spain sternly requested Buckingham to send back the Protestant members of his retinue to England. Negotiations carried on in this spirit were bound to collapse. James chafed at his dreary "widowed life," separated from his favorite. In October, 1621, he recalled his "baby and dog." Londoners were so delighted at this rupture, and at seeing their Prince return still unwed and un-Romanized, that they gave Charles and his mentor an enthusiastic welcome. Their plaudits alone sufficed to fling the vain, flimsy Buckingham into the anti-Spanish camp, and suddenly the detested favorite became the popular leader for a war desired by Englishmen. Parliament itself declared that no man had ever deserved better of his King and country, and James, notwithstanding his pacifism, had to yield. From that time until King James died in 1625, and even during the early years of Charles I's reign, Buckingham had the power, without the prudence, of a king.

Chapter III

Buckingham and Charles I

To scrutinize in Van Dyck's portraits the sad and beautiful features of King Charles I is to be the less surprised at his woes. His face showed nobility, honesty, timidity, but also a sort of somber obstinacy. Charles was pious and chaste. He blushed at hearing an improper word, and fell silent when someone's demeanor displeased him. Devoid of imagination, he never foresaw the reactions of his subjects, and when these were hostile, the surprise set loose the blind violence of a timid man. He was sincerely eager to act well, but had contrived for himself a system of ideas which neither argument nor experience could ever alter. He died, it has been said, repeating all the affirmations of his lifetime. It was his misfortune that at the beginning of his reign he found himself associated in the public mind with Buckingham, whose vanity and volatility were riling to the best Englishmen, and whom they compared to those unhealthy mists which rise from the fields and veil the setting and the dawning sun. Notwithstanding the differences in their nature, perhaps because of them, Charles had an unabashed fondness for this "Steenie," with whom he had spent his youth, and who had lent to his life something vivacious and fanciful which he could not give it himself.

It was Buckingham who, after the projected Spanish marriage, suggested and negotiated for the King a marriage with Henrietta Maria, the youngest daughter of King Henry IV of France. To bring a Catholic Queen, with a foreign retinue, into a country still quivering from the shock of Gunpowder Plot, was a grave error. The Protestants pointed out that no French Queen had ever brought great happiness to England. Later they fancied that there was some fatality in that name of Maria, which the King preferred using to his consort's other name. Admittedly

Charles was at pains to declare that the future Queen would have religious freedom only for herself and her attendants, and that there would be no change in the position of the English recusants; but by a secret clause in the marriage contract, the King actually pledged protection for the Catholics. The beginnings of his married life were unfortunate. The fifteen-year-old Queen sided with her followers against the English. She went to pray for the Catholic martyrs beneath the Tyburn gibbets. Charles wrote to Buckingham that if his wife was to be kept away from dangerous influences, it was urgent "to put away the monsieurs," and he soon ordered their deportation to their own country, by agreement if possible, by force if necessary. With this crisis overcome, the royal pair was destined to become one of the mose affectionate and united in history, but the unhappy start made a breach between the English and French courts, a rift which was dangerous for Buckingham, who was anxious to secure a French alliance against Spain.

Buckingham was neither a diplomat nor a general, and his foreign policy was as inconsistent as it was rash. When the quarrel with Spain broke out, he had for some time dallied with the rôle of champion of the Protestant nations; and this won him loud plaudits in London. But to play this part in earnest on the Continent would have needed a powerful army. England, however, was a small country, with no desire to be a military power. The expeditions which tempted Buckingham into Holland and to Cadiz all ended in disaster, through lack of organization. A policy of alliance with Catholic France would have been conceivable, as hatred of the House of Austria might incline Richelieu to seek allies in the Reformers' camp. But to promise Richelieu—as Buckingham was bold enough to do—the support of Protestant seamen against the Huguenots of La Rochelle, was sheer folly. Having discovered that he could not count on a close alliance between Charles I and Louis XIII, Buckingham avenged himself on the latter by openly making love to his wife, Anne of Austria. And then, having made certain foes of Spain and France, the two great powers of the west, and lacking the money to support such a struggle, he found himself forced to apply to Parliament.

The Parliaments of Charles I had a growing list of grievances and were more skilled in tactics than their predecessors. Their members, nearly all cultivated and devout squires, knew and respected the common law. Amongst them sat a great lawyer, Sir Edward Coke, a former judge, and a man of formidable character who had been able successfully to assert the principle of the subservience of the King to the Law. These members of Parliament respected the traditional forms and knelt respectfully before the sovereign, but they realized that in the last resort supremacy must belong to Parliament. A new theory was taking shape in their minds, that of ministerial responsibility. The King can do no wrong; if he is in error, the guilt lies only with the Minister who ought to have enlightened him; and this minister, even if approved by the King, deserves the impeachment formerly reserved for traitors. One eminent Parliamentarian, Sir John Eliot, asserted this principle in connection with Buckingham's foolish attack upon La Rochelle: "My Lords," he said, prosecuting the Minister in the name of the Commons before the Lords, "I will say that if His Majesty himself were pleased to have consented, or to have commanded, which I cannot believe, yet this could no way satisfy for the Duke, or make any extenuation of the charge, for it was the duty of his place to have opposed it by his prayers, and to have interceded with His Majesty to make known the dangers, the ill consequences, that might follow." Charles I, who had admired the courts of France and Spain and believed, like his father, in the divine right of kings, would not admit this doctrine, and appealed to his own sovereign responsibility. He would not allow the House to discuss his servants, and least of all the one now beside him. But how was he to secure obedience? When he sent Eliot to jail, the energy of Parliament secured his liberation. Could the King rule without Parliament, depending on freewill gifts or forced loans? Such devices only produced slender revenues in a time of mounting expenditure. After humiliating defeats at the hands of France, particularly at the Île de Ré, the House of Commons had perforce to be recalled.

This 1628 Parliament, elected in anger, set about the task of requiring due respect from the King for the law of the realm. It drew up the famous Petition of Right, largely drawn up by Sir Edward Coke, which was a clarified reiteration of what were supposed to be the principles of Magna Carta. The original feature of the Petition of Right lay in the fact that it sought to fix definite bounds between the royal power and the power of the law. It recalled all the earlier conventions made between the English people and their sovereigns. Men had thought that there would be no more forced loans, that no free man could be imprisoned without lawful reason, but all such principles had been violated. Furthermore, Parliament complained of the conduct of Buckingham's soldiers and sailors, of the obligation laid on citizens to lodge these undisciplined troops, and of the irregular application of martial law; and His Most Excellent Majesty was respectfully begged to remedy these matters. For a long time the King hesitated. He had a deep dislike of the ideas upheld in this petition, but the Lords themselves joined with the Commons in its presentation. In the end he answered as Parliament wished him: *"Soit droit fait comme il est désiré"* ("Let right be done as is desired") and the Petition became a fundamental law of the realm. It placed conspicuous reins on the King's prerogative. In particular, it checked the right to billet troops and the exercise of martial law.

If Parliament was right in its insistence on respect for the laws, it erred unreasonably in foreign affairs. It called upon the King to uphold the Protestants of the Palatinate, but refused him the necessary subsidies. The country gentlemen and lawyers assembled at Westminster knew little of Europe and understood nothing about the rise of prices. It would be unjust, therefore, to attribute the breach only to the King and his intransigence. Macaulay has said of Charles I that, infatuated by His Majesty, he felt it incumbent on his honor to retain the tone of tyranny whilst calling for the help of liberty. But an examination of the original texts will show that Charles did not adopt the tone of tyranny, and that liberty refused its help. After giving way on the Petition of Right, the King could justifiably hope that tunnage and poundage would be granted to him for life. But it was not so. Actually, the desire of the Commons was not just to revive the old liberties, but to acquire new ones, and to become the sole power in the realm. Such a defeat and such new ideas the Crown could not possibly accept without a struggle. The death of Buckingham, who was stabbed by one Felton in August, 1628, did not relieve the tension. From the windows of his palace the King witnessed the delight of the London crowd and men drinking the murderer's health. To save the Duke's body from outrage at the mob's hands, it had to be buried in secret. Charles was too dignified to show his feelings, but he never forgot that flaunting of hatred. In the next session the conflict with Parliament was resumed. And this time it wore a mainly religious aspect.

Puritans and Ritualists were still striving for control of the Church of England. The King favored the High Church faction, partly because of his wife's influence, and partly because the High Church clergy were absolutists in their political views and supported the King's intervention in ecclesiastical matters. Confusion reigned in men's minds. A Calvinistic cleric would set the communion table in the center of the choir, and then a sacramentalist would come and place it in its old position. One rejected the surplice, another wore it. Laud, Bishop of London and later Archbishop of Canterbury, made it his custom to consult the King on all such matters, and even on the punishments that should be inflicted on sinners. He prepared for the King a list of the clergy, marking their names as Orthodox or Puritan, "O" or "P," and thereafter only an "O" received high preferment. But the mass of the people and Parliament were of Calvinist hue. Laud and the court accepted the views of the Dutch theologian Arminius (1560-1609), and believed in the doctrine of free will, whereas London and Parliament inclined to predestination. Calvinist apprentices and Arminian courtiers insulted one another in the street. The free-will cause became confounded, as Trevelyan points out, with that of despotic government, and that of predestination with the defense of Parliamentary privileges. "Whosoever squares his actions by any rule either divine or human, he is a Puritan. He that will not do whatsoever men will have him do, he is a Puritan." Theological, political, and fiscal questions became inextricably mingled. If the King was not to have power to oblige his people to have the altars at the east end of their churches, or to use the surplice and the sacraments, he must be refused tunnage and poundage, failing which he depended on a Parliament of Puritans.

From this situation arose the curious and well-known "three resolutions" voted by Parliament in 1629. They laid it down, first, that whosoever might seek to introduce Popery or Arminianism into England would be regarded as an enemy of the commonwealth; second, that whosoever might advise the collection of taxes unauthorized by Parliament would be similarly regarded; and third, that any merchant or other person paying such taxes, not voted by Parliament, would be a traitor and a public enemy. Startled by the trend of these resolutions, the Speaker declared that he had been ordered by the King to close the sitting of the House before they were passed. Two members of Parliament seized him by the arms and held him down in his chair. Another bolted the door and pocketed the key. When an official knocked in the King's name, nobody opened it. The motions were carried. It was a scene of revolution. Charles retorted by a revolutionary action, and after the session imprisoned nine members of the House, contrary to the Petition of Right. The most distinguished of them, Eliot, died in the Tower three years later. Like all martyrdoms, that of this stanch Parliamentarian helped to sanctify the cause to which it testified—Puritanism. Charles was now determined to dispense with Parliaments. Had not the Tudors long done without them in the past? There remained the eternal question of how the King was to obtain money. On that, ultimately, the stability of any government depends.

CHAPTER IV

King Without Parliament

So now Charles I was alone in his palace of Whitehall with his young French Queen. By this time the shy King loved her with a fond and sensuous love which had a much deeper influence on him than it had while Buckingham was alive. Where could he look for support in his rule, now that he was deprived of the contact with public opinion which annual Parliaments might have given him? He found two men who shared his authoritarian creed and believed that firm wielding of the royal prerogative could insure the people's happiness: one was William Laud, Archbishop of Canterbury since 1633, who directed ecclesiastical affairs and then had added financial matters to his charge; the other was a former member of that dangerous Parliament of 1628, Thomas Wentworth, created Earl of Strafford in 1640.

Strafford suffered undue calumny. Because he had been a friend of the rebel Parliamentarians, like Pym and Eliot and Hampden, they regarded his rallying to the royal cause as treachery. "You are going to be undone," said Pym; "but though you leave us now, I will never leave you while your head is upon your shoulders." A striking phrase, which, as things turned out, had a prophetic ring. But where was the treachery? From the start of his career Wentworth had made plain where he stood: his rule, he declared, would be not to "contend with the prerogative out of Parliament." He held that popular trust and royal authority were two indispensable elements in any healthy State, the King being the keystone which could not be touched without bringing down the edifice. Charles at once recognized the gulf that separated this Government man from the Opposition. Wentworth, he said, was an honest gentleman; and taking him into his service, the King intrusted him with his most exacting missions.

[274]

He made him President of the Council of the North, and then sent him to pacify Ireland. If he had been employed in England from the first, it is possible that Strafford would have raised the standing army without which the Crown's prerogatives were shadows, not substance, and that in this event the destiny of England would have had more affinities with the France of Louis XIV. But Charles made profession of Strafford's doctrines without having either his strength of character or his organizing genius. When at last the King decided to set him in the highest place, the game was lost for both.

Laud, too, was a stern man, but a man of good faith. This authoritarian prelate was ill-suited to rule Englishmen! he genuinely believed that firmness of Church doctrine was worth more than freedom of opinion. He wanted to impose forcibly a perfect uniformity of beliefs and ritual, and he was disdainful of patient persuasion. Throughout his life he had followed this same rigid line. At Oxford he had scandalized the Calvinist theologians by telling them that Presbyterians were as dangerous as Papists. As he genuflected before the altar and bowed his head whenever the name of Jesus Christ was spoken during the office, these symptoms had encouraged the Pope to offer him a Cardinal's hat. But Laud declined it, so long as Rome remained what it was. An Aristotelian, he considered that habit was already nature, and that uniformity of ceremonial seemed necessarily to lead to unity of faith. He strove hard to impose both. He had no cruelty in his nature, and used neither stake nor rack, but administratively he was a tyrant in the Church.

Using the ecclesiastical courts, and the Court of High Commission in particular, Laud carried out a purge of the universities and the clergy. He kept an eye on sermons too Protestant in color, and had them shortened. He forbade the malcontent communities from calling in "readers" to supplement Anglican preaching. He closed the private chapels of the Puritans and forbade their pious meetings. In 1618 James I had issued a circular known as the *Declaration of Sports*, which encouraged his subjects to continue their Sunday games in defiance of the Puritan Sabbath. In support of this view he offered very sound reasons: excessive strictness might easily drive men away from religion, as sports were good for bodily health and served to prepare men for war. The declaration horrified the Puritans, who refused to read it in their churches. James did not insist, but Laud tried to compel them. The true Protestants were grieved to observe that, owing to the Queen's influence, the Catholics were now enjoying some degree of toleration, whereas they themselves were being persecuted. The wars on the Continent were turning out favorably to the Catholic powers. In despair, many Puritans thereupon decided to banish themselves and live in America, remote from Lauds and Popes. Over twenty thousand went forth to join the *Mayflower's* Pilgrim Fathers, forming the nucleus of New England, where they introduced the most characteristic English institutions of their age. Had it not been for the strictness of Laud, North America might never have been an Anglo-Saxon civilization. But this remote consequence of the persecutions could not have been foreseen, and there were keen resentment and daily anguish in thousands of English homes, where Puritans strove to sustain their faith by daily reading of the Scriptures.

What taxes could actually be raised by a monarch who respected the law, at least in form? There was tunnage and poundage. But this depended on the volume of trade transactions, and for six months the London merchants protested against the wrongful imprisonment of Sir John Eliot by refraining from buying and selling. Traders refusing to trade! This was indeed a portent, but it was not understood. With the help of lawyers probing into ancient texts for archaic rights, the King produced taxes which had fallen into disuse. He laid claim to "voluntary" gifts, to the obligation on those who for centuries had been settled in royal forests to purchase their lands outright from the Crown, to the sale of titles of nobility, to compulsory knighthood, to "coat and conduct money," to a tax on hackney coaches, to the sale of monopolies to courtiers, which filled both the Treasury and the pockets of the concessionaires at the expense of the public. Charles sought to impose on his subjects the use of a particular soap, indifferently manufactured by a corporation of monopolists. This preparation, which injured both linen and washerwomen's hands, was called "the Popish soap," and London housewives believed that these injuries were symbolic, and that its use was also deleterious to the soul.

And so a high wall of prejudice and grievance and silence arose between the royal couple, secluded in Whitehall amongst the fine Dutch and Italian paintings which the King purchased from abroad, surrounded by lace-collared courtiers with wide-brimmed plumed hats on their long curling hair, and, on the other side, the London merchants with their short-haired apprentices and staid, gray-clad Puritan wives. Public opinion was hostile and had no safety valve. With no Parliament, there were no public speeches; writings were censored; sermons were pruned by Laud; public meetings were forbidden. Despite the unpopularity of these measures, no serious outburst took place for a long time. The people were deeply respectful of legality and a century of Tudor monarchy had accustomed them to regard the sovereign as a sacred figure, so that rebellion against the King still seemed to them a monstrous proceeding. To break down this fearful awe the most extreme errors had to be committed by the Crown.

Amongst the old levies revived by the King's servants was one known as ship money. It had always been customary for the maritime towns to be called upon to participate in coastal defense by providing ships and ships' crews. Charles I enforced this obligation on the whole country, and demanded, not ships, but money to build ships. It was not an unreasonable request. For lack of an effective fleet, the English merchant marine had been at the mercy of pirates since the time of James I. The Barbary corsairs even ventured to attack vessels in English waters and to make slave-raids on the Irish coast. When Strafford assumed his duties in Ireland, his personal effects were captured by pirates. A letter from Charles to "the Mayor, Commonality, and citizens of Our City of London" spoke of "certain thieves, pirates, and robbers of the sea, as well as Turks, . . . wickedly taking by force and spoiling the ships, and goods, and merchandises, not only of our subjects, but also the subjects of our friends . . ." and required the City of London to provide him with one warship of nine hundred tons, four others of five hundred, and one of three hundred, complete with guns, gunpowder, and crews. But utility was not enough to secure Englishmen's acceptance of a tax; it had also to be voted by Parliament. So ran the Charter of English liberties, and such was the thesis upheld by certain citizens, the most famous of whom was John Hampden. In 1637 the sheriff of his county claimed thirty-one shillings and sixpence from him in respect of one of his properties, and twenty shillings on another, as ship money. He refused to pay, not because of the sum (his fortune was substantial), but on principle. He allowed himself to be brought before successive courts, and although in the end the Court of Exchequer gave judgment against him by seven votes to five, he was acquitted and idolized by public opinion.

Notwithstanding the strict censorship, pamphlets attacking the court were rife. William Prynne, a Puritan pamphleteer, concerned with reforming the morals of his time, had written against the long hair worn by courtiers, which he declared to be contrary to the laws of Christ. In 1632 he published a tract on stage plays. Unluckily for him, the Queen and her ladies had themselves lately acted a comedy; the Star Chamber held the pamphlet to be an attack on the Queen, and sentenced Prynne to a fine of £5,000 and to have his ears cut off. He was put in the pillory, and his ears were cut off by the common hangman. This cruel punishment did not stop him from writing, and in 1637, for an attack on Laud, he was again placed in the pillory, along with a clergyman and a doctor. The stumps of his ears were leveled down, and his cheek was branded with the initials "S. L."—"seditious libeler." The London crowd viewed with just horror this barbarous treatment of three respectable citizens. When the hangman laid hands on them, a great shout of anger rose. The wrath of the English people was waxing greater, a grave situation in a State wherein the sovereign's sole mainstay was the affection of his subjects.

The crowning folly was an attempt to impose Anglican prayers and ritual on the Scots, the ardent defenders of their Presbyterian Kirk. Charles, King of both kingdoms, was even more ignorant of Scotland than of England. Although his father, James I, had given bishops to the Scots, the Kirk remained essentially Presbyterian. The Scottish Church, in the opinion of Laud, had not been reformed, but deformed; and this scandalized him. But when the bishops, at his bidding, introduced the new ritual to Scotland, the congregations would not allow the service to go on. All classes in the land, nobles, burgesses, peasants, signed a pact, or Solemn Covenant, vowing fidelity to their Kirk as constituted. Charles set about breaking this religious league by armed force. But dragooning without dragoons is a perilous expedient. To what army could the King intrust his cause: To the trained bands, or militia? But they were not trained. To the country gentlemen? But they were far from approving the cause. When the King put in the field a few Englishmen he had been able to muster against the excellent Scottish army (many of whose 20,000 men had served abroad under the Protestant princes and were commanded by a lieutenant of Gustavus Adolphus), the troops in both camps came to terms. If this "Bishops' War" did not end in disaster, it was only because the Scots were halted by negotiation.

The King had one last hope—Strafford. He was the one strong man of the regime. In Ireland he had put into practice his watchword—"Thorough." He was blamed for his harshness; but he had at any rate tamed the country, assembled a shadowy Parliament, and obtained troops and money. He had even contrived to send the King £20,000 for his Scottish campaign. When Charles consulted him, he advised firm action. Parliament should be summoned, and subsidies should be obtained by revealing the intrigues of the Scots with Richelieu. Then war would be waged wholeheartedly. Strafford himself hurried to Ireland, raised eight thousand men there, and returned ill but resolute. The Parliament convoked by Charles in 1640, the first for twelve years, had not forgotten old grudges. Far from granting support for a new war, the Commons demanded redressment of their grievances. Pym recounted all Charles's failings, and the Parliamentarians negotiated with the Scots. On Strafford's advice this so-called Short Parliament was dissolved after only eighteen days of session. In Strafford's view, Charles had placed himself in such plight that if he could be saved at all, which was doubtful, it could only be by a pitiless despotism, working outside of the customary rules of governance. "Pity me," he wrote to his friend George Radcliffe, "for never came any man to so lost a business. The army altogether unexercised and unprovided of necessaries ... our horse all cowardly, the country from Berwick to York in the power of the Scots, an universal affright in all, a general disaffection to the King's service, none sensible of his dishonor. In one word, here alone to fight with all these evils, without anyone to help. God of his goodness deliver me out of this, the greatest evil of my life. Fare you well."

CHAPTER V

The Long Parliament

WITH neither money nor loyal troops, beaten by the Scots, who occupied the northern counties and demanded for their evacuation not only religious liberty (which none could refuse them), but an indemnity as well, Charles I had to bow to the will of the most resolute among his subjects. The Lords invited him to summon a new Parliament; a petition signed with ten thousand names obtained by Pym requested likewise; he yielded. Never had any election roused such strong passions. Pym, like a party leader (a new function) traversed the countryside, holding meetings and forming local committees. Hampden, now one of the most highly respected men in the kingdom, lent the weight of his authority to Pym. It was the wish of these men to secure the election of true Puritans, ready to struggle against absolutism. The second Parliament of 1640 was not a reforming Parliament: it was a revolutionary Parliament. But it was not a demagogic assembly. The members of the Long Parliament (as it came to be called) were to a great extent gentlemen and landowners, staid, devout, cultivated men, and anxious to return as soon as possible to their family estates. Such men have no liking for turbulence, and only regretfully call in the help of the crowd. Far from being hostile to the institution of monarchy, they envisaged no other. But they felt bound to settle two issues with Charles, one political, the other religious, which had been poisoning the bloodstream of England since the house of Stuart came to the throne.

It was Strafford whom Pym and the Parliamentarians feared, much more than they feared the King. Their hatred of him was all the greater because he had once been in their camp. Above all, they knew that between themselves and him it was a duel to the death. Either Pym would bring Strafford to the block, or Strafford would one day send Pym to the scaffold.

One of the first acts of the new Parliament was to impeach Strafford for high treason before the Lords. For several weeks Strafford had been aware that if he went to Parliament he was lost. He said so to Charles, who replied that, as he was King of England, he could shield him from any danger, and that Parliament should not touch one hair of his head. Strafford therefore presented himself before the House of Lords just when Pym, leading a deputation of the Commons, came to demand his arrest. Strafford had entered with a bold mien; he had to kneel at the bar of the House to hear the charge against him, and only left it a prisoner. If true justice were done, it seemed as if he could be saved. The impeachment had no legal validity. How could a charge of high treason, a crime against the King, be laid against the King's most faithful servant? But constitutional practice afforded Parliament no other means of getting rid of a minister supported by the sovereign. Attempts were made to compromise Strafford by quoting remarks made by him in the Privy Council; he was said to have suggested the idea of using an Irish army to bring England to subjection. Only one witness, Sir Harry Vane, could be found, and he was none too sure. Pym and his friends realized with irritation that the Lords would not hold a majority to condemn Strafford, who, although his strength was sapped by sickness, defended himself in his own fine, trenchant style. The end of his plea moved the hearts of all who heard it: "Now, my lords," he said, "I thank God I have been taught that the afflictions of this present life are not to be compared with that eternal weight of glory which shall be revealed for us hereafter; and so, my lords, even so, with all humility and with all tranquillity of mind, I do submit myself clearly and freely to your judgments, and whether that righteous judgment shall be life or death, *te deum laudamus, te Dominum confitemur.*"

The accusers, seeing their prey escaping them, fell back on the simpler and more brutal procedure of a bill of attainder, voted by Parliament and sanctioned by the Crown. This deprived the accused of all the safeguards of a court of justice. Considering the legal proofs alone, it is impossible to justify the conduct of Pym and his friends. They murdered Strafford with a few legislative formalities. In their defense it may be urged that, if Strafford had lived and recovered his freedom, he would not have failed to be "thorough" in destroying his foes. Perhaps it would have been wiser for Pym and his associates to admit frankly that a civil war had begun, and to abandon the hypocrisy of legal form. Lord Digby, in a speech that did him honor, declared that he could not vote for the bill. "God keep me," he exclaimed, "from giving judgment of death on any man, and of ruin to his innocent posterity, on a law made *a posteriori*. . . . I know, Mr. Speaker, there is in Parliament a double power of life and death—a judicial power and a legislative. The measure of one is what is legally just; of the other what is prudentially and politically fit for the good and preservation of the whole. But these two under favor are not to be confounded in judgment. We must not piece upon want of legality with matter of convenience, nor upon the defailance of prudential fitness with a pretense of legal justice." To what a pitch passion had risen may be gauged by the fact that this admirable speech was burned by the hangman, and the King was asked to confer no further honors upon Lord Digby, and to employ him no longer in any capacity. The bill of attainder was passed in the House of Commons by 204 votes to 59, and the names of the minority, which, according to the rules of the time, should have remained unknown, were posted up in London as those of Strafford's men and enemies of their country. The City shops closed. Masters and apprentices trooped to Westminster to threaten the supporters of Strafford. Under this mob pressure, even the Lords voted the death penalty by 26 to 19 votes.

The King had vowed that Parliament should not touch one hair of Strafford's head. Would he sanction the act duly passed? The bishops, infected by the general panic, advised Charles that, as King, he should have two consciences, one public, the other private. The London crowd massed round Whitehall, and became so menacing that the Catholic courtiers made confession and the bravest captains made ready to die in the defense of the staircases and corridors of the old palace. On May 9th the turmoil increased, and about nine o'clock that night the King signed. "If no less than his life can satisfy my people," he wrote a day or two later, "I must say 'Fiat Justitia.'" Strafford was taken aback by the King's desertion, but he had the nobility to write and tell his master that he gave his life gladly. But he is said to have cried out: "Put not your trust in princes nor in the sons of men, for in them there is no salvation." On the way to the scaffold, the aged Archbishop Laud, himself now a prisoner, came to his window to bless his friend, who died with such unaffected courage that even the City apprentices kept a resourceful silence. Thus vanished a great man, whose crime it had been to wish for a monarchy aided, not dominated, by Parliament. From the date of this trial, it may be said that the King ceased to be the State, as it was on account of loyalty towards the sovereign that Strafford was deemed a traitor to the country.

By condemning Strafford, Parliament had eliminated the one man capable of transforming the English monarchy into an authoritarian government on the model given to Europe by Spain or France. To make the victory of absolutism forever impossible, it now had to forbid the King to govern, as he and his father had over long periods done, without a Parliament. It is a weakness of elected assemblies that when they come into conflict with a permanent executive, they can be dismissed by the latter. Their only defense is to impose upon the executive methods, and fixed dates, of convocation. Pym and his friends obliged the King to approve certain measures accordingly. Firstly there was an act insuring the regular summoning of Parliament, at least once in three years; if after three years the King still refrained from so doing, the meeting of Parliament could take place without reference to him; and no Parliament could be dissolved before it had lasted for fifty days, or be prorogued beyond three years. Secondly, an act withdrew the King's power to raise taxes without Parliamentary sanction: which meant the end of tunnage and poundage, and of ship money—in a word, of any taxes not agreed to by the Crown's subjects. Thirdly, the powers of the King and his Council were greatly diminished, and the courts of prerogative (the Star Chamber and the like) yielded to the common law. The ecclesiastical Court of High Commission, which Laud had used against the Puritans, was abolished. The Crown was being made subservient to Law.

The religious problem was more complex than the political. On one point alone most of the Parliamentarians were agreed: as Protestants, they feared Popery. But many of them hated Laud's bishops, who had tried to lead Englishmen back to ritualism, whilst others were attached to the old hierarchies. The former wished to extirpate episcopacy from the Church, "root and branch," the latter, Episcopalians or partisans of the bishops, had the advantage of being more united than their opponents. Among the enemies of episcopacy, distinctions should be made between the Erastians, followers of the German theologian, Thomas Erastus (1524-1583), who subordinated Church to State in temporal matters, and made lay commissioners take the place of bishops; the Presbyterians, supporters of a religious democracy in the Scottish or Genevese style, with elders and synods; and the Sectarians, or Congregationalists, or Independents, who maintained that God was present with every group of true believers, and who thus, despite their extreme narrow-mindedness, became unwitting precursors of freedom of conscience.

In the counties, supporters of the episcopal Anglican Church predominated; in London, the Presbyterians had the backing of the Scots soldiers who had been installed in the capital since the victory, and whom Parliament, seeing them as allies against the King, was in no haste to disperse. The Independents held that Episcopacy and Presbyterianism were merely two forms of tyranny. These religious and political disputes, be it remembered, went on from morning to night, in a city seething with theological passion. All day long the Parliamentarians debated, and often at night, by candle-light. Pym and Hampden and Hyde could be seen pacing to and fro in the graveyard at Westminster, or meeting at supper to go on discussing their great concern. Any rumor might make the merchants and apprentices put up the shutters and hurry up to Westminster or Whitehall. There was no armed force to hold this throng in check. Indeed, it was the crowd which actually protected Parliament. The King, for his part, retained a few long-haired officers, captains on half-pay whom the City youths jeered at as "Cavaliers"; they accepted the nickname with pride, whilst the Queen, looking down from a window at the Protestants with their cropped hair, asked who were these "Roundheads." And both names stuck.

Historians have generally reproached Charles I for his conduct during the Long Parliament. But how could he have envisaged the compromise which, during the following century, was to create a constitutional monarchy? As things stood, the King could see no way out of the dilemma: either he must forcibly restore his authority, or he must become a phantom sovereign. Civil war was inevitable because, as there was no responsible minister interposed between King and Parliament, these two parties were in conflict. The idea that a minority could in such a case bow to the majority and leave it to govern, was not admitted, nor even conceivable. Once the country found itself seriously divided, civil war was the only solution. In any case, the principle of majority rule would never have solved the essential question of those days. It was religious. Interests may compromise; conscience does not.

But it must be admitted that the King aggravated disorder by playing a double game. Charles meekly confirmed the measures voted by Parliament, and secretly conspired against both laws and Parliament. But he regarded himself as being in a state of war, in which everything is permissible. He went so far as to ask for support from the Scots, who were still the best soldiers in Britain, against the English. They promised their aid if he would, for his part, accept the Presbyterian Covenant for England. Being a convinced Anglican, he could not accede to this, and had to renounce a Scottish alliance. He had one momentary glimpse of deliverance. The Parliamentarians, united in opposition against him, were split on the religious issue, some wishing to abolish all ritual and even alter the Prayer Book, the others being hostile to episcopacy but attached to the noble Anglican prayers. Thanks to this rift, an Anglican and royalist party took shape again, directed by men like Edward Hyde, whom the King might have made his counselors. A Great Remonstrance to Charles secured a majority of only eleven votes. The prestige of King Pym was lessening; it was restored by a blunder of King Charles.

On January 3, 1642, the Attorney-General suddenly demanded of the Lords the impeachment for high treason of five members of the House of Commons, including Pym and Hampden. It was an unlawful step, as the right of impeachment pertained to the Lower House. The Lords showed hesitancy. The King proceeded in person to the Commons to arrest the five members. They had been warned, and the City had undertaken their concealment. It was a painful scene. The King entered the House followed by Cavaliers and took the Speaker's chair. Members were standing bareheaded. One glance showed the King that "the birds were flown." He left amid an excited and hostile crowd, who cried out, "Privilege!" as he passed. The City militia was mustered and assumed the protection of Parliament. A clash between the two forces was becoming inevitable. The King deemed it wiser to leave London.

CHAPTER VI

The Civil War Opens

THE time had come for Englishmen, one and all, to choose their side. But most of them would gladly not have chosen. This revolution was not one of those tidal waves which uplift the great masses. It cut across the classes rather than opposing some against others. Thirty peers were left at Westminster: eighty had followed the King; twenty stood neutral. Like the peers, the squires and yeomen were also divided between both camps. London, a Protestant and censorious city, sided with Parliament, but the cathedral towns stood behind their bishops, and therefore behind the King. The rural population was to a great extent indifferent. So long as they could sow and reap and go to market, it mattered little under what government. In some countries, Puritans and Anglicans, Royalists and Parliamentarians, signed covenants of neutrality. It was not until later, when the undecided found that both armies treated neutrals with no favor, that they grudgingly took one side or the other. Sometimes it was one single, determined squire whose lead was followed by all the gentry of his neighborhood. The farmers followed their landlords. Pleasure-loving men sided with the King because the Puritans stood for austerity; the sectarians championed Parliament because they hoped, mistakenly, for religious freedom. It may be said that the Catholic north and the west of England inclined to the King, the south and east to Parliament; but these lines were ill-defined. At no moment did the campaigning armies number more than one fortieth of the country's population, and in the most important battles of the Civil War there were at most 20,000 combatants on each side.

It may seem surprising to allege apathy at this revolutionary time in a country which, in other circumstances, had shown such passionate feelings. But in 1641 the doctrines and intentions of both parties were confused. Nobody in the Parliamentary camp, at the start of the war, wished to strike down Charles Stuart. Nobody supposed that he could be dispensed with. Parliament only wished to be sure of the King's person, to separate him from his evil counselors, to persuade him not to link his cause with that of the bishops. Essex himself, the leading general of the Parliamentary forces, advised his troops to be prudent, on the grounds that the King, even if beaten, would still be king, whereas they, if beaten, would merely be rebels or traitors. The idea of the sacred character of royalty, imprinted on men's minds by two centuries of respect, remained intact. When the King raised his standard near Nottingham at the beginning of the war, the symbolic ceremony deeply affected many men whom reason inclined to the Parliamentary side.

And yet the scene went wrong. It was raining, and Charles, with the finicking pedantry of the Stuarts, kept on correcting the herald who read the proclamation. The wind blew down the standard into the mud. Many a man thought, like Sir Edmund Verney, that, friendly though he might be to Bible and Parliament, he could not abandon in the hour of need a king whose bread he had eaten. There were many who thus upheld for loyalty's sake a cause which no longer appeared to them just. Amongst the neutrals, some approved the political ideas of the Parliamentarians, but would not tamper with the Book of Common Prayer, whilst others, hostile to the Anglican Church, felt well disposed to the King. So much confusion could not kindle enthusiasm. In point of fact, the issue was not primarily one of a real revolution, which is nearly always provoked by some great economic disorder; it was rather, in this rich and relatively happy country, something which today would be termed a party struggle. Through a lack of constitutional machinery, this Parliamentary debate took the form of a pitched battle. It needed the evils of civil war to give birth to political tolerance, just as in other countries it took the horrors of persecution to compel tolerance in religion.

The active participants in this war, in both camps, were the pick of the nation; and the struggle was to prove reasonably humane. The battles were costly in life and limb because the men who fought were brave, and the prisoners, except for the Irish and Catholic priests, were well treated. Each side extolled itself for having the virtues of a Christian army. Before an engagement, religious services were held by the commanders. Each camp reproached the other for its sinfulness. In the Royalist army, said one of its number, men had the sins of mankind, loving wine and women; among the Roundheads, they had the sins of the devil—spiritual pride and rebelliousness. The courage and faith of the contestants were outstanding; but military science, at least in the early stages, was mediocre. The long peace of the Tudors had drawn a veil of oblivion over the art of war. A few leaders, such as Charles's nephew, Prince Rupert, son of the Elector Palatine, a great horseman and a poor tactician, had held commands on the Continent. Others, like a certain Oliver Cromwell, in the Puritan armies, had read the texts of strategy. Most of them fought as the fighting came. The intelligence services were so halting that the armies had some difficulty in meeting each other. At the outset Charles had a plan, which was to encircle London; Parliament had none, except to capture the King alive.

Once again, in this war, cavalry proved to be the decisive arm. It formed about two-thirds of the armies. The infantry consisted of pikemen and musketeers, the latter being very vulnerable to flank attack by horsemen, because, before the days of bayonet and magazine-loading, they were left disarmed when they had discharged their salvo. The musketeers' tactics were to take cover for reloading inside a square of pikemen, but they had not always time to do this and were apt to be cut down by the sabers. Rupert was the first to carry out the full cavalry charge, with sabers drawn. But being too bold, he neglected the rest of the army; his charges triumphed, his battles were lost. Throughout the war the confusion of uniforms reflected the bewilderment of minds. To recognize friends or foes in the mêlée the combatants had to use rallying-cries. "God with us!" cried the Roundheads; "Have at you for the King!" answered the Cavaliers. Many of the former wore orange scarfs; in some battles the Cavaliers had handkerchiefs in their hats, and in one night attack they let their shirts fly out behind them, the white linen guiding the horseman following. During the whole campaign Parliament, with the London merchants behind it, had the advantage of raising subsidies easily. It also had the mastery of the sea, as the Protestant sailors retained their hatred of Spain, absolutism, and Cavaliers; and sea power enabled the rebels to maintain communication with the Continent, which saved London's trade and the customs revenue.

The first moves favored the King, who was able to concentrate three

him that the royal cavalry would hold the upper hand, and that if the Parliamentary army was to win, it must be made up of soldiers devoted to its cause, not of mercenaries or the indifferent. "A few honest men are better than numbers," he said. What he wanted was a body of shock troops, a battalion of death, like that of the men of Gideon.

To a soul tormented as Oliver Cromwell's was, those years of war were satisfying enough. In action he found a spiritual peace. Following his idea of creating a model army, he raised fourteen squadrons, in all about eleven hundred men after his own heart, disciplined, united, responsive to his will. Cromwell did not require them to be Presbyterians, cross-grain Puritans. He considered that the State need not be concerned suppr the opinions of men whom it chose for its service: if they were ready to serve it loyally, that was enough. In choosing officers he took little account of birth. "I had rather have a plain russet-coated captain that knows what he fights for and loves what he knows, than what you call a 'gentleman' and is nothing else. . . . Better plain men than none." He imposed the strictest discipline on all, in camp as well as on the battlefield. Cromwell's Ironsides neither gambled nor drank, and the villages knew no fears on their approach. The sight of this disciplined troop rejoiced Cromwell's heart. It was, he said, a "lovely company," and would win the respect of any who saw it. Cromwell's men played the rôle of "the Party" in the authoritarian regimes of our own time.

The longer the war dragged on, the more the country suffered and chafed. Shortly before his death, the once-popular Pym was hooted at by the women of London. The execution of Laud, legally murdered after Strafford, separated Charles more drastically than ever from Parliament. If victory were delayed, the City train-bands would end by expelling from Westminster the very men whom they had so long shielded there. But if Parliament were to win a speedy success, it would require an army as strong in all its parts as Cromwell's Ironsides. Cromwell, indeed, made so bold as to tell the Parliamentarians bluntly that their army could not be victorious until members of Parliament ceased to command troops. Soldiers, not politicians, were needed. Cromwell's insistence was met by the passing of the Self-denying Ordinance, and the New Model army was established under the command of Sir Thomas Fairfax. Off the battlefield Fairfax was a taciturn man, halting in speech, but a fiery fighter and respected by all for his loyalty. Henceforth the pay of the troops would be regular, their arms of consistent quality, their uniforms of compulsory type. Cromwell himself was deprived of his command by his own Ordinance, but by special legislation he was authorized to remain Fairfax's lieutenant, with command of all the cavalry.

In June, 1645, the New Model army defeated the Royalist forces decisively at Naseby, in which victory Cromwell clearly discerned the hand of God. In the following year Fairfax marched on Oxford, and Charles had to flee. This was the end of royal resistance. In vain the Queen wrote urging him to buy Scottish support at the price of abandoning Anglicanism. He could not bring himself to this. "I am doubly grieved to differ with thee in opinion. . . . But I hope thou wilt not blame me at all, if thou rightly understand the state of the question. . . . For I assure thee I put little or no difference between setting up the Presbyterian government, or submitting to the Church of Rome." When he left Oxford on April 27, 1646, he first thought of going to London. "Being not without hope that I shall be able so to draw either the Presbyterians or Independents to side with me, for extirpating the one or the other, that I shall be really king again." In the blend of their heroism with naïve duplicity, these words were entirely characteristic of Charles. What matter to him if he deceived Presbyterians and Independents at once? He despised both equally. And at the eleventh hour he changed his mind and chose to deliver himself to the Scots.

CHAPTER VII

Army against Parliament

WITH Oxford taken and Charles in flight, Parliament was the victor. But in a civil war, problems are not all solved by military victory. The King's defeat made the despotism of the Crown impossible; but it did not authorize the despotism of Parliament. The country was still monarchist, longing for the time when the villages were not invaded by soldiery, and having no love of the harsh religion of Cromwell's men. Many of the King's partisans, notwithstanding their defeat, looked forward confidently to the time when England would return to her older, kindlier ways. Nevertheless, in the eyes even of the Cavaliers and neutrals, the New Model army stood for order. And if in its hour of victory it had shown some moderation, it would have met with an almost unanimous acceptance. Unfortunately, it expected the victory to be the dawn of a new era. The army consisted mainly of Independents and other sectarians, passionate enthusiasts, every one of them a preacher and a prophet, democrats who had scuffled in battle with Royalist Cavaliers and now had no respect for the hierarchy of birth. And where was Parliament, they argued, without their army? What authority had Parliament to impose a new national Church on these victorious soldiers, who asked for freedom of belief and were no more inclined to accept Westminster's Presbyterianism than the Anglicanism of Whitehall?

Caught up between a conservative populace and a radical soldiery, Parliament understood neither people nor army. Like any assembly left too long in power, it tended to become a collective autocracy. In the folly of pride, Parliament felt strong enough to persecute both Anglicans and Independents. Against the new Presbyterian Church, with clumsy stupidity, it arrayed the Cavalier gentry by threatening their property, and the Roundhead soldiers by threatening their pay. Bereft of Pym and Hampden, the Long Parliament had lost that sense of possibilities which is indispensable to governance. It first of all tried to make fresh terms with King Charles, whom the Scots, tired of this English quarrel, had now surrendered. Held captive by the Parliamentarians, he was presented with nineteen proposals as terms of peace: he had, for instance, to accept the Covenant, to abolish episcopacy, to hand over to Parliament for twenty years the supreme authority over army and navy, to allow Parliament to appoint the chief officers of State, and to consent to the proscription of numerous Royalists. Charles did not believe that it was his duty to play a straightforward game with the rebels. So neither refusing nor accepting, he continued to negotiate with France, with Scotland, with Presbyterians against Independents, and with Independents against Presbyterians.

To be able to conclude a valid treaty, Parliament would have had to wield the essential power. But this was in the hands of the army. Thirty thousand men under Fairfax and Cromwell were anxiously waiting to learn their destiny. It was Parliament's desire, firstly, to disband them as soon as possible, retaining only the troops necessary for garrison duty, and for a campaign in Ireland rendered more and more urgent by disorder in that country; secondly, to keep the Presbyterian officers and retire the Independents, whom it viewed as suspect; thirdly, to refrain from paying arrears of pay. Cromwell, Parliamentarian as well as soldier, but predominantly a soldier, was seriously perturbed by the rising tide of feeling against the army which he saw at Westminster. He was baffled by Parliament's refusal to allow the right of being Christians according to their own light, to victorious soldiers who had fought only to win that right. Troubled, unhappy, anguished, he took as his confidents two younger men—Sir Harry Vane, and Thomas Ireton, his own son-in-law, both of whom were likewise revolted by the ingratitude of the Presbyterian Parliamentarians. Still, the idea of ranging the army against Parliament had not yet entered Cromwell's mind, and he had a genuine horror of civil war and of any military dictatorship.

But the army's discontent grew more and more serious. Soldiers' councils were set up in certain regiments. Parliament sent four members from Westminster, Cromwell and Ireton among them, to negotiate with the malcontents. Cromwell might possibly have restored discipline among them if he had not learned, during the discussions, that the Parliamentarians, whilst feigning interest in the grievances of the army, were making plans to attack it. They were arming the citizens of London and forming Presbyterian train-bands; they were calling in the Scots to the rescue; and they were now offering the King a full restoration if he would accept Presbyterianism for three years. The soldiers resolved not to leave the trump card in the hands of Parliament—possession of the King's person. Cornet Joyce set off with his horsemen to Holdenby near Northampton, where the King then was, and invited Charles to follow him. The King asked to see his commission. Joyce pointed to the horsemen behind him. "It is as fair a commission, and as well written," said the King, "as I have seen in my life: a company of as handsome, proper gentlemen as I have seen a great while." Then the King, who seemed very cheerful, left with Joyce for Newmarket. The sight of his foes disputing for his person made him feel that the hour of retribution was at hand. When Parliament proposed to disband the army with one week's pay, which was simply mockery, Cromwell decided to leave London and join the soldiers. He was now ready to use the army in order to outplay the Parliamentary plots. His conduct may have run counter to ideas which he had often voiced, but it is sometimes wise, for a man on the side of order, to take the head of a movement which he deems dangerous. It is better to guide than to be driven. Cromwell doubtless had less fear of the reactions of an army disciplined and commanded by himself than of the upheavals of blind revolt.

Under his leadership twenty thousand men marched on London: twenty thousand men who prayed long to the Lord God before they started, twenty thousand men who saw eye to eye with their officers in their demand for justice. A letter drawn up by Cromwell was addressed to the lord mayor, who might have put up some resistance. In this he voiced his soldiers' claim to profess their own religion. Read before the House of Commons, it was listened to with respect and apprehension. Next came the Declaration of the Army, drawn up by Ireton, a manifesto declaring that the source of all power resides in the people, that an elected oligarchy can become as dangerous as a tyrannical monarchy if it claims absolute power, and that, accordingly, the army insisted on Parliament being purged of eleven members deemed undesirable by the soldiers. Parliament refused. The army moved nearer to London, and when it came near enough the eleven members fled. The military agitators wished to advance on Westminster, but Cromwell preferred to negotiate, arguing that they would thus avoid the reproach of having used force to obtain the assent of Parliament. The army received Parliamentary sanction to enter the City, and Fairfax was appointed Constable of the Tower. A few days later the clash between Parliament and soldiers broke out again, sharper than ever. "These men will never leave," exclaimed Cromwell, "till the army pull them out by the ears."

Cromwell's mind was slow-moving, vigorous, and straightforward. Parliament had been the faith of his youth; he had lost that faith; he made a move towards the King. After all, was not Charles, like the army, apparently demanding tolerance for all Christian men? And would not the fixing of limits to his power suffice to leave it innocuous for the future? Cromwell and Ireton drew up certain proposals, which, had the King accepted them, would have established constitutional monarchy in England. But Charles was blind to realities, and in no humor to reach an understanding. Holding his court at Hampton Court, where he received with admirable dignity the army leaders, with their wives and daughters, promising Cromwell the Garter but reserving for him, if need be, a hempen rope, he persisted in regarding himself as indispensable in intriguing with all parties. These balancing feats were dangerous, and disheartened the King's friends. A new faction was forming in the army, styling themselves the Levelers. Inspired by a Puritan pamphleteer, John Lilburne, they were advancing republican doctrines. Interlaced with plentiful texts from the Bible, their argument was that natural power came only from the people, that the Crown and the House of Lords were vain excrescences, and that government should reside only in one Chamber, elected by universal suffrage.

Lilburne was eloquent, violent, credulous, and vindictive: one of those men who can catch the ear of the masses and lead them to ruin. In Fairfax and Cromwell he was confronting leaders who could forcibly defend a moderate and reasonable position. Cromwell's straightforward, muscular mind could not be affected by such abstractions as the natural rights of man. To believe and to understand, he needed tangible, actual institutions: whence his attempts to treat with the King. But Charles forfeited Cromwell's sympathy, just as he had nullified the hopes of all who espoused his cause. On November 11, 1647, he disappeared from Hampton Court. His warders found his cloak under the gallery and letters on the table: the King had fled with three followers. It was shortly learned that he was in the Isle of Wight. His flight roused distrust of Cromwell among the Levelers. A few days later there were mutinies amongst the troops, and some men appeared in the ranks wearing Lilburne's tract, *Agreement of the People,* stuck in their hats. Cromwell drew his sword, rode along the mutineers, and had them arrested by trusty men. The mass of the soldiers dared not move. These rebels were tried by Court-martial, and one of them, chosen by lot, was shot by Cromwell's orders. The rebellion was quashed.

But Charles had fled his captors only to fall into the hands of another. In Carisbrooke Castle he had hoped to find a refuge. He found a prison. He still corresponded with the King of France, with the Scots, but with Oliver Cromwell no longer: he had learned to mistrust Charles. An intercepted letter to the Queen revealed that he was again trying to bring a Scottish army into England. Faced by the danger of a Royalist rising with Scottish support, Parliament and the army joined hands. And in the second civil war (1646) Cromwell's victory was swift and complete. In his triumph he saw the hand of God. If the Lord had used Cromwell's army to smite the King's troops, was not this the sign of God's having chosen the army and Oliver Cromwell to strike down a once-sacred power? Meanwhile, released from all fears by this victory, Parliament was negotiating with Charles, whom it regarded as henceforth harmless. The King accepted most of the Presbyterian conditions with the firm resolve not to put them into force.

The position of the Independents and the army was becoming dangerous. The mass of the nation, critical in temper, only awaited a sign of weakness to turn against them; London, the chief source of State revenue, and Parliament, the only lawful power, were hostile to them; and the Levelers were still snarling. Many a Puritan officer was beginning to say that no real peace could be secured so long as Charles Stuart, "that bloody man," remained on the stage of action. But Fairfax was still a loyalist, and Cromwell himself hesitated, with prayer and weeping. What was the Lord's will. Where lay duty? What was to be done with this King? Brought back victorious to London, he would not have spared his foes. Kept a prisoner in the Isle of Wight, he would still be plotting. To execute him would perhaps provoke a Franco-Scottish invasion. Whatever was to be done, it was necessary to act, or to perish. The army marched against Parliament. On December 6, 1648, Colonel Pride and his musketeers posted themselves at the doors of the House of Commons, with lists in their hands, stopping suspects, and sent the forty most dangerous members to a tavern popularly known as "Hell." They left at Westminster only about fifty men of their own. It would now be certain that this Rump Parliament would vote whatever the army leaders bade them vote. There remained the King. Cromwell saw clearly that to sacrifice the life of Charles Stuart would lead to a deep cleavage between the army and the nation. Besides, the Prince of Wales was in France, quite prepared to come forward as lawful claimant, so that the death of Charles I would not even discourage the Royalists. But Cromwell felt convinced that no peace was possible for the children of Israel so long as this mischief-maker lived.

His decision was sudden, and he attributed it, as ever, to divine inspiration. On January 20, 1649, the trial of the King was opened. The charge laid against him was that, having been trusted "with a limited power to govern by and according to the laws of the land, and not otherwise," he had sought "to erect an unlimited and tyrannical power to rule according to his will, and in pursuance of this design had levied war against the present Parliament, and the people therein represented." It was further alleged that he was to be held responsible for all the bloodshed and rapine issuing from that war. The charge had no legal force. "I would know," said Charles, "by what power I am called hither . . . by what authority, I mean lawful; there are many unlawful authorities in the world, thieves and robbers by the highways . . . and when I know what lawful authority, I shall answer. Remember, I am your King, your lawful King, and what sins you bring upon your heads, and the judgment of God upon this land; think well upon it I say, think well upon it, before you go farther from one sin to a greater." This insistence on the word "lawful" was sincere, and characteristically English. It was this same idea of lawfulness which, years after Charles's death, brought his son back to the throne of England. "I never," he also said, "took up arms against the people, but for the laws." Condemned to death, he wrote to the Prince of Wales a fine letter wherein he advised him to be good rather than great, and faithful in matters of religion: "For I have observed," he said, "that the devil of rebellion doth commonly turn himself into an angel of reformation." Right up to his last moments he stood fast by the political ideas for which he was dying. He desired the liberty of his people as much as any man, he urged; but that liberty consisted in having a government and laws whereby their life and property could be called their own. It did not consist in the self-government of the people. Government did not pertain to them. That, indeed, was the whole issue in the trial. The case then seemed to have gone against the King. In the following century, the doctrine of Charles Stuart would be taken up again by Bolingbroke.

CHAPTER VIII

Cromwell in Power

CROMWELL, the Rump, and the army were now left at the head of England. The country was hostile and outraged, but it had to be governed. No lawful power now remained in a country where law was venerated. By condemning Charles I, Parliament had declared that the Commons of England assembled in Parliament were the supreme power, and that anything willed by them had the force of law, even without the assent of the Lords and the King. But this fiction deceived nobody. How far was the nation represented by these fragments, chosen not by the people but by the military, of a Parliament already over eight years old? These men were at Westminster because the army had kept them there; the people hated the army; and the army despised Parliament. It is a sorry spectacle to see a country submitting in fear to a hated government. The Independents, and Oliver Cromwell, kept on urging that they were the Lord's elect; and certainly, it has been said, no other mode of election would have enabled them to represent England.

In March, 1649, the Rump Parliament abolished the House of Lords and the office of king, the latter as being "unnecessary, burdensome, and dangerous to the liberty, safety, and public interest of the people." Henceforth England was to be a Commonwealth, or Republic. But if the word were to have a real meaning, an election would be necessary, which the Independents could not venture upon. Royalists and Presbyterians would have joined hands to oust them. These Republicans were forced to maintain a military dictatorship in flat contradiction to their principles, and justified themselves by quoting from the Bible. Pharaoh's daughter, finding Moses in his cradle, had sought out the child's mother to rear him. The new-born Republic was to be reared, until it reached adult age, by those who had brought it into the world. They were certainly quite capable of winning obedience, if not affection. The Commons set up a Council of State, comprising squires, lawyers, and soldiers, which proved competent in its administration of finance, the army, and the navy. Mazarin's ambassador in London, though hostile to these regicides, admitted their ability in his dispatches: "they are economical in their private concerns and prodigal in devotion to public matters, wherein they toil as doggedly as if in their own interests." Cromwell himself was characteristically English in his blend of cautious realism and forceful passion.

A military dictatorship presupposes that the dictator can count on the army's favor. But here the army, who had supposed they were making a democratic revolution, soon grew vexed at having set up an oligarchy in power. The army's leaders had drawn up a Republican constitution in the *Agreement of the People* (1648): biennial elections, a wide suffrage, and freedom of conscience. The Rump greeted this document with the courtesy due to well-armed citizens, and paid no heed to it. It was not long before hostility to the Government became almost unanimous. The Royalists still felt themselves impotent, but hoped for a speedy revenge. They circulated an account of the King's death, a book entitled *Eikon Basilike*, which made a martyr of King Charles in the popular mind. The Presbyterians regarded Parliament as heretical. The demagogue John Lilburne, the eternal malcontent, started a campaign at the head of the Levelers against the new Government. It was said of him that "if the world was emptied of all but John Lilburne, Lilburne would quarrel with John, and John with Lilburne." But this intolerable pamphleteer won the masses' favor, and they dubbed him Honest John. Every revolution throws up men of two types—the born leaders and the born rebels. Cromwell belonged to the first, Lilburne to the second, class. But governance is a craft which makes unchanging demands on those who practice it; the new masters may justify these demands by original principles, but obey them as their predecessors have always done. And Oliver Cromwell, like King Charles before him, had Lilburne arrested. Honest John refused to doff his hat before the Council of State, which, he declared, had no more lawful authority than he had himself. No jury would condemn him. London was now as hostile to the Rump as it had been to the King; and when the Republican Government, in April,

1643, had a mutineer executed in the city, all the citizens were sporting the green ribbon of the Levelers.

Cromwell was bound to be intolerant of this equalitarian agitation. He believed in the necessity of an aristocracy, which he would have defined in terms of faith rather than of birth. He hated all disorder. "You must break these men, or they will break you," he kept telling the Council of State. But conscience pricked him. In the days of Pym and Hampden, he himself had trusted to law and Parliament; and although nowadays he might impose the rule of the sword, reassuring himself by calling it the sword of the Lord God, he could not always convince himself. His remedy for moral perturbation had always been—action. The battlefield revived his common sense and his practical virtues. And opportunities for action were still at hand. In Ireland a Catholic party had been in control of the country for several years, and English Protestants had been murdered there. And to Ireland Cromwell proceeded, at the head of a New Model army, in almost regal state. He annihilated the forces on the spot, and avenged massacre with massacre; a soldier of Jehovah, he rigorously and wholeheartedly applied all the warlike methods of the Old Testament. He settled Protestant soldiers in the eastern parts of the country, and with the same instinct as the old invaders he pushed the Irish back towards Connaught, in the west. Then began the long martyrdom of Ireland. The land was handed over to foreign and often absentee landlords. The yeomen planted there by Cromwell never took real roots. Some leased out their farms to Irishmen and returned to England; others married Irishwomen and became Irish. One grave outcome of this war was the substitution of a theocracy for the Irish aristocracy which it destroyed. It was the Protestant Cromwell who handed over Ireland to Catholic clericalism. But meanwhile the military victory seemed complete.

In Scotland things looked more dangerous. The execution of Charles I, a king of Scottish blood, had reconciled the Kirk and the Scottish nobility in a common hatred of the regicides. The Prince of Wales, at the age of nineteen, was proclaimed King under the title of Charles II, and signed the Covenant. An invasion of England by a Royalist army became probable, and Cromwell advocated a preventive war. The loyal Fairfax refused to take part, declaring that it would be a violation of the solemn league previously formed. "Your Excellency will soon determine," replied Cromwell, "whether it is better to have this war in the bowels of another country or of our own." Fairfax withdrew, and Cromwell became commander-in-chief. A decade of war had made a great general of this country squire. About the art of war he held few theories, but in organizing and in training men he was admirable; and in battle he was a tactician who kept an open mind and could seize the right moment to make a crowning stake. His moves against the Scots were bold. He allowed them to enter England, moved between them and Scotland, and defeated them heavily at Worcester in 1651. The young Charles II, who had fought courageously, had to flee. It was symptomatic of the loyal feelings of the English people in general that the youthful King found plenty ready to shield and hide him, and in the end to send him safe and sound across the Channel. Scotland, like Ireland, seemed to be mastered, but her old Parliament was revived at the Restoration. The unity of Great Britain was now complete, and for some weeks the victory made Cromwell popular. Parliament gave him a royal grant, and the Palace of Hampton Court. When London, which a couple of months before had been booing him, welcomed him now with salvos of muskets and shouts of delight, he remarked to his lieutenants at the sight, that this vast crowd would be vaster still to see him hanged.

Somber words: but notwithstanding his victories Cromwell was, and remained, somber. He knew all too well that this country which he would have wished to see governed by saints was being exploited by the unscrupulous, that the army of 50,000 men, useless after having defeated the foes without, was ruining the country, that debtors filled the prisons and beggars the roads. He realized that this was the moment to revert from military to civil law, from force to justice. But by what means? Prayer and meditation notwithstanding, Cromwell could not discern a remedy. Bereft of action, his mind became confused. He had no money. His soldiers now were costing the nation a hundred times what it had paid for King Charles's ships, the cost of which had been a prime cause of the revolution. For a long time Ireton had been Cromwell's brain, but Ireton had died in 1651 and was no longer there to guide him.

What could he do? Order an election? But did he not know that if he allowed *all* the citizens to vote freely, they might recall the Stuarts? True, when Edmond Calamy told him that nine Englishmen out of ten were opposed to him, he asked whether he ought not to disarm the nine and put a sword in the hand of the tenth. Besides, he would have to be in agreement with the tenth man; and Cromwell was weary of the intolerance of his friends. He was beginning to have some shadowy picture of a Protestant England, united and imperial. What other solution was there? To disband the army? It would mutiny. Or to set up a monarchy again? The thought ran through his mind: suppose a man were to take it upon himself to stand forth as king? But whatever happened, the Rump must be dismissed; the army was tired of it. On April 20, 1653, the Lord-General Cromwell entered the House of Commons and took his seat on one of the benches. He listened, grew restive, and rose. "Come, come," he said, "I will put an end to your prating. You are no Parliament. I say, you are no Parliament. . . . Some of you are whoremasters. Others are drunkards, and some corrupt and unjust men. . . . It is not fit that you should sit as a Parliament any longer. . . ." Then he lifted up the Mace, the sacred emblem of Parliament's power. "What shall we do with this bauble?" he said; and cried to an officer, "Here, take it away!" And having driven all the members out, he set padlocks on the doors. A soldier bore away the keys and the Mace, and the Long Parliament vanished, as one witness said, as quietly as a dream.

After the Crown, the Mace; after the sovereign, the Parliament: no trace was left of this country's long history of freedom. But, once again, how was government to be carried on? By a republic, said some; by a monarchy, said others. But Cromwell's choice was for the saints. He dared not trust to an election, but called upon the Independent churches to select good men, and thus set up a Parliament of one hundred and fifty members. It was called the Barebones Parliament, from the name of one of its members, Praisegod Barebones, a leather-merchant of Fleet Street. Sir Harry Vane refused to become one of this assembly, saying that for the company of saints he preferred to await Paradise. Cromwell himself soon tired of these men whom he had drawn forth from obscurity, and would doubtless have sent them packing in their turn if they had not dissolved themselves.

A new constitution was drawn up by the army leaders. This Instrument of Government, as it was called, is conspicuous for the boldness of its ideas, so novel that they could not then be put into practice. More fully even than modern England, this document was a foreshadowing of the United States as we know them today. Supreme authority was to be vested in a Lord Protector, a Council, and a Parliament, shortly

OLIVER CROMWELL

Engraving of a portrait
by Jan van de Velde, Netherlands School.

Gul. Faithorne ad Vivum

Delin. et sculpsit

Joannis Miltoni Effigies Ætat: 62.
1670.

JOHN MILTON
Engraving of a portrait by W. Faithorne the elder
in the London National Portrait Gallery.

completed by a House of Lords. Any measure voted by Parliament became law, even after the Protector's veto, provided that it was not contrary to the fundamental ideas of the Republic. The British Parliament in the twentieth century was to be, theoretically at least, all-powerful, and could, if necessary, modify the constitution of the realm by its vote. The Protector's Parliament, like the United States Congress, was subject to this constitution. For the first time England, Scotland and Ireland found themselves united under the same laws. English judges sat in Scotland, and order was maintained there by English soldiers under General Monk; the Westminster Parliament would legislate for Scotland. Ireland too was represented in the common Parliament, and across St. George's Channel the English settlers were expropriating the native population. But this forcible "union" remained precarious, and with the Restoration the old Parliaments of Scotland and Ireland reappeared. Most of the measures passed at this time were likewise ephemeral, because they were premature; but many of them (such as free education, a public postal service, the freedom of the Press, female suffrage, secrecy of the ballot, a national bank) were to be revived in time, and to triumph after long eclipse. These frail Parliaments of the Protectorate were animated by a reforming zeal, like a sick body flushed by fever.

The conflicts of Cromwell with his Commons were as grave as those between Charles and his Parliament had been; but the Protector had something which Charles had lacked—a good army. On one point only Parliament and Protector were agreed: they both desired order. Every intelligent rebel who attains power becomes a Government man. Cromwell was one by instinct. This country, he told himself, had suffered enough. What was now needed was the binding up of wounds and the revival of traditional England. This, too, was very much what Parliament felt. But the Commons urged that, above all things, the constitution should not be imposed on Parliament by a military leader, and Cromwell was refusing to allow them to discuss the essential features of the Instrument of Government as drawn up by the army. The Parliamentarians demanded control of the armed forces, and it was Cromwell's belief that to place these in the service of factions would have meant the revival of civil war. Finally, Cromwell desired some measure of religious toleration (in 1655 he even tacitly authorized the return of the Jews, banned from England since the time of Edward I); Parliament was opposed at once to toleration and to military despotism. The sword won the day. England was divided into military regions, each set under the authority of a major-general. The austere discipline of the Puritans was imposed by stages over the whole country. They had closed the London playhouses, and now they imprisoned strolling players, forbade the village sports, and closed ale-houses. Shakespeare's England became virtuous by compulsion, and sighed for the old Cavalier justice of the peace, who had at least been jovial. For a long time this regime inspired England with a horror of standing armies.

Englishmen had no love for their army, but abroad their army and fleet made the name of England respected. The chief foe for many years was Holland. These two countries were rivals in trade and in mercantile traffic. The Navigation Act of 1651 forbade the importation of goods into England except in English ships. The Dutch refused to salute the English flag in English waters. A conflict ensued in which two great admirals, the Dutchman Van Tromp and the English Robert Blake, were confronted. Their fighting fleets were evenly matched, but Holland's trade was the more vulnerable and she suffered more than her rival. After peace with the Dutch was concluded in 1654, Cromwell's chief enemy abroad was Spain. Against her he made alliance with France, who, although a Catholic power, was carrying on a Protestant foreign policy on account of her hatred of the House of Austria. Cromwell seized Jamaica from Spain, and his "plantation" there of English settlers created a prosperous colony. He was the first English statesman to have the idea of maintaining an English fleet in the Mediterranean, and to insure its safe passage he fortified Gibraltar. Maritime and Mediterranean power enabled Cromwell to intervene effectively in Continental broils; he shielded the Vaudois Protestants against the Duke of Savoy, bombarded Tunis, and was able to demand indemnities from Tuscany and the Pope. Cardinal Mazarin sought his alliance and the Ironsides garrisoned Dunkirk. But these wars were costly, and notwithstanding all his successes on land and sea, Cromwell's foreign policy was unpopular.

Ruling three kingdoms, feared throughout Europe, the Protector now had as enemies only his former friends. And they were irreconcilable. Having climbed to power on the shoulders of a republican army of fanatics and "levelers," he would gladly have used it to restore the old English hierarchy. But the army was rebellious in temper. If Parliament wished to make him King of England, his soldiers threatened their enmity. If, as a prince *de facto*, he maintained a real court, the Puritans grumbled that it was a court of "sins and vanities," all the more abominable because it called continually upon the name of God. When Oliver Cromwell died in 1658, still only fifty-eight years old, the victim of melancholy and fever, the whole edifice which he had hastily erected in an attempt to make a substitute for traditional England, was shaken to its foundations. In the roaring of the great wind which blew on the night of his death, he was heard praying for his country: "Give them consistency of judgment, one heart, and mutual love; and go on to deliver them, and with the work of reformation; and make the name of Christ glorious in the world." And when the end was near, they heard him murmur, "My work is done." It did not survive him.

As his successor Cromwell had named his son Richard, a harmless but uninspired man, who proved powerless to resolve the latent conflict between the army and the civil power and incapable of smoothing out the even graver discords between the rival army leaders. There followed eighteen months of anarchy, during which Parliament and officers were at grips. At last only two generals were left in the lists—the Republican Lambert, and Monk, a secret Royalist. Monk came to London, and John Milton was among those who urged him to restore the Long Parliament for the saving of the Commonwealth. But the aspect of the streets showed clearly enough how Englishmen felt. The citizens and apprentices were burning the Rump in effigy in bonfires. The energetic and reasonable Monk acted with cautious deliberation. Although the return of the King was desired by Cavaliers and Presbyterians alike, that is to say by the great mass of the nation, it was difficult to prepare this lawfully, since only a Parliament could recall the King, and only a king could summon Parliament. Monk convoked as many of the Lords as he could, and called on the electors to return a House of Commons. The King later confirmed this summons, the jurists maintaining the legal fiction that the monarchy had never ceased to exist. In actual fact, an illegal Parliament had set up a king. The Restoration was achieved without civil strife, because Monk took the precaution of promising the troops their pay. The soldiers knew how public opinion was running; they were at loggerheads with their officers, and glad to bring matters to a head. Within two years of Cromwell's death his whole edifice, like himself, was dust.

CHAPTER IX

The Puritan Heritage

ENGLAND's spiritual life in the days of the saints is one of the most surprising phenomena of history. Oriental narratives and poems, thousands of years old, provided a Western people at this time with its only reading, the language of its political discourse, and its religious faith. To this legal-minded people it seemed only natural that the letter of a law should be constantly respected, and as the Bible presented the Law of God, men should live in accordance with its literal Word. Because the Israelites slaughtered the Amalekites, Cromwell was prompt to slaughter the Irish. Because he had stoned certain offenders, the cry of "Stone him!" was raised in the Commons. Because the Psalms are often warlike poems, the Puritans were ever ready to bear arms against the enemies of Jehovah. Because the Bible exalted the people of Israel above all others, the English race, convinced that they were a new Israel, felt growing within itself the pride which the Hundred Years' War had engendered. A Milton believed that, if God had some exacting task to be carried out on earth, He would appeal to His Englishmen. The sentiment is one which will be seen again, during the nineteenth century, in a Curzon or a Rhodes.

Next to the Old Testament, the Puritan's favorite reading was the Epistles of St. Paul and the writings of Calvin. His God was not the God of the Gospels, Who died for all men, but the terrible God, the jealous God, who saves only His elect. The Puritan, anxiously scrutinizing the inner workings of his soul for the signs of Grace, could only be hostile to pleasures, intolerable as these are when behind them glow the flames of hell. Cromwell wrestled with the Evil One all his life long, and bowed himself to the dust before the Lord. For every decisive step he awaited the divine inspiration. "A man drunk with God," he has been called. But this doctrine, though it darkens life, powerfully strengthens those who profess it. The deliberate sacrifice of everything that the men of the Renaissance called pleasure or happiness, makes for seriousness and courage, and produces such a dread of sin that soldiers are disciplined, tradesmen faithful to their bond, workmen industrious. Such men demand much of others, but no less of themselves. When Cromwell's veterans were disbanded, they did not drift into mendicancy or thieving. Even the Royalists admitted that in honest industry they prospered beyond other men, and that if a baker, a mason, or artisan was conspicuous for his sobriety and zeal, he was in all likelihood one of Oliver's old soldiers.

Certain sects went farther than Cromwell's Independents in the interpretation of Holy Writ. The Fifth Monarchy Men believed in the return of Christ to earth and an imminent millennium. The apocalyptic seventh chapter of the Book of Daniel was their gospel, and as one of its verses foretold the reign of the saints, they claimed the governance of England by a Sanhedrin. The Anabaptists rebaptized adult men and women in streams at twilight. At this time, too, George Fox founded the Society of Friends, who acquired the name of Quakers from the occasional physical tremors which testified to their faith. To the Quakers, religion should be only an inner spiritual experience, and it was therefore superfluous to ordain clergy or build churches. Contrary to the Puritans, the Friends held that every man, in his own life, can be fully victorious over sin. They showed more serenity and kindliness than most other sects. But their refusal to take an oath or to participate in war, and their denial of clerical authority, made them rebels despite themselves.

During the reign of the Puritans, life, in so far as they could control it, was overshadowed. They banned the Englishman's favorite enjoyments, such as the theater, horse-racing, cock-fighting, and the ale-houses. Gambling-houses and brothels were shut down. On Sundays the streets were patrolled to compel the closing of taverns. That day had to be spent at home, reading the Scriptures and singing psalms. In 1644 Parliament forbade the sale of foodstuffs on Sunday, and likewise traveling, transport of goods, any everyday work, participation in any contest; it forbade also the ringing of church-bells, shooting-matches, markets, ale-houses, dancing and sports, under pain of a fine of five shillings for each person over fourteen years of age. Parents or guardians paid for children found guilty of these offenses. Religious services were stripped of whatever might recall the pomp and beauty of Catholic, or even Anglican, ritual. Evelyn noted in his diary that he was arrested on Christmas Day for having observed the superstitious festival of the Nativity. Such fear was there of being "Popish" that moderation and decorum were lost. John Evelyn described them reading and praying without method, and saw a whole congregation wearing hats during their psalm-singing. In some conventicles they did not read the Scriptures at all, but spoke insipid prayers, and were given sermons which were understood neither by listeners nor preachers. Many churches, Evelyn noted, were being filled with pews in which worshipers sat isolated in threes or fours. The pew survived, a sign of Puritan individualism, and a subject of dispute between the High and the Low Churchmen.

Notwithstanding its scorn for beauty, Puritanism produced two great writers, who did, however, write their principal works after the fall of the Commonwealth. The first was John Milton (1608-1694), who in youth was a polished poet in the direct line of the great Elizabethans, but renounced pagan versification in the time of political conflict and entered the "frozen element of prose." During the Commonwealth he became Latin secretary to the Council of State, a faithful partisan of Cromwell, and then, stricken with blindness, he dictated after the Restoration his two epic poems, *Paradise Lost* and *Paradise Regained*, and also a drama, *Samson Agonistes,* a spiritual autobiography in which the vanquished and blinded hero laments his lot among the triumphant Philistines. He was the last survivor of the Renaissance, the only one in whom were combined the grace of paganism with the solemn sublimity of Puritanism. The second great writer was John Bunyan (1628-1688), whose *Pilgrim's Progress* found the same fame in England as the *Iliad* in Greece. This itinerant tinker, tormented by visions now of hell fire, now of the celestial, had the simple but inspired idea of interpreting the abstract progress of the Christian soul towards salvation as an imaginative narrative of an earthly journey. Christian, the central figure of the story, is doubtless Bunyan himself, seeking the path towards the Everlasting City, which in the end he reaches, despite his foes. The naturalness of the story and dialogue, the transformation of spiritual happenings into concrete drama, enabled simple and sincere readers to understand, better than from books of devotion, the nature of the religious life.

Puritanism, like all movements seeking to alter the moral code, had in it a strain of tyranny. A minority submitted by conviction, but the majority through fear, and the submission of the latter was apparent rather than real. To read the letters of Dorothy Osborne to Sir William Temple is to realize that in many a manor-house there were still men and women trying discreetly to live a humane and sensible life. The most obdurate Royalists, for all their hatred of the rebels, sought after a term of wandering abroad to return home and settle there. The Pretender himself encouraged them to do so. It was better for him to have supporters on the spot. Evelyn tells how he decided to open his manor-house again because there was so little hope of any change for the better, with everything entirely in the rebels' hands. While Cromwell still lived, the Restoration, near at hand though it proved to be, was foreseen only by the wisest heads.

After the Restoration the Puritan temper had its own taste of persecution. But it was destined to survival. The dissenter, the man who refuses conformity, examines all questions for himself, and keeps faith with his settled conviction even at peril of his happiness or his life, remained a highly significant type of Englishman. Sometimes he would stand fast on a religious issue, sometimes on a political one. Always he would be stanch, obstinate, incorruptible. This was the man who battled against slavery, against war, the man who maintained even into our own time the gloom of the English Sunday. To him the English character has owed some of its finest traits, and also those which have made it sometimes disliked. Earnestness and trustworthiness are among his attributes, but self-deception also, human nature being a more complex thing than the Calvinists would have it. The truth is, not that some men cherish God whilst others cherish Satan, but that in each one of us God and Satan are at war. Unable to accept the inevitable evil in their thoughts, the Puritans strove to interpret them by pious discourse. They came to impose a mask of morality upon selfish interests. In this as in much else, a great many Englishmen were destined to preserve Puritan modes of thought and feeling, and Disraeli, two centuries later, had to recognize that no man could govern England on lines counter to the Nonconformist conscience.

[311]

Chapter X

The Restoration

The new sovereign whom England had so long proscribed, but now awaited as a savior, was in no way the seraphic character imagined by the fervent adherents of his father, the Martyr King. Charles II had not the noble, sorrowful face of his father; his heavy, sensuous lips, his sturdy nose and laughing eyes, were reminiscent rather of his grandfather, Henry IV of France. From him he inherited his gayety, his wit, his taste for women. Long exile had not soured him, but had given him an experience of poverty, and a firm determination not to set out again "on his travels." In spite of pressure from his mother and his sister Henrietta, who were both Catholics, he had not renounced his Protestantism. Catholicism had attracted, perhaps convinced him; but remembering the Puritan passions, he was reluctant to compromise his throne. To safeguard him against the dangers of the Papist court of Saint-Germain, his faithful counselor, Edward Hyde, took him to stay with his sister Mary, wife of William of Orange, in Holland. There he fell in love with a young Welsh refugee, Lucy Walters, and by her had an illegitimate son, whom he made Duke of Monmouth. The life of a prince in exile is a hard one: Charles borrowed money from the courts of France and Spain, and his precarious existence made him more charming than kingly, and adroit rather than scrupulous. If ever a day should come when life smiled on him, he was firmly resolved to enjoy it. And that was clear enough when he was indeed King, and his Ministers, seeking him on State business, would find him playing with his dogs or fondling his mistresses. When he landed at Dover on May 25, 1660, the mayor presented him with a Bible, and Charles replied that it was the thing he loved above all things in the world.

London gave him a warm welcome, with flowers and carpets in the streets, peals of bells, fountains of wine. John Evelyn tells how, seeing it, he thanked God, for all had been done with no drop of blood spilled, and by that same army whose rebellion had driven forth the King. Charles turned with a smile to one of his entourage and remarked that it was no fault but his own if he had been so long absent, as he met nobody who would not have wanted his return. The changeable moods of nations are surprising. Everything in Charles's character ought to have shocked his subjects. In his train he brought back a beautiful mistress, Barbara Palmer, later Lady Castlemaine, and in her company, cynically, he spent his first night in Whitehall. Ere long he lived surrounded by a veritable seraglio, and court morals imitated the King's. But a touch of folly was not displeasing after the constraints of Puritanism. Dissipation seemed to accord with loyalty, as gravity had done with rebellion. The King's wandering youth had induced habits of idling and irresponsibility. All real power he left to the servant of his exile, Edward Hyde, whom he had made Earl of Clarendon, and the beginnings of this administration were cleverly handled. An act of indemnity reassured those who had taken part in the Great Rebellion, and only a few regicides were executed, in a repulsive butchery. The bodies of Oliver Cromwell and some others were exhumed, hung up, and then buried at the gibbet's foot. As in the case of every restoration, the men who had stood fast during the dark days felt that they were ill-treated. The law of amnesty disappointed them. "Indemnity for the King's enemies, oblivion for his friends," they said, sourly. The policy of moderation vexed a few die-hard Cavaliers, but was quick to rally the Cromwellian squires to the monarchy. A restoration could abandon a few heads to the avenging executioner, provided that it did not tamper with fortunes acquired. Clarendon was shrewd enough to pay in full all wages due to the Commonwealth soldiery, which enabled him to disband this formidable army without a clash. Fifty thousand of Cromwell's veterans were suddenly loosed on England; and to their honor be it said that none was seen asking alms or behaving ill. Puritanism had its good side.

To avoid any more of his "travels," Charles was resolved upon lawful rule. He greatly admired Louis XIV, and his secret desire was to fortify his prerogative as much as possible, and pave the way, so far as was possible, for emancipation of the Catholics—but all without forcing the issue. In 1661 he summoned a Parliament. In the body which had re-called Charles, Presbyterians and Cavaliers shared the seats. This time the country sent to Westminster a Parliament which has been described as more Royalist than the King and more Anglican than the bishops, entirely devoted to the interests of landed property and the Established Church. The members were mostly young. The King remarked that he would keep them until their beards grew; and in point of fact he re-tained this one for eighteen years. But so deeply ingrained was the jealousy for English liberties that even this House showed its resolve to grant the King no standing army; nor were his revenues sufficient so he could not dispense with Parliament, nor any courts of royal prerogative. The King, on his side, remembered the history of his father and was careful not to step across these bounds. No constitutional check had been laid on him, and no responsible Cabinet was interposed between Crown and Parliament. But Charles, when his Ministers became unpopular, always managed to dismiss them just in time. Thus Parliament was the ruler *de facto*, if not *de jure*. The French ambassador at the time con-sidered that this was not a monarchic regime, and was astonished at hearing the Thames bargemen discussing politics with the "milords." During the following century Montesquieu mentioned his surprise at seeing a slater reading a news-sheet on the roof. England's political edu-cation had begun much sooner than that of the Continental nations.

If the Puritans expected religious tolerance from the new King, they were disappointed. Parliament and Lord Clarendon both showed a stern front against independent sects, and even against the Presbyterians. A series of enactments known as the Clarendon Code enforced strict con-formity. These measures forced all mayors and municipal officials to re-nounce the Presbyterian Covenant and to receive the Anglican sacraments; obliged all clergymen to be ordained by a bishop, to use the Prayer Book and English liturgy; forbade any religious service except the Anglican whereat more than four adherents were present; and required noncon-formist ministers to retire at least five miles from any important town or from any parish where they had preached. These laws deeply influenced English life. They won the final support of the squires for Anglicanism, as the ban against dissenters holding political or civic office forced the sub-mission of anyone having ambitions or important interests. From this time dates the traditional alliance of parson and squire in village life. But many of those who surrendered still had a dissenting temper, and in later years they became politically the supporters of the Whig party, in alliance with the skeptics and rationalists. The Clarendon Code made Presbyterianism almost impossible in England, although other sects, less highly organized, survived. By isolating a class to which it refused political rights, this Code created the dissenting type—a type of great importance in English history—a breed of men who, out of loyalty to their principles, accept the prospect of conflict with established authority and are not afraid, in any circumstance, of offending public opinion. In various forms this dissenter appears in the subsequent centuries, and his active strength is considerable because his intellectual courage is unbounded.

Clarendon wore himself out quickly in power. In a youthful and cynical court, he was a pompous, gouty old servant, forever moralizing. The King's ladies laughed at him; in private, the Duke of Buckingham mimicked the Chancellor; and Charles himself, though not ungrateful, laughed. Only a pretext was by now needed to get rid of this battered survival; and the course of events produced several. It happened that the King's brother James, the heir to the throne, had fallen in love during his exile with Clarendon's daughter, Anne Hyde. He married her, secretly at first, and then publicly. From this union sprang two English sovereigns: Mary, who married William of Orange, and Queen Anne. At the time of its celebration the marriage roused popular hostility, and there was strong feeling against Clarendon, who feigned disapproval himself. Furthermore, Clarendon was responsible for the marriage of Charles II with Catherine of Braganza, a Portuguese and Catholic princess, who proved, moreover, to be sterile. A Portuguese marriage was a less heinous offense than a Spanish one, but not much, and the highly improbable allegation was made that Clarendon had chosen a sterile Queen so as to place his own grandchildren on the throne. Another charge was laid against him that he sold Dunkirk to the French for a large sum, and himself pocketed a commission. The public mind was also deeply affected by the terrible plague which ravaged London, with its swarming, dirty streets, during the summer of 1665, and also by the Great Fire which destroyed two-thirds of the City a few months later. And this second disaster (because the people insist that great events must have great causes) was laid at the door of the Papists, the French, and Lord Clarendon.

A final blow was the arrival in the Thames of a Dutch fleet, which came as far as Chatham and burned English ships. Panic spread quickly among a people unnerved by plague and fire. The capricious London mob was by now looking back with regret to the days of stout Oliver, when the coasts were protected and the army was strong. It was of no avail that the Treaty of Breda (1667), which ended the Dutch war, gave the English New York, with the whole of the American coast joining Virginia with New England. Englishmen felt they had been betrayed, and in that same year Clarendon, the public enemy, was exiled.

His place was taken not by one Minister, but by a group of confidents known as the Cabal—the word happened to be formed by the initial letters of their names: Clifford, Arlington, Buckingham, Ashley, and Lauderdale. The first two were Catholics, the rest skeptics. The most remarkable, but most suspect, was Ashley, who shortly became Earl of Shaftesbury, and was depicted by Dryden in a famous satire as Achitophel, the treacherous son of King David. With the help of the Cabal, the King not only reigned but ruled. To outward appearance he still idled and fooled with dogs and doxies; but actually, with hidden tenacity, he was pursuing a great project: to secure money and troops by an alliance with Louis XIV, and with this foreign support, perhaps to re-establish Catholicism.

Charles had a sincere admiration for France and her governance. There he found what he would have liked, but did not dare, to be—an absolute monarch. Realizing that such omnipotence was made possible only by harmony between the sovereign and the Church of Rome, he desired to achieve this harmony and to imitate his cousin. These sentiments were strengthened by a new French mistress, Louise de Kérouaille, whose child-like face disguised real adroitness. Notwithstanding Parliament's desire for alliance with the Protestant powers of Sweden and Holland against France, who was taking Spain's place as the supreme power on the Continent, Charles II signed a secret treaty with France, and against Holland, in 1672. Parliament refused subsidies for this unpopular war, and the Dutch defenses were effective. In 1674, much against the grain, Charles had to negotiate with Holland, and three years later his niece Mary, daughter of James and Anne Hyde, married William of Orange. That French treaty was the last move made by Charles personally on the board of foreign policy, and it was checkmated.

He still had hopes of achieving his great plan in the religious field. Early in his reign he had tried to impose on Parliament a Declaration of Indulgence, thinking to make Catholic emancipation acceptable in return for a corresponding measure for dissenters. But even the dissenters, Protestants before all else, opposed the measure, and it was rejected by Parliament. Later, Charles tried to give effect to the measure in spite of Parliament, in virtue of his prerogative. But he chose the wrong moment, when hatred of Popery and fear of France had both been quickened by fire and pestilence. Once again it was a period when foreign affairs are determined by internal policy. In days gone by, Spain had symbolized persecution in Protestant eyes; now, France personified absolutism and the loss of the subject's liberties. Once more travelers contrasted the wealth of the English farmer with the poverty of the French peasant. Popery and wooden shoes—the combination haunted men's imaginations. Parliament stood fast and refused to recognize the King's right to settle such matters by ordinance. Charles wavered, remembered the rebellion and his "travels"—and yielded. But part of the Cabal had sided against him, and made him accept the Test Act, a national and Protestant retort to the French alliance and the Declaration of Indulgence. This law excluded from public office any who would not swear allegiance to the King's supremacy and to the Anglican faith. Catholic peers under a further act had to leave the House of Lords. The King's brother himself was obliged to own himself a Catholic. The King, and tolerance, were beaten.

His reasonable acceptance of defeat gave grounds to suppose for a time that tranquillity would be restored. But even the wise live at the mercy of events. Within a few days everything was changed by a lie and a mystery. Titus Oates, formerly an Anglican cleric, was a convert to Catholicism more for self-interest than by conviction, a man of base and contemptible character, who had made enemies wherever he went. Expelled from the English Jesuits' college at Saint-Omer, he returned to England penniless, and in 1678 concocted an accusation against the Jesuits, who, he averred, were plotting to set fire to the City, murder the King, set up his brother James, Duke of York, in his place, subdue England with Dutch and French help, and re-establish Catholicism. He sent one copy of this denunciation to the King, another to Sir Edmund Berry Godfrey, a well-known justice of the peace in Westminster. The excitement caused was prodigious, in a London still nervous after the plague and the Great Fire, with memories of Gunpowder Plot and an unreasoning terror of Jesuits and Popery. A search among the papers of the Duke of York's secretary revealed a compromising correspondence with Father La Chaise, the confessor of Louis XIV. Calumny had accidentally come upon an authentic intrigue. And at this point came the dramatic discovery of the murdered body of Godfrey, at the foot of Primrose Hill. Panic ran riot. Armed Jesuits were reported everywhere. Women went out-of-doors carrying daggers. The King was incredulous about the plot, remarking that none would be so foolish as to murder him to put his brother on the throne; but he was obliged to feign alarm and to double the guard at Whitehall. A few steady heads vainly argued the personal baseness of Titus Oates, and the absurdity of a pointless crime, as Godfrey held no more than a copy of a document which had already produced its full effect. But, victimized by a sort of public blackmail, they soon found themselves forced to believe in Oates, through fear of being mistaken for Papists. A veritable reign of terror began.

Since the Restoration, parties had been forming in embryo, engendered by the passions of the Civil War. Englishmen had grown used to taking interest in public affairs, and the habit remained incurable. Some favored the King like the Cavaliers in the past; and their adversaries dubbed them "Tories," the name of certain Irish freebooters, implying that they were merely Papists disguised; but the King's party wore the insult as a cockade. They, in their turn, nicknamed the King's opponents "Whigs," an abbreviation of "Whigamores," a Covenanters' faction in the west of Scotland. The Whigs were rebels born, the devil their sire, Shaftesbury their chief; but this was a rebellion of aristocrats. The Tories represented landed property and the Anglican Church; the Whigs, the dissenters and the mercantile classes. When the King ordered an election in 1679, the first for seventeen years, the two parties invested it with the character which an appeal to the country has today, with its meetings, processions, violent speeches. These were noisy methods, but doubtless their infusion of the spectacular and competitive element into politics made for the enduring success of parliamentary rule. Halifax compared these battles of Whigs and Tories to a children's snowballing fight. In the election of 1679 the Whigs won the day by taking their stand, in all bad faith, on the calumnies of Titus Oates; and after their success they made the first experiment in constitutional government. A Privy Council of thirty members was to serve as intermediary between King and Parliament, directed by Shaftesbury, Sir William Temple, Lord Russell, and Lord Halifax. The 1679 Parliament is best known for the amendment of the law of habeas corpus which set up the most stringent precautions against the arbitrary imprisonment of any English subject. No measure shows more clearly the distinction between despotic and free systems of government. Habeas corpus was never suspended except in times of emergency. In 1815 it was even put forward by Sir Samuel Romilly in favor of the captive Napoleon.

The Whigs' victory had been due to dread of Catholicism, a cause which was associated with that of the Duke of York. As partisans of radical measures, therefore, the Whigs felt that the King's brother ought to be excluded from the royal succession, while the Tories, as good legitimists, held that it would suffice to set limits on his powers. In this matter, however, the Whigs themselves were divided, some favoring the Prince of Orange, the Duke of York's son-in-law, others inclining to the Duke of Monmouth, the natural son of the King. Charles himself supported his brother against his bastard. Very speedily, with their surprising fluidity, the English populace tired of the Whig terror and forgot Titus Oates. In 1681 Charles, having no need of Parliamentary subsidies as he received funds from Louis XIV, was able without undue outcry to dissolve the last Parliament of his reign, which sat at Oxford in order to be at safe distance from the London crowd. The Tories were winning.

Englishmen had not yet learned the parliamentary game whose rules, universally accepted, enable political foes to alternate in power, without the victory of one leading to an instant massacre of the other. The triumph of Crown and Tories was followed by a persecution of Whigs. Shaftesbury was prosecuted for high treason, and although acquitted by a jury had to flee to Holland, where he died. The other leading Whigs, Russell and Algernon Sidney, died on the scaffold, Essex cut his throat in the Tower. A wave of mystical devotion to royalty had swept over England. The Tories proclaimed the doctrine of non-resistance to the King, which protected them at once from a counter-attack by the Whigs and from the independence of the Calvinists. Robert Filmer published his *Patriarcha*, asserting that as the King was the successor to the patriarchs and the father of his subjects, any revolt against him was parricidal. In this fever of servility all the barriers against the Duke of York were forgotten.

With impunity, during his last years, Charles II lived unblushingly on French subsidies, and regardless of English interests allowed Louis XIV to pursue his aggrandisement in Flanders and the Rhineland. And thus the monarch who had with so much charm betrayed England, two Churches, his wife, and all his mistresses was able to preserve to the last his luxuriant, perilous equilibrium. He wondered what his brother would do when he himself had left the scene; it seemed all too likely that James would be forced upon further "travels." But he would take good care, said Charles, to leave him his kingdoms in peace. On his deathbed, for the first time, he summoned a Catholic priest, and received extreme unction.

CHAPTER XI

James II and the Revolution of 1688

CHARLES II bequeathed to his brother a despotic and almost unquestioned power. The Church of England preached divine right and non-resistance to the tyrant. A Tory Parliament was ready to vote life-taxes to the King. Discreetly Charles had begun to recruit a standing army of ten thousand men, and James was to double the strength—a great novelty for an English sovereign. The country let matters drift, wishing only to be quiet. Even the new King's Catholicism roused no violent opposition. Anglicans and dissenters were agreed that he might practice his religion provided that he did not seek a national conversion. If James II had been a man ready to compromise, like his brother, he might have reigned undisturbed. But he was obstinate, energetic, dutiful, and rather unintelligent. Comparing the two brothers, men reached the conclusion that Charles II could have understood things if he chose, whereas James II would have liked to understand them if he could. He was ingenuous enough to suppose that, because it preached non-resistance, the Church of England would not resist if he should seek to deprive it of its privileges; but the Anglican Church discovered the weakness of the doctrine precisely when this coincided no longer with its interests. James also believed that he could count on the support of dissenters against the Anglicans because he promised tolerance to the former as he did equally to the Catholics; but this was the moment of the revocation of the Edict of Nantes (1685), when the Huguenot fugitives were coming into England with tales that did not provide a heartening example for the English Protestants.

It could be seen at once that repression under the new reign would be merciless. Rebellions, headed in Scotland by the Duke of Argyll, and by the Duke of Monmouth in the west of England, were fairly easily suppressed, and their leaders were put to death. Hundreds of hapless rustics who had followed Monmouth shared his fate, and the "Bloody Assize" of Judge Jeffreys became notorious. Everywhere the rope, the lash, the dungeon, and even women were sent to their death. The days of Mary Tudor seemed to have returned. Having established an armed camp near London, King James felt secure from any rising and had no qualms about violating the law. Unable to obtain from Parliament the abrogation of the Test Act, he declared it inapplicable to Catholics, by virtue of his royal prerogative, and so was able to fill civil and military posts with Catholic officials and officers. Within the Church of England he favored crypto-Catholic prelates, and amongst the nobility he sought proselytes. When the Duke of Norfolk, bearing the Sword before him, halted at the door of the Catholic chapel, the King said to him: "Your father would have come farther." "And your father, who was a better man," said the Duke, "would not have come so far." And when the young Duke of Somerset, instructed to bring the Papal nuncio into the King's presence, said, "I am informed that I cannot obey Your Majesty without infringing the law," James was furious. "Do you not know that I am above the law?" he exclaimed. And the Duke replied: "Your Majesty, perhaps; but not myself." For the spirit of resistance showed itself amongst the peers rather than amongst members of the Commons. The great Catholic families themselves, well aware of the national character and foreseeing dangerous reactions to come, refused to accept high appointments offered them by the King. Pope Innocent XI advised moderation. But James, zealous and blind, hurried boldly on towards the abyss.

To rule, he needed middle-class support. But the middle classes no longer contained Catholics. James thought to rally them by a Declaration of Indulgence comprising the dissenters. This was the old, ineradicable fallacy of supposing that Catholicism could be restored by taking advantage of internal conflict among the Protestants. The Anglican clergy were ordered to read this declaration from the pulpit, but the whole Church refused. A petition was addressed to the King by the Archbishop of Canterbury and six bishops. They were sent to the Tower. On the barge which bore them down the river the soldiers knelt and asked for the bishop's blessing. When they were acquitted by a jury London was illuminated, and seven-branched candlesticks were seen in the windows, the highest of the stems being for the Primate. Next, the King sought to impose a Catholic president on Magdalen College, Oxford; when the Fellows refused, he expelled twenty-five of them, and had his way. The old clash between the Stuarts and their subjects was starting again, but by now in an emancipated world where rebellion against the King no longer appeared as something incredible and monstrous. People were patient, however, so long as the King had no heir male. The heiress to the throne was Princess Mary, a good Protestant, and the wife of William of Orange. Such a couple, it was felt, would one day restore order in the realm. But despair fell on the country when James's second wife, Mary of Modena, gave birth to a son in 1688. The child was rumored to be supposititious: there had been no legal witnesses of the confinement, and besides, it was a Jesuit plot. The King seemed ready to send an Irish Catholic army into England, and the streets echoed to the strains of "Lullibullero," a song of hatred against the Irish, who would cut the throats of Englishmen. By now, far more than in 1640, the spirit of revolution was rife.

William of Orange, meanwhile, was engaged in mortal strife with Louis XIV of France, and believed that unless England remained Protestant, liberty in Europe was doomed. Neither he nor his wife had any scruples about declaring against their father or father-in-law; keeping constantly in touch with the English parties, they only awaited a definite invitation before taking action. On the day when the seven bishops were acquitted (June 30, 1688), an invitation to William and Mary was signed by several peers—amongst them Danby, and the wise and attractive Halifax—who risked their lives, and had the support of numerous officers, including Lord Churchill, court favorite though he was. Louis XIV had recently invaded the Palatinate, thus giving Holland several weeks of respite. William landed in Torbay on November 5, 1688, and advanced towards London. James had an army, but it was untrustworthy. Seized with panic, he made concessions. It was too late. The militia were mustering in the counties, their password "a free Parliament and a Protestant religion." The great landlords were siding with William, and James had powerful interests against him. The Church and the universities had everything to fear from this Catholic sovereign. Princess Anne, the King's second daughter, took her stand with the rebels. James felt deserted. If he had fought, William's position would perhaps have become difficult, as the English people in general were in no mind to reopen a civil war. Instead of trying to make James II captive, his adversaries were at pains to open the door to flight for him. He took the chance and crossed the Channel, casting the Great Seal into the Thames in the hope of preventing the transaction of State business. But a Seal can be replaced; and so can a King.

To assure the lawful transmission of power was not easy. The Whigs maintained that, as monarchy was a contract between people and sovereign, the people or its representatives had a right to reject James II and his sons as unworthy of confidence, and to summon William of their own free will. The Tory bishops, true to the doctrine of divine right, could not accept this method and urged a regency. A legal compromise, put forward by Danby, considered the fugitive King as having abdicated and proclaimed Mary as having inherited the throne. But this plan clashed with the wishes of the royal couple, Mary being unwilling to reign without her spouse, and William not wishing to become a prince-consort. In the end an agreement recognized them both in February, 1689, and the reign was that of William and Mary. After this compromise the question of the divine right of kings in England could not be raised again. But it enabled this conservative revolution to be effected without civil strife, without proscriptions, without the common hangman. Slowly, the English were learning the difficult art of living in a society.

Chapter XII

The Restoration Spirit

THE pendulum of human nature swings on either side of fairly steady sentiments. Puritan rigidity in morals was bound to be followed by laxity. The Cavaliers, pestered for twenty years past, had a comprehensible horror of the morality and notions which had plagued them; so much so that, in their reaction, they toppled over on the other side. At Charles II's court the hatred of hypocrisy really became a contempt for decency. Now that an end was made of the gloomy faces and cropped heads which had reigned at Westminster, Whitehall longed for the taste of vengeance. The palace was open to all, and everyone could see the royal lewdness for himself. Every night the sentries could see the King crossing the gardens to join his mistress, the all-powerful and shameless Lady Castlemaine. Subjects imitated their ruler. Women in men's clothing, groups meeting to dance in nakedness, cynical wantoning with chambermaids— here were all the usual characteristics of those periods of debauchery which generally follow a great social upheaval. Restoration England is like the age of the Directoire in France or like the post-war Europe of Morand's *Ouvert la Nuit*. The memoirs of the Chevalier de Grammont present a picture of the time, but it was probably more crude in character than Hamilton described it. The English Rochester is more typical of that world than the Frenchman Grammont. An intimate of the King, who delighted in his bawdy talk, impudent enough to snatch a kiss from the favorite herself, libertine enough to rent a tavern with the Duke of Buckingham for the seducing of the most respectable women of the neighborhood, he is like some degraded image of the great Elizabethans, with the same violence, but applied to less worthy ends.

Those young Cavaliers of 1660 had not received, as their fathers had, the solid upbringing which a family of well-to-do squires can give its sons. They had lived with grooms while their fathers followed the king's standard, and they had drifted through the disreputable parts of Paris and Amsterdam. Drunkenness was fashionable. Rochester boasted of having been drunk for five years on end. A capable civil servant like Pepys tells unblushingly of his toping. In London the taverns and brothels multiplied. Coffee and tea, lately introduced into England, were the pretext for opening coffee-houses where more brandy was drunk than coffee. It was in the coffee-houses, and their rival ale-houses, that seditious talk went the rounds, and where scandalous tales of Lady Castlemaine had their currency. Brutal displays of cock-fighting or bull-baiting were hardly enough to quicken the pulse of onlookers who thronged to the executions of the regicides. And the stage mirrored the cynicism of the time. Pepys could still take pleasure in *The Tempest*, but regarded *A Midsummer Night's Dream* as a highly ridiculous performance. Amongst the fashionable dramatists were Deaumont and Fletcher, with Congreve and Wycherley in the field of comedy, to which they transplanted the themes of Molière in a cruder style. The audacity of these Restoration comedies was to startle the nineteenth century; Taine, in his disgust, wondered that any public ever tolerated them. The more amoral twentieth century was to discern afresh their vivacity and comic quality, and in 1935 London audiences were applauding a play of Wycherley's which, in 1865, would have caused dire scandal. Such are the variations of modesty; but Taine was right in judging Wycherley's humor as less healthy than Molière's. Fundamentally, the Puritan still dwelt within these emancipated Englishmen of the Restoration age, and there is a somber violence in the efforts of these comic writers to shock the creature.

In the sixteenth century, Italy was the chief foreign influence in England; in the seventeenth, it was France. Many of the Cavalier poets lived out their exile in France, where they knew and admired Boileau, Molière, Bossuet. French poems and romances found English translators. King Charles II himself was French, not only through his mother, but in his memories and his mode of life. From Louis XIV he received "a pension, a mistress, and examples." An Englishman of the Restoration mingled French phrases with all his conversation: one more reaction, it seemed, against the Puritans. It was at this time that the English language was augmented by words expressive of shades of mockery—"to burlesque," "to droll," "to ridicule," "travesty," and "badinage." The religious poem was succeeded by the satire. One of the great successes of the time was Samuel Butler's *Hudibras*, which has been styled a *Don Quixote* of Puritanism, but to a French reader is reminiscent of Scarron rather than Cervantes. Dryden, in his sparkling satire, combined the Gallic form with biblical allusions, and depicted the hapless Monmouth and the treacherous Shaftesbury under the names of Absalom and Achitophel, the sons of David. The madrigal flowered side by side with satire. Numerous Cavalier poets composed love songs, often charming. Literature was aristocratic. The mysticism of a Milton or a Bunyan found no place in this court, which knew all too well what sort of morality would be imposed upon it by mysticism. It was correct in England, about the year 1670, to be graceful, light-hearted, and reasonable.

Descartes was the fashionable philosopher. The reign of Reason, that un-Britannic divinity, was opening. Seventeenth-century science was Cartesian, and could be so because it dealt with mathematics, astronomy, and optics. These modes of discipline produced a man of genius in Sir Isaac Newton, whose discovery of certain laws of mechanics confirmed the rights of Reason. The King himself, and the second Duke of Buckingham, were men of science. In 1662 the Royal Society received its royal charter for the advancement of Knowledge of Nature, a nucleus of all who were interested in scientific investigations, from the King to the cultivated middle class. There Halley described his comet, and Newton expounded light, Roy demonstrated his botanical classifications, and Boyle the theory of sound. The principles of scientific research, set forth previously by Bacon in his *Novum Organum*, were at this time productive of such results that men began to presume that self-confidence which, during the eighteenth century, led them to seek rational solutions for the problems of politics, morality, and economics. Nevertheless, English rationalism, before Locke, was different from its French counterpart. The great thinker of the Restoration period was Thomas Hobbes, who regarded human societies as purely mechanical systems set in motion by our appetites and desires. In his view, self-interest is the mainspring of the moral law; but socially organic life brings about a war between conflicting self-interests, and this clash causes the transformation of the natural state of war into a lawful system of agreements. Hobbes's political philosophy is one which would naturally arise from an era of civil war such as that which he had himself witnessed. Since men hate each other and are incapable of living in peace, a strong master is the sole remedy. And Hobbes's *Leviathan* is simply the totalitarian State of the modern dictatorships, with the sovereign as its dictator.

Even the Church at this time became rationalistic. The fierce, devouring faith of a Cromwell satisfied the deepest craving of certain Englishmen, but most of them preferred religion of a less violent kind. The leading Christian thinker of the Restoration, Isaac Barrow, was a mathematician, and propounded a scientific theology and a utilitarian morality, demonstrating the obvious advantage to mankind of insuring eternal bliss at the cost of a few quite trifling sacrifices. Tillotson, a preacher so much admired that his widow was paid £2,500 for the copyright of his unpublished sermons, expounded the wisdom of being religious, showing this wisdom by practical arguments ranged with geometric precision. There was no fire, no imagination, nothing of the style which lends æsthetic value to a Bossuet, a Bourdaloue, a Massillon—but a house well built and wind-proof.

This kindly, reasonable religion had a strong hold on the English people. It would be very misleading to infer from comedies and court memoirs that the whole country, during the Restoration period, was given over to cynicism and debauchery. Such immorality is always confined to a few, to the idle, who employ their energies in artificial love-affairs in default of having proper work to use them in. Family life in the manor-house, the shopkeeper's home, the farm, remained as it had always been. Private letters give us glimpses of excellent households, united in sober affection. Samuel Pepys, during a walk on the outskirts of London, came across an old shepherd reading the Bible to his boy. The libraries were full of books of theology, and in the reign of Charles II sermons sold more freely than poetry.

There is no resemblance between the English Revolution of 1688 and the French Revolution of a hundred years later. The latter was one in which classes came into conflict; peasants and townsmen revolted against king and nobles. There was nothing like this in England. The two great conflicts of the Revolution in England presented the picture of a religious and a political clash. Who was to dominate? King or Parliament? Which Church was to mold the souls of Englishmen? Roman, Anglican, or Independent? But there was also a third, and less obvious, conflict. It was fiscal in character. Who was to pay for State expenditure? Charles I, with his ship money, had stood for direct taxation. The Revolution certainly meant the triumph of Parliament, of the Anglican Church, of the Common Law; but it also indicated the triumph of the propertied class. For some years, in the time of the New Model and the Levelers, it looked as if a Puritan and equalitarian opposition might come to birth. But such fear tended to unify the great landlords who supported Parliament with those who upheld the King. The former came to be Whigs, the latter Tories; but between them was a tacit agreement to keep from power any group whose ideas were too extreme. And so Puritanism, which acknowledged only the authority of conscience, was kept out of practical politics.

The Stuart adventure brought about the victory of the Common Law, no less than that of Parliament over Crown. After that dynasty, England saw no more of administrative rights and courts of royal prerogative. There was one law for all, as strict for the State as for individuals; habeas corpus closed the last gates of the domain of justice against "reasons of State." In France the various revolutionary assemblies at the close of the eighteenth century, and later the National Assembly of 1871, having overturned monarchy or empire, were to attempt the immediate creation of a strong State. In contrast, the Revolution of 1688 in England was directed only towards limiting State powers for the benefit of the rights of the subject. Parliament summoned William and Mary, imposing its own terms on them. The truth was that England, shielded from foreign armies by her girdle of sea, and from internal disorder by the law-abiding temper of her people, was not forced primarily to protect her frontiers against invaders nor her counties against anarchy, but simply to defend the religion and freedom and prosperity of her people against the arbitrary interference of their government.

In years to come, Burke called the events of 1688 a "happy and glorious revolution," and it was indeed a piece of good fortune for England that she could thus achieve the greatest alteration in her history, the transition from despotism to constitutional monarchy, without an unbridgeable gulf being made between Englishmen of opposing views. If Cromwell had remained in power and himself founded a royal dynasty, England would probably have remained for many years divided, as France was after 1789; the dispossessed descendants of the Cavaliers would not readily have forgiven their defeat by the Roundheads. The comparative temperate-

[329]

ness in political conflict during the eighteenth and nineteenth centuries is largely attributable to the indulgence shown at the Restoration of Charles II, to the fact that both parties were at one in defending Protestantism at the time of James II's flight, and also to the circumstance that, after 1788, the last legitimists rallied to the existing monarchy because the legitimate line of kings had come to an end. Whereas in France, in the days of the Terror, a vendetta between Left and Right was opened which has never yet been forgotten, in England, after 1688, political passion never reached the compelling fervor of a religious sentiment.

Book VI

MONARCHY AND OLIGARCHY

theoretic glorification. With the Declaration of Right accepted by the King, few grounds for conflict remained between Crown and Parliament. But a method had not yet been found for insuring coöperation between the Executive and the legislature. Nobody as yet imagined that unity of government would be achieved by a homogeneous group of the King's counselors (the Cabinet), who would hold the high offices of State, belonging to the dominant party in the Commons and following the fortunes of that parliamentary majority. When William, influenced by the "ingenious" Sunderland, tried to form such groups of Ministers, Parliament was startled, talked of juntas and cabals, and brandished its old weapon of impeachment. But impeachment provided no adequate control over the Executive. It made possible the punishment of Ministers after a failure or a blunder, but could not forestall a rash act. For several generations England puzzled over this difficult problem of Ministerial responsibility without finding its solution.

William III preserved, in theory at least, the executive power; but he was far from having the personal prestige which Charles I, even to the scaffold, had retained. A fairly numerous party remained loyal to James II. A great nobleman to whom William refused some favor was very likely to enter into secret correspondence with the refugee court at Saint-Germain. Several bishops, and four hundred clergy who remained true to divine right, refused to give their oath. They were called the non-jurors, and had to resign, their places being taken by "latitudinarian" bishops like Burnet and Tillotson. If William had been able to do so, he would have imposed religious neutrality upon England. But the opposition roused by this new-fangled notion forced him to compromise. A measure granting comparative freedom of worship was passed in 1689, but Catholics and dissenters were still excluded from public office. Some Nonconformists consented to become communicants in the Established Church, in order to take municipal posts, and this was termed "occasional conformity." It angered the Tories, who regarded the pretense as impious.

Party frontiers became more definite. The Tories were the party of landed proprietors, the Jacobite squires, and adherents of the Anglican Church. The Whig party was made up of three elements: aristocratic families with an anti-Jacobite tradition (such as the Cavendishes, Russells, Pelhams); City merchants, nabobs from the Indies, moneyed men, who at this time were growing rapidly richer and bought themselves seats in Parliament; and dissenters, who had hardly any link with the two former groups beyond a common fear of the Stuarts and of religious intolerance. In the time of James II the Tories had found themselves, to their despair, forced to choose between Church and King. To avoid Rome they chose The Hague. Some regretted it, and dreamed of an impossible restoration. On the other hand, under William, a curious reversal made the Whigs the most stanch supporters of the sovereign. They supported without reserve his wars against France because he undertook them as head of the Protestant princes; because opposition to Louis XIV meant opposition to the Stuart Pretender, from whom the Whigs had everything to fear; and because their City supporters, during and on account of this war, were enjoying unheard-of prosperity.

Since the early years of the seventeenth century there had existed at Amsterdam a famous bank, at which all the great merchants of Europe had their accounts, so that transfer payments could be made, although the procedure was too cumbersome and the restrictions were too many for comparison to be made with a modern bank. England was still content with private bankers having narrower resources. The goldsmiths of the Stuart period were pioneers of a new banking technique, dealing in gold, lending to the King and to private persons, and accepting deposits of precious metals in return for receipts (goldsmiths' notes), which were the first form of banknote. Even the Exchequer borrowed from the goldsmiths. During the wars against Louis XIV taxation and loans proved inadequate to cover expenses, and it was then that the Whigs invented the National Debt, the Bank of England, and speculation in stocks. "Dutch finance," sneered the Tories, who hated these new devices, politically as aids to the maintenance of Whig power, economically because State expenditure was facilitated by State borrowing, and morally because such loans increased the power of moneyed men at the expense of the country gentlemen, the backbone of the country.

The Bank of England was created only to enable William to carry on his wars. A number of capitalists raised a sum of £1,200,000, all of which was lent to the State at a rate of interest totaling £100,000 per annum. The bank established to carry out this operation undertook at the same time to open accounts for private persons, as did the Bank of Amsterdam. It had no reserves, its capital being lent to the Government, but was given the privilege of issuing paper notes up to a sum equivalent to its capital, such notes being payable in gold. The Bank was able to fulfill these obligations by means of its trading profits and annual interest paid by the government. Its notes at first roused deep distrust. Then the public were glad not to have to borrow from the goldsmiths, whose interest charges were high. The State loan of 1694 was the beginning of the National Debt. It resulted in strengthening the links which united William III with the City and the Whigs. If ever Louis XIV and the Pretender proved victorious, the loans would certainly not be repaid. Thus to the House of Orange, the Bank of England became what the spoliation of the monasteries had been to the Tudors: it allied political passions with economic interests. The founding of the Bank, the increase of large-scale business, and the close connection with Amsterdam all helped to make London the financial and commercial center of the world. England would soon challenge the productive wealth of France, with hardly a quarter of France's population. Dutch finance soon realized that it had raised up a dangerous rival.

William was no general; Massillon said of him that "he was happier instigating wars than in fighting them, and more formidable in conclave than in command." But he waged war all his life. As King of England he had to defend himself against the dethroned James II, who, with French naval support, effected a landing in Ireland and was aided by the Irish Catholics. With this Catholic army James tried to occupy the Protestant counties of Ulster, treating their people with cruelty. In 1690, at the head of an Anglo-Dutch army, William won the battle of the Boyne and drove James from the kingdom. Ireland was conquered. William would gladly have granted Ireland some measure of liberty, but here again his desire for tolerance ran counter to old and fierce prejudices. Harsh laws were passed against the religion, and even the trade, of the Irish. English manufacturers and breeders feared Irish competition; the rivalry between Irish cattle and English cattle was not the least of the obstacles to reconciliation between the two islands. The Scottish Highlands, loyal to the Scottish house of Stuart, had likewise sided with James, although the Lowlands had accepted the Revolution after 1690. It was not until 1707, under Queen Anne, that the Act of Union united the English and Scottish Parliaments; and thereafter Scotland had the right of trade with the British colonies. Her success was remarkable: Glasgow became a rival of

London, the Clyde as busy as the Thames, and Scotsmen princes in the City.

To William III, Continental problems were paramount. Elizabeth had constantly suffered from the dangerous proximity of the Spaniards in their Flemish domains. She had then supported the Dutch against Spain, and during the following century the port of Antwerp had become weakened by the rise of Amsterdam and Rotterdam. But Spain, when the eighteenth century opened, was no longer the powerful monarchy which had formerly dominated Europe. Her invincible foot soldiers had shrunk to a few thousands; her navy was a tenth of that of Philip II; her arsenals were ruined, her coffers empty. The long struggle with the Moors had left her in a regime of protracted feudalism; no middle class had grown up on her territories; amidst adult States, she remained politically adolescent. The power of Spain had been stricken, but another had risen, that of France: far more dangerous to Holland and England because now, between the mass of national forces and the Netherlands, there existed no great buffer state. It was Louis XIV's ambition to make the Rhine the frontier of France, a trustworthy and neutral boundary. The Dutch and English merchants considered that if Antwerp were held by France, who was already mistress of Europe's resources, they would be ruined. William was determined to oppose this, and accordingly pursued England's traditional policy—the defense of Flanders, mastery at sea, the formation of a league against the strongest Continental power. At first the excellent French fleet commanded by Tourville scored victories over the combined English and Dutch navies. But France was hard put to it to control both the Mediterranean and the Atlantic, the sea and the Continent. Colbert was no longer there to fit out the French navy. A fiscal system which exempted the clergy and nobility from taxation deprived Louis of the financial sinews of war. The French seamen finally succumbed at La Hogue, and Louis XIV was prepared to negotiate. At the Congress of Ryswick he showed wisdom and moderation, agreeing to renounce the Netherlands and recognize the House of Orange in England. This, he felt, was better than allowing Spain to rebuild the Empire of Charles V with English support. William III, for his part, had succeeded in restoring a Continental balance between the Empire and France. After Ryswick, in 1697, European peace seemed to be assured.

Fate raised a troubling hand, and human wisdom was diverted by the mischief of circumstance. The one outstanding danger-point was the question of the Spanish succession. The King of Spain, the half-witted Charles II, shortly afterwards died without issue (1700). Who was to succeed him? A son of the Emperor, a French prince, or the Elector of Bavaria? With the Empire straddling Spain and Italy, France would again find herself encircled. Louis XIV, anxious for peace, proposed to let Spain go to the Elector of Bavaria, to satisfy himself with Naples, the two Sicilys and Tuscany for the Dauphin, and to yield Milan to Austria. It was a reasonable solution; but "death had not signed the treaty." The Elector of Bavaria, a child of five, died; the Dauphin and the Archduke alone were left at grips; the compromise was null and void. Fresh negotiations opened between Louis XIV and William III, who were both willing to dismember Spain for the preservation of peace. The Spanish Ministers were not willing, and, believing that the most valuable, because the nearest, support for an enfeebled Spain, was that of France, secured from their dying King a testament naming the Duke of Anjou and the Duke of Berry as his successors. If these princes refused, the Austrian prince was to be substituted. This forced the hand of Louis XIV. He could no longer refuse the kingdom of Spain for his grandsons without himself restoring the Empire of Charles V. He accepted the perilous honor, sent his grandson to be Philip V to Spain, and manned the strongholds of the lower Rhineland with French garrisons alongside the Dutch (1701). William III was furious. He felt that he had been tricked, and began negotiations with the Emperor. As a reprisal, and contrary to the Peace of Ryswick, Louis recognized the exile James III as the true King of England.

Death checked William just when he was preparing, along with the Empire and Prussia, a new plan of campaign against France (1702). His wife, Mary, had died in 1694, and the Princess Anne, second daughter of James II, had become heir-apparent. She had lost all her children at an early age (the last surviving one died in 1700), and probably would have no more. Accordingly, in the last year of William's reign the important Act of Settlement had laid down the order of the royal succession. All the male heirs, being Catholics, were excluded, and it was decided that the crown should pass, after Anne, to the Electress Sophia of Hanover, granddaughter of James I, and to her descendants, provided that they were Protestants. And it is this act which still orders the succession to the English throne today.

CHAPTER II

<hr>

The Reign of Queen Anne

QUEEN ANNE had never had the same friends as her brother-in-law, William III. He had upheld the Whigs because they were untainted by Jacobitism, because they supported his policy abroad, and because they showed more tolerance in religious affairs than did their opponents. Anne was insular, narrowly Anglican, fiercely Tory. She was said to be stupid; her letters show, rather, a vein of obstinacy. It has been said that she set up three aims in her life: to be Queen, to favor the right wing of the Church, and to give her husband, Prince George of Denmark (of whom Charles II had said, "I have tried him drunk and I have tried him sober, but there is nothing in him"), posts which he was quite incapable of filling. A fourth should be added: to satisfy her favorites. In the course of her life, Anne had friendships with two women, which had many of the marks of love. The first of these passions was for Sarah Jennings, who became by marriage Lady Churchill, and then Duchess of Marlborough. ". . . Nothing ever can express how passionately I am yours," wrote Anne to Sarah; and in order to avert obsequiousness, she adopted in this correspondence the name of "Mrs. Morley," Sarah Churchill becoming "Mrs. Freeman." But Mrs. Freeman, although she accepted the shower of advantages which poured upon herself and her husband from the Queen's morbid affection, was stern in her judgment of Anne: in ordinary matters, she wrote, the Queen's conversation was in no way brilliant or witty, and in matters of moment she spoke hurriedly, and with a vexatious manner of keeping close to such advice as had been given her, showing no intelligence or judgment. During the last third of the Queen's life, Sarah Churchill's place was taken by Abigail Hill, who became Mrs., later Lady, Masham, and ruined the fortunes of the Marlboroughs.

[340]

The Reign of Queen Anne

The career of John Churchill (who became Duke of Marlborough in 1702) presents an odd blend of amoral adroitness and genius. The son of a squire, Winston Churchill, he began as a page to the Duke of York, thanks to the protection of his sister Arabella, a mistress of James II. He himself became a lover of Lady Castlemaine, Duchess of Cleveland, and accepted her gift of £5,000. This ill-gotten money was well invested, young Churchill handing it over to Lord Halifax in return for an annuity of £500. It was the foundation of a great fortune. This clever lover and prudent capitalist happened also to be a great soldier. In James II's day John Churchill had reached high military rank. During the Revolution of 1688, like most men in that difficult age, he played a double game, supporting William III but taking out counter-insurance at Saint-Germain. The accession of Queen Anne, who protected the husband through love of the wife, made him the most powerful man in the country, and his fortunes, due to favor, were consolidated by merit. Not only was Marlborough an excellent general, attentive to detail, careful of the health of his troops, but he was also the wisest and least partisan of politicians. Tory by birth and habit, he consented to work with the Whigs because they were supporting him, as they had upheld William III, against Louis XIV. The two great figures of Anne's reign, Marlborough and Godolphin (or, as they were styled, the General and the Treasurer), were experts set above party divisions, an excellent type of man, but one which partisan passion always strikes down in the end.

The Queen's first Parliament was composed of full-blooded Tories. Thereupon the General and the Treasurer found themselves driven towards the Whigs by the demands of their foreign policy. They tried to rule with mixed Ministries, but it was "mixing oil and vinegar." Political and religious controversy became as violent as they were brilliant. The new-found freedom of the Press allowed the publication of pamphlets from the pens of the foremost writers. This was the time when Steele and Addison, both Whigs, were issuing the *Tatler* and the *Spectator*, when Swift, the friend of the Tories and the High Church, wrote the *Tale of a Tub*, while Daniel Defoe voiced moderate opinion. These "paper cannon-balls," loaded with explosive prose, brought the wars of the factions into quarters hitherto unreached. Passions rose high. The blend of oil and vinegar, of Whiggery and Toryism, such as Charles II, James II, and William III had been able to impose, appeared scandalous.

Spontaneously the country was moving towards the alternation of parties which turns civil strife into a chronically benignant malady.

The War of the Spanish Succession lasted until 1713. The English objective, now as always, was to maintain the balance of power in Europe, prevent Louis XIV from uniting the forces of France and Spain, and compel him to quit Flanders and the estuary of the Rhine. France had the advantage of being in occupation of the disputed territories at the start of the war, but she was exhausted by half a century of campaigning, and, what is more, she did not hold the mastery of the sea. Furthermore, England had robbed her of two of her allies—Savoy (alienated, according to Saint-Simon, by the tortuous maneuvers of Louvois), and Portugal (after the Methuen Treaty of 1701, which gave England the friendship of the court of Lisbon, a taste for the wine of Oporto, and hereditary gout). The Allied generals, Marlborough and Prince Eugene, taking advantage of the fact that Louis XIV's armies had ventured beyond the lines fortified by Vauban, shocked conventional ideas by substituting a mobile war for a strategy of sieges. The flintlock and bayonet, in both of the opposing armies, had replaced pike and musket. Losses on both sides were severe; Marlborough overwhelmed the French at Blenheim in 1704, and then reconquered Flanders at Ramillies in 1706.

But the Whigs, although they had won the war, were unable to make the peace. To halt a campaign before victory becomes exhaustion, is difficult and demands foresight. In 1709 and after, the English might have been able to obtain a treaty which would have freed them from all fears, so far as Flanders was concerned. But they wanted more, and wished to see the King of Spain expelled from that country by his own grandfather, Louis XIV. This was an insult which rallied Frenchmen to their King. Their courage was rekindled by a noble letter which he addressed to his people. The battle of Malplaquet was not nearly so fortunate for the Allies as those which preceded it, costing the victorious side more than a third of their effectives, and Marshal de Villars retreated in such good order that pursuit was impossible. In England, public opinion began to sag. Marlborough was now trying to have himself appointed by the Queen as generalissimo for life. Such a claim alarmed Parliament. Would another victorious army produce another Cromwell? The Tories plucked up fresh courage.

The Tory reaction had several causes. Firstly, there was war weariness.

In his pamphlet, *The Conduct of the Allies,* Swift wrote that "after ten years' war with perpetual success, to tell us it is not yet possible to have a good peace, is very surprising." He attacked those who sought to impose too harsh a peace on France. "After the battle of Ramillies," he said, "the French were so discouraged with their frequent losses and so impatient for a peace, that their King was resolved to comply upon any reasonable terms. But, when his subjects were informed of our exorbitant demands, they grew jealous of his honour, and were unanimous to assist him in continuing the war at any hazard, rather than submit. This fully restored his authority; and the supplies he has received from the Spanish West Indies . . . have enabled him to pay his troops. . . . All this considered, with the circumstances of that government, where the prince is master of the lives and fortunes of so mighty a Kingdom, shows that monarch not to be so sunk in his affairs as we have imagined, and have long flattered ourselves with the hopes of."

Secondly, there was a religious incident which crystallized the latent discontent of Englishmen. Anniversaries have always provided a soil too fertile for the germination of passion. At this period England observed three dates of political significance: January 30th, the martyrdom of King Charles I, May 29th, the restoration of King Charles II, and November 5th, the Gunpowder Plot. And on November 5, 1709, a violent sermon was preached at St. Paul's Cathedral by Dr. Sacheverell, denouncing the tolerance and tepidity of the Whigs, and all liberal tendencies. Its success was prodigious: forty thousand printed copies were sold. The Whig ministry made the mistake of demanding the impeachment of the preacher, and Sacheverell became a popular hero. When Queen Anne drove out from her palace, her coach was surrounded by a crowd shouting: "God bless Your Majesty! We hope Your Majesty is for Dr. Sacheverell!" The Doctor was convicted at his trial, but Tory reaction triumphed.

In the third place, these Tory sentiments were at one with the Queen's. A bedchamber revolution coincided with the religious outburst, and Mrs. Masham supplanted the Duchess of Marlborough. The Queen chose Tory Ministers to serve her—Harley (later Lord Oxford) and St. John (later Lord Bolingbroke). Marlborough, just when he thought he had Louis XIV at his mercy, was recalled. An unforeseen event strengthened the Tory resolve to treat with France: the unexpected death of the Emperor of Austria, which threatened, in the event of Philip V's abdication, to place on the Archduke's head the crown of Spain as well as that of Austria. The balance of power was upset; Spain was in Flanders; all that England had feared for a century was coming to pass. Cynically adopting the balancing tactics which were to become the favorite, and perhaps necessary, device of her foreign policy, she abandoned and betrayed her allies, who were defeated by the French at Denain in 1712.

The Treaty of Utrecht, concluded in 1713, had to face severe Whig attacks; but it was not a bad treaty. The Emperor lost his hope of reconstituting the Empire of Charles V, and Louis XIV his hope of uniting the two crowns. In the Mediterranean, England secured two valuable bases in Gibraltar and Port Mahon. She further augmented her empire with Newfoundland and Hudson Bay, handed over by France. Unable to wrench from Spain the vast colonial domain on which England's merchants had so long cast envious eyes, she nevertheless obtained privileges therein. England was henceforth entitled to import a certain number of slaves into South America. Moreover, she could send there every year a shipload of her products, which gradually, by shifts and devices, became a whole fleet. Finally, by the Treaty of Utrecht, France bound herself to give asylum no longer to the Pretenders, James III and his son Charles Edward. This treaty marks the beginning of England's preponderance in Europe. She had enfeebled all her Continental rivals, and had acquired, for the time being at least, a mastery of the seas greater even than that of the Dutch. This small island was becoming arbiter of the world. This peace concluded at Utrecht, deemed by the Whigs too favorable to France, was the type and pattern of an English peace, flexible enough to preserve the enemy from despair, firm enough to enrich England and her commerce. In this reverse of fortune, Louis XIV showed modesty and prudence in his policy. Having sacrificed in time conquests which he could not defend, he left the frontiers of France stronger than he had found them.

To secure the approval of the House of Lords, with its Whig majority, for the Treaty of Utrecht, the Queen had to carry out a real *coup d'état* and create a dozen Tory peers—a famous precedent in the country's constitutional history. So high did political passions rise that Marlborough, the conquering general, was hooted in the streets of London. "Stop thief!" they cried after him, for he was accused of taking commissions on army contracts. He had to take refuge on the Continent. Reaction spread everywhere. Tory unbelievers stood forth as champions of the Established Church and threatened the Nonconformists with persecution. Oxford, too moderate for his party's taste, was dominated by Bolingbroke, who drafted an electoral law which would have enabled him, as he believed, to install the Tories in power forever. But he was warring against a foe more powerful than the Whigs—time was against him. Queen Anne was old, and obviously had not long to live. It would have been prudent to pay court to the future King, George of Hanover, but that was not easy for Ministers of Anne. The result was that only the Whigs made advances to Hanover, and it soon became clear that if the Queen died, the Whigs would hold power. What could Ministers do? Come to terms with James III? But the Tory squires would not have supported a Catholic King, and it was a hopeless position for legitimist Ministers to advance the claims of a lawful sovereign whom they knew would not be accepted. The end came with dramatic suddenness. The Queen, after a discussion with Oxford when she insisted on his surrendering office, had an apoplectic stroke. The two parties faced each other across her deathbed. Marlborough, over at Amiens, was recruiting soldiers to defend the Protestant cause; Bolingbroke, wielding power without having been officially invested, was planning a legitimist Ministry, declaring that within six weeks he would be ready. Ready to do what? To proclaim James III as King? None knew, as Bolingbroke never entered the Promised Land. "The Earl of Oxford was removed on Tuesday: the Queen died on Sunday," he wrote to Swift. "What a world is this! And how does Fortune banter us!"

An unknown sovereign was arriving from Hanover. Bolingbroke, whom the new King did not even consent to receive, prudently sought exile in France. Thereafter he lived in retirement, partly at Chanteloup, near Amboise, and partly in England, where before long he was allowed to return, his successors regarding him as harmless. Barred from office, he expounded his doctrine by political writings, the most famous of which, *The Patriot King,* inspired the actions of George III and the doctrines of Disraeli. In this Bolingbroke defended a renovated Toryism. He strove to free his party from ideas which had become outworn—divine right and non-resistance—but maintained that the rule of a strong King, based on wide popular support, can be more beneficial to the mass of the people than the governance of a parliamentary oligarchy. What had the great

Whigs given to the English people? A Venetian oligarchy, Dutch finance, and French enmity—so Disraeli was later to answer, rather unfairly. This was already, more or less, Bolingbroke's thesis. But even more than for his writings, which are somewhat disappointing, he was remarkable for the part he played during the eighteenth century as an intellectual link between England and France. It was at his house that Voltaire met Pope and Swift, and there that the young Frenchman learned to understand institutions to which Marlborough's victories had given a European luster.

Chapter III

The Age of Walpole

THE mediocrity of the first Hanoverian sovereigns gave them historical importance. It completed the transformation of the British monarchy into a constitutional monarchy. On the heads of these foreign Kings, the crown ceased for over a century to be the object of any fervent emotion. It was now ridiculous to speak of the divine right of kings. George I was certainly the great-grandson of James I, but at the time of his accession there were plenty of other princes who, but for the Act of Settlement of 1701, would have had a better title to the throne than he. If George reigned, it was by the free consent of the nation. There was no trace of English origins in this German princeling. If he had had to choose between the throne of England and the Electorate of Hanover, he would have preferred the latter. He was fond of his small Hanoverian capital, his small Versailles—Herrenhausen by name—his small army. But a matrimonial tragedy must have spoiled his memories of Hanover. There he had repudiated his wife, Sophia Dorothea, for adultery with the Swede Koenigsmark, who was supposed to have been strangled, and buried beneath the floor boards of the castle. Since this episode, the Princess had been a State prisoner, and George I had consoled himself with mistresses who compensated for the dullness of their wits by the vigor of their charms. Any woman could please him if she were complaisant and plump, and those who aspired to his favors amplified themselves as best they could. The people of Hanover endured them because they cost the treasury little. The harem which arrived in England with the new King caused more smiles than frowns. In the eyes of George's German retinue, England was merely a country from which riches must be extracted. Of one favorite Walpole said that she would have sold the King's honor for an additional shilling. Nobody in the royal entourage spoke English, and Latin was the only tongue by which the court and the Ministry could communicate. *"Mentiris impudentissime,"* was a cry heard in the palace corridors. It may well seem surprising that the nation consented to this farce. But it was the Whigs who made the miracle possible, because they stood in need of the Hanoverians. Without George, they would have had only a king-dom without a King; without the Whigs, George would have been merely a King without a kingdom. George I was no more than a rather ludicrous convention; but the peace of the lieges depended on the accept-ance of that convention.

At the date of his accession, George was already a man of fifty. His habits were set, his ideas fixed. Regarding home affairs in England, he was ready to trust to his English Ministers. He was only vaguely ac-quainted with the laws and constitution of his new kingdom. And as he knew no English, he soon ceased his attendance at meetings of the Cabinet Council. From this fortuitous circumstance sprang in due course a form of government destined to enjoy lasting success—that of a Cabinet respon-sible to the Commons. Before George I, the idea of Ministerial responsi-bility remained in the void, because, with the King present at the Council's deliberations, its decisions were always deemed to be his. Fre-quently, too, Ministers had been chosen by the King from both parties; and this had made collective responsibility impossible. With the Hano-verians began a long period of purely Whig Ministries. On the accession of George, the Whigs rendered the Tory party impotent by exiling Bolingbroke for some months, and by sending Oxford to the Tower for a couple of years. Then they consolidated their position in the Commons by manipulating the "rotten" boroughs and by corruption of the elec-torate. Being now sure of the Commons' support, they extended the duration of the Parliamentary mandate from three to seven years—a measure modified in 1911, when the period was shortened to five years.

The Cabinet, a body of Ministers collectively responsible to Parliament, was, like nearly all British institutions, not an *a priori* conception, but the creation of time, chance, compromise, and common sense. It was simply a group of Privy Councilors, and Ministers had no other official standing. There was no thought of creating a Prime Minister: Parliament disliked the name and the idea. But as the King, through ignorance of the lan-guage, could not preside over the Council, his place had to be taken by one of the Ministers. It happened that this Minister, Walpole, was a master of the art of governance, and his colleagues came to acknowledge his authority as a matter of course. He admitted that he derived this authority from his agreement with the existing majority in the House of Commons, and when he lost the confidence of the House, he resigned, contrary to all precedents. This withdrawal, in the King's view, was an encroachment on the prerogative of the Crown, and the other Ministers did not follow Walpole into retirement. For a good many years yet the King was able to keep in the Council Ministers who were not part of the Prime Minister's group. Not until the days of the younger Pitt did the office of Prime Minister begin to resemble its present form, and not until the twentieth century were the title and function officially recognized.

The Walpole era did not open precisely with the new reign. The Stanhope-Townshend Whig ministry successfully crushed the Jacobite rising of 1715, but two major errors led to its downfall. Firstly, with a view to insuring Whig stability in both Houses of Parliament, the Ministry proposed to limit the King's right to create new peers. This was a dangerous step, which would have made the House of Lords quite independent of the Crown and the country, blocked access to the peerage "except through a coffin," and fostered irremediable conflicts between the two Houses in the future. Walpole opposed the project and secured its defeat. Secondly, there was the great financial scandal of 1720, the South Sea Bubble, which discredited a whole generation of politicians. The South Sea Company, in 1711, had been given a monopoly of British trading with South America. Later, its directors offered to take over the whole of the National Debt in return for certain concessions and annuities. What profit could they obtain for themselves? They borrowed at a lower rate of interest than the State, proposing to give creditors of the latter, in exchange for their scrip, shares in the company at the current quotation. (These shares had risen from 121½ at the beginning of the year to about 1000 in July.) This speculative frenzy, resembling that which seized France about the same time under John Law's scheme, subsided as rapidly as it had risen. August saw the shares down to 135, and thousands were ruined. An investigation showed that Ministers, including the Chancellor of the Exchequer, had been bought. Walpole himself had speculated successfully, selling his holdings at top price, but in his speeches he had denounced the peril. And now, as happened at the end of the nineteenth century in France after the Panama scandal, a younger generation of men were suddenly forced upward into power by the folly and collapse of their elders. This happened to Walpole after the South Sea Bubble. The prudence of his speeches was praised, the propriety of his conduct envied. He became First Lord of the Treasury and Chancellor of the Exchequer, and held these offices for twenty-one years, exercising, in fact, the functions of Prime Minister.

Sir Robert Walpole was one of the greatest of English Ministers, although he fought shy of all the attributes of greatness. Son of a Norfolk squire, he had the tastes and manner of a country landowner. He opened his gamekeeper's letters before those from his colleagues. He hated books and music, but liked gay suppers and gallant company, and was capable of standing up to King George for hours on end, talking dog Latin. His cynicism made him suspicious of exalted ideas, and he laughed aloud when his adversaries spoke of their patriotism. Hating doctrines and crusades, he distrusted anyone who sought to dictate his conduct to him in accordance with the history-books, and conducted affairs of State, like a good business man, from day to day. He worked with such skill that he seemed to be idling when he was doing most. His great principle was *"quieta non movere,"* or to let sleeping dogs lie. In the loyalty of partisans he had no faith, and used to advise his young disciples "never to say *always*." He has been condemned for saying that "all men have their price," but he really said "all *these* men have their price," referring to opponents of whom it was quite true. If he governed by corruption, as Macaulay said, it was because in his age there was no possibility of governing otherwise.

Walpole never propounded plans or programs to the nation, but his common sense amounted to genius. Throughout his twenty years of power his political system was simple; a weak State, he argued, ought to shun adventures, and in order to consolidate a dynasty devoid of prestige it was his duty to play for time. He therefore sought to maintain peace by an understanding with France, to lessen taxation, to keep the Church of England apart from the Jacobites, and to keep the Tories out of power. These may not have been exalted aims, but by attaining them he gave his country several years of unmatched prosperity. It was Walpole who deprived party conflicts of their former ferocity. When at last he lost power, he let himself be overturned by men whom he might easily have sent to prison. Regarding politics skeptically and mankind with humility, he did as little harm as possible during his tenure of power, but his lack of fervor was distasteful to the young and ardent.

In international politics Walpole's pacific tendency was helped by circumstance. The Treaty of Utrecht had left none of those wounds to self-respect which call forth the futility and cruelty of revenge. The age of religious wars had passed; that of nationalistic wars had not begun. For five-and-twenty years the French Ministers, Dubois and Fleury, impelled by the fear of Spain revived by the strange Alberoni, sought alliance with England. France and England in unison have nearly always been invincible. They now maintained a comparative degree of peace. The principle of non-intervention in Europe could not be unreservedly applied by Walpole, whose sovereigns had their Hanoverian interests outside of Britain, and whose supporters at home had commercial interests in the Spanish dominions. His policy, he said, was to keep clear of all engagements as long as possible.

During the summer of 1727 George I died of an apoplectic stroke. It looked as if Walpole might fall from favor. The Prince of Wales had always been on bad terms with his father, and now, as George II, it seemed probable that he would desire a change of Ministry. But very soon the courtiers were surprised to find Sir Robert more welcome at court than ever. The new King, however, was not easy to win over. Miserly, malicious, fantastically methodical, he would wait with his watch in hand for the hour to join his mistress, because he wished to be with her at nine o'clock punctually. He had shown signs of physical courage in his earlier life, but Walpole put him down as the greatest political coward who ever wore the crown. Happily for the Minister, and for the country, George II let himself be led by Queen Caroline, who had intelligence and some culture and a stoical patience. Tirelessly, for seven or eight hours a day, she listened to the flood of words pouring from the poor King, pontificating about war or genealogy. Her sole compensation for these trials was the knowledge that she ruled the country and could uphold her dear Sir Robert. Thanks to this prop, Walpole survived. The great storm during his tenure of office was an extraordinary revolt of public opinion against the excise laws. The question was simply one concerning an excise duty to be levied on tobacco and wine. The country was as furious as if Magna Carta were being attacked. London bellowed: "No slavery! No excise! No wooden shoes!" These wooden shoes had obsessed Englishmen since the days of Sir John Fortescue. Walpole, who was completely in the right, did not deem the affair worth spilling blood for. "This dance will go no farther," he said. Whig government has been described as an oligarchy tempered by riots. Actually, the threat of rioting was enough. On the night that Walpole yielded, London was illuminated. But the Minister retained power.

After twenty years of respite, the great peacemaker at last found himself forced into war. Commercial chauvinism was increasing. Under cover of the treaty entitling England to import slaves to the Spanish colonies and to send one ship there annually, a large contraband trade had grown up. The single vessel was followed by a whole flotilla which, on the pretext of carrying supplies, replenished her with fresh merchandise. The Spanish coast guards were furious and searched all English ships. The Opposition exploited these "atrocities" to attack the inertia of Walpole, and, as they said, his passion for negotiating. A certain Captain Jenkins came to the bar of the House of Commons and told how his brig, the *Rebecca*, had been boarded by the Spaniards, who had cut off his ear, and how he had "committed his soul to God, and his cause to his country." To settle this affair Walpole reached an equitable agreement with Spain. It was denounced as dishonorable by a youthful member of Parliament named William Pitt. The truth was that the Minister's opponents were anxious for war with Spain, not without thoughts of acquiring some part of her colonies. This would be their war, Walpole told them when, in 1739, he had at last to resign himself to it, and he wished them joy of it.

This war of "Jenkins's ear," as Walpole foretold, was troublesome. The Opposition, after demanding it, refused the government the wherewithal to win it. Sir Robert, it was said, wanted an army, did not want war, and could not get peace. At last the Minister, suffering from the stone, exhausted, beaten in the Commons by the help given to the Opposition by members from Cornwall and Scotland, resigned, and went to the House of Lords with the title of Earl of Orford. His departure gave rise to a curious agitation against the office of Prime Minister. Thirty-one peers drew up a resolution setting forth that this office was not allowed for by the laws of England and was incompatible with the constitution of the country. But the "wise and excellent" minister had achieved his task. By prolonged tranquillity he had given the dynasty firm roots and enriched the country. This new wealth was throwing up new men. Avid for conquest, England was coveting an Empire. She desired no longer peace, common sense, happiness, but news of victory, lists of captured towns, triumphs, adventures. The age of Walpole was over.

With Walpole also passed two of his favorite conceptions: the homogeneous Cabinet, and the alliance with France. The Whig Ministers who succeeded him (Carteret and the Pelhams) took into their Cabinets a few Tories, in order to end "these unhappy distinctions of party." This reopened the issue (not yet finally decided after two centuries) between the totalitarian State and the parliamentary State. Carteret, for all his fine gifts, soon fell through faults of pettiness. Despising the systematic corruption practiced by Walpole, he let it be seen that only higher politics interested him, and that he would waste no time in busying himself with jobbery. Those who sought place or profit turned to men of greater leisure. Contrary to Walpole's maxims, Carteret engaged in Continental concerns. The Emperor Charles VI, by the Pragmatic Sanction, had bequeathed to his daughter Maria Theresa all his dominions (Central Europe, Belgium, Italy): a heritage which was bound to quicken covetousness. In Charles's death Frederick II of Prussia claimed Silesia for himself. By what right? By the right, it has been said, of vigorous troops, full coffers, and a greedy mind. England, unwillingly allied through her dynasty with Hanoverian interests, also plunged into this welter. Before long the seconds were involved. In May, 1745, war was declared between France and England; and the Young Pretender, Prince Charles Edward, sailed from France and landed in Scotland.

There, once more, a Stuart found the astonishing loyalty of the Highlands to his family; and once more it was proved that the Scots were the best soldiers in Britain. With 6,000 men Prince Charles was able to enter England and advance as far as Derby. With the support of an English rising, he could in his own person have restored the Stuart dynasty to the throne of England, and grave confusions would have arisen. But the episode showed the amazing indifference of the mass of the people to this dynastic issue. A few thousand Highlanders had been able to invade Britain; a small army recalled from abroad sufficed to save London, and Charles retreated. In Flanders the war turned in France's favor. Freed from the Austrian menace by the victory of Frederick of Prussia, Marshal

Saxe inflicted a resounding defeat on the English at Fontenoy in 1745. If the English had not controlled the seas, if their corsairs had not ruined French trade, and if the Protestants had not driven forth Prince Charles, Louis XV might have hoped for great things indeed. But in April, 1746, defeated at Culloden, Charles fled to France and the Highlands were at last subjugated, not without harshness. Before long regiments recruited from amongst the clansmen—such as the Black Watch—proved to be amongst the bravest and most loyal units of the British army.

Between 1740 and 1748 England and France were at war not only in Europe, but in Canada and India as well. In North America, the French were anxious to occupy the Ohio and Mississippi valleys, which would have cut off the English coastal colonies from their hinterland. In India, the two rival Companies maintained small armies, which they placed at the service of the native princes whenever they saw an opportunity of extending their territories. There two great men came into conflict, Clive and Dupleix. The Frenchman held the upper hand at first, and seized the English town of Madras, but had to restore it by the Treaty of Aix-la-Chapelle in 1748. But the peace did not prevent the rival Companies in India from continuing the struggle, under cover of helping local potentates. Clive, despite his youth and a scanty force of soldiers, won conspicuous victories over the native princes. His defense of Arcot in 1751, and his great victory at Plassy in 1757, founded a British Empire in India. His personal fortune, as well as the territory of the East India Company, was enormously aggrandized, and in India the English discovered treasures comparable to those which in bygone days the Spaniards had brought from South America. The Indian princes, to gain the goodwill of their conquerors, lavished gold and precious stones upon them, and private fortunes of Indian provenance henceforward played a leading part in English elections.

The Peace of Aix-la-Chapelle satisfied nobody. As had long been happening when an Anglo-French war ended, each party had to restore its conquests because the other held valuable stakes. To obtain withdrawal of the French troops occupying Flanders, the English Government had to abandon the island of Cape Breton which commanded Canada. In the Spanish colonies, England secured a renewal for four years of the *Asiento*, the right to import slaves, as also of the annual trading ship; but Spain reserved the right of search, a source of future complications. In Canada and in India, the Anglo-French conflicts were far from being settled. None of the great European countries accepted the existing map of the world. All the old systems of alliance were collapsing. France and Austria wondered whether their traditional enmity was justified by any real clash of interests, or whether, on the contrary, the rise of Prussia did confront them both with a formidable threat. France and England began to realize that, so long as the question of the mastery of the sea and the colonial issue remained unsettled, there could be no lasting peace between them.

CHAPTER IV

The Spirit of 1700-1750

NEVER had England's prestige in Europe been so extensive. The triumphs of her armies, the foresight of her Revolution, inspired other peoples with a desire to study her ideas and institutions. John Locke, the philosopher of the Whigs, became the master of all his European colleagues. He has been described as the theorist of the Revolution of 1688. It was his aim to oppose what he termed natural right against the Stuart theory of divine right. Whereas Hobbes, who regarded the natural state of man as brutish and dangerous, deduced from the natural evil of the species the necessity of a strong State (the "Leviathan"), Locke argued that the natural man, a reasoning creature, respects the great laws of morality. In Hobbes's view, the contract binding sovereign and subjects was imposed on the latter by their own weakness; to Locke it appeared as a contract freely entered into by free beings having the right to impose their own terms. A theologian might say that Hobbes believed in original sin, whereas Locke denied that doctrine. From Locke's optimism, in due course, would spring Rousseau's *Social Contract*, the French declaration of the Rights of Man, and the American Declaration of Independence. The rationalistic, anti-historical spirit of the eighteenth century is largely attributable to the essays and treatises of John Locke.

It may be wondered why the English townsfolk and peasantry, at a time when philosophers were teaching that men were born free, submitted so readily to the authority of a landed aristocracy who did not even possess, as their feudal predecessors did, military strength. This was due, firstly, to the fact that Englishmen regarded concrete realities as more important than abstract rights; Locke's influence was deeper in France than in England because ideas are given more credit and potency by Frenchmen. There was also the fact that England, in Locke's time, had no grave causes of discontent. Englishmen observed that their local institutions, notwithstanding inevitable hardships, were efficient and tolerable. The justice of the peace tempered the measures enacted by Parliament. He was bound to do so: for how could he have enforced them without the assent of the parishes, when his only police consisted of the village constables? His very weakness was a pledge for his relative equity. The penal laws were certainly of archaic severity; vagabonds and poachers were treated as dangerous felons. But the landowners lived on their own lands and respected an honest farmer. Competent agriculturists, the English squires worked in close contact with their cowmen and shepherds. A personal relationship was better than an administrative one. Eighteenth-century England was an oligarchy tempered by familiarity.

The merchant classes, so often humiliated on the Continent, could keep their own pride in England. Noblemen and self-made commoners minded their own concerns; their families became linked by marriage. We have already noted this revolution, the most difficult of all, but one which in England is several centuries old. The testimony of language should also be noted. "During the centuries," wrote Tocqueville, "the sense of the word 'gentleman' has completely altered in England. Even by the year 1664, when Molière wrote the line in *Tartufe, 'Et tel que l'on le voit, il est bon gentilhomme,'* it would have been impossible to translate this literally into English. If you seek another application of the science of language to that of history, trace through time and space the destiny of the word 'gentleman,' which sprang from the French *'gentilhomme.'* You will see its meaning spreading in England in proportion as social classes approximate. With successive centuries, it is used of men standing a little lower in the social scale. But in France the word *gentilhomme* always remained strictly confined to its original meaning. The word was preserved intact as serving to indicate the members of a caste, because the caste itself had been preserved, as much separated from all others as it ever was."

The squire, with his silver-buttoned coat, his wig, his hunters, his family pew where he dozed in church—the figure was an essential part of the background of English life, in the eyes even of the country folk. Not until they were in the midst of the industrial revolution did the masses transplanted to the towns cease to regard a Parliament of country gentlemen as part of the natural order. In the early eighteenth century they were gratified to see some approximation of the mode of life in the manor to that in the cottage. The squire then was a countryman, using the oaths of his rustics and drinking with them if need be; on polling-day they would insult his son, pelt him with mud, and then acclaim him. Electoral contests at this time have been described as a national sport, as popular as horseracing. The people of the countryside were not then wretched. Well fed, they lived the lives their fathers had led, and knew no other; the village was still their universe. In the towns, too, the apprentice was still regarded, in many a merchant's or artisan's home, as one of the family. "The humble classes in England," wrote a Swiss traveler, "hardly call for particular description: in most respects they seem to me part and parcel of this nation, having more or less the same enjoyments as the nobility, the merchants, and the clergy, with the same virtues and the same vices." During the second half of the century this balance was to be upset by the development of machinery and the drift into the towns.

Stability in the social organism, during the eighteenth century, was matched by stability in literary forms. The classical mode was then, as it were, a Church, having Horace and Boileau as its fathers. Like the latter, Alexander Pope, the great poet of the age, wrote his *Lutrin*—the *Dunciad* —and epistles and satires, excellent in themselves and traditional in their form. More original, and so more characteristically English, were Swift and Defoe. Steele and Addison fixed the enduring form of the English essay. And art was no less classical than letters. Grace and simplicity of line are the characteristics of Wedgwood's pottery, the furniture of Chippendale and Sheraton, the architecture of the Adam brothers. Great painters like Gainsborough, Romney, and Reynolds continue for the great noble families (such as the Spencers) the galleries of portraits begun by Holbein and Van Dyck. Handel, coming from Hanover in 1710, where he had been a *Kapellmeister*, became in England a composer of oratorios on Biblical themes, this type of work being fashionable, and *The Messiah* was first performed in Dublin in 1742. In 1741 David Garrick had made his first appearance on the stage, in *Richard the Third*; and he became not only a great actor, but a fine conversationalist, admired by Samuel Johnson. In this new Augustan age painters, musicians, writers, and politicians formed a real society of their own, forgathering in the coffee-houses or chocolate-houses, or in clubs. Some of the most famous clubs date from this time—the Kit Kat, the Beefsteak, the October clubs were all famous in their different ways. Addison depicted them, with their pleasing stiffness, in a *Spectator* essay.

In shaping the spirit of talk and molding ideas in general, the club and coffee-house performed for England the function which in France was fulfilled by the *salon*, although their flavor was less subtle. If the age had its Gainsborough-Reynolds side, it had also a Hogarth side. "The commonest pleasures of the English," wrote the Swiss traveler again, "or at least of Londoners, are wine, women, dicing—in a word, debauchery. Certainly, they seek no fine shades, so far as women and wine are concerned. These they delight to combine, but without much subtlety or appreciation; they may be said to drink simply for drinking's sake. They wish their wenches to drink likewise, and are overjoyed when they find one who can keep pace with them." Since the Methuen Treaty with Portugal, the wealthier classes had drunk port to excess. Bolingbroke, Carteret, and Walpole were all heavy drinkers, one-bottle, two-bottle, or three-bottle men, as the contemporary classification of statesmen had it. A Minister was not ashamed to come drunk into the royal presence, nor a squire to fuddle himself in his daughter's company. The common people drank gin, of which two million gallons were distilled in 1714 and five million in 1735.

Violence spread with drunkenness, all the more dangerous in the absence of a police force, and with an army reduced after the Treaty of Utrecht to 8,000 men for the whole of Great Britain. People were terrorized in the London streets by a gang of young bloods known as the Mohocks. Mounted highwaymen robbed travelers on the water-logged highways. About 1725 a certain Jack Sheppard was the talk of the town, a sort of eighteenth-century Capone, who specialized in robbing the rich in the most gentlemanly manner, and was a lavish spender. His last journey through London, from Newgate Jail to the Tyburn gallows, was like a triumphal procession. On such a bandit's life, John Gay wrote a comic opera, a parody of the Italian mode, set in Newgate Jail, the famous and successful *Beggar's Opera*. Like *The Marriage of Figaro*, it is one of those works which are famous for both their æsthetic value and their historical significance. It depicts, albeit fantastically, an immoral society, unable to master its bandits and even, with a touch of wildness, admiring them.

Gambling was another vice of the age. Play went on in all the clubs, as also amongst women. In a single night one lady lost her jewels and estate. Whist, hitherto best known amongst the clergy, became fashionable. Teachers gave lessons at a guinea each. Those who did not play cards laid wagers or speculated. Rogues preyed upon the lust for lucre, and shady financiers formed companies for the most absurd purposes. One went so far as to ask two guineas a head for a project which would only be revealed after subscription. In one day he received two hundred guineas, and bolted. This was the atmosphere which made possible the South Sea Bubble.

Drink, play, and gallantry gave rise to quarrels, and these often ended in duels. Meetings took place in all sorts of places, in ballrooms and coffee-houses, even in the corridors of theaters. The custom of killing a man for a chance remark did not completely disappear before the century ended. In 1775 "the wicked Lord Byron," in a stupid duel, killed his man, the uncle of Mary Chaworth. But after 1730 the duel was tending to vanish, through the influence of a man who left a curious mark on English ways—Richard, or "Beau," Nash. In 1705 he had become master of ceremonies at Bath, a watering-place which had enjoyed high repute since Roman times, but where visitors suffered prodigiously from ennui. Nash proceeded to enliven it. With unlimited and self-invested authority he imposed strict and sensible rules. He was the first to make English people of different classes grow used to mixing when they came to take the waters; and it was he who forbade the carrying of swords at Bath. This restriction, at first confined to Bath, later became general, which at least prevented impromptu dueling. Furthermore, Nash set the fashion of silk stockings and open shoes for men; indeed, as Goldsmith said, Nash gave a certain ease of manner and mien to a people whom foreigners generally accused of being awkward and reserved. The gentry brought their Bath polish back to London, and thus, thanks to Nash, the tone became more refined. It was easy to smile at the master of ceremonies, with his white hat and his coach-and-six; but "although ceremony is not the same as politeness, no nation ever acquired politeness without having first been ceremonious." In those pools at Bath, where men and women, with handkerchief or bouquet or snuff-box floating in front of them on wooden trays, relieved their ennui by fleeting love-affairs, the grossness of Wycherley became the wit and frivolity of Sheridan.

Throughout Europe, during the first half of the eighteenth century, men had many traits in common. Frivolity, sensuality, skepticism, and the other characteristics of societies where men are too fortunate, were all to be seen in London as they were in Paris. In 1729 Montesquieu noted: "In England there is no religion. When some one said in the House of Commons, 'I believe this is an article of faith,' every one burst out laughing." David Hume, the fashionable philosopher in two capitals, was typical of his century in his hatred of enthusiasm, and especially religious enthusiasm. His contemporary, Voltaire, in his last years, came to realize that man cannot live without enthusiasm, and that he must ceaselessly be moving "from the convulsions of anxiety to the lethargy of ennui." In England, as in France, ennui and hunger for emotion were to bring, after half a century of skeptics and egotists, the sentimental revolution of romanticism. True, skepticism itself had often masked a new mysticism. "It is chimerical," Bernard Faÿ has said, "to imagine an eighteenth century ruled by an implacable logic, the master of men's hearts and imaginations; like all other ages, this one was borne along by dreams and passions which molded the forms of intelligence and imposed their discipline upon it." Just as the doctrines of Locke, apparently so logical and reasonable, enabled the Whigs to rationalize their political fervors, so Freemasonry, which was then swiftly spreading throughout England, after the foundation of the Grand Lodge of London in 1715, provided a spiritual haven for deists who still craved for ritual and mysticism. But Freemasonry remained an aristocratic or middle-class affair; the emotional needs of the masses were better satisfied by the teachings of John Wesley, as will shortly appear.

CHAPTER V

The Elder Pitt

"As STUPID as the peace," men said in France after the Treaty of Aix-la-Chapelle; and certainly that peace had settled nothing. In the colonies the war went on. How could the governments have resisted it? In bad weather it took two months to reach New York, six to get to Calcutta. Orders from London or Paris arrived when battles were already lost or won. In India, Pondicherry stood in rivalry with Madras, Chandernagore with Calcutta. In America the French governors were striving to join up Louisiana with Canada, the Mississippi with the St. Lawrence, by coming in the rear of the British Colonies, which would thus have been encircled between the Alleghanies and the Atlantic. The rivals had come to grips in the Ohio Valley in time of peace, and the French, having driven out the English settlers, built Fort Duquesne.

Despite these victories, the position of the French in Canada was far from safe. Since the days of Charles II, who had acquired the Carolinas and the State of New York (ceded by Holland under the Treaty of Breda), the English Colonies had formed a fairly homogeneous and populous belt along the coast. They counted about 1,200,000 inhabitants, as against the bare 60,000 of French settlers in Canada. England, with her powerful merchants, was determined to hold her colonies, and to this end was prepared for sacrifices to which France would not have consented. On the other hand, the Anglo-Saxons in America were more divided than their French neighbors. These States peopled by dissenters, prickly and none too loyal, were jealous of one another; they seemed unlikely to unite for a common end, whereas the French colonists, ably administered by faithful soldiers of their King, were capable of forming large plans and carrying them into practice.

Not only were the colonists of both countries, in various quarters of the globe, fighting in defiance of peace treaties, but English squadrons at sea were stopping and attacking French ships. Two able Ministers of Marine, Rouhier and Machault, had made a new navy for France, and the English Admiralty was perturbed. Without a declaration of war, they gave chase to French vessels. The pacific Louis XV was content to dispatch diplomatic notes, a practice which, throughout the thousands of years since men have been coveting one another's property, has delighted and encouraged aggressors. Actually, since the accession of William III, a new Hundred Years' War had begun. The stake was no longer the Angevin or Anglo-French Empire, but the Empire of the world. It would inevitably belong to whichever adversary obtained mastery of the seas. Now, to devote all her strength to the refashioning of a navy, France required peace in Europe; all that England needed, on the contrary, was to have, according to her tradition, a soldier on the Continent. Time and again experience had shown that naval and colonial victories were unavailing if France could occupy Flanders, as it was then necessary, when negotiations began, to restore captured colonies in order to obtain the evacuation of Antwerp. The question remained, to choose the soldier. Up to 1748 England had poured subsidies into the coffers of Austria, but since the last war George had been an admirer of the King of Prussia, Frederick II, who was less expensive than Maria Theresa, and also a better strategist. England therefore reversed her alliances, and at the same time, partly for this reason, France shifted hers around. The traditional rivalry of the Bourbons and Hapsburgs was transformed into an alliance, to the deep perturbation of the masses in France. This Austrian alliance marked the beginning of the divorce between the French monarchy and the French people. Nor did the reversal at all affect the principles of British policy—to form a Continental coalition, provide it with money and some troops, and wage war in the colonies. But in the course of this struggle with France, England produced a statesman who would now view war in Europe as a side issue and devote the main resources of the country to the colonial struggle.

William Pitt was born in 1708. His grandfather, a Governor of Madras, had brought home a great fortune from the Indies and purchased parliamentary boroughs, including the famous Old Sarum, a constituency with virtually no electors. His grandson, a young cavalry officer, entered the

House of Commons in 1735 as member for Old Sarum, and soon made an impression on members by his dramatic, ironic, impassioned eloquence. Adversaries were awed by the gleaming eyes and the long, threatening beak of this young man. They might hate his grandiloquence, but had to admit his authority. Walpole declared that the young fellow must be tamed. But Walpole's usual methods had no hold on William Pitt, an incorruptible. One problem was dominant in his mind—the formation of an overseas empire for England's benefit. Hanover, Prussia, Austria—the Continental chessboard had little intrinsic importance to Pitt; these matters were only pawns, useful to safeguard the greater pieces, India and America. One fact above all seemed to him inadmissible—Spain's grip on the South American trade. So long as Spain had tolerated English contraband, it had been an endurable evil; but when she tried to apply the treaty terms strictly, the English merchants waxed wroth and Walpole's passivity brought about his downfall. Pitt sided against him. "When trade is at stake," he told his fellow-countrymen, "it is your last intrenchment: you must defend it or perish." Such language pleased the City. Defeated by Pitt, Walpole at once advised his successors, Henry Pelham and his brother, the Duke of Newcastle, to make room for this young man in their Ministry. "Pitt," he told them, "is thought able and formidable; try him and show him." His office was a modest one, that of paymaster-general of the army. His honesty took men by surprise. Hitherto the paymasters, having substantial sums in their keeping throughout the year, had generally pocketed the interest themselves. Pitt paid these sums into the treasury, and declined the commission which his predecessors had received on loans. For some years it looked as if he would remain in this junior post. King George II disliked the young Minister because, in his hostility to Continental engagements, he opposed any Hanoverian policy; moreover, cruel attacks of gout kept Pitt down at Bath, crippled by pain. His advent to power was made possible, and necessary, only because of grave English reverses.

Pelham was no less anxious for peace than Walpole. His brother and Minister for Foreign Affairs, the Duke of Newcastle, was the prince of Parliamentary corruptors, and the worst of all geographers (he was so surprised on finding that Cape Breton was an island that he went off and told the King). He sent barrels of beer, with his compliments, to Madame de Pompadour, but the piracies of English seamen belied these lands of Brittany themselves were in British hands. Choiseul saw that he must now come to terms.

If Pitt had remained in power, he would have imposed a harsh peace indeed upon France. England's history, he said, would not again be stained by a fresh Treaty of Utrecht. But George II died in 1760, and his throne was taken (Frederick, Prince of Wales, having died in 1751) by his grandson, George III, a young man of twenty-two. Opposed to foreign adventuring because he wished to push forward a new policy at home, the new King immediately wanted the war to end, and showed scant patience with Pitt's omnipotence. In 1761 Pitt was ready to declare war on Spain, who had just concluded a pact of mutual aid with France; he urged that an end must be made of the House of Bourbon, and that Spain was a harmless adversary because her resources came from her colonies, from which the English fleet would cut her off. Not only Spain, but the world at large, would learn how dangerously presumptuous it was to seek to dictate terms to Britain. With a hundred and fifty ships of the line, in a world where no other great navy existed, Pitt felt prepared to claim a colonial monopoly. But the Council was nervous, the King did not support Pitt, and the country was beginning to think that if England appropriated too much territory, she would soon have a whole Continental coalition against her. Pitt's colleagues declined to collaborate in his new war plans, and when he threatened to resign, one of them answered that this would cause no distress, as if he did not, they would have to leave him.

And in October Pitt did resign. The King appointed in his stead Lord Bute, a favorite of his, reputed by gossip to have been the lover of his mother, the Princess of Wales. The Peace of Paris, signed in 1763, gave England Canada, Saint Vincent, Dominica, Tobago, and Senegal; France undertook to evacuate Hanover and Prussia, and—a painful condition —to dismantle Dunkirk. England restored to France Belle-Isle, Guadeloupe, Martinique, Marie-Galante, Saint Lucia, the French trading-stations in India, Saint-Pierre and Miquelon, and likewise the Newfoundland fishing rights. Spain, for ceding Florida to England, was given Louisiana by France as compensation. The King of Prussia, being no longer useful, was thrown over. It was a harsh settlement for France, but less so than Pitt would have desired, his wish being to keep all the colonies, both Spanish and French. He came himself to Parliament and protested against the terms granted by his successor. Propped up on crutches, walking with the help of servants, his legs wrapped in flannel and his hands in thick gloves, he spoke for three hours, despite acute pain, claiming for his country a monopoly of world trade, preaching hatred of the House of Bourbon, proclaiming the imminent greatness of the House of Brandenburg. A tragic, magnificent scene; but a vain speech, as the treaty was ratified. "And now," said the Princess of Wales, "my son is King of England."

The case of Pitt is one where the firm resolve of one man seems to have altered the stream of history. What would have happened without him? One English historian has envisaged Dupleix consolidating France's empire in India, Montcalm extending French control across to the Mississippi, and France becoming the mother-country of the United States. In 1755 these developments seemed probable. By 1761 they were impossible. Pitt had passed across the arena. But the achievements of great men are lasting only inasmuch as they have made allowance for the main currents. England, in the eighteenth century had more opportunity than France for gaining the mastery of the seas, and so a colonial empire. And this for several reasons. First, as an insular power, freed by the sea from having to maintain a great army, she could spend more on her fleet than could the Continental powers. Second, her acquired form of government allowed her, with impunity, to raise far higher taxes on the rich and influential than the Continental monarchies commanded: English Parliaments voted with hardly a murmur the huge subsidies asked for by Pitt, whilst the non-elected Parliaments of France were refusing to abolish the fiscal immunity of the privileged orders. Third, the merchant classes, well knowing the value to themselves of India and the colonies, gave Wolfe and Clive the support of their votes, their cash, their admiration, whereas mercantile interests were held of scant account by the ruling classes in France. Sooner or later, even if Pitt had not existed, these deeper causes would have produced their effects.

Europe had undergone a period of Spanish predominance, then one of French. With the Seven Years' War began a period with England paramount. But this burst of splendor was soon to be overshadowed. Intoxicated with triumph, Englishmen became more overbearing than ever. In their pride, they did not fear making enemies simultaneously of France and Spain and Austria. Meanwhile France, though stripped, was still a great power. A day might come when she would crave for vengeance on those whom Choiseul called "the tyrants of the sea."

CHAPTER VI

George III and the American Colonies

"BORN and brought up in this country, I glory in the name of Britain. . . ." From these words and facts George III expected to enjoy a popularity such as his ancestors had never known. "Britain," he said rather than "England," not to hurt the feelings of the Scots; but in appearance, manners, speech and character he was English. To him, Hanover was only a family memory. It was said that he could not even find the Electorate on the map. But whereas the first two Georges, foreign and rather comical kings, enjoyed straightforward reigns, the third, a man more worthy of respect, put a severe strain on the monarchy itself. Brought up by his father, Frederick, and then by his mother, to despise his nerveless grandfather, he had been well primed with the Bolingbroke doctrines of *The Patriot King*. Why should he obey the orders of a Cabinet, of a few great families, of a Parliament, none of them representative of the people? No: his duty was to champion his subjects against oligarchies. "On him the eyes of a whole people are fixed, filled with admiration and glowing with affection."

Such ideas, inciting the King to restore personal power, exposed him to grave conflicts with Parliament. But George III thought that, if the Whigs had dominated the House of Commons by purchasing seats and votes, he could play the same game equally well. He therefore strove to create a party of "the King's Friends," hoping to be aided in this by the new frame of mind amongst the Tories. The squires and clergy had abandoned their Jacobite leanings since the startling defeat of Prince Charles. Instead of remaining loyal, as some of them had done since 1688, to an outworn code of ideas, and giving way to a handful of Whig grandees with moneyed interests behind them, the Tories were eager now to become a part of the Government. The King might advantageously have used Toryism in this new guise to oppose the Whigs, who were becoming divided after too long a monopoly of power. But his temperament ruined his chances. "Farmer George" was an honest man, a good husband, thrifty and chaste; but he was both vain and vindictive. What he did not forget he did not forgive, he used to say; and he had a precious good memory. At his accession, the war which was heightening the prestige of Pitt was not favored by George. England had one Patriot King: a William, not a George. And such was George's hatred of William Pitt that soon he would have accepted defeat abroad if it could have brought him victory at home. In his first speech he proposed to refer to "this bloody and expensive war," and it needed all Pitt's authority to induce the King to say merely "just and expensive."

Determined to choose his own Ministers, George tried to foist on a country which adored Pitt, the unpractical Lord Bute. Hooted by the London crowd, who were doubly vexed because their idol was subordinated to a newcomer—and that newcomer a Scotsman—Bute soon lost heart. Londoners burned tartan bonnets and other Scottish emblems in their bonfires, and the Minister, thoroughly alarmed, resigned. His successor, Grenville, was treated no better by the public. He deplored the public loans necessitated by the war and asked the House where he would find the money; and the terrible Pitt rose in his place, mimicking Grenville's plaintive voice and murmuring the refrain of a fashionable ditty: "Gentle shepherd, tell me where . . ." The nickname of the "Gentle Shepherd" clung to Grenville for the rest of his days. One member of the House of Commons, John Wilkes, a brilliant and witty pamphleteer, criticized the Speech from the Throne of 1763 in number 45 of his publication, the *North Briton*. By the King's command he was arrested, by means of an open warrant against "any person" responsible for the publication. This arrest was contrary to Parliamentary privilege. The courts of justice upheld Wilkes, and condemned the Secretary of State to a fine of £800. London was illuminated and houses showed forth the gleaming figure "45." George II learned, like the Stuarts before him, the necessity for even the most Patriot King to respect the traditional liberties of Englishmen.

Graver events were set in motion in the Colonies through the defense of these liberties. In America the original thirteen "plantations" now had a population of three million, a people prosperous and jealous of their independence, who had gradually obliged the royal governors to leave real power to the local Assemblies. The several stages of this conflict were very much what they had been in England, and the assemblies won because they held the purse-strings. But during the Seven Years' War these Colonies had had to defend themselves against French Canada. The troops and money necessary for this war had been provided by London; and when it was over, a permanent force had to be maintained in America to guard against a possible rising of French Canadians. Grenville proposed that one-third of the upkeep charges of this small army should be raised in the Colonies by a stamp duty. The project did not seem outrageously unjust, but the Americans, like all taxpayers, hated taxes, and found support against this one even in London. "No taxation without representation" had been one of England's political maxims since the Middle Ages; and the Colonies were not represented at Westminster. True, many of the large English towns themselves had no members there; but at least it could be argued that the county members covered all "interests" within their constituencies, whereas the few active spokesmen for colonial interests were unofficial, and indeed owed their seats to English electors.

The Colonies' point of view had other arguments in its favor. They had contributed to the prosperity of English commerce; they had been exploited according to mercantile principles, that is to say, in the interests of the mother-country. The doctrine of the mercantile system required, firstly, that a Colony should import and export all merchandise in English ships; secondly, that Colonial commerce pass through English ports, even if the Colonists themselves should receive better prices in France or Holland; thirdly, that the Colonies should be forbidden to build factories capable of competing with those of England. Pitt himself had threatened that if America made one strand of wool, or one horseshoe, he would fill her towns with soldiers. To estimate the real contribution of the Colonies to the revenues of England, it was therefore necessary to add, over and above the direct taxes voted by the Assemblies, the profits of English manufacturers and merchants, themselves taxable.

The mercantile system might be endured, if absolutely necessary, by the Colonies in the South, where the Colonists grew tobacco and other products which England would buy from them; they would thus obtain the gold which would enable them, in turn, to acquire the manufactured products sent out to them from England. But to the Colonists in the North, whose products were not adjuncts to, but rivals of, England's, this state of affairs was intolerable. Here lay the direct cause of the War of American Independence. Englishmen had hitherto regarded a colony as an investment yielding immediate returns for capital. The idea of empire, they had not yet conceived. Now, the conquest of Canada could hardly be lucrative. Pitt had acquired this territory in despite of the mean-spirited who were "capable of selling anything they can, even truth and conscience, in the name of commerce." The mercantilists could not even imagine a colony which, far from being a source of revenue, would involve England in actual expenditure; and they proceeded to make the older Colonies pay part of the cost of this new empire. The said Colonies were quite willing to share in the advantages of empire, but not at their own expense. A duty imposed on molasses annoyed the distillers who sold rum to the Indians. And then the Stamp Act drew into the fiscal coffers the small stores of gold possessed by the Colonies, and made their commerce almost impossible.

Early in 1766 Pitt intervened. Since his retirement he had lived at Bath, helpless with gout. Although he could not walk without crutches, use a fork at table, or even write legibly, he appeared in the House to advocate the suppression of this taxation. In his opinion, England had no right to tax the Colonies. "The gentleman tells us America is obstinate," he said; "America is almost in open rebellion. I rejoice that America has resisted. Three millions of people so dead to all the feelings of liberty, as voluntarily to let themselves be made slaves, would have been fit instruments to make slaves of all the rest. . . . In such a cause even your success would be hazardous. America, if she fell, would fall like the strong man Samson. . . . The Americans have not acted in all things with prudence and temper. The Americans have been wronged. They have been driven to madness by injustice. Will you punish them for the madness which you have occasioned?" The Act was annulled, and George III reluctantly had to offer Pitt the Ministry. When the crippled statesman entered the royal presence, he was once again the most powerful, and the most idolized, man in the country. But popular favor can be lost by one mistake, one gesture, one word. Pitt was almost out of his mind with physical pain; he left the House of Commons and

George the III, King of Great Britain, &c. &c.

GEORGE III

An engraving from a portrait by J. Meyer.

JOHN WESLEY

An engraving from a portrait by J. Jackson.

was made Earl of Chatham. When it became known that he had accepted the Ministry, illuminations were prepared in London; when the word went round that Pitt was going to the House of Lords, they were canceled. It was foolish to style Pitt a traitor. To go from the Lower House to the Upper was no crime; but for the Great Commoner it was a mistake. Perhaps Chatham could have overcome opposition and regained his popularity if he had not been an exhausted man; but disease made him a nervous wreck and he became unapproachable. The King himself sent emissaries; but they found merely a madman brandishing a crutch. An obstinate King, a headless Ministry, a paralyzed leader—such was the Government of England for several months.

Lord North, who in 1770 agreed, as Prime Minister, to mask the personal rule of George III, had the cynicism of Walpole, but not his shrewdness or vigor. In the matter of the Colonies George III made a practical concession by suppressing the Stamp Act; but to safeguard the principle involved, he maintained certain small duties on secondary articles, such as glass and tea. This showed little understanding of the Colonists. Many of them had inherited the strong dissenting spirit of their forefathers, and the principle was precisely what they could not admit. In the end, by a majority of one, Lord North's Cabinet decided to retain one tax only, that on tea. And for the paltry sum of £16,000 Britain lost an empire. When the Americans refused to buy tea on which duty had to be paid, orders were given to the East India Company to ship a cargo of tea to Boston. The matter might still have been settled if only this tea had been intrusted to the ordinary merchants. But the Company sought direct sales to the consumer, and thus upset the traders as much as it annoyed the free-born tea-drinkers. Warned by sympathizers in London, a number of protesting Americans, disguised as Indians, boarded the ship and pitched the tea-chests into Boston Harbor. This act of rebellion led to hostilities. The Colonists bound themselves, like the Presbyterians of old, by a solemn covenant. But they were far from being unanimous. Out of 700,000 men of military age, only one in eight enrolled to fight. In no battle did George Washington have more than 20,000 men behind him. The aristocracy of Virginia, the common folk, and the middle classes stood out for resistance; but the well-to-do farmers and the more solid men of the liberal professions remained loyalists.

The most experienced heads believed that the Colonists would soon be put down. They had no fortified towns, no trained regiments, no ships of war, no credit. Neither in financial nor in military resources were they a match for England; and besides, if they forfeited the protection of England, they would be exposed to attack by the other maritime powers. The Americans, it was officially believed, were a weak people who would

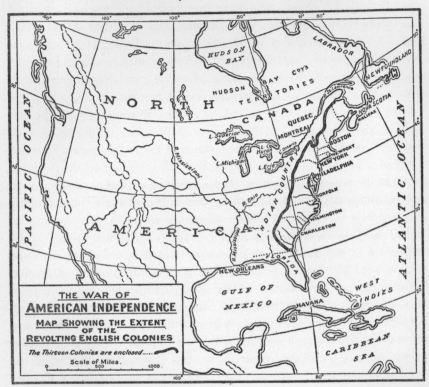

require the protection of maritime power for several centuries to come. And perhaps, in spite of Washington's genius, they would indeed have been defeated if they had not been supported by France, who was delighted to find this opening for revenge and was carried along by a current of public enthusiasm. This intervention was folly on the part of the French monarchy: it completed the ruin of the royal finances, provided Frenchmen in general with the picture of a republic triumphant, and taught them a vocabulary of democracy. In England, the whole nature of the dispute was altered by French intervention. The dying Pitt felt his hatred of the House of Bourbon revived, and came down to

Westminster to deliver the most dramatic speech of history. All in vain. The French fleets, reorganized by Choiseul, ruled the seas. Their admirals won victory after victory, and the military triumph of the Americans was determined by the naval battle of Chesapeake Bay.

When Lord North learned of Lord Cornwallis's capitulation at Yorktown, he flinched like a man struck by a bullet. "It is all over," he said. English public opinion suffered a reaction and desired the independence of the Colonies to be recognized. Parliament itself, although filled with the King's servitors, abandoned him. In 1780, John Dunning secured a majority in the House of Commons for a motion declaring that "the influence of the Crown has increased, is increasing, and ought to be diminished." George III's attempt at personal rule was ending in disaster. Ireland was heading for revolt, and had to be appeased by the grant of complete legislative independence to the Parliament in Dublin, although it was a strangely formed body, Catholics being excluded and sixty seats being in the hands of three families. In England itself, the growing towns were protesting against the archaic electoral system of the boroughs, and their consequent lack of Parliamentary representation. The collapse of military efforts in America led to a gradual decline of Lord North's majority in the Commons. At length, in March, 1782, he felt obliged to resign, though much against the King's inclination. The King had perforce to summon his enemies the Whigs, whose leaders were Rockingham, Edmund Burke, Shelburne, and Charles James Fox, Lord Holland's younger son. Fox, a man of gifts, widely read and a fine orator, a delightful and generous friend, had also faults and vices which always prevented him from ever holding supreme power. His cynical father deliberately turned him into a libertine and gambler, which made him distasteful to the sober George III. So zealous was his support of the American and the Irish insurgents that he virtually desired the defeat of his own country at their hands. Always crippled by debts and always rich in friends, turning from the gaming-tables at Brooks's to Theocritus or Virgil, he was loved, but not trusted. Through him and Shelburne was negotiated the peace which ended this disastrous war.

Month after month it had gone on with shifting fortunes. Spain, Holland, and even Russia had taken a hand against England; but in Rodney England found a great admiral, and notwithstanding a siege by French and Spanish ships in conjunction, she was able to save Gibraltar. The

Peace of Versailles in 1783 nevertheless gave France her full revenge for the Treaty of Paris, and inflicted a humiliating peace upon England. She acknowledged the independence of the American Colonies, restored Minorca to Spain, and St. Pierre, Miquelon, St. Lucia, Tobago, and Senegal to France. "The sun of England's glory has set," said young William Pitt, the son of Chatham. To many intelligent men it looked as if England's day were indeed over. At home things seemed to be breaking up; the Parliamentary system was becoming tyrannical, corrupt, nerveless; personal rule had led to defeat. The triumphant England of 1815 was then quite unpredictable.

The immediate results of the American war were serious. In the first place, England conceived a deep and destructive hatred for the French monarchy, and in preparing the ground for the French Revolution, English money was to play a large part. Secondly, the two great Anglo-Saxon democracies were sundered, and for a considerable time remained at enmity. Many historians regard this course of events as beneficent, arguing that it would have been beyond human power to govern such large masses at such great distances. True, but it is possible to envisage the United States as a member of a British Commonwealth, and exercising a preponderant influence therein: a solution which might possibly have been more favorable to the settled peace of the Old World. And thirdly, England's trade with the newly formed United States, instead of waning, waxed greater, after the Treaty of Versailles; and many English merchants began to wonder whether the possession of a colonial empire was in fact desirable. Another result of the loss of America was that India, which had been saved during the war by Warren Hastings, became a vital center of English trade.

The defeats suffered by England in America probably saved her constitutional monarchy. If the King and his friends had succeeded, personal rule would have been maintained, and this would have led, as it did in France, to a revolutionary conflict. But military reverses brought about the downfall of Lord North, and thereafter England had no other Ministries responsible to the king alone. Cabinets were to rise and fall at the will of the majority in the Commons. A Fox-North alliance, with no moral basis, was short-lived. The younger Pitt, second son of the Earl of Chatham, who had shown at the age of twenty-one the full stature of his great father, lent his prestige to Parliamentary government. Molded from boyhood by his father, he made so brilliant a start in the

House of Commons that the highest posts were at once within his reach. In contrast with Fox, and in spite of his youth, Pitt seemed a prodigy of dignity and prudence. He had inherited his father's impeccable honor and irresistible force of character. Numerous sinecures were his for the asking, but he remained a man of modest means. When the King, in defiance of the Whigs, made Pitt Prime Minister at the age of twenty-four, the prestige of the head of the Government soon outstripped that of the sovereign. For over twenty years on end Pitt was to rule England; and into political life he introduced a new and valuable quality—that of purity.

Had it not been for the memory of the elder Pitt, this accession of a stripling to power might have been impossible. But his personal virtues would have sufficed to justify it. At twenty-four he showed the wisdom of maturity. He made the Tories into a genuine party, independent of the Crown, with its own electoral funds, its own boroughs, its own program of peace, retrenchment, and reform. He restored to the office of Prime Minister the power and status which Walpole had given it. He strove to deprive the Whigs of the support of the moneyed men. He fought against corruption, and controlled the rising tide of national debt by the creation of a sinking-fund. His Budgets are still cited as models of ingenuity. But his attempts to reform the electoral system were less successful. The House of Commons was obviously no longer representative of the country, and Pitt proposed a moderate scheme of reform. He wished to allot seventy-two seats to London and the larger counties, these seats being obtained by abolishing the "rotten" boroughs which had mere handfuls of electors. But too many vested interests were affected, and Pitt was rebuffed. Hitherto he had ruled without a majority. In the election of 1784, partly owing to the money of the Anglo-Indian nabobs, he defeated Fox and his friends, who fell by the dozen and were referred to as "Fox's martyrs." Pitt's opponents believed that they were totally undone, when King George III showed clear symptoms of insanity; and when the sovereign began to mistake a tree at Windsor for the King of Prussia, a Regent had to be appointed. The Prince of Wales favored Fox as against Pitt. But happily for the latter, the King's madness was intermittent; and the sovereign was already on the way back to normal health when an event took place which has been described as the most important in the history of eighteenth-century England—the capture of the Bastille.

CHAPTER VII

The French Revolution and Napoleon

HOWEVER great their wisdom, statesmen are less the rulers of events than ruled by them. Pitt, like his father, was to become a great war Minister, but he desired nothing so much as peace. A first-rate financier, he was more concerned with his Budgets than his armed forces. The opening years of his Ministry were years of commercial prosperity for England: between 1784 and 1793 exports rose from ten to eighteen million pounds; in 1783 the three-per-cents stood at 74, in 1792 at over 96. During this same period Pitt had tried to impose a generous policy on his Tory friends. If he could have had his own way, the Catholics and Nonconformists would have been emancipated from the outmoded clauses of the Test Act. He obtained some partial relief for these classes, but seeking to go farther, he came into collision with the Anglican bishops. When he united England and Ireland in 1801, thus forming the United Kingdom of Great Britain and Ireland, he would again have been ready to grant emancipation to the Irish Catholics and entitle them to sit at Westminster; but, unfortunately, he could not convince either his sovereign or his party, and in defiance of all justice and prudence a Protestant minority continued to represent Ireland. But a state of mind hostile to any reforms had been created in Parliament by the anti-Jacobin reaction.

The French Revolution, in its earlier stages, was hard for Englishmen to understand. They did not anticipate its violence because they knew little or nothing of its nature and causes. England had not herself engendered those intense enmities between the landed gentry and the peasantry, between court circles and the merchant classes, which had been produced in France by the watertight barriers of caste. Inequality there was in plenty, but a career was open to talent and laws were binding on

every class of citizen. Between 1789 and 1792 Englishmen honestly believed that the French were on the way to achieving, with no undue
disturbance, institutions roughly analogous to those of Great Britain. When
Fox heard of the capture of the Bastille, he greeted the event as the most
important and happy one in the world's history; and many thinkers
and writers believed likewise. Even Pitt at first refused to side with the
crowned heads of Europe against the Revolution. On the contrary, there
is a likelihood that he favored it. His feeling, like that of Tory England
in general in 1789, was that a rival power was, fortunately, going to be
weakened by internal dissension, and would emerge from the fever re-
generated. Burke believed, and wrote, that for a long time to come the
martial faculties of France would be stifled. This was a few months before Valmy, a few years before Bonaparte. In 1792 Pitt reduced the
British navy to an establishment of two thousand men, and said: "Un-
questionably there never was a time in the history of this country when,
from the situation in Europe, we might more reasonably expect fifteen
years of peace than at the present moment." Prophecies endanger prophets.

The execution of Louis XVI and the occupation of the Netherlands
by France changed this benevolent optimism into open enmity. When the
Terror began, all the sympathies of the ruling classes in England were
with the fallen monarchy, and so with the European powers attacking
the Revolution. The only sympathizers with Revolutionary France were
some radical republicans, such as Tom Paine, and a small body of advanced Whigs grouped round Fox, Sheridan, and Grey. Burke himself
was by now showing feelings of hatred for the French Revolution which
at times seemed like an obsession. This attitude on the part of the ruling
classes may perhaps be explained by horror and fear. But on the part
of the people at large it is surprising. Why was the contagion of revolutionary ideas so slow in reaching the English working-people, rural or
urban?

The explanation of this phenomenon should not be sought in the contentment of the English nation, which had indeed been gravely affected
at the close of the eighteenth century by an agricultural and industrial
revolution. It had various causes. Firstly, as we have already shown,
landlords and peasants in England were linked by certain approxima-
tions in the mode of life. In France, the landlord had preserved his
privileges but lost his functions. As Tocqueville said, "he no longer

[379]

ruled, but his presence in the parish prevented the establishment of a sound system of parochial government which might replace him." The English rustic was perhaps poorer than the French peasant; he certainly believed that he was more free. In the second place, France was England's hereditary enemy: every idea emanating from France seemed suspect, any invective against France found an answering echo in Englishmen's hearts. Thirdly, the very nature of the "principles of '89" was distasteful to the English spirit. In the French Assemblies, lawyers and men of letters had drawn up abstract declarations, enumerated the Rights of Man, and paraphrased Rousseau's *Social Contract*. Burke refused to enter into "metaphysical distinctions," hating, he said, their very names: "no moral question is ever an abstract question." Fourthly, the French Revolution was destroying the structure built up, through the centuries, by the monarchy, and sought to rebuild another solely with the materials provided by Reason. But essentially the English intelligence was, as it still is, based on a historic sense. Burke kept repeating, in countless forms, that man is incapable of living on his slender capital of reason, and that the individual must ask some credit of acquired wisdom from the funded reserves accumulated through the ages by countless generations of men. And finally, Englishmen had been offered a new spiritual sustenance by the religious revolution known as Methodism. The French Revolution was deistic, anti-Christian, and this feature damned it in the eyes of the middle and lower classes, "who were afraid of losing their religion," as did its violence in the eyes of the aristocrats, who were afraid of losing their lives.

After 1793 the Whig party was cleft asunder and ceased to count; a national coalition took shape round Pitt to combat the plague of subversive ideas and the militant spirit of the French Revolution. In London the French agent, Chauvelin, intrigued with the malcontents, incited the Irish to action, set up dissentient cells in the army, and worked hard to prepare an English Revolution. There was a quick reaction. The rights of foreigners in the country were limited by law; Habeas corpus was suspended; the publication of lampoons was severely punished. Every village formed its loyal associations. But Englishmen would still have refrained from declaring a war of principle, as the European monarchies had done, against the French Revolution, if the latter had not been itself so aggressive. As long as it seemed possible, Pitt declared his desire to remain a spectator and "to enjoy neutrality." His patience was clearly proved by the fact that he let Antwerp fall without making it a cause of war. When the Convention in France assured the English Revolutionary delegates that ere long France would be able to lend her aid to an English National Assembly, Pitt was still tolerant of the provocation. But when France decided to open Antwerp's river, the Scheldt, to navigation, and thus to ruin the Dutch ports, he was forced to act. Holland was safeguarded against such a threat by solemn treaty. This had been confirmed by Pitt himself in 1781, and by France in 1785. The Convention did not deny the existence of the treaty, but maintained that stern necessities overruled contracts. War with France became inevitable. Pitt solaced himself with the idea that, for reasons of finance, the campaign would be brief. It was to last for twenty years.

The general character of this great war is simple enough. To begin with, England followed her traditional policy and defended her Dutch allies, refusing to allow Antwerp and Belgium to remain in the hands of a major European power. She conquered new colonies and defended the old. In particular she waged a stern campaign in the West Indies, which cost her, through disease rather than battle, some forty thousand men, a price justifiable only by the importance then attached to the sugar-cane plantations, a great source of wealth. Then, after the figure of Napoleon began to dominate the stage, England's aim became no longer that of victory over one country or another, but the downfall of this conqueror who threatened to destroy the balance of power in Europe. For the third time in her history she battled against the strongest power on the Continent, and the struggle against Napoleon became the natural sequel to the wars against Philip II and Louis XIV.

England's methods of war were likewise unchanging. Primarily she strove for mastery of the seas. And this she secured because she had a powerful fleet, and a group of first-rate admirals—Hood, Jarvis, and Nelson—to whom the American war had given experience of sea-fighting. In contrast with the current practice in the British army, it was competence, not birth, which opened the way to high command in the navy. Collingwood was the son of a Newcastle merchant, Nelson of a country clergyman. One outstanding advantage over the Continental navies was that Kempenfelt had lately provided the fleet with his signal book, whereby an admiral was able to direct the movements of his ships even during an engagement. Mastery of the seas enabled Britain to repulse any invasion, to transport her troops wherever their presence seemed useful, and also to prevent any supplies from reaching hostile ports.

At the same time England was making full use of her other favorite weapon—subsidies to Continental coalitions. The method seems distasteful and Bonaparte spoke scornfully of "Pitt's gold." But England had only ten million inhabitants against the twenty-seven of France. Poorer in man-power, she needed sailors rather than soldiers, and it was quite natural that, for this Continental war, she should seek out mercenaries. She helped the allied States in two ways: direct gifts, and agreed loans. Both methods were in fact identical, as neither principal nor interest of these war debts was ever paid. The total of Pitt's subsidies from 1792 to 1805 amounted to ten million pounds. The increase of the national debt between 1793 and 1802 amounted to 336 million pounds, on which the Treasury received only 223 million, for the three-per-cent funds in 1797 stood at only 47. Pitt tripled all taxes, appealed for voluntary contributions, and finally established an income tax, on a very wide basis of incidence, the rate of which was about ten per cent. For this war, then, the country had once again to strain every muscle, and only its vast riches enabled it to sustain an effort in which, at certain moments, England found herself confronting the whole Continent of Europe.

The war opened badly for her. The Revolution was producing a new and strong type of army. As Wellington said in later years, the French system of conscription mustered average men of every class, whereas the British armies were composed of "the scum of the earth." At sea the French were joined by the Spaniards, and then by the Dutch; England found herself barred from the Mediterranean, and this deprived her of much of her potential pressure on the Continental powers. Permeated by the notions of equality then preached in Europe, English sailors mutinied. They had always been ill-paid, ill-fed, ill-treated. In 1797 certain crews drove away their officers and hoisted the red flag. This happened just when the Continent, after four years of war, was making peace with France. England was isolated, Ireland in revolt, the navy mutinous. Pitt was insulted in the streets of London, and had to be protected. But the situation was saved by a truly English combination of sternness and indulgence. The mutineers became victors, and in the same year the battle of Cape St. Vincent delivered Pitt from the Spanish fleet, and the battle of Camperdown from the Dutch. Could he reconquer the Mediterranean? Since losing Minorca England had had no base within the Mediterranean: whence the importance she laid on the port of Toulon, which she captured only to lose again. Bonaparte, on his way to Egypt, conquered Malta, the best naval base of that time, and thereafter felt assured that he could refashion the empire of Alexander in the East. But no overseas conquest can be retained by a power which has lost naval supremacy. Bonaparte's fleet was destroyed by Nelson at the battle of the Nile, and this victory gave to England both Malta and the East. Leaning upon Malta and his Neapolitan allies, Nelson was able to exert pressure on Austria, whose Italian possessions he threatened. Once again, mastery of the Mediterranean would enable England to form a Continental coalition.

England lorded it at sea, but Bonaparte was still invincible on land. In 1801 he conceived the idea of closing the markets of Europe to "perfidious Albion." A league of armed neutrality was formed between the Scandinavian powers, Russia, and Prussia, as a protest against the right of search which the English claimed to exercise at sea. In order to break up this league, which might deprive Britain of primary naval necessities (timber, sail-cloth, and ropes), Nelson attacked the Danish fleet. The Northern league collapsed, and the project of a blockade became chimerical. The First Consul and the Prime Minister now realized the limits of their respective powers. Peace was obligatory on both. But it was made difficult by the critical and doctrinaire attitude of England towards the French system. Only Fox appreciated the greatness of Bonaparte. The Tories viewed him merely as a sort of Corsican bandit, about whom the most grotesque legends were current. Grenville wrote insolently to Talleyrand that His Majesty's Government could have no confidence in the First Consul's peaceful assurances. This was unreasonable: if Bonaparte was not sincere in his desire for peace, the only means of proving his insincerity was to accept peace. In 1801, unable to secure the King's consent to the admission of Catholics to the House of Commons, Pitt resigned office. His successor, Addington ("Pitt is to Addington, Like London to Paddington," ran a song), entered into negotiation, and in 1802 the Peace of Amiens was signed. It was a serious diplomatic defeat for England. She retained a few distant conquests, like Ceylon; but

France remained in possession of the left bank of the Rhine and of Belgium, a state of affairs which was the less tolerable to England as Bonaparte immediately began to examine ways and means of making Antwerp a naval and military base. In the Mediterranean England abandoned Minorca and promised to restore Malta to the Knights, which would again have deprived her of any base. It had been necessary to make terms, as England needed a breathing-space, however short; but whereas to Bonaparte the Peace of Amiens was "final," to Pitt it was only a truce. France's acquisition of Louisiana, the expedition to San Domingo, and the alliance with Holland finally brought English irritation to a head.

In point of fact, nobody observed the Peace of Amiens. England kept Malta; Bonaparte, despite his promise to respect the *status quo* in Europe, became head of the Republic of Italy, annexed Piedmont, imposed his protectorate on Switzerland, and took the chief part in the reshaping of Germany. The *Moniteur* published an ominous report on a "trade mission" under Colonel Sebastiani to the East, from which the English learned that the First Consul was renouncing neither Egypt nor India, and their resolve to keep Malta, treaties notwithstanding, was correspondingly strengthened. After an ultimatum from Addington in 1803 hostilities were resumed. This time Bonaparte, planning to strike at England itself, assembled at Boulogne an invading force of 400,000 men, and fitted out a flotilla of flat-bottomed boats to convey this army across the Channel. Like the Duke of Parma with his Armada, and like Choiseul in more recent times, he would have needed, for success, to have his transports shielded for at least a few hours by a squadron. But the French and Spanish fleets were blockaded in the ports of Toulon, Rochefort, Brest, and Cadiz, by Nelson, Cornwallis, and Collingwood. There they remained helpless until the summer of 1805, unable to obey the orders of the Emperor (as he had now become) to effect a concentration. In October, when Napoleon had abandoned his projected invasion of England and was forcing the Austrian general Mack to capitulate at Ulm, the defeat of the Franco-Spanish fleet at Trafalgar—the last great battle of sailing-ships—in which Nelson died, gave England for a full century the uncontested mastery of the world's seas. Two years later, in time of peace, the Danish fleet was seized at Copenhagen by the English, who thus completed the ruin of Europe's maritime forces.

After Trafalgar, and throughout the nineteenth century, the idea of attacking the British fleet was to appear an absurdity to all heads of States, and to Napoleon himself. But if the naval superiority of the mother-country was an essential and sufficing condition for the stability of colonial empires, that superiority was not in itself enough to resolve Continental problems. At Trafalgar Napoleon lost his colonies, and all hope of getting control of the sea-route to India; but he was nevertheless master of Europe. In vain did Pitt, in power again, conjure up coalition

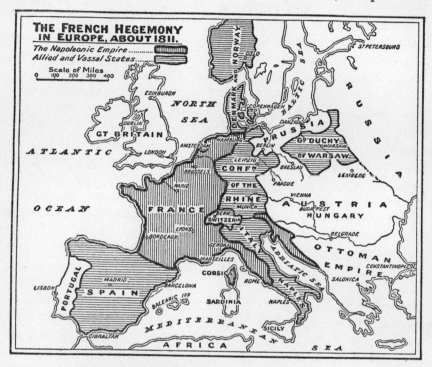

after coalition. After Austerlitz he had to recognize his powerlessness. It was then that he pointed to a map of Europe and said: "Roll up that map: it will not be wanted these ten years!" He died in 1806, worn out and broken-hearted, murmuring (it was said): "O my country! How I leave my country!"

In this great duel Pitt had won at sea, the Emperor on land. Master of Austria and Prussia, allied with Russia, Napoleon now sought to strike at England's naval and commercial power by indirect means, and forbade the Continental ports to admit any English ships. To this Berlin

Decree which opened the Continental blockade, England retorted with orders-in-council, stopping all sea-borne traffic which did not pass through her own ports, even trade with the United States of America. On both sides these measures caused much hardship. They brought about a war between Britain and the United States in 1812. As Europe could not dispense with English products, smuggling became universal, and was so profitable that severe penalties failed to check it. The Emperor himself had to resort to fraud in order to provide cloaks for his Grande Armée. Such Continental industries as cotton, which depended on imported raw materials, were ruined, to the enrichment of their English rivals. England, on the other hand, went through a grave industrial and commercial crisis. Europe, deprived of products to which she had become accustomed (such as sugar and tobacco), tried to produce them from her own soil. Beet sugar supplanted the cane sugar of the West Indian plantations, to the grave detriment of the latter. In 1810-11 there was serious unemployment in England, with menacing riots. If the Tsar Alexander of Russia had not broken the Continental blockade in 1811, England might perhaps have yielded.

But the Continental blockade brought about the downfall of Napoleon because it forced him, for all his anxiety for peace, to carry the war on and on. Having tried to bend Spain to his will, he found there a country of guerillas, "where either a large army starved or a small one was beaten." British troops landed in Portugal—a country very useful to England as a landing-stage in Europe; led by Wellesley (later the Duke of Wellington), they forced the French to concentrate. Whenever Soult or Suchet turned his back on a Spanish province in order to face Wellington, that province revolted. The Emperor's marshals succeeded in driving Wellington behind the fortified lines of Torres Vedras; but he was able to make use of circumstance, and by the creation of an extended field of fire, he put up a successful resistance along these lines. Wellington's tactics were defensive. The mass of his troops held a covered position; only the skirmishing riflemen, in advanced positions awaited the enemy columns. In 1813 Spain was lost to Napoleon. Meanwhile he had had to attack Russia, who was refusing to maintain the blockade. And there he lost the flower of his troops. Backed by English subsidies, Russia, Prussia, and Austria, after the battle of Leipzig in October, 1813, pushed Napoleon back into France; and there, notwithstanding the amazing victories of the campaign on French territory, he had to abdicate, in 1814. Whilst the Allies debated the fate of France at the Congress of Vienna, Napoleon, who had not been sent farther away than the island of Elba, returned, expelled the Bourbons without a struggle, and marched on Brussels. Wellington, with a small army of combined British and German troops, defeated him at Waterloo in 1815. Wellington's "thin red line" had checked the columns of the Emperor, and the charges of Ney had been shattered on his squares.

Waterloo broke the armed Revolution. Although Napoleon had married an archduchess, his "good brothers the Emperors and Kings" had never regarded him as anything but a dangerous upstart. It was the aim of the sovereigns of Russia, Austria, and Prussia, at the Congress of Vienna, to shut off with a wall of buffer states this nation which had so long intimidated them. They created a kingdom of the Netherlands (Belgium and Holland), which lasted in that form until 1830; they intrusted the safe keeping of the left bank of the Rhine to Prussia; that of the Alpine frontier to a kingdom of Piedmont and Sardinia; that of northern Italy to Austria. Talleyrand, in his efforts to set limits on French sacrifices, found an unexpected ally in the British emissary. Lord Castlereagh. Once again, to maintain the balance of power, after the triumph of a coalition inspired by herself, Britain was taking the side of the vanquished. She did not want France to be too weak, nor Russia too strong; she was not, like the Central European powers, in a state of reactionary panic; she had obtained what she wanted—the Cape of Good Hope, Malta, Ceylon; and above all, she had laid low the man who had resisted her and had tried to achieve hegemony in Europe. She could rest content. But Napoleon himself she treated with little generosity. After his second abdication he threw himself on the hospitality of "the most generous of his foes," who, however, left him, until his death on St. Helena, in a state of truly pitiable destitution. This pettiness roused the indignation of Byron, amongst many other Englishmen.

Freed now from its fears, the British Government would gladly have stood apart from European affairs. But it could not. The victorious powers had formed a league for the maintenance of the Treaty of Vienna and of the principles of legitimacy; and England, rather grudgingly, had to form part of the Holy Alliance. It was not long before she began to come into conflict with her partners. The achievement of the Congress of Vienna may have been more enduring than such diplomatic edifices usually are, but during the nineteenth century it crumbled away. The negotiators at Schönbrunn had made full allowance for the two ideas which seemed to them fundamental—legitimacy and European equilibrium. They had reckoned without those nationalist sentiments whose growing strength would, in thirty years' time, burst through the framework constructed in 1816.

Chapter VIII

The Agricultural and Industrial Revolution

THE Black Death of the fourteenth century, by abruptly reducing the population of England by one-third, had favored the emancipation of the serf peasantry and the division of landed property. In the second half of the eighteenth century a sudden increase of population caused the development known as the inclosures. About 1700 the inhabitants of England were estimated at about five and a half million; the figure rose slowly up to about 1750; and then suddenly, during the reign of George III, it doubled itself, until in 1821 it reached fourteen million. The causes of this increase were numerous. Parochial aid was granted to large families. The rapid development of industrial manufacture provided employment for children and encouraged the poor to multiply. The drift of rural workers into the towns pushed them into unduly small and overcrowded houses, which weakened the traditional sense of decency and restraint. And while the birth rate rose, the progress of medical knowledge diminished the death rate, and in time ended the vast epidemics which obliterated hundreds and thousands at one stroke. Mothers and infants were better cared for at the time of confinement. Hospitals were opened in most towns. A larger population needed more food. And thus came the need for increasing both the yield and area of cultivated land, and securing assured profits for landowners.

The great landlords, unfortunately, were alone to reap the profit from this agricultural prosperity. Every government favors certain economic interests. Under the Tudors the great merchants had prospered; under Cromwell, the shopkeepers and Puritan artisans; under Charles II, the dominance of the country gentlemen to whom he owed his restoration. The eighteenth-century Parliaments were composed of great landlords and squires, and the laws which they enacted often bore hardly on the country folk. Farmers holding long leases were often supplanted by tenants liable to eviction at six months' notice. All local rates were raised. To become a member of Parliament or a magistrate, to hold rank in the local militia, to obtain shooting rights, a man had to be richer than ever. The old popular institutions of the parish were replaced by the more aristocratic ones of the county. At the time of the French Revolution the justices of the peace became harsher. And finally the great landlords were even tempted to use their political and administrative power to expand their own estates, in which they succeeded the more easily because their personal interests seemed here to coincide with the national weal.

The cultivation of the common fields, still numerous and extensive in 1750, was certainly a very primitive method of husbandry. One neglectful worker could spoil the work of the rest by not killing his weeds. The peasant spent his life in moving from one strip to another. The use of marl or manure was difficult because the workers of such small strips of land lacked the capital to buy these products. Yet meanwhile, in Holland and France, scientific agriculture was coming to birth, and its principles were being spread in England by such men as Jethro Tull and Lord Townshend. The latter, leaving political life, himself became a skilled agriculturist. Instead of leaving his fields fallow every three years, he alternated tap-roots (turnips or beet) with cereals and sanfoin or clover, thus preparing supplies of winter fodder for livestock. The small farmers were skeptical: it was all very well, they grumbled, for a gentleman to sow clover, but how were they to pay their rents? But they were wrong, and the most productive method won in the long run. Coke of Norfolk, a famous agriculturist whose model estate attracted visitors from all over Europe, succeeded by skillful use of fertilizers in growing wheat on land hitherto sterile. Bakewell improved the breeds of cattle, goats, and sheep. Realizing that the demand for meat would increase with a growing population, he tried to rear herds of fat stock instead of the long-legged cattle which had been practical when the land was marshy and brambly. These experiments diverted an age avid for science and novelty. Throughout the eighteenth century farming and stock-breeding were fashionable. Self-made men invested in landed property. Doctors, clergymen, and lawyers became farmers whenever they had leisure, and

Arthur Young commented that the farmer tribe was now composed of all classes, from dukes to apprentices.

At the beginning of the eighteenth century vast areas were still common land or open heath. Under George III landlords became more and more eager to inclose their fields; and in the process they acquired for their own use much of the peasants' plowland and great stretches of commons, grazing and waste, as well. Their instrument was the private act of Parliament. There were no fewer than 3554 such inclosure acts during the King's reign, and about four million acres were thus made available for the new methods of farming. To obtain such measures from Parliament only needed the agreement of three-quarters of the landowners in a parish. But the three-quarters was reckoned by superficial area, not by the number of individual owners, so that in many parishes the squire by himself formed a majority. For decency's sake he joined with a few of the larger proprietors to lay his proposal before Parliament, and the common folk often discovered that their common lands had ceased to exist without their being consulted. These inclosures made possible the formation of large farms with lands joined up, the adoption of scientific methods, and increased productivity. England became one of the grain-producing countries of Europe. But the small peasantry suffered severely from this spoliation. The disappearance of the commons deprived them of the strip of meadow where they could graze a cow, or of the belt of wood where their pigs grubbed acorns, and where they themselves had always found their firewood. They lost heart in their toil, and drifted into idleness or drunkenness, or into the North Country towns where the swift growth of industry was causing a demand for workers. Then the excellent Elizabethan law was abrogated which forbade the building of a cottage without at least four acres of land; and this opened the way for the growth of those clusters of slum hovels which disgraced the large towns of England even into the twentieth century.

At a different period the yeoman would have resisted and clung to his soil. But besides the towns, the colonies were luring him. Between 1740 and 1763 England had acquired the greater part of France's colonial domains. Canada, sparsely populated, and the prosperous American colonies, offered a refuge to the bolder farmers. Those who stayed at home entered the service of the landlords. In 1821 William Cobbett observed that all over the country he could find one farm only where three had been before. In 1826 he noted, in one village, that fourteen had been displaced by one. The very name of yeoman began to be forgotten. Three centuries earlier it had meant both the tenant-farmer and the independent owner, whereas now these classes were both known as farmers, and the whole class was coming to be dependent on the gentry. Dependence soon led to imitation. The big farmer of the 1820's was no longer simply the leader of his workers, but a well-to-do man who wished to live a gentleman's life. And when the farmers become gentlemen, cried Cobbett, their laborers become slaves. During the Napoleonic wars the high prices of produce still permitted the survival of such of the small farmers as had been able to keep their land. Waterloo was their death blow, and England then witnessed the almost total disappearance of that rural middle class which had so long been her military and moral backbone.

The agricultural laborer himself, in the early part of the nineteenth century, was in dire plight. Wages had risen more slowly than prices. Formerly every village, and almost every house, had been able to live a self-supporting life. With the growth of large-scale industry the village craftsmen disappeared. Before long farmers were refusing, not only to give, but even to sell, grain to their laborers. The divorce between production and producers created an abstract economics totally unknown to the Middle Ages, and fostered the growth of the most hideous poverty. The best of the country magistrates tried hard to remedy the situation by a more liberal administration of the Poor Laws, but their good intentions led to formidable consequences. In 1794 a number of justices of the peace, meeting at Speenhamland, decided to fix a sum to be taken as the vital minimum necessary for a family. It was to be the equivalent of twenty-six pounds of bread weekly for every adult man, with thirteen allowed for a wife and each child. If the father's wage did not reach this minimum, it was to be made up by a grant provided by the poor-rate in each parish. The immediate results of this were deplorable: landlords and farmers found laborers willing to work for a very low wage because this would be made up by the parish, and the small farmer, employing only his own family, was ruined by this indigent labor which, as a ratepayer, he had himself to support. The Speenhamland system, charitably conceived, resulted in transforming the rural population of what had once been Merry England, into a mass of wretches fed, and ill-fed, by public charity.

Big-scale manufacture developed side by side with big-scale farming.

The industrial revolution was not, like a political revolution, a sequence of events compressed into a fairly short time, but the transformation, slow at first but gathering speed between 1760 and 1815, of the whole economic system. With the disappearance of the guild system had begun the development of capitalism, or the exploitation of collective labor by a man of business. This tendency towards large undertakings was accelerated during the eighteenth century by the increased number of consumers in England, and by the opening up of new markets, especially in the American Colonies, and by mechanical inventions. In the textile industry the invention of the mechanical shuttle (1733) increased the productivity of the weavers and the demand for thread. Hitherto wool had been spun at home by the weaver's wife and daughters; but now, to meet the increased requirements of the weavers, Hargreaves, Arkwright, and Crompton succeeded in bringing into simultaneous action ten, and then a hundred, spindles, controlled by a single workman with the help of piecers. Spinning thus became faster in output than weaving, and the invention of power-looms met this new need. Then the steam-engine supplanted the power supplied by men or water, and coal-mines became the essential wealth of the country. France might have been England's fortunate rival in this conquest of markets, but was held back at the critical moment by her internal customs system, by lack of coal (in 1845 France was producing only five million tons as against England's thirty-five million), and by being deprived of cotton through the Napoleonic wars and the Continental blockade. The new cotton industry became exclusively English. In 1784 England was using four million pounds of cotton, in 1833, three hundred million. The substitution of coal for charcoal in ironfounding led to the shift of the great English factories from the wooded south to the coal-bearing north.

All these developments in town and country called for improved means of transport. Over large parts of England during the eighteenth century travel was only possible on horseback. The trouble was that every parish was still, as in mediæval times, responsible for its own roads, and local autonomy, useful enough in its day, was preventing the creation of a road system properly conceived by central authority. After 1760 fairly good results came from the system of turnpike roads, concessions being made to trusts which recovered their expenses by their right to extract payment from travelers using them—very much as is done on certain

[393]

motor roads on the Continent today. But little real progress in actual road construction was made until after 1815. A Scottish engineer, John McAdam, conceived the idea of laying a water-resisting surface on roadways, and, thanks to him, the speed of the stage-coaches rose from four to seven, and then to over ten, miles per hour, although these speeds were exhausting to the horses, of which very large numbers were used. In 1831, when coaching was at its heyday, about 150,000 horses were employed over some 3,000 stages. (After the 1830's, coaching declined as railways began to spread.) It was also during the closing years of the eighteenth century that the Midlands and the north were threaded by canals intended mainly for the transport of coal. Concomitantly grew up the auxiliaries of trade—banking and insurance. Edward Lloyd's coffee-house in London, towards the end of the seventeenth century, was frequented by a group of men willing to insure shipowners against maritime risks. The institution thus begun came to be the greatest society of underwriters in the world; but with the usual English conservatism it retained for generations the name of Lloyd's Coffee House—and is still Lloyd's.

The industrial revolution prepared and necessitated a political revolution. Liverpool, with 4,000 inhabitants in 1685, had over 40,000 in 1760, and was to reach 517,000 in 1891 and 803,000 in 1936. Manchester, from 6,000 in 1685 rose to 40,000 in 1760, 93,000 in 1801, 505,000 in 1891, and 800,000 in 1936. The political map of England no longer coincided with the map of its population. The north, formerly sparsely populated, Jacobite and Catholic, was now swarming with radical miners and mill-workers. The growth of large industries created two new classes: the rich manufacturers whose fortune, matching the expansion of new markets, was comparable to that of the great landed proprietors and who insisted on having their share of influence; and the urban working class, very different from the old village craftsmen, more accessible to agitators because it was concentrated, and more ready to claim political power because it was conscious of its strength. Between these "Two Nations" (as Disraeli later named them) the current system of political economy raised a doctrinal barrier.

Every great social change finds its own theorists, who attribute transitory results to permanent causes. The theorist of the industrial revolution was Adam Smith. Inspired by the French physiocrats, this Glasgow professor wrote a book, *The Wealth of Nations,* which became the economists' Bible for over a century. In it he expounded the doctrines of *laissez-faire*, free competition, and trust in the spontaneous currents of economics. In the eyes of Smith and his followers, a benevolent Deity had so ordered the world that the free play of natural laws insured the greatest happiness of the greatest number. This freedom might possibly cause temporary hardships, but a balance would in time be automatically restored. The theory soothed the consciences of the wealthy by representing poverty and unemployment as natural and heaven-sent counterweights. This had not been the view of the Middle Ages, which held a closely corporative view, nor was it that of the mercantilists of the seventeenth century. The latter believed that a State's prosperity was measured by the positive balance of its foreign trade, and that the State should constantly intervene to protect the trade balance (a doctrine which lost England her American Colonies). But in the nineteenth century these views were discredited; economic liberalism triumphed because it accorded with the temper of an age of expansion when all new producers were finding markets. It became dangerous as soon as the markets of labor, or of production, reached saturation point. Free competition then engendered disastrous evils, and England, like the rest of the Western World, was to see the beginnings of a protectionist reaction, holding views of State and autarchic authority which would have astounded François Quesnay or Adam Smith.

CHAPTER IX

The Sentimental Revolution

"THE eighteenth-century mind was a unity, an order; it was finished, and it was simple. All literature and art that really belong to the eighteenth century are the language of a little society of men and women who moved within one set of ideas; who understood each other . . . who lived in comfort, and, above, all, in composure. The classics were their freemasonry." As was shown elsewhere, this description, quite commonly accepted, portrays only the surface of ideas and morals. It is improbable that human minds were untroubled by any agonizing problems. Although Gibbon and Johnson were authentic figures of the eighteenth century, their deeper passions were violent; actually, they strove to justify these passions by rational explanations and to give their ideas a classical form. But the intellectual equilibrium then sought by the wisest of the aristocracy and upper middle classes, as well as by men of letters, could not satisfy the much more numerous classes whose economic balance was overturned by the agricultural and industrial revolutions; they needed a religious or a political faith in order to escape from an intolerable actuality.

The Anglican Church itself was too rational to satisfy the ardor or anguish of men's souls. The eighteenth-century theologians tried hard to show that reason and religion did not clash. Providence willed it that Christian morality should be the most certain path of temporal salvation. William Paley (1743-1801), so dear to Shelley's father and to so many souls eager for simple soothing certainties, was typical of these optimist philosophers who proved the existence of God as by a geometrical theorem. The Church of England at this time became a class Church. Nearly all its bishops belonged to aristocratic families, Whig or Tory, and reflected the party in power. The lesser clergy held their livings from the

Crown or from the local squire. Out of 11,000 livings, 5,700 were in the hands of patrons, who naturally gave them to men of their own social circle and often enough to members of their own family, sons or nephews or cousins. To take holy orders the Anglican cleric did not need to pass through a specifically theological college. An ordinary Oxford or Cambridge degree sufficed. Their culture, so far as they had one, was as much classical as Christian. They were gentlemen, with the tastes and failings, and the virtues, too, of their class. The fox-hunting parson shocked nobody. Frequently, he was a justice of the peace and sat on the magistrates' bench with his kinsmen. The religious structure of the country thus doubled and amplified the political. In both, the main element was formed by the landowning class, and the Church of England thus became linked with the local authority of the ruling classes, but lost most of its contact with the common people. Many wealthy rectors of parishes were not resident, and were even pluralists, holding several livings and leaving their parochial duties to ill-paid vicars. In 1812, out of 11,000 parish clergy, 6,000 were non-resident. The vicar himself did his best to live a gentleman's life and please the squire.

If the kindly and reasonable religion of eighteenth-century Anglicanism harmonized excellently with the more fortunate part of the nation, it brought no spiritual nourishment to the town toilers or country laborers, soured and perturbed as they were by dire want. The profound changes gave rise to a sense of injustice and instability. Wounded and unhappy souls starved on logical proofs of an abstract God. In days gone by the dissenting or Nonconformist sects had held sway among the populace with their more equalitarian teachings. But in the early eighteenth century the older of these denominations—Presbyterians, Independents, and Catholics—had themselves grown humdrum. Persecution quickens faith; tolerance drugs it. Although there were still laws against the dissenters, they were scarcely enforced. "Occasional conformity" was all that was needed for them to take part in official activities. The Calvinist doctrine of predestination, the stern religion which had so deeply imbued the Scots, became attenuated in England, the land of compromise. The country still had some violent and convinced Calvinists, but these, being certain that they were the Lord's elect, did not proselytize.

Possibility lies near to necessity. The middle classes and the poor contained countless souls craving for a more ardent religion, and as neither

Anglicans nor dissenters could satisfy their need, a man was bound to appear who would give these great masses what they wanted. His name was John Wesley. As a young man at Oxford he had been a latitudinarian, regarding faith as a reasoned consent. But such teaching did not fully satisfy the fervor of his spirit. Does reason, he wondered, ever cease to reason? How shall a man be certain of having at last found truth and salvation? Cannot one feel grace? And must not grace be sought with more fervor? There was some surprise in Oxford in 1726 when a few young men founded a Holy Club, whose members fasted, prayed, visited the poor, preached in the open air, and confessed their sins to one another. Wesley and his friends were ridiculed, and dubbed "Methodists." The nickname was to become the name of a Church which today counts millions of adherents. In vain did Wesley's father, a Church of England rector, implore his son to renounce these follies and succeed him in his parish. John Wesley felt called to a higher mission—that of converting a listless world to Christianity.

For several years he led a life of intense activity. He first went off with his brother to the American Colonies. The narrative of his misfortunes gives glimpses of a violent, sensuous nature. His zeal in converting young women had in it something of the most genuine religious fervor, and something also of physical desire, perhaps unknown to himself. The Christians in the Colonies did not like this aggressive religion, with its fiercely personal preachers. Wesley had to return to England rebuffed, without having yet found his true path. He had gone to America to convert the Indians, he said, but who would convert himself? On board ship he came into contact for the first time with members of a German sect, the Moravian Brotherhood, and fancied he might find amongst them what he sought. He went to visit the Moravian communities in Germany, but felt their faith to be too genial. Wesley's soul needed a hotter flame. On May 24, 1738, in a moment of illumination, he saw the true faith, a living link and not a working of reason. From that day he had but one object in life—to bring men into that state of spiritual trance and total communion with God.

Thereafter began a life of preaching. With his friend George White-field, he preached in the fields, in barns, in working-class districts. Wesley alone preached 40,000 sermons and traversed 250,000 miles. At first he was often received with hostility by the crowds; but soon the news spread of the astonishing conversions which he wrought. His physical influence was extraordinary. Men and women trembled, swooned, and revived infused with the Holy Ghost. Wesley himself, traveling in all weathers and with little sleep, at last tamed an all-too-human temperament by a mode of life which would have killed most men. How did he view his mission? He would have liked to remain within the Church of England and infuse it with new vigor. He believed himself to be completely an Anglican, fulfilling his duty rather better than other men. But the rational, aristocratic bishops of the time could only eye with scornful annoyance these open-air meetings and neurotic crowds. They closed their churches to Wesley, and refused to endorse his preaching or to ordain his preachers. It was only in the last years that Wesley, despairing of making his peace with the Established Church, resigned himself to ordaining his own ministers, and so, against his own inclination, founded the dissenting sect of Wesleyan Methodists, which, by 1810, could already show some 230,000 adherents.

The Methodist influence on the religious life of the English people was far-reaching. To thousands of men and women, and to those who most intensely needed it, religion once more became a living thing, in an almost primitive form. Like the early Puritans, these first Methodists condemned the tolerant, self-indulgent philosophy of the age. They helped to maintain the sabbatarian tradition. In opposition to an emotional force which threatened their own, they delayed the emancipation of Catholics in England. Inside the Church of England, the "evangelical" influence permeated the whole of the Low Church party, whose clergy, like Wesley's preachers, made their appeal to the common people. The dissenting sects were startled by the headway made by the Wesleyans, abandoned their traditional Puritan anarchy, and formed church organizations. All religion became more emotional. And as this awakening absorbed the vital forces of the suffering lower classes, they were less tempted by revolutionary doctrines than the populace of the Continent. Want and inequality were accepted, for a time at least, as scourges of divine origin, to be counterbalanced by inner happiness and salvation. At the close of the eighteenth century the aristocratic and upper classes in England may have been cynical, dissolute, and often atheistic, but the common people revered the Holy Bible.

The revolution in sentiment, however, was not only religious. In England as in France, the eighteenth century began with the cultivation of a refined but artificial civilization, and then, discovering the complexity of man and the power of sentiment, craved for a return to nature. Whilst Fielding observed human beings as a great classic novelist, Richardson, like Rousseau, strove to depict their anxieties and passions. Goldsmith, and then Sterne, made fashionable a gentle, calm sensibility, "a constant tremolo," a new humanitarianism. Scott, rather later, gave his readers an escape into the past. Urbane verse was succeeded by a personal, mystical poetry. Cowper, Wordsworth, Blake, and Coleridge prepared and proclaimed romanticism. They were already romantics, as there were no definite boundaries between these aspects of the age, and Dr. Johnson was still a young man when Richardson published *Pamela.* The outbreak of the French Revolution shocked political philosophers like Burke, but it deeply moved some of the greatest of England's poets. Shelley defended its principles, and when Byron learned of Wellington's victory at Waterloo, he wrote, "Well, I am damned sorry for it." The youth of both countries craved a sort of rejuvenation. The youth of France remolded a whole society by their deeds and Europe by their wars, and this transformation in a world of fact allowed them to dispense with literary forms of escape. In England, on the other hand, the young felt the oppression of a society whose framework had been tightened up by the dread of Jacobinism. They fled into the world of fancy: fled also in fact, and Italy became a rallying-ground for the great rebels of English romanticism. Chesterton pointed out that the close of the eighteenth century, which in revolutionary France produced the classical paintings of Boilly and David, was in England the period of Blake's transcendental visions, that Coleridge and Keats would certainly have shocked Danton, and that if the Committee of Public Safety had not beheaded Shelley as an aristocrat, they would have locked him up as a lunatic. No period gives a better idea of the "compensatory" character of artistic activity. One of these two countries made a political, the other an æsthetic, revolution.

The various revolutions of the eighteenth century, industrial, political, and sentimental, are reflected in the mirror of the English language. Between 1700 and 1750, according to Pearsall Smith, there emerged the words "banking," "bankruptcy," "bulls and bears"; after 1750, "consols," "finance," "bonus," "capitalist." The word "ministry" dates from Queen Anne, "budget" from George II. From the French Revolution England acquired such words as "aristocrat," "democrat," "royalism," "terrorism," "conscription," "guillotine." The "London season," the "club," the "magazine," the "Press" are eighteenth-century words. "Interesting" first appears in its present sense in Sterne's "Sentimental Journey" (1768), almost simultaneously with "boring." The vocabulary thus shows man becoming more aware of his own emotions; and this applies likewise to the word "sentimental" itself, which came to birth in England in the middle of the century, to be adopted immediately by the French, together with the mood that it indicated.

CHAPTER X

Conclusion

THERE are many resemblances between England and France in the eighteenth century. In both countries a cynical freedom of morals was blended with a cult of sensibility. But the temperaments of both peoples, molded by climate and history, remained profoundly different. It would be hard to imagine, in the France of the 1760's, a figure like Dr. Johnson, a vigorously reactionary Tory, proclaiming his love of hierarchies and hatred of liberty, and yet being the friend of Burke, sitting down with Wilkes, and admiring Fox. The Protestant Puritan, a rare and uninfluential type in France, is still one of the most important elements in the composition of England. His religion colors the ideas of all classes, even of those which in other countries are the least religious. Compare the life of an Adrienne Lecouvreur or a Sophie Arnould with that of a Mrs. Siddons, a great actress who was virtuous, respected, and always rather solemn. If England seemed to have turned cynical under Charles II and in the intoxication of the Restoration, her evangelistic side resumed its sway in the time of the Regent, notwithstanding the extravagances of a few dandies. It is curious to observe in the dying Byron the symbolic triumph of an hereditary Calvinism, rooted deep in the soul, over a quite intellectual synicism.

Three important characteristics of the period between the Revolution of 1688 and the battle of Waterloo may be noted. First: the change from monarchic rule, under which Parliament had only a legislative part, to an oligarchic Government in which Parliament, contrary to Montesquieu's belief, was also the source of executive power. That change took place because of the invention (or rather, the spontaneous engendering) of a Cabinet responsible to both Houses, which made possible the peaceful alternation of parties in power. Second: the struggle with France, aimed primarily at preventing a Continental hegemony inimical to England, whether controlled by Louis XIV or by Napoleon, aiming also at securing for England the mastery of the seas, and resulting indirectly in the almost unintentional formation of a new colonial empire. Third: the agricultural and industrial revolution within the country, which by at once ruining the small landholders and accumulating a huge wage-earning class in the towns, made a political revolution inevitable. As Pollard has pointed out, every economic regime has a corresponding political one. The pastoral economy produces a family or tribal form of government; a primitive agricultural economy implies a feudal system, as the scattered tillers of the soil require protection; the age of merchants is the age of plutocracy, and the age of industry, during the nineteenth century at least, was to be that of democracy.

Power in eighteenth-century England had belonged to a mixed class, consisting of the aristocracy descended from a defunct feudalism and of a new plutocracy. This class itself had split into the two great parties. In 1800 or thereabouts, out of the 658 members of the House of Commons, 487 were virtually nominated by that class. As we saw, this system of governance was accepted because those who wielded power kept in contact with the rural classes, because local institutions to some extent mitigated its injustices, and because this privileged order was open to talent, or at least to success. The system, highly unjust though it became, had the advantage of making the authority of Parliament accepted by the ruling class. And if Parliament, even when it became democratized during the nineteenth century, never had to face hostile prejudice from the ruling class, this was because during the eighteenth century they had become used to regarding Parliament as their own preserve. That is one reason, perhaps the most important, for the success in England of the Parliamentary system, which elsewhere failed for lack of such roots. But this aristocratic monopoly could not hope to survive when the industrial revolution, by massing the workers in the towns, compressed within narrow limits immense forces which had to find an open safety-valve, and if not, would have blown up the existing system. The House of Commons squires had neither life nor ideas in common with the workmen of Leeds or Birmingham. What could "the parish," in its true sense, mean to a slum-dweller? The population of England had doubled in sixty years, and the younger generations who peopled the great towns about 1815 had never known that rural life which created and explained the country's constitution. It was only natural that these generations should grow restive, irritable, and insistent on reform.

These feelings were all the more keenly felt because the fears roused by the French Revolution were making the aristocracy less inclined to compromise. The militant, contagious aspects of the Revolution awakened resentment in England which was slow to die down. The wars which it provoked upset the normal development of the country. The towns were growing up at a time when the Government's absorption let the principle of hygiene in their building go by default. Every period of change and invention at first involves much distress, but this intolerable misery of the poor could have been in great measure avoided, especially in the country districts. Discontent ran high. The monarchy itself lost prestige. Even on the morrow of the victories of 1814 the Regent was hooted in the London streets. But national loyalty upheld the Tories against "Boney"; and after Waterloo the peace gave freedom to men's consciences and the pent-up grievances of five-and-twenty years broke out into open disturbances.

The Government was powerless to resist popular pressure. True, it had the greatest navy in the world, but a navy cannot maintain domestic order. After the war the army was largely disbanded, and what remained was quite insufficient to occupy a whole country. The yeomanry were unresponsive, and the voluntary constables declined to be sworn in. The magistrates were thus disarmed. But England, it will be seen, nevertheless escaped the vain and bloody shocks of revolution and reaction. She owed this immunity to three forces: firstly, the power of opinion, which through the Press, the jury system, and the workers' associations, imposed the necessary reforms on an oligarchic Parliament; secondly, the existence in the Whig party (thanks to the enduring influence of Charles James Fox) of a liberal element proud enough of the privileges of birth to hold political privileges of less account; and thirdly, the currents of evangelism, which made for a gentler morality and diverted men's passions into other courses. The independence of the judiciary, the lofty liberalism of the Whigs, and a measure of Christian charity, all helped the country to traverse the most difficult tract in its history without civil warfare.

Book VII

FROM ARISTOCRACY TO DEMOCRACY

CHAPTER I

A Post-War Age

A LONG war, even if victorious, is naturally followed after the brief relaxation of triumph by a period of discontent and confusion. A people which has made great sacrifices for victory expects great rewards. But, almost inevitably, the upsetting of the artificial equilibrium attained during war brings about an economic crisis which speedily becomes political in character. The years 1816 to 1821 were dark ones in England. After the peace, prices fell. Wheat, which had gone as high as 120 shillings per quarter, dropped to under 60 shillings. The fall meant ruin to farmers who had supposed these high prices to be everlasting and tied themselves by onerous leases; and of these there were great numbers, only a tenth of the land belonging to small landowners since the time of the inclosures. Squires and farmers called out for reduced taxation. The Chancellor of the Exchequer had to drop the income tax and fall back on loans. When a bad harvest suddenly sent wheat up to 103 shillings, it was the turn of the working class to protest. The manufacturers accused the Government of forcing them to raise wages by a policy of "dear bread." In factories and manor-houses alike, prosperity was dead. There were no more military orders. It had been supposed that the production of the new machinery would be absorbed by the Continent, but the Continent, worn out by years of war, refused English goods. Quarter-of-a-million demobilized soldiers were vainly seeking work. As always happens in a period of rapid and many-sided invention, machinery was robbing men of their employment. The infuriated handweavers smashed the mechanical looms, and sometimes even fired the factories. Want and unemployment forced the poor-rate up from five to nine million pounds sterling. Were these the boons of a long-awaited peace?

The interests of manufactory and manor-house seemed to be contradictory; but when popular agitation became violent, when the ricks blazed up after the mills, landowners and manufacturers were reconciled by alarm. Not being electors, the work-people in the towns and the laborers in the countryside were becoming rioters. None of their defenders had any chance of being elected to Parliament. Only freeholders having land of forty shillings value voted in the counties, and the list of parliamentary boroughs had not been revised since Tudor times, so that large towns of recent growth remained without representation. In such a plight, on whom could the townsmen count? Hardly on the King. Since 1810 the aged George III had been blind and insane. True, his madness, by making him the most constitutional of monarchs, had at last made him unreservedly popular. But in practice the throne was occupied by his son, the Prince Regent (later George IV), for whom the English had little or no respect. Prince George was neither bad nor foolish; he patronized the arts, appreciated Jane Austen, upheld Byron and Scott, made Sheridan one of his best friends, sat for Lawrence, and sent £200 to Beethoven. He was to some extent responsible for the planning of Regent Street and Regent's Park; he rebuilt Buckingham Palace, and restored Windsor Castle. His polished manners made him, if not "the First Gentleman of Europe," at any rate the prince among his own dandies. But he was selfish and petty, and in an age of prudent virtue his debauchery made him unpopular. Having secretly married the Catholic Mrs. Fitzherbert before his official marriage with Caroline of Brunswick, from whom he separated after a year to return to his morganatic spouse, he deceived two wives; not even through bigamy could he escape libertinism. Failing the intercession of a sovereign, could the people have intrusted their cause to Ministers? A Tory Cabinet was in power, hostile to reform, of whom it might have been said, as of Metternich, that if they had been present at the creation of the world, they would have beseeched God to preserve Chaos. And what of the Opposition? The great Whig Lords had not yet made alliance with the reformers. There remained only rebellion, the oldest and most undeniable right of Englishmen, a weapon all the more formidable as England had no great police system, and as the rapid growth of the cities had not allowed the local authorities to acquire experience of the mob. When Chateaubriand spoke to the Prime Minister, Lord Liverpool, about the solidity of English institutions, the latter replied: "What solidity is there with these huge towns? One serious rising in London, and all is lost."

Towards rebellion the people were being pushed by several radical groups. Some, like Henry Hunt, advised them to claim universal suffrage; others, like Sir Francis Burdett and Major Cartwright, to demand a vote for every payer of direct taxes. William Cobbett, a man of yeoman birth who had been made a radical by his observation of the sorry lot of the English peasantry since the inclosures, published a small journal, strongly reformist, the *Political Register*, written in admirably pungent style. There grew up various "Hampden Clubs," and, in imitation of the methods which had served Wesley so well, the country was traversed by numerous political preachers. Their meetings, together with the violence of the machine-wreckers and the symptoms of similar destructive outbursts, startled the Ministry. The French Revolution was not yet a thing of the distant past. When the propertied classes beheld Henry Hunt at his meetings, preceded by one man bearing a Phrygian cap on a pike and another upholding the green-blue-and-red banner of the future British Republic, they trembled. Fear is always cruel: the rebellious workmen and rustics went to the gallows or to Botany Bay.

How was order to be maintained in the towns? In many counties the justices of the peace fell back on the soldiery. The Horse-guards were sent out into the country districts; and blood flowed more than once. The most serious of these massacres was that near Manchester in 1819, when the troops fired on the crowd, leaving eleven dead and numerous wounded. From the place of meeting, St. Peter's Square, the Government's victory was ironically known as "Peterloo." After this it was decided by Lord Sidmouth's famous Six Acts, to prohibit any assembly aiming at exercises of military character, to give justices of the peace the right to seize weapons dangerous to public safety and arrest their holders, and to circumscribe the freedom of public meeting and of the press. A plot to assassinate Ministers, the so-called Cato Street Conspiracy, fostered by government police spies, brought matters to a violent head in both camps. The wealthy called for military rule and counted on the Duke of Wellington; the poor openly prepared for revolution. Five years after victory, England seemed to be on the brink of civil war.

She was saved by two unforeseeable circumstances—a scandal, and an economic recovery. The latter came, as usual, just when the economists despaired of it and were suggesting the most drastic remedies, including inflation. The scandal broke out when old George III died and was succeeded by the Regent with the title of George IV. His wife Caroline, who had for a long time been leading a rather shady life abroad, suddenly made up her mind, from vanity and in hatred of her husband, that she would be crowned Queen at his coronation. Legally she was within her rights; morally she was far from queenly. The King, highly vulnerable himself, would have been wise to avoid any moral debate. But in his determination to hold off Caroline, he showed such obstinacy and clumsiness that his Ministers sometimes wondered whether he had not inherited his father's madness with his crown. He even went so far as to engage in divorce proceedings before the House of Lords, undertaking to expose the Queen's dissolute life. London forgot electoral reforms to savor this indecency. The populace had sided with the Queen, and cheered her in the street. The testimony against her hardly affected her, as it came mostly from foreign servants. This infatuation, however, was short-lived, and the Queen herself died in 1821, to the vast relief of her husband.

Thanks to this diversion, tempers were cooled a little. The intransigent Tories had given way before some younger men in their ranks who wished to bring their party back into the reforming tradition of Pitt. Amongst these newcomers Robert Peel, Huskisson, and Canning were prominent. Peel, the son of a Lancashire manufacturer, owner of one of the largest seven fortunes in England, had been brought up, like Pitt before him, to be Prime Minister. At the age of five his father lifted him on to a table and made him recite speeches; at twenty-one he was found a seat in the House of Commons; at twenty-three, he was a Secretary of State. Worthy of respect and winning respect, he was the arbiter between the advanced wing of the party, with such men as Canning, and the resisting wing, grouped round Wellington. As Home Secretary Peel did excellent work. In particular, he abolished the death penalty for numerous crimes and offenses which did not deserve so ruthless a punishment. The incredible severity of the laws, excusable in times when a weak government had everything to fear from lawlessness, had become useless and shocking in an age of abler administration and gentler manners. Children especially had hitherto been treated by justice with a cruelty as offensive as it was unavailing. Peel reformed all this. Huskisson meanwhile was giving relief to the manufacturers by suppressing the protective tariffs on raw materials, wool and silk; he would gladly have abolished the duty on corn likewise, but in this he clashed with the numerous and vigilant country gentlemen of his party. Finally, Canning, who took charge of the Foreign Office after the suicide of Castlereagh in 1822, pursued a "liberal" policy from within a Tory Ministry. (That was a new word, brought into currency by the Spanish revolution of 1823, when the partisans of absolute monarchy were called the "serviles," and their adversaries the "liberales.") The Tories had shown some apprehension in intrusting this high office to Canning, something of a political adventurer who had often betrayed and mocked them; but he had genius, and that was what the party lacked.

The position of Castlereagh after the downfall of Napoleon had been difficult. The Continental sovereigns, perturbed by the phenomenon in so many European countries of an insurgent younger generation, consisting of half-pay subalterns, students with Byronic tendencies, and romantic conspirators, had built up the Holy Alliance to ward off a counter-attack by the French Revolution. Although England formed part of the victorious alliance, her interests were different, her fears less acute. She had been obliged to pledge herself, along with Austria, Prussia, and Russia, to resume hostilities against France if the latter restored Bonaparte or committed an aggression against her neighbors. But Castlereagh was reluctant to become a policeman for the European counter-revolution. He sought to oppose the despotic tendencies of his allies, and did not always succeed. Even Canning, when France was intrusted by the Holy Alliance with the throttling of revolution in Spain, had to let things take their course, having no army for a new Peninsular expedition. But such is the effect of reputations that Castlereagh was deemed reactionary by the public and his liberal actions were overlooked, whereas the conservative concessions of a Canning, supposedly a liberal, were forgotten. Yet Canning's hatred of the Holy Alliance was due not to its reactionary character, but to the fact that it was not English. If "England" were substituted for "Alliance," he declared, the keynote of his policy was clear.

If he failed, for lack of armed force, to protect the revolution in Madrid, he took his revenge when the Spanish colonies in South America declared their independence. Once war goes overseas, maritime supremacy makes victory certain. It was to the British fleet as much as to the moral support of President Monroe, that the South American republics owed their salvation. This episode made Canning extremely popular. It was one of those lucky cases where the commercial interests of the City coincided with the sentimental sympathies of the British public. Since the days of Drake and Elizabeth, the London merchants had chafed at their exclusion from one of the world's finest markets. The Peninsular War and the European blockade under Napoleon had enabled them to make a breach in the walls. The Minister who opened the markets wide, whilst defending the cause of liberty, satisfied both Whig doctrinaires and Lancashire cotton-spinners. Only old Tories like Wellington blamed him, the men who feared demagogy abroad as much as at home. And when Canning in 1827, despite the wrath of the Holy Alliance, gave recognition to the Greek rebels attacked by Egyptians and Turks, this Tory Ministry became the prime favorite of the liberal elements in every land. And when, after Liverpool's resignation through illness, he formed a Ministry in which Wellington and Peel declined to serve, it was the Whigs, along with some of his personal friends, who upheld him. But after attaining power in February, 1827, Canning died of dysentery in August, without having been able to show his full stature.

His death caused a bewildering situation. Since 1815, whenever an English sovereign found himself in a quandary, he thought of "the Duke." The victor of Waterloo was venerated in the Tory camp, whilst the Opposition, after long fearing that Wellington wished to set up a military dictatorship, came to see that, like most great soldiers, he held civil war in horror, and that in Parliament he was an honest, clumsy, not very dangerous adversary. The Duke feared all the fashionable reforms as much as the King did—Catholic emancipation, extension of the franchise, free trade. His ideal would have been to change nothing. But his political campaigns consisted only of retreats. As he always gave way in the end, rather than engage in battle, he became, despite himself, the best ally of liberalism. It was under his Ministry that Admiral Codrington, fulfilling old instructions from Canning without asking for new ones, destroyed the Turkish fleet at Navarino, although the Duke, in this matter, was favorably disposed to the Turks. Again, it was the Duke who accepted the abrogation of the Test and Corporations Acts, exempting dissenters from communion according to the Anglican rite as a condition of holding municipal or State offices. And he likewise it was who, having begun with the emancipation of dissenters, was brought face to face with the graver question of Catholic emancipation.

The right of Catholics to vote and sit in Parliament had been promised to the Irish at the time of the Act of Union (1800). Only the opposition of King George III, who made it a point of conscience, had prevented the promise from being kept. Thereupon the Irish had founded a league, raised funds, and chosen an eloquent leader in Daniel O'Connell. They were certainly within their rights. In England itself the younger men of both parties, tired of what seemed to be outworn quarrels, favored emancipation. But the Catholics had foes within the Cabinet, amongst whom was Peel, a member for the highly Anglican University of Oxford. For several years Ireland breathed the air of civil war; the Catholic Association and the Protestant squires of the northeast were at daggers drawn. In despite of the law, O'Connell was elected in a Parliamentary contest, and the sheriff did not dare to declare either him or his opponent a duly elected member. Wellington grasped the danger of this situation. He was not personally hostile to Catholics; civil warfare seemed to him even more undesirable than change; he advised the King to give way, and in the end, though with difficulty, convinced him. Finally the Duke's prestige overcame all resistance within his own camp, and once again he carried out a victorious retreat. Catholic emancipation was passed in 1829. After some delay O'Connell was able to sit at Westminster, and in the House of Lords the Duke of Norfolk and other Catholic peers resumed their long-lost seats. The only remaining religious inequality in England was that affecting the Jews. The first bill dealing with them was laid before Parliament in 1830, and in 1860 they obtained full rights as British citizens. The first Jewish peer—not converted to Christianity—was Lord Rothschild (1886). After Catholic emancipation the Duke found himself being blamed by his friends and praised by his foes: a man greater than Cæsar, as the Tory *Edinburgh Review* said, who did not destroy in peace what he had saved in war.

CHAPTER II

The Reform Bill

KING GEORGE IV died in June, 1830, and the First Gentleman of Europe left no regrets. The Duke, in charge of the obsequies, found round the King's neck a medallion miniature of Mrs. Fitzherbert and ordered this to be buried with him. George was succeeded by his brother, the Duke of Clarence, who reigned as William IV, an elderly and fairly popular man, with a long and honorable service in the navy behind him. He showed himself irresolute and not very intelligent, but impartial, and as a constitutional sovereign very sound. That year 1830 was one of revolutions in Europe. Charles X of France was supplanted by Louis-Philippe after the July rising. Belgium blazed up in protest against the union with Holland imposed on her by the treaties of 1815, and would gladly have accepted union with France, or at least a French sovereign, the Duke of Nemours. But England had made up her mind never again to allow a great European power to be installed in Flanders. To avoid war, Louis-Philippe agreed that the new kingdom should be given by the Powers to Leopold of Coburg (the son-in-law of George IV and then of Louis-Philippe), a wise and active monarch.

In 1830, also, revolutionary agitation pervaded Spain, Italy, and even England, where a new peasants' revolt took place in the southern counties. The rural laborers claimed a minimum wage of fourteen shillings, which was just; but they did so collectively, which brought them within grasp of the Riot Act. They broke up threshing-machines, held a few hated landowners to ransom for a few pounds, called on the clergy to renounce part of their tithes, damaged some workhouses, but hurt nobody. After their suppression, three were hanged and four hundred sent to transportation. Many of these died of despair. But the insurrection showed up the real weakness of aristocratic rule. To most moderate minds among the middle classes it was clear that electoral reform was a necessity.

After the overturning of the Wellington-Peel Ministry, an old Whig leader, Lord Grey, long a supporter of reformist projects, consented to emerge from the rural retirement where he brought up his eleven children, and formed a coalition Government, of Whigs and friends of Canning. A general election was held. True to family traditions, the Whigs had chosen to ally themselves with the reforming Radicals and the middle-class Nonconformists, which made them a party of popular interests. When a footman in Holland House opened the door and announced, "Mr. Macaulay," the nineteenth century, said Chesterton, took the decisive turn. In the opposite camp the Duke found weakened support from the Tories, who were resentful of his moderation. He had been loved for his shortcomings; now his virtues were held up against him. Notwithstanding their "rotten" boroughs, the Tories lost their majority. In the counties, where freedom of voting was greater, sixty out of eighty-two members were Whigs. For fifty years the Tories had been ruling the country; and the formation of a new team was a great political event. Devonshire House and Holland House came into their own again. The less perspicacious Whigs imagined that the great days of the eighteenth century and the "Venetian" government were come again. In their first Ministry ten holders of office were peers, with only four commoners. The great Whigs may have chosen to join hands with revolution, but they certainly seemed anxious to make the revolution a family affair.

Immediately Lord Grey let it be known that the first aim of his Government would be a measure of electoral reform. Indispensable as this obviously was, it was more or less certain that the project would meet with violent opposition. The holders of "rotten" boroughs were resolved to protect their threatened seats, and could count on the support of the House of Lords. The middle classes in the towns, on the other hand, favored reform—the merchants, bankers, and people of independent means, who felt it anomalous and humiliating to have no vote whereas, in certain country towns, every owner of a small house had full citizenship, and in others even stones and mortar had their voice. The Reform movement, between 1830 and 1832, was a middle-class movement, aiming at victory by lawful methods. The first bill, put forward by Lord John Russell, had a majority of only one vote in the Commons—not enough to force so important a measure on the Lords. In agreement with the King, Lord Grey decided to dissolve Parliament and hold an election.

He returned to power with a Whig majority of 136. The country felt that Reform was as good as gained, and rejoiced accordingly. In all classes of the population men were expecting wonders from a suffrage law. The middle classes hoped thereby to give platonic satisfactions to the common people, whose turbulence had been alarming them for quite fifteen years. As to the extent of the reforms, employers and employed would not have seen eye to eye; but regarding the need, their agreement was wonderful. It is difficult to bring men together for constructive action, but easy enough to league them against a minority. In the early nineteenth century the owners of the "rotten" boroughs—three or four score families in all—fulfilled the rôle which a century later was to be held by industrial magnates and international financiers. Sydney Smith satirized the sentiment: "All young ladies imagine they will be instantly married. Schoolboys believe that currant tarts must ultimately come down in price; the corporal and sergeant are sure of double pay; bad poets will expect a demand for their epics; fools will be disappointed, as they always are."

The Tories had supposed that the Whigs, men of their own class, would put forward mild projects of Reform. When Lord John Russell's bill appeared, they were stupefied and outraged. Here were the Whigs, formerly so exclusive, deliberately playing into the hands of the middle classes. Boroughs having fewer than two thousand inhabitants were abolished; towns with a population of between two and four thousand were to lose one out of every two representatives; and the 144 seats thus left open were to be shared amongst the more important towns. London gained ten seats; Liverpool, Manchester, Birmingham and Newcastle each obtained two members. Broadly speaking, the distribution of seats favored the industrial north at the expense of the rural south. It was obvious that this new balance of representative power would involve the suppression of the duties on corn. In the towns, the vote was given to all occupiers of houses having an annual value of £10 or over, and in the counties, to owners and tenants on a correspondingly wide basis. In fact, the bill would create an electorate of lower middle-class townsmen and of small farmers. Factory workers and agricultural laborers were still unrepresented. The Whigs declined to enforce a secret ballot, as open methods of voting maintained the squire's political control over his farming tenants.

The Lords inclined to tolerate Reform in some attenuated shape, but were infuriated by this electoral revolution. In October, 1831, they threw out the bill. Then, faced by popular agitation, and with the country ringing to cries of: "The bill! The whole bill! Nothing but the bill!" they passed it in part, but not integrally. The clauses for the abolition of "rotten" boroughs were cut out. Lord Grey, being in a minority in the Upper Chamber, resigned. But when the Duke, who for all their disappointments, was still the supreme hope of the Tories, tried to form a Government, the country rose. The tocsin was sounded from church towers, and work stopped in factories. At Bristol the town hall was burned and the bishop's palace pillaged. Lord Stanley, the most brilliant of the younger Whigs, jumped onto a table and declared that if the Lords stood fast, His Majesty could put coronets on the heads of a whole company of his Guards. The walls were plastered with posters calling upon Englishmen to withdraw their money from the Bank and so check the Duke. The Bank of England was the only institution held in greater respect than the Duke. The rebellion of depositors overwhelmed that of the great landlords. Wellington, as usual, avoided civil war. And when the King, who already saw himself taking the road to exile, if not to the scaffold, again summoned Lord Grey, the latter consented to take office only if the King gave him a written promise to create, if necessary, as many peers as would secure the passage of the Reform Bill. The Duke and his friends abstained from attending the debates, and on June 4, 1832, in a half-empty House, the Bill was at last passed into law by 106 votes to 27. The new act was certainly far from being what is nowadays termed a democratic measure. By granting a few members to the industrial centers it certainly diminished to some extent the influence of the rural aristocracy. But it gave the suffrage to a larger number of farmers dependent on that aristocracy. The Whigs had served their party interest without seriously endangering their class interest.

This electoral reform, desired by the masses and dreaded by the ruling classes, produced neither the hoped-for miracle nor the predicted disaster. With the battle fought and won, the agitation subsided. The new electorate proved reasonable, and even, to the chagrin of the Radicals, conservative. The traditional families remained in power. When the

Chartist agitation between 1835 and 1841, by means of giant petitions, meetings, and processions, sought to revive enthusiasm for a more revolutionary program (universal suffrage, secret ballots, equality between constituencies, annual Parliaments and payment of members), the campaign met with some success amongst the working class, who until 1850 remained unreconciled and regretted their thwarted revolution. But the middle classes sided against the Chartists; and when the agitators had recourse to rioting, when soldiers had to drive off a crowd armed with sickles which tried to seize the town hall at Newport, they remained loyal to the Government. In the north, the most dangerous region, the troops were fortunately commanded by an excellent general, Sir Charles Napier, who combined firmness with humanity. Thanks to him, an almost inevitable massacre was averted. And when the Chartists in 1848 threatened to imitate the February revolution of that year in France, 200,000 citizens enrolled as voluntary constables to maintain order. The nineteenth-century Englishman remained more law-abiding than ever, and as capable as his ancestors of spontaneous organization. Speaking of the Newport revolt to Lord Stanhope, the Duke, whose common sense, like Walpole's, often amounted to genius, remarked that there was one thing which should always be borne in mind about England—that when Englishmen know they are wrong and acting contrary to law, they become alarmed and run away. In France, he said, things were different: how else could it be explained that thirty men, at Newport, routed six thousand?

For many years after 1832 the membership of the House of Commons changed little in character; but although men were slow to recognize it, the constitution had in fact been profoundly modified. Henceforward the last word in politics was with the electorate, and Ministries came and went, not to the orders of Parliamentary managers, but to those of the county and borough voters. And at once the Whigs and their new manufacturing friends had to proffer some reforms to the people who had expected so much from them. The most important, but most imperfect, was that of the Poor Law. In Elizabethan times, as we have seen, the acts of 1597 and 1601 had distinguished between willful idleness, that of incorrigible rogues and vagabonds, and the plight of those hapless men who were incapable of earning their living through reasons independent of their own will—indigence, old age, insanity, sickness; and we have seen also how, during the eighteenth century, the inept Speenhamland system, by supplementing wages according to a fixed scale, inevitably reduced nearly all agricultural workers to pauperdom, ruined the small farmer, and raised local rates. At the time of the Reform Act, the condition of the poor in town and country was appalling. Disraeli and Dickens depicted these "Two Nations" in their novels—the nation of the rich and the nation of the poor, living side by side, each heedless of the other. The rural laborer's cottage was often a mere hovel, round which ran children in rags and tatters. These villagers just contrived to keep body and soul together by eking out their wretched pittance with poaching and alms. The happy race of yeomen, who numbered a full million in 1688, had almost vanished. Lord Grey's Government appointed a commission of inquiry, under the guidance of Nassau Senior and Edwin Chadwick, both men with questionable but firm preconceptions on the problem.

Senior believed that the best way to abolish poverty was never to help the poor. With serene, unwitting cruelty, he argued that if the poor know that they must either work or starve, they will work; if young men know that they will be helpless in their old age, they will save; if older men know that they need their children, they will take pains to secure their affection. Wherefore, no help should be given except to those who really have no family or means of existence. There must be no partial aid: all or nothing. For such as are old enough or strong enough to work—the workhouse. And lest the workhouse become a favored haven, it was important, argued Senior, to make life therein less desirable than the life of the most hapless of independent workpeople. Considering what was then the lot of these, it seems almost impossible to evolve anything more wretched. But this cruel program was put into operation, and the workhouse became "the Bastille of the Poor," a loathed and dreaded place. In 1838 there were 48,000 children under sixteen living in workhouses, too often in company with adults of the basest type, and even with half-witted creatures. After the passing of the Poor Law Administration Act (1834), the number of poor receiving parish aid was greatly diminished; expenditure fell from seven million pounds in 1831 to four and a half million in 1836. The commissioners were filled with pride in their achievement, but without justification. The result was actually due to the horror inspired by the workhouses and to the growth of industry. In any case, was such a result in itself a mark of progress?

However that may have been, the suffering inflicted on innocent people in the name of sound economic principles was unpardonable.

Amongst other Whig reforms, two should be noted. Firstly, there was the Municipal Corporations Act of 1835, which replaced the old-fashioned system by more democratically constituted municipal bodies elected by all payers of local taxation. This applied only to towns, and country districts remained under the administrative authority of the justices of the peace until a later act, in 1888, set up the County Councils. The municipal corporations, with State aid, gradually came to administer means of transport, schools, and the supply of light and water. Secondly, there was the abolition of slavery in British colonial possessions. The history of this reform began in 1772, when Lord Mansfield laid it down in a judgment that the Common Law did not recognize the status of slave, which at one stroke freed some fifteen thousand negroes brought by their owners into the British Isles. It was more difficult to secure the abolition of the trade in slaves, which had been the basis of the fortune of ports like Bristol and Liverpool, and without which Nelson himself maintained that the British mercantile fleet could not live. It is to the honor of Parliament that, despite the pressure of the interests at stake, Bishop Wilberforce and Charles James Fox, with a powerful tide of Quaker and Methodist opinion behind them, and aided also by Pitt, managed to secure the prohibition of this traffic in 1807, at a time when the crisis of the Napoleonic wars was at its height. There remained the slaves in the British colonies, and on this point the West Indian planters continued the struggle with desperate obstinacy, spending vast fortunes on the purchase of "rotten" boroughs. The anti-slavery movement thus became a political issue, as it was linked with electoral reform; and it became also a religious question, as the planters were persecuting the missionaries who taught the negroes that all races of men were equal before Christ. Upheld by liberal and Nonconformist forces, the reform was finally voted in 1833, and was welcomed by the dissenting churches as a great victory. An indemnity of twenty million pounds was granted to the planters, but the production of sugar fell by one-third, that of coffee by half, and for a long time the islands were ruined.

Lord Grey resigned in 1834, partly because O'Connell and his group of Irish members made his life intolerable, but chiefly because there could be no enduring union between the moderate Whigs and the Radical

Nonconformists who had made up the victorious coalition of 1832. His place was taken, after a short interregnum under Peel, by Lord Melbourne, a Whig of the old school. Husband of Byron's too-famous Lady Caroline Lamb, he was through her allied to Devonshire House. A witty skeptic of eighteenth-century temper, he governed with something of Walpole's unobtrusiveness a country still perturbed by the backwash of the Reform agitation. Enthusiasm, a bad counselor, makes, nevertheless, a good partisan. Like most skeptics, Melbourne did little harm, but he enfeebled his party. Under his rule the English electors ceased to regard the Whigs as "advanced." The great event of his Ministry was the death of King William and the accession of the young Queen Victoria, who was to reign from 1837 until 1901. She was welcomed by the English people, whom she saved from her uncle, the Duke of Cumberland, the very unpopular brother of King William. For more than half a century her reign would make loyalty a chivalrous duty. But the accession of a Queen had another happy result. The Kingdom of Hanover was not transmissable through the female line; it was inherited by the Duke of Cumberland, and so the country was freed at once from a hated prince and from a symbiosis which compromised Britain in European affairs. England had long ago broken with spiritual internationalism; she now cut free from the dynastic community of Europe. The young Queen was quick to show a tenacious will of her own, which amounted even to obstinacy. At first Melbourne had grounds for hoping that he would convert her to easy-going gayety; but when she married her cousin, Prince Albert of Saxe-Coburg, she learned from him the professional sense of sovereignty and that respect for the domestic virtues which in years to come saved the British monarchy. In a kingdom which had to defend its institutions against republican ideas, and had also to adapt itself to the liking of the industrial middle classes, the absolutism of the Stuarts and the dissoluteness of the Hanoverians could not have saved the Crown. In England as in Belgium, the Coburgs made monarchy worthy of respect. It was under Queen Victoria that Englishmen came to regard the family life of the sovereign as something bound up with their own private family lives. The influence of Prince Albert's stiff morality, and the strictness of Court life, influenced the whole tone of English life as deeply, and at least as widely, as Wesley had done in an earlier age.

CHAPTER III

Free Trade Triumphant

THE Whigs had told the people that Parliamentary reform would end all their ills. The people had forced reform on the Lords, and the ills were worse than ever. The people were grumbling, and the Whigs tottering. The Tories had both weapons and leaders capable of depriving the Whigs of the favors of the new electorate. As the Duke nowadays preferred popularity to power, party leadership had passed into the hands of Sir Robert Peel, who dropped the label of Tory and styled himself Conservative, a name better contrived to attract the middle classes. They were bound to like Sir Robert, a man closer to factory and shop than to manor or cottage. Alongside Peel, though opposed to him on occasion, a so-called "popular" Conservatism had its representatives within the party, in the small "Young England" group, whose spokesmen were an orator of genius, Benjamin Disraeli, son of a Jewish man of letters but baptized in the Anglican Church as a child, and Lord John Manners, son of the Duke of Rutland. Disraeli and his friends turned back to the doctrines of Bolingbroke regarding the traditional constitution of England. They condemned a doctrine which, instead of maintaining a natural hierarchy of classes involving rights and duties equally, allowed the automatic laws of economics to control the relations of employers and workers. They urged that salvation lay in a return to a society built up like that of the Middle Ages, wherein every man, be he lord or peasant, knew his place and accepted it. According to Disraeli and his associates, the rôle of a Conservative party was at once to save such elements of the past as still had vitality in them, and to prepare the future by a policy of generosity.

John Bull smiled at Young England. This clique of young gentlemen

[422]

in white waistcoats, claiming to persuade the working classes into feudal ideas, seemed an oddity. The professional politicians had no faith in it. The theories of Bentham, Malthus, Ricardo, Cobden, and James Mill were then accepted as articles of faith. All, or nearly all, serious people believed with the utilitarians that human societies strove to achieve the greatest happiness of the greatest number, and could attain this only by allowing free play to the personal interest of the individual. The clash of interests would bring about, not a perfect justice, but the nearest possible approach to perfection. Any State intervention should, therefore, be avoided. The slightest restriction or competition was deemed heretical. Prices should be fixed automatically by the law of supply and demand; the profits of business men and the wages of workmen were automatically adjusted to their proper level by competition. Wages rose, according to Cobden, when two masters sought one workman, and fell when two workmen sought one master. The wage-earner could control wages only by deliberately restricting the population. What was true of individuals was true also of States. The rule of buying as cheap, and selling as dear, as possible, which every business man applied in his private life, was also the best rule for the trade of a whole nation. Customs barriers always distorted the laws of supply and demand. Actuated by the highest motives, men like Richard Cobden, manufacturer and statesman, the prophet of the Manchester School, strove to persuade the English people that their distress was caused by trade restrictions and protectionist duties, and in particular by the Corn Laws.

The anti-protectionist campaign was one of the first in England to be waged by those weapons of propaganda—in newspapers and speaking tours—which were to transform political life during the nineteenth century. In public meetings the orators of the Anti-Corn Law Association displayed three loaves, different in size but costing the same in three countries—France, Russia, England. England's loaf was the smallest, and Englishmen were therefore being cheated. These demonstrations were particularly successful with manufacturers like those in Lancashire, who imported both their cotton and their corn. On the other hand, they alarmed the agricultural interests. "Abolish the duty on wheat," repeated the farmers and squires, "and you will kill English farming." "That matters little to us," retorted the Manchester School. "If other countries are in a position to produce corn more cheaply than we can, let them plow and reap for

[423]

us, and we shall spin and weave for them. All trade must be a cycle. We cannot sell if we do not buy. To bar our shores against imports would mean the end of our exports."

The Conservative party, consisting largely of country gentlemen, was bound to be hostile to Free Trade and favorable towards maintaining the duties on corn. But Sir Robert Peel, its leader, showed dangerous sympathies with the opposing doctrine. He was a man of good faith, high intellectual courage, great administrative and financial skill, but domineering and not in close contact with the House. In 1842 he attacked the tariff, and reduced the number of dutiable articles from 1,200 to 750. To make up for the losses thus caused in the Budget, he instituted an income tax of sevenpence in the pound on incomes above £150. In 1845 he further reduced the customs list to 450 heads. He was moving towards Free Trade by leaps and bounds. These successive reductions had astonishing effects. Not only were the State revenues undiminished, but they were actually increased by the augmented volume of trade and by the taxable profits. Peel was thus emboldened. But he had not yet ventured to touch agriculture, the citadel of his party. Disraeli had twitted the Prime Minister on his conversion to Free Trade: "The right honourable gentleman," he said of Peel, "caught the Whigs bathing and walked away with their clothes." The House laughed and cheered. In 1845 and 1846 Ireland was twice in succession stricken by a failure of the potato crop. Before long Peel was using the word "famine," because half of that over-populous island lived mainly on potatoes. A shortage of corn in England prevented help of that kind being sent to Ireland, and so the only solution, he said, was to abolish the duty on corn and at last authorize the free import of foodstuffs into Great Britain.

This abruptness and panic came as a surprise. Lord Stanley, the most influential member of the Cabinet after Peel, confessed that he could no longer understand his leader: nothing certain would be known about the harvest for two months yet; the admission of foreign grain would not feed the Irish, who had not a penny to pay for it; and Peel was proposing to maintain moderate rates of duty for three years, whereas in three years' time the famine would be a thing of the past. But Peel's decision came from instinct rather than argument. What the Tories called treason was in his view simply a pious conversion. The Queen and Prince Albert, Free Traders both, kept telling him that he was saving the country.

BENJAMIN DISRAELI, LORD BEACONSFIELD
From a painting by L. Bogle
in the London National Portrait Gallery.

QUEEN VICTORIA WITH PRINCE EDWARD, HIS GRANDFATHER, EDWARD VII, AND HIS GRANDMOTHER, QUEEN ALEXANDRIA

Against him a group of Conservative Protectionists took form within his own party, the attack being led by two men of widely different character, Lord George Bentinck and Benjamin Disraeli. Nobody would have imagined that this young Jew, known only as a brilliantly sarcastic orator, would become the leader of the country gentlemen and overturn the all-powerful Sir Robert Peel. But so it befell. In a series of dazzling philippics, rich in imagery, Disraeli denounced the Prime Minister's "treason." The abolition of the Corn Laws was passed because, for that division in the House, the Whig and Free Trade opposition voted with Peel's supporters; but the same night saw the defeat of Peel by an alliance of ungrateful Free Traders and vengeful Protectionists.

For twenty years this split was to keep the Conservative party out of power, except for short intervals. Peel's friends never became reconciled with the men who had overturned their leader. Peel himself died as the result of a riding mishap in 1850. The leading Peelites, and in particular the most conspicuous of them, William Ewart Gladstone, allied themselves with the Whigs and Liberals. The Conservatives were now headed by Lord Stanley (later Lord Derby), a great landowner of intelligence and culture, and devoid of personal ambition, and by Disraeli, who, notwithstanding his genius, was not for a long time accepted by his party as their leader, but ultimately secured their merited confidence. The government of the country was carried on by Lord John Russell, then by Lord Aberdeen and Lord Palmerston at the head of Whig and Peelite coalitions. Meanwhile, Free Trade and Protection had ceased, with surprising suddenness, to be controversial politics. The abolition of the Corn Laws had not ruined agriculture, as Disraeli and his friends had prophesied it would. For many years longer England imported only about a quarter of the grain she used. In spite of inevitable times of difficulty, the years between 1850 and 1875 were a period of great general prosperity, due to the increasing population, the development of railways, and the furnishing of the Empire overseas. Farmers shared in the profits, and ceased to complain. Protection, said Disraeli, was not only dead but damned. His political heir, at the close of the century, discovered that it was only in Purgatory. Meanwhile Gladstone, who had become the great financier of the Whigs, transformed the fiscal system by a series of budgets which were held in high repute because they coincided with years of plenty. Abolishing nearly all import duties, his action had by 1860 reduced the 1,200 dutiable commodities to a mere 48. He simplified taxation, retaining only the income tax, land tax, and, among duties, those on tea, coffee, wine, beer, and spirits. Between 1825 and 1870 the per capita taxation dropped from £29.3 to £1.18.5½.

Post hoc, ergo propter hoc: the adoption of Free Trade principles had coincided with England's enrichment, and now economic liberty became an article of English faith. But the swift development of industry had produced grave abuses. It could not be expected that a House of Commons which was little more than a club of gentlemen-farmers, fully occupied with the wars against Napoleon, could have imposed strict and sound regulations on the factories and towns during the years of their growth. But the outcome was a disgrace to a rich and free country. The Irish famine had discharged into Liverpool alone over 100,000 starving people whose advent only intensified the squalor of the slums. When Engels visited Manchester in 1844, he found 350,000 workpeople crowded in dank and dirty little houses, breathing a sodden, dust-laden air. In the mines half-naked women were employed as mere beasts of burden, and children spent their days in the darkness of a pit-gallery, opening and shutting air-vents. In the lace industry infants of four years old were employed. True, these evils were not universal, and perhaps the writers of the time depicted the worst examples; but their exaggeration was useful in rousing public opinion.

Despite the *laissez-faire* prejudice, Parliament at last intervened. A Factory Act of 1819 had controlled the employment of children under nine years of age, who at the beginning of the century had worked as much as fifteen or sixteen hours daily in the cotton-mills. An act of 1833 limited the employment of workers under eighteen, and set up the first factory inspectors. In 1847 the hours of work for women were limited to ten, and this soon brought a corresponding modification for men. The textile industry in 1850 adopted the Saturday half-holiday (a system widely known abroad as the "English week"), and this transformed the life of the English workman by enabling him to indulge his interest in sport on Saturday afternoons. The campaign for limiting hours of work had been directed by Lord Ashley (later Lord Shaftesbury); and in 1842, after the publication of a report which inspired shame and disgust in the public conscience, he also pushed through legislation to prevent the employment of women and children under nine in the mines. By these more humane laws, by the general prosperity in which they shared, and also by the attraction of the Nonconformist chapel, large numbers of English workmen were diverted from movements of a revolutionary character. It was in England that the coöperative societies and trade unions for bettering conditions were brought to birth. The trade unions had existed since the eighteenth century, but they were not strictly legal. They became so in 1824. One of the most conspicuous was the Amalgamated Society of Engineers, founded in 1851, and counting 30,000 members in 1865, at once a trade union in the strict sense and a mutual-benefit society. Its first head, William Allen, was the typical trade-unionist of the Victorian period.

The administration of the new laws touching factories, mines and sanitation, and Peel's creation of a regular police force in 1829, necessitated the growth of that central bureaucracy which England, a country of local government, had previously lacked. In 1815 the Home Office had only eighteen officials. With the Post Office, the railways, factory inspection, the number of officials rose to 16,000 in 1853. The question of the recruitment of the Civil Service is never an easy one to solve in a democracy. If posts are at the disposal of politicians to reward their partisans, no Government can keep a steady control over its servants. In America the "spoils" system, which upsets the whole administration of the country after every election, and in France the abuse of political recommendation, are examples of dangerous error. One reason for the success of England during the nineteenth century was the creation of an excellent Civil Service, non-political in character and taking no direct part in politics. During the first half of the century the regime of political influence throve. The old Whigs held on to the gift of place as one of the attributes of power, and when an open system of examination was laid down as essential for the Civil Service, this new-fangled idea shocked them profoundly. They were soon to realize that it gave good results. Civil Servants showed themselves loyal executives for every successive Government, whatever its party color, and by keeping scrupulously aloof from partisan disputes insured the continuity of national traditions.

CHAPTER IV

Palmerston's Foreign Policy

ENGLAND, as we have seen, was no willing partner in the European Alliance, and English opinion approved Canning only where he combined the defense of oppressed nations with that of British interests. After Canning, the great Foreign Secretary for twenty years, was Lord Palmerston, who was not a Whig, but had supported the Reform movement and so quarreled with the Tories. To foreign affairs Palmerston brought intelligence, a strain of gayety, a very definite view of England's duties in the world, and an obstinacy which endeared him to his fellow-Englishmen. Since 1815 no real danger had threatened the country. At sea no power could vie with England; on land there were still certain sensitive spots where tradition and prudence called for a close watch. England wanted an independent Belgium, had succeeded in creating one, and was resolved to protect it. She did not wish to see a French prince on the throne of Spain, and although Palmerston could not prevent the Duke of Montpensier's Spanish marriage, the downfall of King Louis-Philippe soon freed him from anxiety in this respect. Finally, public opinion in England favored the cause of peoples struggling for liberty, and Palmerston accordingly sided with the Hungarians and the Italians, and supported the Sicilians against the King of Naples, and the Sardinians against Austria. In any international discussion Lord Palmerston's usual argument was the British fleet. He thus annoyed the Court, which he embroiled with other Courts, perturbed the peace-loving, who feared that this bluff might one day lead to war, but delighted the average Englishman, who beheld his flag honored without fighting, listened rapturously to Palmerston's speeches on the theme *"civis romanus sum,"* and honestly believed himself a defender of right when the Foreign Secretary sent an

[428]

ultimatum to Greece to protect a certain Don Pacifico, who was not even English, and another to China in defense of merchants whom he refrained from disclosing to be opium-traffickers. But when Palmerston allowed himself to approve the *coup d'état* of Napoleon III in 1852, without consulting the Queen or the Cabinet, he was obliged to hand over his portfolio to Lord John Russell. The incident, however, only increased his popularity, and not long afterwards he himself became Prime Minister.

The fact remains that Palmerston's masterful policy did not involve Britain in any hostilities, whereas the vacillations of Lord Aberdeen produced the Crimean War. The famous Eastern Question was primarily the question of Turkey. Many European statesmen in the mid-nineteenth century believed that the Ottoman Empire in Europe could not survive much longer. "We have a sick man on our hands," said the Tsar to the British ambassador, "and we must not let him disappear without settling the succession." The Tsar's idea of the settlement was that he himself should take the Balkan provinces, whilst he offered Egypt and Crete to Britain. If Britain and Russia could agree in this matter, he said, it mattered little what anybody else thought or did. But Britain desired the convalescence of the sick man more than his inheritance, and viewed with anxiety the growing strength of Russia, an Asiatic power formidable to India, an autocratic power hostile to liberal nations. France, on her side, had recurrent quarrels with the Tsar concerning the Holy Places, of which both countries claimed to be protectors. The storm broke when the Tsar demanded that the Sultan should intrust him with the protection of all Christians in the Levant. The British ambassador in Constantinople, Stratford Canning, joined France in encouraging the Sultan to resist this. British foreign policy became strangely confused. Lord Aberdeen, the Prime Minister, wanted peace; the Foreign Office wanted peace; the ambassador in Constantinople may have wanted a diplomatic victory; public opinion, ruffled by the Tsar's arrogance, wanted war. For the first time an attitude was imposed on the Foreign Office by an emotional campaign in the country. This was one consequence of a widened suffrage and the freedom of the Press. On March 27, 1854, France and England declared war on Russia, who had invaded Turkish provinces. French and British ships sailed up the Bosphorus and forced the Russian fleet to take refuge in Sebastopol.

Public opinion had the war it clamored for. Was public opinion right?

Admittedly the Tsar could not be allowed to slice up the Ottoman Empire to suit himself, but he might perhaps have been prevented by a more dexterous diplomacy. It was a paradoxical success—the triumph of sentimental liberalism making England the ally of one "despot"—Napoleon III—to support another despot—the Sultan. British campaigns had generally opened with a spectacular lack of foresight, and the Crimean war was the most brilliant of these exhibitions. The medical and commissariate services were so far beneath requirements that, in a war employing only small numbers of troops in the field, twenty-five thousand British soldiers died whilst the country spent, in vain, seventy million pounds. Fortunately the new power of the Press stirred up public opinion. A great journalist, William Russell of *The Times*, followed the campaign as a war correspondent and described the sufferings of the troops. Lord Aberdeen, attacked by every party, had to resign, and his place was taken by Lord Palmerston, who had the good fortune to come on to the stage when circumstances were at last turning in the Allies' favor. After a lengthy siege Sebastopol was taken (1855). Napoleon III, already reconciled with Russia, was anxious for peace in order to pursue his other great projects, and especially to further the unity of Italy. Lord Palmerston would have liked to bring Russia to her knees and force her away from the shores of the Black Sea. Had his views prevailed, the war might have lasted for many a long year, and for very remote and ambiguous objects. But already a volatile public opinion was wavering, and beginning to wonder whether it had not backed the wrong horse.

In 1856 the Treaty of Paris was signed, known to the malcontents as the "Capitulation of Paris." "We made a peace, but not peace" said Clarendon. It was decided that the Ottoman Empire would be left intact, and that Russia should no longer be entitled to have a fleet in the Black Sea. The Sultan promised certain reforms, and to show more benevolence towards his Christian subjects; and a whole generation of Englishmen believed that the "sick man of Europe" had been made a better man. Disillusion was at hand: the check to the Tsar's European ambitions resulted in his turning towards Asia, which implied danger to India, and the Sultan's conflicts with his Balkan provinces were to cause disturbance in Europe for over half-a-century.

The most important decision reached by the Congress of Paris was the adoption of new international regulations concerning the freedom of the seas in time of war. Four essential principles were laid down: the right of pursuit was held to be abolished; the flag of a vessel covered its cargo, except as regards contraband of war; neutral merchandise could be seized only if carried under an enemy flag; blockade, to be obligatory, had to be effective. These safeguards for neutral commerce in wartime contained the seeds of grave incidents, even of future wars. One remote and unforeseen consequence of the Crimean War, in England, was women's suffrage. At the time when the medical services were in a state of collapse in Russia, the only person who proved capable of reorganizing them was a woman, Florence Nightingale; and this brought into currency entirely new ideas of the education of women and of their place in society, which paved the way for the women's suffrage movement.

During the Crimean War, Napoleon III had been insistent that the Sardinians should be authorized to join the Allies. The romantic strain in the Emperor of the French had been attracted by the idea of nationalism. He was eager to help the Italians to liberate themselves from Austria, and to make the House of Savoy, which ruled over both Sardinia and Piedmont, the pillar of the new Italy. Palmerston and English opinion favored the idea, but the Court was suspicious of the Emperor. Prince Albert kept saying that Napoleon was a conspirator, and that this was the key to all his actions. In 1859 Napoleon III embarked on his Italian campaign. Anxious though he was to liberate Italy, he. nevertheless wished to keep that country divided so as to make his own power felt there, and in particular he wished to preserve the temporal sovereignty of the Pope. Palmerston and his Foreign Secretary, Russell, forced Napoleon's hand and lent their support to the Sicilian expedition of Garibaldi, thus facilitating the total attainment of Italian unity. The aim of this policy was threefold: to satisfy liberal and Protestant opinion, to insure the friendship and gratitude of the new Italy (Anglo-Italian friendship was to last unbroken from 1860 until 1935), and to prevent France from acquiring too much authority beyond the Alps. Palmerston had been alarmed by the annexation to France, after a plebiscite, of Nice and Savoy; and he took pleasure in beating Napoleon III with weapons of his own forging.

When the Southern States of America, in 1860, declared their intention of secession from the Union, England was in two minds about this grave issue. A certain number of Radicals and dissenters sided with the anti-slavery campaign waged by the Northern States, but London's fashionable world, the small aristocratic clique which controlled British policy, was wholeheartedly in favor of the South. There indeed manners were more agreeable and accents more refined; thence, also, came the cotton which England urgently required. When Abraham Lincoln declared that the aim of the war was not the abolition of slavery, but the maintenance of the Union, British sentiment ceased to conflict with prejudices in favor of the South. If the Southern States only wanted their freedom, did not the principles of nationalism call for this being granted? In 1861 and 1862, with Lancashire stricken by a veritable cotton famine, Palmerston's Government was on the point of recognizing Southern independence. Only the decisive victories of the Northern armies in 1863 prevented this rash step. But the attitude of the English newspapers had deeply wounded the Northerners, whose annoyance almost brought open war when the British Government authorized the building in England of ships supposedly for mercantile purposes; several disguised warships, such as the *Alabama*, were put in the service of the Confederates and wrought havoc in the Northerners' trade. After the victory of the Union side, England was forced to renew her friendship with America by payment of large sums as reparation for the heavy damage done by the *Alabama*. For many years this episode poisoned the relations of the two countries; in the course of the next fifty years, moreover, North America received a flood of Slav, Latin, and Irish immigration, and ceased to be a predominantly Anglo-Saxon community, becoming the great melting-pot of races that it continued to be until the war of 1914.

"I am setting an example which probably, in a very short time, Prussia will be glad to imitate," Cavour had said to the Court of Berlin; and Berlin did not gainsay him. The danger of the policy of nationalities lay in its liability to be constantly calling in question the map of Europe, and in its tendency to rouse sentimental sympathies which expressed themselves more vehemently than effectively. The Poles had rebelled against Russian oppression in 1863. British opinion warmly supported them. Napoleon III, approving the principle of nationality, supported Britain, who sent the Tsar a peremptory note. The Tsar replied in a tone of haughty sarcasm. Everybody expected war. When the British Government admitted that a momentary error had led it along a mistaken path for three or four months, and that it never intended to go beyond an exchange of notes, Napoleon found himself in a very false position. And the most obvious results of this high-minded agitation were, first, that the Russian Minister, Gortchakoff, who had been responsible for the insurrection and its brutal suppression and, until Russell's intervention, was on the point of being disgraced by his Emperor, suddenly became the most powerful and popular statesman in Russia; and second, that the squares of Warsaw were strewn with dead and wounded. Such, said Disraeli, were the results of a policy which was neither fish nor flesh nor fowl.

A few months later the Germans threatened to invade Denmark, and (of course in the name of the principles of nationality) to rob it of the Duchies of Schleswig and Holstein. Lord Palmerston vehemently declared in Parliament that if Danish independence were threatened, the attackers would find that it was not with Denmark alone that they would have to measure their strength. Reading this speech, the Danes took great comfort and assumed a bold front. Once again the whole of Europe believed that England would intervene with armed force; once again public opinion, in the goodness of its heart, was encouraging the Government to side with a small State bullied by a stronger State. Palmerston asked Napoleon III for the support of the French army, but the Emperor had been abandoned by Britain in the Polish affair, and was now distrustful. While Britain and France played this inopportune game, the Germans marched into Denmark. Hopefully the Danes turned to Lord Palmerston: had not he said that Prussia would not have to reckon with Denmark alone? But at the eleventh hour public opinion discovered the perils of intervention. The Cabinet met and decided against war. What could be said to the Danes? It was explained to them that Lord Palmerston had spoken without consulting the Cabinet, and therefore had not pledged the Cabinet. In 1864 Schleswig and Holstein were annexed by Prussia. A new Power, strong and exacting, was arising in Europe, and secretly aspiring to hegemony. Prussia, in the years that followed, was helped by the uncertainties of British policy, which, deriving at once from the masterful imperialism of Pitt, from the aggressive liberalism of Canning and Palmerston, and also from the pacifism of the Cobdenites, wavered dangerously for half a century between contradictory positions.

CHAPTER V

Victorian England

AT NO stage in human history did scientific invention so rapidly alter
manners, ideas, and even landscapes as in the first part of the nineteenth
century. The scientific method, the method of Francis Bacon, had suddenly produced effects which the Englishman of Bacon's day would have
deemed miraculous. Man seemed to have mastered Nature. Steam was
replacing the strength of men's arms, of animals, of the wind. In 1812 a
steamboat puffed its way up the Clyde; in 1819, the first steamship crossed
the Atlantic; in 1852 the *Agamemnon*, the first armor-plated screw-driven
warship, was launched. In 1821 Stephenson built his first locomotive
engine; in 1830 the Duke of Wellington opened the railway between
Manchester and Liverpool; in 1838 Prince Albert, having come from
Windsor to London by rail, asked the driver at the end of the journey
kindly not to go so fast next time. The boldest minds were impressed
by the vastness of the railway stations and the busy districts growing up
round them. Companies had been formed to exploit the invention; men
from every walk of life—retired officers, merchants, schoolmasters—were
becoming directors of railway companies. In 1842 a boom began, and
shares and salaries went soaring up. *Punch* displayed the locomotive-
juggernaut "Speculation" running over its worshipers; and it did in
fact crush them, for in 1847 the total value of railway shares dropped, as
vertically as it had soared, by over seventy million pounds. Speculation
in shares, which had been only a transitory sickness in the eighteenth
century, was now becoming a regular occupation; in many large enterprises, the joint-stock company (foreshadowed by the older colonial companies) was supplanting the individual and responsible master.

About the same time the penny post gave an impetus to the writing

[434]

habit among new classes. The newspapers, costing less since the stamp duty was lowered by the Whigs from fivepence to one penny, increased their circulations. From 1837 onwards, towns and continents were brought nearer by the telegraph. The planet shrank, as it was said, to the dimensions of an English warehouse. Like a spider in the center of the world's commerce, England threw a vast web of cables round the globe. Because she lived in peace, because she had the largest fleet and the richest coal-mines, because her prosperous and free middle class was ready to make the most of new inventions, she grew richer more quickly than any other people. In 1830, at a time of economic crisis, the historian Macaulay had chanted a hymn of triumph and announced that in 1930 these same islands would see a doubled population enjoying a doubled wealth. Rash though the prophecy seemed, it was certainly outstripped by fact.

The Victorian era in England, like the age of Louis-Philippe across the Channel, was the reign of the middle classes. Enriched by the application of scientific discovery, they might at that time have assumed power by force, had it not been that the Whigs surrendered the aristocratic citadel to them without a blow. As Elie Halévy has written: "the political masterpiece of England in the nineteenth century was the perpetuation of the tradition of aristocratic parliamentarianism. But on what condition was this feat carried out? On condition of continual adaptation of that policy to the needs of a society in course of industrial and democratic conversion." The alliance of the Whigs and the middle classes had deep and lasting effects on England's moral standards. Many of the wealthy men who formed the new industrial oligarchy sprang from Nonconformist stock. Even those among them who no longer held the faith of the Puritans retained a Puritan austerity, and this blend of moral strictness with commercial success was not fortuitous. Temperance, Sabbath observance, the strict observance of the marriage bond, were virtues with worldly as well as heavenly rewards. Religion, indeed, proved frequently to be a direct occasion and secret of worldly success: Thomas Cook, who founded the famous travel agency, was a Baptist missionary who began by organizing excursions for temperance meetings and Sunday schools; the Cadbury and Fry families were Quakers and built the most prosperous and beneficent chocolate-works, cocoa being a powerful ally of preaching in the struggle against "strong drink." In deference to their political allies the Whigs abandoned their cynicism, and, outwardly at least, their pleasures. The aristocracy, Bagehot noted in 1867, lived in terror of the middle classes, the grocer and shopkeeper. By 1850 a correspondence like that of Byron with Lady Melbourne would have been almost inconceivable. Together with Free Trade and electoral Reform, the Whigs, reluctantly no doubt, had added Virtue to their program.

The Queen herself, wedded to the prudish Albert, had been transformed. Her Court had become serious and domestic. "This damned morality will end by spoiling everything," grumbled Melbourne. But Melbourne belonged to a vanished epoch, and Gladstone, prosperous and pious, solemn and domestic, was a better emblem of the reign. Novels and plays took on a tone suitable for a youthful Queen, a virtuous wife and mother, and contained nothing to bring a blush to the cheek of the young. *Punch* was extolled as a paper fit for family reading. Vice and crime were banned from literature, unless veiled with sentimentality or humor. The monarchy, the aristocracy, and literature had realized that, in this new world, excesses of frivolity or sincerity would endanger their privileges. To impress the mass with a sense of their safe respectability, the ruling classes assumed, if not always the reality (which would have been beyond human nature), at least the conventions and semblance of respectability. And to a great many these appearances became habits. Reading Gosse's *Father and Son*, one observes how closely the temper of certain Victorians approximated to that of Cromwell's "saints." The blend of solemnity, reserve, and strength which was characteristic of that age reappeared in the black frock-coats and high collars and ties of the men, as it did in the legendary black silk gowns and bonnets of Queen Victoria.

And whilst the Whigs, in this alliance, sacrificed their free-living ways, the bourgeoisie abandoned their radicalism. The Victorian middle class professed an essentially conservative form of snobbery, accepting the structure of aristocratic society, and respecting that framework all the more as it offered chances for outsiders to take their place inside it. Every middle-class person liked to know people of title, and if he denied this, it was not to be believed. For a long time the servility of the new electorate nullified the effects of electoral Reform. Cobden declared that, day by day, feudalism was resuming its place in both political and social life. Bagehot analyzed this peculiar deference: strange as it might appear, he said, there were nations where the ignorant majority desired to be ruled by the competent minority, and abdicated in favor of their superiors, and England was a typically deferential nation. About 1850 it did indeed appear as if the people were consenting to leave the privilege of the vote, not even to the few and fortunate, but to the middle classes, and that these classes themselves preferred to be represented by professional aristocrats. Middle-class people seemed to regard themselves as spectators enjoying the spectacle of a sumptuous life presented to them by excellent actors on a superb stage. Thus the great English families still preserved for many years longer their noble parks, their almost royal state, their Wren or Inigo Jones mansions, without having to face any vehement opposition. At Chatsworth, at Belvoir, at Woburn, the dukes held court. In June, 1832, on the morrow of the Reform Act, Disraeli had written that the reign of the dukes, which had seemed eternal, had collapsed. He was soon to learn that the dukes whom he thus buried were still in good health, and was himself seeking alliance with them.

This upper-class life, widely tolerated and fabulously rich, is all the more astonishing because the lot of the poor was then so deplorable. The fine English breed of the eighteenth century, comfortable, vigorous, full-blooded, well-nurtured from its own fields, had been succeeded by a pallid, urban proletariat. Mortality in the working-class quarters of the large towns was appalling. In the East End of London it was double what it was in the West End. At Bath the normal lifetime of a gentleman was fifty-five years, of a workman, twenty-five. G. M. Young has depicted the squalor and dirt in which thousands of families then lived: the drinking-water polluted by ordure, the pestilential courtyards where even grass would not grow, the cellars, sometimes flooded with stagnant water, where ten or twelve people slept. Rural England, indeed, was not altogether dead. In 1861 the proportion of urban to rural population was as five to four; not until 1881 did the town population become double that of the country district. But the rural population itself did not recover its equilibrium. The farm worker was henceforth better off on the great estates, where "the dukes" built sound cottages, than on small properties which, except in periods of high prices, were hard put to it to make both ends meet. As for the urban workers, their lot grew slowly better throughout the long reign of Victoria. The worst period was at the beginning of the century. Until Peel's time, the people's foodstuffs were expensive. Free Trade lowered the cost of living, and in the early '50's wages began to rise. Wages in 1865 were 20 or 25 per cent higher than in 1845; prices had risen, but bread, for instance, was barely 12 per cent dearer. The purchasing power of the working-people had increased; and coöperative societies and savings-banks helped them to tide over hard times. It is noteworthy that from 1850 onwards they abandoned direct action; and like the middle class in general, the English workman adopted the hope that machinery and scientific discoveries would bring in a new Golden Age.

And so progress became the faith of all the Victorians, rich and poor. Science filled them with a religious awe. The Middle Ages had seen the universe solely as the outcome of the free will of God; the eighteenth century had tried to reconcile a system of rational laws with a reasonable faith; in the nineteenth century many scientists believed they were observing an entirely mechanical world. Lyell's *Principles of Geology* and Darwin's *Origin of Species* shattered the Biblical theories and gave their contemporaries the illusion of having discovered, from the evolution of living creatures, laws as exact as those of the material world. Philosophy itself became materialist. Herbert Spencer, a man of simple and fallacious mind, was as universal as Comte, but as summary as Comte was brilliant; gifted, as it has been said, with an extraordinary faculty of building general ideas round insignificant facts, he conquered not only the British public, but the average reader all the world over, with a philosophy of evolution applied to all the sciences, not to mention morality and politics. This era of universality, of faith in scientific and material progress, of pacifism and industry, found its perfect expression in the Great Exhibition of 1851, organized by Prince Albert with truly German solemnity and thoroughness. The vast size of the Crystal Palace, the enthusiasm of the crowds, the atmosphere of national reconciliation after the turmoils of Reform and Chartism, deeply impressed the English people, many of whom, on that occasion took their first railway journey and for the first time beheld their capital city.

Inevitable reactions appeared against social and scientific materialism. The reign produced its romantic waves, sometimes religious, sometimes literary in character. Not only did the Methodist movement make further headway, but the Anglican clergy worked devotedly at the evangelization of the new industrial towns. The Oxford Movement, which began about 1833, strove to invest the Anglican faith anew with the historic and poetic glamour of Catholicism. Its most famous figure, John Henry Newman, himself became a convert to the Church of Rome, and in his later years a Cardinal. Carlyle led the charge against utilitarianism, and showed that people were wrong in supposing that Manchester was becoming richer— it was only the less desirable figures of Manchester who were doing so. Ruskin attacked the ugliness of industrialism and supported the Pre-Raphaelites, some of whom joined with William Morris in founding an æsthetic form of socialism. Finally there was Charles Dickens, in himself the most redoubtable wave of attack, who did more than all the professional philanthropists to teach the England of his day that true generosity which is fundamentally imaginative. But even Dickens, to make his realism acceptable, had to blur its outlines with humor and sentiment, and provide happy endings for his tragic stories. For such was the Victorian compromise.

CHAPTER VI

Disraeli and Gladstone

THE Reform of 1832 satisfied the middle class, but left the working classes with no means of expression. To voice their grievances they fell back on riot, a method old and efficacious, but perilous. The violent campaigns of the Chartists had shown how grave the dangers of such a situation still were. True, this ebullition had been stifled by the wave of prosperity which began about the middle of the century; wise minds knew that it could revive, and that a safety valve then would be desirable. The new masters of law-abiding England, who in any case had maintained their former masters in power, felt no desire to enlarge the electorate further; but the most far-seeing statesmen in both parties, Gladstone in the Liberal, Disraeli in the Conservative camp, believed this to be the only remedy. Each party desired the honor and the fruits of a new reform. In 1852 a *Punch* cartoon showed a sleeping lion which the politicians tried to awaken by prodding it with red-hot pokers, each of them labeled "Reform." But what sort of Reform? A Tory government proposed granting the vote to every elector paying more than £10 rent; to which the Whig Opposition retorted that this was shameful, that £8 was the proper frontier of the Rights of Man. Or a Whig Parliament proposed £7, and Lord Derby, through the mouth of his prophet, Disraeli, declared that this was handing over England to all the perils of demagogy. The real problem was to know which of the two great parties would harvest the new voters. But Gladstone fumed at politicians who thus pored over electoral statistics and gauged popular forces like those of an invading army: these people, he declared, were in truth their brothers, fellow-Christians, men of their own flesh and blood. Whereupon a Tory asked why flesh and blood stopped short at £7 rental.

A group of about thirty Whigs were determined to bar the road against any new advance of democracy, and in 1866 refused to vote for Gladstone's Reform measures. They were called the Adullamites, because of the cave of Adullam, where David was joined by "every one that was in distress, or everyone that was in debt, and everyone that was discontented." Lord Derby and Disraeli, with the passive aid of the Adullamites, overturned Russell and Gladstone. Regaining power in a minority, they proceeded to give the Conservative party a modern color, no longer hostile to any change as the old Tory party had been, but prepared, if new conditions demanded it, to renovate the old national institutions (the monarchy, the House of Lords, the Church of England), even although they stanchly upheld them. Disraeli's efforts to educate his party were successful, and to him the Conservative party owed a new and prolonged youth. By reminding the aristocracy that its traditional rôle was not to restrain but to lead the people, he enabled the families which had so long governed England to continue their function in a transformed society. Making concessions to the Liberals on points of detail, he induced the Commons to pass the new Reform Act of 1867. As in the Act of 1832, the vote still depended on the ownership of a house, or on a sum of rent, but the limits were lower, especially in the boroughs, and more than a million new voters were added to the electorate, mostly from the urban working class. What political attitude would they adopt? This was unpredictable, and Derby himself admitted that the new law would be "a leap in the dark." But he prided himself on having robbed the Whigs of a favorite theme, and, like Disraeli, he put his trust in the common sense of the English workingman. In the long run, the Conservatives had no reason to regret their move, but the next general election (1868) brought a Liberal victory.

When the Conservatives returned in 1874, Lord Derby, in failing health, handed over the Premiership to Disraeli. About the same time Gladstone became the undisputed leader of the Liberal party, and the two men who, since the fall of Peel, had always differed from each other now found themselves in direct conflict. The Gladstone-Disraeli struggle, apart from its human interest, is also of exemplary value as a study: it illustrates the importance of a certain dramatic quality, for a parliamentary regime to be successful. If physical strife was to be replaced by revolutions in a debating-chamber, these rhetorical battles must in themselves offer a noble spectacle. Thanks to the widely different but equally admirable talents of Gladstone and Disraeli, the Parliamentary battles of the next two decades were battles of giants. Two philosophies, two mental attitudes, were at grips. On one side, solemnity, seriousness, conscious rectitude; on the other, brilliance, wit, and—under the guise of superficial frivolity—a faith no less living than Gladstone's. The latter believed in government *by* the people, wished to receive his inspiration from the people, and declared his willingness to accept all the reforms desired by the people, even if they should destroy the oldest traditions of England. Disraeli believed in government *for* the people, in the necessity of keeping intact the framework of the country, and would concede reforms only in so far as they respected certain essential institutions linked with unchanging traits of human nature. Admirable symbols of the two attitudes were to be seen in Gladstone at Hawarden felling trees with his own ax, and in Disraeli at Hughenden refusing to let a single one be cut down.

Gladstone was Prime Minister from 1868 to 1874, Disraeli from 1874 to 1880, and then Gladstone returned from 1880 to 1885. During these eighteen years great changes took place in Europe. Neither Gladstone nor Disraeli was able to realize that the balance of power was about to be upset by the new power of Prussia. Palmerston had tolerated the annexation of Schleswig-Holstein; Disraeli and Gladstone did not react when confronted by the Austro-Prussian War, nor by the Franco-Prussian War, which achieved the hegemony of Prussia and brought about the creation of the German Empire. Russia in her turn denounced the Treaty of Paris, which had ended the Crimean War, and reorganized her Black Sea fleet. Here again Gladstone let things take their course. But the danger of concessions is that they whet the appetite and boldness of those who take advantage of them. England seemed to have fallen asleep, and the weakest Powers believed that they could now pull the British lion's tail with impunity. In the long run public opinion chafed at this weakness. A stage performance showed Gladstone receiving an embassy from China asking for Scotland. The Prime Minister reflected, and said there were three possible replies: to hand over Scotland at once, to wait a little and then hand over Scotland, or to appoint an arbitrator. The public saw in this a true enough picture.

Disraeli's foreign policy, however, was bold; it was more dramatic, and also more dangerous, than Gladstone's. Whereas the Liberal leader desired peace at any price, took up a disinterested view even regarding the Empire, and, by his desire to see his country endowed with a moral rather than an imperial prestige, gained the name of "Little Englander," Disraeli and his friends declared themselves Imperialists. The conception of Empire, eclipsed since the death of Chatham and the loss of the American Colonies, was reborn in the romantic imagination of Disraeli. Before Rhodes, before Chamberlain, before Kipling, he tempted Britain with a positively Roman image of her destiny and duties in the world. Against the wishes of the majority of his party, who distrusted changes whatever they might be, he brought the Queen, who ardently desired it, to assume the title of Empress of India. In 1875 he secretly bought from the Khedive, for £4,000,000, 177,000 shares in the Suez Canal. The majority of the shares remained in French hands, but Britain thus acquired a share in this undertaking, of high importance to her as determining in future the shortest route to India and China. In that same year, Disraeli, a tired and aging man, went to the House of Lords as Lord Beaconsfield. Europe continued to be perturbed over the conflict between Turkey and her Christian provinces, which Russia, to obtain them, defended. There was nothing that Disraeli dreaded more than to see the Russians in the Mediterranean. In his view the prime axiom of British policy was to maintain free communications with India. By land, this communication was possible only through a friendly Turkey; by sea, it must now be kept through the Suez Canal, which would be highly vulnerable if the Turkish provinces in Asia were in hostile hands. He therefore sided with Turkey. But when atrocities were committed by Turks in Bulgaria, Gladstone kindled British opinion against them by pamphleteering and speech-making which Disraeli found absurd, but which touched the religious masses by their fervor. The wave of feeling was such that Disraeli had to abandon intervention.

Before long Russia was able to force the Treaty of San Stefano on the Turks. Turkey-in-Europe disappeared almost completely, and an expanded Bulgaria gave the Russians access to the Mediterranean. Lord Beaconsfield held that this treaty was unacceptable to Europe and sent an ultimatum to Russia. Exhausted by the war, and alarmed by the arrival of troops from India and the dispatch of the British fleet to Constantinople, Russia bowed. This negotiation in the Palmerston manner, the fleet first with diplomacy following up, was refreshing to British pride. The Congress of Berlin in 1878 revised the Treaty of San Stefano. Bulgaria was bisected, Bosnia was promised to Austria, and Britain obtained Cyprus. The Treaty of Berlin seemed a complete triumph for Beaconsfield, who was rewarded with the Garter. In point of fact Cyprus was never of much use to Britain; Turkey continued to maltreat the Christian subjects restored to her, and it was the Bosnian problem which precipitated the war of 1914. In 1879 the hostility of Russia, whose Ministers had returned from Berlin in high dudgeon against England, precipitated a clash on the Indian frontier. When a war followed against the Zulus in South Africa, the public began to feel that, although Gladstone's pacific policy might be inglorious, Disraeli's Imperialist line had its dangers. In 1879 Gladstone again conducted a great oratorical campaign, with prodigious success. He told the electors that it was no longer a question of approving this or that political measure, but of choosing between two systems of morality. For five years past they had heard of nothing but the interests of the British Empire, of scientific frontiers, of new Gibraltars—and with what result? Russia was aggrandized and hostile, Europe in ferment, India at war, Africa stained with blood. And why? Because, said Gladstone, there was something beyond political necessities, there were moral necessities. Let them remember that in the eyes of Almighty God the sanctity of human life was no less inviolable in the villages of Afghanistan than in their own towns. That noble hawk-like face, those powerful piercing eyes, that voice of miraculously sustained vigor, this lofty and religious doctrine, impressed his devout audiences with an almost awful admiration: they seemed to be hearing the divine word, to be gazing upon a prophet inspired. In the election of 1880, Disraeli and his party were swept away.

It is easier to preach peace than maintain it. Gladstone was sincere in his hatred of force, but found himself constrained to use it, and to use it the more fully because his initial weakness heightened the general danger and disorder. The first troubles rose in South Africa. There had been clashes there between the Dutch farmers and the English settlers ever since England annexed the Cape during the Napoleonic wars. In 1877 they had further annexed the Dutch republic of the Transvaal, and in 1881 the Boers revolted, overwhelming the small British army of occupation at Majuba Hill. Gladstone bowed to the force of circumstance and restored Boer independence. Meanwhile in Ireland, a rebel, republican, anti-English party was secretly gathering strength. In the House of Commons the Government was constantly harried by the eighty Irish members, partisans of Home Rule, led by the brilliant, enigmatic Parnell. In Ireland itself Parliamentary action was backed up by a policy of direct action which culminated in murder. The peasantry refused to pay rent. Gladstone vainly tried to support their cause by a Land Act which gave special tribunals power to adjust leases; and, also unavailingly, he released Parnell and some of his associates who had been arrested for incitement to lawlessness. Within a few days violence was again abroad. Public opinion in England was outraged and the Cabinet was forced to put forward fairly effective repressive measures.

After the Transvaal and Ireland, came Egypt. The Khedive's bad administration had led Britain and France to undertake a joint control of finance and the administration of the Egyptian Debt. After the massacre of some Europeans in Alexandria, the French Government, with more timidity than wisdom, withdrew the French fleet. Gladstone would have willingly done likewise, but the Press and public forbade him. British troops entered Cairo. This conquest, undertaken "in a fit of absentmindedness," made Gladstone popular, although he disapproved of it. Theoretically, this occupation of Egypt was temporary, and it was jealously scrutinized by France. Actually, Sir Evelyn Baring (later Lord Cromer) was soon administering the country under the nominal sovereignty of the Khedive. A British army of occupation remained "provisionally" in Egypt. When a Moslem fanatic proclaimed himself as the Mahdi in the Egyptian Sudan, rallied the Dervishes and drove out the Egyptian soldiery, General Hicks was dispatched there, and his force was cut to pieces. Gladstone decided to evacuate the Sudan, and rashly intrusted the operation to General Gordon, an extraordinary personage who had won a great reputation during the campaigns in China, a man as fanatical in his own way as the Mahdi. Instead of evacuating the Sudan, Gordon shut himself up in Khartum and called in vain for reinforcements. When Gladstone at last decided to send them, it was too late. The Mahdi massacred the General and his garrison of 11,000 men. Gordon had all the virtues necessary to become a national hero; his tenacity appealed to the Imperialists, his love of the Bible pleased the pious, his whimsical qualities touched the English imagination at large. His death

[445]

brought the Government down. But the murder was not avenged until Kitchener's expedition in 1898.

At home, Gladstone had been removing some of the last of the country's religious inequalities. He disestablished the Anglican Church of Ireland, which the Catholic Irish had no reason to maintain; and he opened the Universities of Oxford and Cambridge to Nonconformists, who since 1836 had had access to the younger University of London. Forster's Education Act of 1870 gave England at last the embryo of a national system of schools. Prince Albert had been shocked by the number of illiterates in England, who were far more numerous than in Germany or France. In Manchester in 1838, out of a hundred persons entering into matrimony, forty-five could not sign their own names; in 1849, 33 per cent of men and 49 per cent of women were illiterate; in 1861, 25 per cent and 35 per cent, respectively. Victorian complacency declined to accept the necessity for imitating the Continent in this respect. The upper and middle classes sent their sons to the public schools or grammar schools; the common people in England for a long time had only the schools maintained by the Church. At last the Forster Act of 1870 set up State schools in villages and districts where there was no non-ecclesiastical school. The new schools were Christian, but not sectarian. It was in 1891 that education became compulsory; and in 1912 it became gratuitous.

In 1877 Disraeli had given the vote to the urban working class; in 1884 Gladstone gave it to the agricultural laborer. Bills for a secret ballot and to stifle electoral corruption had ended the plutocratic control of polling. After 1884, out of seven million adult males, five million were on the register. Almost the only exceptions now were those sharing their masters' houses (servants) or their fathers' houses (sons living with their family), and all women. Local government was now mainly carried out by elected bodies, and the justices of the peace had lost the administrative power which they had held since Tudor times. Within fifty years England had passed, with no great upheavals, from oligarchy to democracy. But at the same time the independence of the House of Commons had been weakened. Under the old aristocratic system, a rich landlord in his own borough (or his nominee) knew himself invulnerable; and his vote in Parliament was free, because the Prime Minister had no hold over him, unless by corruption, which honorable (or extremely rich) members resisted. But under the democratic system all seats became uncertain; no member could be absolutely sure of re-election by a wide and capricious electorate, and a threat of dissolution therefore became the whip which the Prime Minister cracked to bring straying members to heel. A Liberal association founded by Joseph Chamberlain at Birmingham became the pattern of what was called, from American usage, a "caucus." The parties became powerful organizations, each choosing its candidates, collecting election funds (provided, on occasion, in exchange for titles), and setting forward its chosen leader as the Premier to be summoned to office by the sovereign. Barring some unforeseeable accident, a grave personal mistake or a party split, a Prime Minister with an electoral majority was now increasingly certain to retain power for the duration of a Parliament. In this way, as an unforeseen outcome of electoral reforms, the executive was increasingly strengthened, and the English system became more akin to the American, although it was freed from the dangers raised under the American Constitution by the twofold currents of Presidential and Congressional elections.

The two great traditional parties seemed now to be part of the eternal verities; and it would have been a bold man who foretold that one day a Labor party would come into power. English Socialism, from More to Morris, had been utopian and ineffectual. A German Jew, Karl Marx, who had lived in London since the Revolution of 1848, published there his book on *Capital* in 1864, which became to Socialism what *The Wealth of Nations* had been to Liberalism. He described therein the results of free competition, which were quite unforeseen by Adam Smith, and declared that, just as the middle classes had ousted feudalism, so one day the proletariat would expropriate the bourgeoisie. But the class war found few recruits in the prosperous England of those days. It required the long and distressing slump which began in 1875, to bring into being a Social Democratic Federation, founded by the well-to-do H. M. Hyndman. And even he played a far smaller part in the activities of the working class in England than did practical trade-union leaders of the type of Keir Hardie or John Burns. Socialism in England always took peculiar forms. It had been reformist and paternal with Robert Owen, æsthetic with Ruskin; it was intellectual, paradoxical, and temporizing with the Fabian Society; emotional and evangelistic with Ramsay MacDonald. Through this last aspect it was later to draw to the workers' side a good proportion of the Nonconformist middle classes. Just as Bentham and

Mill imbued the Victorian intellectuals with their ideas, and brought about the supremacy of individualist Liberalism, so the Fabians, Bernard Shaw and the Webbs in particular, made the collectivist conception of society acceptable to the Edwardian intellectuals. Fabian collectivism was differentiated from Continental Socialism by two characteristics: it assailed ground rent and large landed estates rather than industrial capital, and it clung to the principles of representative government rather than urging direct rule by the voting masses. Fabian ideas, not very many years after the society's foundation, were to inspire the social and financial policy of advanced Liberals like Lloyd George.

CHAPTER VII

The Empire in the Nineteenth Century

AFTER the loss of the American Colonies, it was common enough to find Englishmen denying the economic value of colonies. Furthermore, Wesley had roused scruples of a religious character regarding the native races, especially when these were becoming converted to Christianity. This indifference and these moral doubts explain the surprising generosity with which England twice, in 1802 and in 1815, restored to France and Holland colonies which her maritime supremacy had enabled her to conquer. France received back her West Indian islands, the fishing rights in Newfoundland, and sundry other possessions. Holland recovered Java, Curacao and Surinam. But some obscure instinct checked the negotiations at certain points, and they retained at least the framework of an Empire. India and Canada were still the two main pieces. The Cape of Good Hope, taken from the Dutch in 1796, was held as a useful stage on the passage to India. Gibraltar, Malta and the Ionian Islands dominated the Mediterranean. In the Antipodes, transported convicts had made the first Australian settlements in the later eighteenth century. Thus the groundwork of the future British Empire was unmistakably sketched out; but nobody supposed that one day these scattered territories would form a Commonwealth of Nations, self-governing, but united by bonds freely accepted.

Nevertheless, if the new Empire was not sooner or later to follow the American example, it must obtain some form of autonomy, at least in those parts where large communities of the white race had grown up. Our study of English history has shown the early and growing attachment of the Anglo-Saxon to his liberties. And this sense he carried with him all over the globe. The English colonist, who quite often had left the

mother-country to escape from religious or social restrictions, was not
the man to surrender in exile the right to share in the government of his
new country. In the colonies as at home, it was essential that respect be
paid to those two great principles which, as H. A. L. Fisher has said,
are the poles of the Anglo-Saxon race: that all rule must be based on the
consent of the ruled, and that a statesman's duty is to avoid revolution
by resorting to reform. But how are colonies to be made into free States
while maintaining Imperial unity? It would have gone against the grain
of the Anglo-Saxon genius to resolve this problem by making one line
of abstract reasoning triumph over another. A fortunate accident created
the first Dominion; success encouraged imitation; and so the Commonwealth of Nations was born. The said accident was the existence in Canada of a French population which, since 1791, had maintained a legislative assembly almost entirely French in speech and sympathies, whereas
the executive power was in the hands of a British Governor, with a
Council composed of British officials. In the event of disagreement—and
in such circumstances disagreement was inevitable—there was revived
across the Atlantic that old conflict between Crown and Parliament
which in England had brought about the fall of the Stuarts.

In 1837 a rebellion broke out in French Canada and spread into the
provinces. It was easily put down, and a blind or obstinate Government
might easily have paid no heed to the signs of discontent. The Whigs
were wise enough to send over to Canada a statesman not afraid of experiments. Lord Durham had generous instincts and an unlikeable
character, quite a good combination in a leader. After a few months in
residence he drew up a remarkable report on the Canadian situation. His
conclusion was the necessity of trying to unite both provinces more
closely, and of setting up in both some form of Ministerial representation.
He had no desire to touch any of the Crown prerogatives, but the Crown
would have to submit to the necessary consequences of representative institutions and govern through the intermediary of those in whom the
representative body put confidence. To many of Lord Durham's contemporaries these ideas seemed revolutionary. They held that this meant
the breaking of every bond between colony and mother-country. And what
was to happen if a conflict arose between the King's representative and
the local government? The risk, however, was accepted. The new Gov-
ernor-General, Lord Elgin, bravely formed a Ministry of reformist Cana-

dians, who then held a majority in the country, and several of whom had taken part in the recent rebellion. The experiment was successful. Confidence fostered loyalty. Thenceforward the principle of self-government was admitted. Theoretically nothing had changed, as the form had to be respected. The British Government retained the right of appointing the Ministers. In practice they made their choice only from among the men who held the confidence of the Canadian Chambers. Thus the greatest colonial revolution was accomplished with no theorizing and no noise. It was a very British solution.

The different States composing Australia and New Zealand also became entitled, between 1850 and 1875, to provide themselves with liberal constitutions. But the solution was more complicated in countries where small numbers of white colonists lived side by side with numerous natives. In these cases it would have been dangerous to grant all rights of control to the white minority, which might misuse its power to oppress the natives. In South Africa a still more awkward problem was raised by the presence of two European races. The original colonists at the Cape, at the time when England occupied that country, were Dutch farmers; these Boers had emigrated first into Natal, and then into the Orange and Transvaal republics which they founded. In 1881 the Boer rising wiped out the British forces at Majuba Hill, and Gladstone had thereupon abandoned the Transvaal. But British penetration of South Africa was carried on by a chartered company, the animating force of which was Cecil Rhodes, the Clive of this continent. When gold and diamond mines were shortly afterwards discovered in the Transvaal, a flood of British immigrants poured into the Dutch republics, where they were granted mining or trading concessions, but not civic rights. In 1895, Dr. Jameson, a friend of Rhodes's, acting under the latter's inspiration, organized in time of peace an armed raid into the Transvaal to overturn the existing government. Repulsed and captured, Jameson gravely compromised the British Government, whom the Boers suspected of having encouraged the raid.

During the second half of the nineteenth century, Africa—that continent "invented by Providence to vex the Foreign Office"—was sliced up by the European Powers. Between 1853 and 1873 Livingstone explored the region of Lake Tanganyika; then Stanley crossed the whole continent. While the new territories were being opened up, Germany, Belgium,

France, and later Italy, all quarreled over them. Officially, Britain for a long time stood aloof from the African game. It was the great Companies —not only Rhodes's British South Africa Company, but also the Niger and the East Africa—which founded the new British colonies of Rhodesia, Nigeria, Kenya, and Uganda. This curious reversion to the Chartered Company system is attributable to the advantage found by the Imperial Government in allowing capitalist enterprise to bear the cost of exploration and pioneering work. If the undertaking was a failure, it was abandoned. If it succeeded, the Imperial Government supplanted the Company. Thus, piece by piece, there grew up in Africa an Empire of such magnitude that Rhodes was able to envisage a railway running from the Cape to Cairo without ever leaving British territory. The only barrier across this line was German East Africa, which Britain was in the end to acquire after the war of 1914-1918.

In India the East India Company, almost despite itself, had continued the conquest of that country after the collapse of the Mogul Empire. It brought over a body of officials who battled as best they could against anarchy and famine. The Reform advocates of 1832 had been anxious to apply their principles in India, too, and an Indian Charter in 1833 laid it down that any subject of His Majesty could fill any post, whatever his race, birthplace, or color. It was a bold theory, and difficult of application. In 1857 a terrible mutiny broke out among the native Indian troops to whom the Company, like the Roman Empire of old, had intrusted the security of the country. After fearful massacres of women and children by the rebels came a ruthless and efficacious repression. The British Government itself took over the administration of India, and the European garrison was increased to 75,000 men. The great period of conquest was by now over. Fresh campaigns in Burma and on the Eastern frontiers led to the final delimitation of territory in 1885.

Rudyard Kipling has sung the praises of the Indian Civil Service. Other writers have attacked it for its racial pride and lack of contact with native life. It is a fact that since the Mutiny India, with its 350,000,000 inhabitants, has been held in peace—except for a few inevitable riots—by 75,000 white troops and 150,000 native troops; it is a fact that British administrators have never numbered more than 5,000, and that the area of land cleared, irrigated, and made healthy by them is immense; and it is a fact that English is the only tongue common to the countless races of

India and is spoken in the political congresses representing the whole country. A large body of Hindus educated on European lines has come to occupy administrative posts. It is only natural that India in her turn should come to desire self-government as granted to the Dominions, or even complete independence. Especially since the Russo-Japanese War, the East has only reluctantly continued to accept the overlordship of the West. Nationalistic movements have come into being, rather coldly received by the British administration, but tolerated by the Imperial Government, which, in India as elsewhere, has worked for compromise. Slowly governmental authority is being transferred into Indian hands. In 1917 public education and most of the internal services were intrusted to Indian provincial Cabinets, responsible to elected Chambers, only the military and police forces being left under British control.

The difficulty for any colonial administration is that the very fact of its complete success loosens the bonds with the mother-country. In Egypt as in India, the stabilization of finances, the spread of education, and increasing wealth and order were bound sooner or later to inspire the native peoples with a greater craving for independence. Nevertheless, it seemed not impossible to envisage free peoples united by pledges of mutual defense, by preferential tariffs, and by links of language and culture. In the twentieth century the new character of the Empire was to be one of the problems of the post-war period. In the nineteenth, that Empire had first to be given its shape, and had to be recognized by rival nations. This twofold task called for a government which believed in Empire, and the opportunity for the Conservatives appeared.

CHAPTER VIII

The Waning of Liberalism

QUEEN VICTORIA respected Gladstone, but deemed him dangerous: in her view he had weakened his country's authority in the world. The Queen had a curious faculty for thinking on all subjects very much as "her people" thought. Since the death of Gordon, many of Gladstone's supporters had lost faith in him, notwithstanding his astounding eloquence. In the election of 1886, after a short Conservative interregnum, he came back with a small majority, holding power only by the support of the Irish Nationalists. And by a paradox of Parliamentary rule, this foreign element became the arbiter in English politics. Soon it was rumored that Gladstone had bought their support by a promise of Home Rule for Ireland. And it was true. In April, 1886, the Prime Minister introduced a bill to grant Irish autonomy and set up an Irish Parliament in Dublin. A single Chamber, composed, however, of two sorts of members, some elected by boroughs and counties, the others nominated for permanent membership, would be intrusted with all Irish internal affairs, while the Imperial Government retained control of the army, customs, and foreign policy. Ireland was to pay Westminster an annual contribution towards her share of the common expenditure. Joseph Chamberlain, Lord Hartington, and numerous Liberal leaders protested; if need be they would have accepted a federalist solution, but they refused a separatist handling of the Irish problem. They maintained that the past record of Parnell and his friends did not justify Gladstone's trust in them. Before long these Unionists, as they then came to be called, left the Liberal party, and, without as yet joining the Conservative party, pledged themselves to support the latter against Gladstone. The Prime Minister appealed to the country, but the polls went against him.

Four hundred Unionists were returned to the House, three hundred and eighteen of whom were Conservatives. The Gladstonians were routed, and Lord Salisbury, at the head of the Unionist coalition, took office.

Robert Cecil, Marquis of Salisbury, regarded the affairs of mankind with a deep, aloof wisdom. In the days when he served under Disraeli he condemned the romantic visions of his leader as severely as he did the idealism of Gladstone. He detested the lofty moral arguments with which most politicians buttress their selfish interests, and regarded human societies as fragile organisms to be interfered with as little as possible. When he left office, after twenty years, he had solved neither the social problems nor the Irish question; but he had prevented them from causing any disorder during that period. In foreign policy, as in his conduct of home affairs, he tried to avoid emotion and to think in "chemical" terms, striving to feel neither sympathy nor antipathy towards foreign nations. A solitary in his private life, he accepted for his country "a splendid isolation." And this attitude remained possible, even reasonable, so long as Lord Salisbury remained in office—that is, until 1902. Thereafter came the time when England was menaced and, as in Pitt's day, had to find an army on the Continent.

Salisbury's long rule was broken only by a brief interregnum. At the election of 1892 the majority in the House of Commons once more consisted of Gladstonian Liberals and Irish Home Rulers. At the age of eighty-three the indomitable Gladstone once more pushed a Home Rule bill through the Lower House. But it was rejected by the Lords, and the measure was not sufficiently popular to justify a decisive battle with the Upper Chamber on that ground. Gladstone's retirement through illness and old age put the premiership into the hands of Lord Rosebery from 1894 to 1896; but the Liberal party was divided between his supporters and those of Sir William Harcourt and the rôle of the Conservatives became easy. This time the Liberal Unionists—Lord Hartington (later Duke of Devonshire) and Joseph Chamberlain—consented to enter the Government alongside Salisbury and his nephew, Arthur Balfour. It was a time of conflicting imperialisms, of jealousy and intrigue. In America, a frontier dispute between Venezuela and British Guiana led the President of the United States to remind the world of the Monroe Doctrine, and might have led to war if Salisbury had not accepted arbitration. In Africa, French military expeditions, pushing up the valleys of the Niger and Congo, were annexing vast territories which cut off the British colonies from their hinterland. France had then no reason to renounce Egypt, which she hoped to enter by way of the Upper Nile, and a mission under the command of Commandant Marchand found its way across Africa towards the Sudan. Britain, for her part, had not renounced Morocco, and at the court of the Sultan a Scottish adventurer, Kaid Maclean, was fostering resistance to French influence. The Siamese frontier, Madagascar, Newfoundland were also points of friction between the two countries.

This latent hostility became acute when General Kitchener, after defeating the Mahdi, avenging Gordon, and occupying the Sudan, came face to face with Marchand's column at Fashoda. The Conservative newspapers in London had a dangerous attack of bellicose fever; the Liberal Press spoke gravely of the moral duty incumbent on Britain to reconquer the Sudan for the Egyptians. Both countries mobilized their fleets. Britain hurriedly moved her ships, which were dangerously scattered, the Mediterranean fleet being partly at Malta and partly at Gibraltar, and therefore liable to be cut into by the French fleet from Toulon. The German Emperor, William II, hoped that this war would break out. But Delcassé, at the French Foreign Office, deemed it wise to yield and thus prepare the way for a reconciliation between the two countries. During the years that followed this episode England's name was hated in France.

Truth to tell, it was hated all the world over at that time, for England was going through one of those periods of vainglorious prosperity which are as dangerous to nations as to individuals. The Imperialist doctrine, propounded by Disraeli in the middle '70's to somewhat protesting Conservatives, was becoming a national religion. Just as the Great Exhibition of 1851 marked the apogee of England's industrial prosperity, so the Diamond Jubilee of 1897 crowned her Imperial glory. The Queen and Lord Salisbury had agreed in making this festivity a private celebration of Empire. No foreign sovereigns attended, but from all the Britains overseas came princes, statesmen and soldiers. For some years past a poet of genius, Rudyard Kipling, had been voicing the feelings of all those Englishmen who, scattered over the globe, strove to uphold in every clime the solid qualities of the British character as it had been shaped by the public schools since the days of Dr. Arnold. To this moral race

Rudyard Kipling supplied moral grounds for cherishing their own renown; conquest became in their eyes an Imperial duty, and they were called upon to take up "the White Man's burden." Another man of genius, Joseph Chamberlain, the Radical who had become the ally of the Conservatives, urged at the Colonial Office that poverty and unemployment were best combated by the development of Imperial trade. He tried by every means to imbue the Dominions, the colonies, and the mother-country with the sense of unity sung by Kipling. A letter bearing a penny stamp could reach, no longer simply the United Kingdom, but the farthest corners of the Empire. The Dominions were encouraged to introduce their products to London. Chamberlain was the first to envisage the collaboration of Canada and Australia in the defense of the Empire in the event of war, an idea which half a century earlier would have seemed wild, and fifteen years later became a reality.

At the time of the Jubilee, Kipling published in *The Times* a poem which surprised the country by its note of bodeful solemnity. At the height of the feasting he traced the warning letters on the wall:

> Lord God of Hosts, be with us yet,
> Lest we forget, lest we forget. . . .

It was a prophetic warning. Within three years of the glorious Jubilee procession, at the southern end of the African continent, the most powerful Empire in the world was being held in check by two small republics of farming folk—the Transvaal and the Orange Free State. England and Europe alike were astounded when the conflict lasted for over a year. It exposed the weakness of the British army, the faulty organization of the War Office, and also the enmities which Britain's policy of Imperialist self-seeking had roused against her all the world over. By forcing the wiser heads in England to ponder this situation and seek a remedy, the South African War exerted a deep influence on European politics in the early years of the new century. For a time it made England suspicious of the domineering diplomacy which Canning and Palmerston had made popular, and which was no longer justifiable by the actual relations of the existing forces. When the victories of Roberts and Kitchener at last enabled a victorious peace to be signed with the Boers, its terms were conspicuous for their moderation. Both republics were annexed; but Britain granted the vanquished farmers a generous indemnity which enabled them to rebuild their farms and replenish their fields. When the Boer generals came to London a few months later they were welcomed with an enthusiasm that surprised them. In 1906 both republics received a measure of responsible self-government, and in 1910 the Union of South Africa was set up, comprising the Cape Colony, the Orange Free State, and the Transvaal Republic. Few things do fuller honor to British policy here than the loyalty with which, in 1914, the South African republics took their part in the defense of the Empire. General Botha and General Smuts, veterans of the war against Britain less than fifteen years before, came to be among her most trusted and worthy counselors.

Queen Victoria did not live to see the Boer War ended. She died early in 1901, after a reign of sixty-three years, the happiest reign perhaps in England's history, in the course of which the country had accepted without civil strife or grave suffering a revolution far more profound than that of 1688, while the Kingdom was becoming, not only in name but in fact, an Empire. Amongst her subjects she could count Dickens, Thackeray, George Eliot, the Brontës, Macaulay, Carlyle, Newman, Tennyson, Ruskin, William Morris, Rossetti, Thomas Hardy, Meredith, Swinburne, Wilde, Stevenson, and Kipling. But literature had interested her (and that very little) only so long as her "dear Albert" was alive. Her own concerns and her greatness lay elsewhere. She had restored and enhanced the royal dignity, besmirched by the later Hanoverians. Thanks to her, constitutional monarchy had become an accepted, tested, desirable form of government. Except in the far-off days of her girlhood, she had always been wise enough to yield when she found herself in conflict with her Ministers; but she retained and insisted upon her three essential rights—to be consulted, to encourage, and to warn. In this way the sovereign, especially after a long reign, was able to exercise a moderating influence upon Ministers, who could not but respect her. Early in her reign, and again about 1870, when as a "professional widow" she seemed to lose interest in the realm, waves of republican feeling rose here and there; but when Victoria died, the country's attachment to the monarchy was as firm as, perhaps firmer than, it had been in the days of Elizabeth. And her successors, by their firm grasp of the craft of kingship, kept that feeling warm and rooted it still more firmly.

Victorianism died before Victoria. A new society had taken shape round the personality of Edward, Prince of Wales. Marlborough House was anti-Victorian by reaction, more free in morals and speech, and more accessible than Buckingham Palace to the new moneyed men, Americans and Jews. The middle classes themselves no longer clung so passionately to the Victorian compromise. It became fashionable to condemn the great poets and novelists of the Victorian age. At the time when the adolescent Marcel Proust was admiring George Eliot, fashionable England was applauding Oscar Wilde. As in France, scientific romanticism and the cult of Progress were followed by doubt and discouragement. Victorian demigods like Spencer and Darwin saw their altars overturned. Samuel Butler made mock of evolutionary and Christian teachings at once. A few sought refuge in the decadent æstheticism of the *Yellow Book*. Other, more vigorous, minds criticized in order to rebuild. A new generation of writers came to the fore, with Bernard Shaw, H. G. Wells, and John Galsworthy to teach the English middle classes new moral and intellectual values. The *Daily Mail,* the first halfpenny newspaper, had been founded by Alfred Harmsworth (later Lord Northcliffe) in 1898, and immediately caught the favor of the masses. The cult of sport spread more and more widely amongst Englishmen of all classes, and at the end of the reign the bicycle came into its own. The motorcar was coming into existence, and Wells proclaimed to an incredulous public that it would one day drive the horse from the roads. Eight years after the death of the Queen the Frenchman Blériot would cross the English Channel in a flying-machine. After the Diamond Jubilee in 1897 the makers of the strange new cinematographic machine were able to show Her Majesty her own picture in motion. Throughout that long reign scientific inventiveness had hardly paused. The strong fever-wave of genius which had been traversing mankind since 1760 was still potent; it would be strange if it did not one day bring about some grave mishap.

CHAPTER IX

The Armed Peace

KING EDWARD VII, on his accession, was nearly sixty. As Prince of Wales he had been kept by his mother at arm's length from public affairs. Public opinion, especially among his Nonconformist subjects, had turned a disapproving eye on a life which hitherto had apparently been devoted to pleasure. But Edward VII had sound sense, bonhomie, and tact. Widely traveled, he knew Europe and the statesmen of foreign countries, and realized also the limitations of Britain's power. While having many friends in Paris, even among Republican statesmen, he was the object of nothing less than hatred on the part of his nephew William, the German Emperor since 1888. In the eyes of the capricious, impressionable, romantic Kaiser the Prince of Wales was the supreme example of that calm English self-confidence which disconcerted and vexed him. In the end, after several public and private affronts, the uncle himself came to have an obvious dislike of his nephew. The antipathy between these two men played a secondary, but very real, part in the development of European politics between 1900 and 1910. In particular, the Kaiser's longing to astound the English and beat them on their own ground hastened the construction of a great German navy which ere long began to alarm England.

The South African War had shown the more clear-sighted of the English that "splendid isolation," from being a source of strength had become a danger; and the isolation, it has been said, was more evident than the splendor. The extent of the Empire was such that England might at any moment be obliged to use a large part of her strength in some distant quarter of the globe. If one of the enemies made by the arrogance of the Palmerstonian tradition chose such a moment to strike at her in India, in Egypt, or even at home, who would come to her defense? Two powers were outstanding as possible allies—Germany and France. Between these two, Joseph Chamberlain hesitated. He had been one of the first to appreciate the perils of this situation. His advances to Germany were repulsed. When Salisbury's place in Downing Street was taken by his nephew Balfour, and the Foreign Office was in the hands of Lord Lansdowne, a reconciliation with France became more practicable; all the more so because the statesmen of both countries were alarmed by the power of Germany and anxious for a more friendly relationship. Steps to achieve this were taken after a visit to Paris by King Edward VII in 1903, which transformed the emotional atmosphere of the negotiations. The essential point was the abandonment by France of any claim to Egypt, in exchange for Britain's recognition of French interests in Morocco, the country bordering on Algeria. The agreement concluded in 1904, the starting-point of an Entente Cordiale, was remarkable in that it satisfied both parties. All the old disputes, in Newfoundland, Africa, and the Far East, were settled. Both governments promised mutual diplomatic support against the claims of a third party in the fulfillment of this agreement. And thus there came about a happy conclusion of the long rivalry which had sundered the two countries since the Norman Conquest. They had been opposed to each other in dynastic, in religious, in imperial interests. Now the quarrels had burned themselves out. Each nation had now an Empire in conformity with its own character and strength. Neither now coveted the other's territories. Although not set down in black and white, it seemed probable that these two countries, now amply provided for, would soon be prepared to support each other against powers less fortunate in the world's goods.

The German Government had observed this rapprochement between Britain and France with perturbation, and in regard to Morocco, where German interests were involved, with annoyance. But they awaited a favorable opportunity for protest. This seemed to come with the Russo-Japanese War in 1904. Russia, in spite of the Tsar's hesitancy, had for about ten years been drawing nearer to France. After her defeat she ceased, for a time at least, to count as a military power. Since the Dreyfus Affair France had apparently been so deeply divided by domestic strife as to make her incapable of withstanding foreign conflict. Would Britain support her if Germany assumed a bold front? The German Government did not believe so. The moment seemed favorable to get rid of Delcassé, whom Germany regarded as the architect of a coalition designed to oppose her. The landing of the German Emperor at Tangier, followed by a thinly veiled ultimatum, roused fears of war. Lansdowne offered Delcassé, not an alliance, but a tightening of the bonds uniting the two countries. Rouvier, the French Premier, was alarmed by Germany's threats and preferred to capitulate. Delcassé was thrown overboard. For some weeks British statesmen wondered whether the Entente Cordiale had been a wise policy. Such were the events of May and June, 1905.

But in England, meanwhile, the swing of the pendulum had come. The education policy of the Conservative Ministry had caused discontent among its Radical-Unionist allies. The non-sectarian schools set up by Forster's act of 1870 had pleased the Nonconformists, but left the Anglicans and Catholics dissatisfied. The Unionist Cabinet, predominantly Anglican, decided that all schools, free or otherwise, should receive State aid, and thus alienated the Nonconformist electorate, which was behind Chamberlain and his friends. Aware of the gathering storm, Chamberlain sought to avert it by launching a new idea—that of Tariff Reform, a program of preferential tariffs designed to tighten the trade bonds between the colonies and the mother-country. "You are an Imperial people," he told the British people. "Let Imperial products come to you freely, and tax the products of other countries." But to protect Canadian wheat, Australian sheep, Indian cotton, meant the reopening of the whole Free Trade controversy. The creed of which Cobden and Bright had been the prophets, and Peel the martyr, was still very much alive. England had waxed rich and fat on Free Trade, and to its principles she owed a century of contentment, abundance, and variety of foodstuffs, and markets for her manufacturers. She kept her faith. In vain did Chamberlain demonstrate that Cobden had erred. The rest of the world had not fallen in with his idea that England was to be the universal workshop, with other countries as her granary. Other countries had countered Free Trade with heavy tariffs. The new factories of Germany and the United States were rivaling, sometimes outstripping, those of England; to save her Dominions and her industries, she must act. These doctrines shocked the Free Traders in the Cabinet, and did not convince them. The appeal to Imperial sentiment made little impression on the electorate; it even displeased them, because the enthusiasm of the early stages of the Boer

War had been succeeded, as the was dragged on, by a wave of pacifist and anti-Imperial feeling. All the Free Traders in the Cabinet handed their resignations to Balfour. Unionism was disunited. The pendulum had swung.

The Liberal party now had some difficulty in forming a Ministry. To avoid quarrels, the old leaders were set aside and the Prime Minister was Sir Henry Campbell-Bannerman, of whom little was expected but who worked wonders. He died, however, in 1908, and his place was taken by Asquith, a great parliamentarian who was also a man of indisputably fine character. The Foreign Office went to Sir Edward Grey, a descendant of the famous old Whig family. This country gentleman with a deep fund of loyalty was destined to direct Britain's destinies at the gravest crisis of her history. The harsh irony of fate willed it that this Liberal Cabinet, peace-loving in tone and hostile to Imperialism and military and naval expenditure, inherited, as Gladstone did in 1880, a situation which demanded firmness. Hardly had Grey settled into the Foreign Office when he had to concern himself with the Algeciras Conference, convoked to deal with the fate of Morocco, and had to authorize the conversations between the General Staffs of France, Belgium, and his own country. Algeciras ended without catastrophe, von Bülow having yielded before the firm attitude of Britain and the hostility of Europe at large. But between 1906 and 1914 alarms came thick and fast. The German navy was increasing so rapidly that the day could be seen when it would equal, then surpass, the British navy itself. The balance of power in Europe was upset. However peace-loving the Liberal Ministry might be, it recognized its responsibility for the country's security and knew that without the mastery of the seas Britain was doomed. After unavailing efforts to reach a naval agreement with the Kaiser and Admiral von Tirpitz, the Cabinet took up defensive measures. An agreement with Russia, supplementing that of 1904 with France, grouped these three powers in a Triple Entente. Germany, in all good faith, declared that she was "encircled." Lord Haldane reorganized the army at the War Office, created the Territorial Army, and formed a General Staff. Admiral Sir John Fisher, supported by Winston Churchill at the Admiralty, strove to regroup the unduly dispersed fleets and to get a powerful fighting fleet into the North Sea. The safeguarding of the Mediterranean was left mainly to France.

This armaments race swallowed up the resources which the Liberal Government had planned to devote to social reform. Its supporters were resentful. To go to the polls without some popular agitation to rehabilitate the party would have been to court disaster. Lloyd George, a young, aggressive, and spellbinding Welshman, was now Chancellor of the Exchequer; and he found an advantageous opening for such an agitation in a revival of hostilities against the House of Lords. The prestige of the peerage had been injured by a widespread knowledge that titles were given in return for contributions to party funds. The Liberals had good reason for resenting the Upper Chamber, which had rejected its most cherished measures, notable Welsh Disestablishment, the development of Nonconformist schools, and Irish Home Rule. But in a country so loyal to tradition, the defeat of the peers depended on their being put unmistakably in the wrong, as they would be, for instance, if they were brought to rejecting the Budget, a step contrary to all precedent. Lloyd George put forward a body of new taxes and social legislation which he styled the People's Budget. He needed money, he said, to pay for new battleships, military expenditure, and old-age pensions; and he would seek it from the rich. More particularly, he appropriated some of the ideas of the Fabians, imposing fresh taxation on large landed estates and in "unearned increment." In 1909, as Lloyd George desired, the Lords threw out this Budget and Parliament was dissolved. The election campaign showed how conservative Edwardian England remained. A nation of voters had to choose between an aristocratic Chamber and a demagogic Budget. The result was surprising. The Liberals lost a large number of their seats, Asquith returned to power in very much the same position in the Commons as Gladstone had stood. He could pass his Budget only with the support of the Irish Nationalists, and had to obtain this by a promise of Home Rule. But if this promise were to have any validity, the veto of the House of Lords must be abolished, as the peers would certainly never vote for a dismemberment of the Empire. Thus the Budget problem passed into the background, the control of the veto into the foreground. How could the Lords be induced to vote their own abdication? This was possible only by the method of 1714 and 1832: a threat to create a batch of new peers. Such a threat in itself required the support of the King; and the King would certainly not grant it without a fresh election.

The Armed Peace

Prudently the Lords passed the Lloyd George Budget. The party struggle was interrupted by the death of Edward VII in 1910, but feeling ran too high for the quarrel to be left where it was. Another election repeated the situation of a Liberal-Nationalist majority, and the New King, George V, obliged the House of Lords by a threat to create new peers, to vote the limitation of its own powers. Since 1911 any financial measure passed by the House of Commons becomes law after one month, even if the Lords refuse to accept it. As regards other legislation, the Lords retain a suspensive veto; but after three favorable votes of the Commons, the Upper House is obliged to yield. These measures, however, have not robbed the House of Lords of all its prestige. It continues to play a moderating rôle, and its debates have often more intellectual and oratorical value than those of the Commons.

This just law was passed in a cloud of hatred. These political battles between 1911 and 1914 were more violent than any which England had known for years. Lloyd George had set class against class, even Church against Church. Amongst the coal-miners and railway workers, powerful trade unions were confronting the autocratic organizations of employers. It was a time of numerous strikes. Scientific progress was increasing the volume of consumable wealth, and the working class demanded its share. But could a readjustment of relations between employer and employed be achieved peacefully? If the Parliamentary regime was to last, there would have to be some indirect representation of the trade unions. The Liberal party was wise enough to prepare for this by a whole series of measures, the most significant of which was one for the payment of members of Parliament, thus putting an end to the House of Commons being regarded as a sort of aristocratic club. The Labor Party, which had only had two members in 1901, had fifty in 1906. Allied with the Liberals, it pushed forward useful laws for the safeguarding of working-class interests. Meanwhile women, eager to secure for their sex the right of the Parliamentary vote, became exasperated by the attitude adopted towards them by the Government and the House of Commons, abandoned peaceful agitation, and tried now to alarm, rather than to convince, the male. Further, the Home Rule Act of 1912 met with impassioned resistance from the Ulster Protestants, who declared that they would never consent to be separated from Britain and vowed to defend themselves, if need be, by armed force. Their leader, Sir Edward Carson, formed a provisional Ulster Government, and organized an army. Open discontent among British officers at the Curragh Camp in Ireland made it look as if part of the Crown forces would eventually refuse to move against Ulster. Dropping the usual prudence of his party, the Unionist leader, Bonar Law, sided with Carson. To avoid civil war, Asquith proposed giving Ulster six years' respite. But Carson stood fast: Ulster, he said, would not agree to a sentence of death with six years' respite. In 1914 the peril was imminent. The act was due to come into force. It required only the assent of the Crown. Great efforts were made to bring George V to refuse his consent and insist on a dissolution. On July 21, 1914, the King in person opened a conference between representatives of the Government, the Opposition, Southern Ireland, and Ulster. After three days, seeing no hope of agreement, this conference broke up. On the same day Austria dispatched her ultimatum to Serbia.

In Europe as in Britain, a period of comparative tranquillity was being succeeded by one of feverish unrest, animated by philosophies of violence. The static conservatism of the Holy Alliance, the ineffective idealism of the revolutionaries of 1848, had been supplanted by the realist politics of Cavour and Bismarck, and by the ruthless class warfare prophesied by Karl Marx and Georges Sorel. Liberalism might be in power in Britain, but its idealist, reformist, rational, and moral doctrines were checkmated at every turn by frenzied woman suffragists, impatient strikers, malcontent Irishmen, rebellious officers. And it was at this juncture that, for four years, the most terrible of foreign wars interrupted the painful, unconscious travail whereby the old nation was giving birth to a new England.

CHAPTER X

The Great War

IN THE middle years of the nineteenth century, indeed until its last decade, a fight to the death between England and Germany would have seemed incredible. These two countries, so willing to recall their common roots and religions, had no conflicting interests, and their dynasties were tied by close family bonds. The rival of Russia in Asia and of France in Africa. England at that time saw nowhere the shadow of Germany across her path. With the opening of the twentieth century, the situation was transformed. Once again, after Philip II, after Louis XIV, after Napoleon, a European sovereign was aspiring to hegemony in Europe, and was anxious to build a fleet capable of opposing the British navy; and once again the policy of the balance of power obviously required Britain to oppose such claims. The successive Ententes with France and Russia after 1905 were a defensive gesture provoked by the threats of Admiral von Tirpitz. "We must seize the trident of Neptune," declared the German Emperor. And that gave food for thought to the holders of the trident.

But although the Conservatives, the Admiralty, and a few clear-sighted Liberals like Winston Churchill, discerned a traditional danger ahead, the British Government at this time was essentially pacifist. Accordingly, no formal promise had been given to either France or Russia before August, 1914. Public opinion, paramount in British decisions, would not have tolerated a war designed solely to preserve maritime supremacy. The immediate cause of the war of 1914 (an ultimatum from Austria to Serbia following the murder of the Austrian heir-apparent) could not in itself affect the British electorate. It required the German invasion of Belgium, in defiance of treaties of neutrality, to release that emotional

[467]

wave which, arising to swell a wave of realism, swept England into almost complete unanimity. In any case, even if Germany had respected Belgian neutrality, Britain would nevertheless have been forced before long to enter the war. She had given no direct pledge to France, but many of her statesmen felt that neither her honor nor her interest could allow France to be crushed. Still less could she tolerate what William of Orange or Pitt would never have allowed—the presence of Germany at Antwerp or Calais. Asquith and Grey were resolved to resign if Britain remained neutral. The violation by Germany of the Belgian frontier determined the dispatch of an ultimatum to Berlin on August 4, 1914, and that night war was declared.

Although the Great War shows certain recurrent characteristics of Continental wars involving England in the past (the guarding of sea routes, a Continental coalition, subsidies to allies, and the dispatch of an expeditionary force to Flanders), there were several new features. In the first place, and for the first time, the masses of men set in motion were such, and the dangers were such, that Britain was forced against all her instincts to fall back on conscription for her armed forces. The main body of British citizens, hitherto screened by professional soldiers and sailors, felt for themselves the evils of war. Secondly, Britain's maritime resistance was nearly shattered by the submarine. At the start of the war, the British fleet easily enough assured the transport of the expeditionary force. But gradually the number and the active range of the German submarines increased. In 1914 there were on the high seas about 8,000 merchant ships, half of them under the British flag. Between 1914 and 1918 Germany sank 5,000 of that total. Out of twenty million tons, eight million were sent to the bottom. At first the losses were made up fairly well by the shipyards, but in 1917 the rate of torpedo destruction rose rapidly and fresh building lagged behind. If remedies had not been found, the Allies might have collapsed about August, 1917, for lack of transports.

It was this situation, fully visible to the Germans, which decided them to torpedo ships at sight, even under neutral flags, and at the risk of bringing in the United States on the Allied side, as indeed happened in 1917. The submarine menace was thwarted by the organization of convoys screened by destroyers, by the use of armed vessels disguised as merchant ships, and by blocking the Belgian coastal bases used by the German submarines. In 1918 the submarine danger was so far obviated that the transport of forty-two American army divisions was carried out with a loss of only two hundred lives. Although the one great naval battle of the war, that of Jutland, was indecisive, Britain kept the mastery of the seas, as the German fleet, in spite of some remarkable exploits by isolated ships, could not leave its base. Without the British navy, the food supply of the Allies would have been broken down.

The first aim assigned by the British Government to its expeditionary force in France was the protection of the Channel and North Sea ports. This could not be completely attained, as the Germans captured Antwerp, Ostend, and Zeebrugge; but the first battle of Ypres saved Calais and Boulogne. When the western front had become stabilized by continuous lines of trench from the Channel to the Swiss frontier, many able minds both in France and in England were bent upon the problem of outflanking this line by making some other front the scene of the main military blow. Some suggested Salonika and a vigorous campaign in the Balkans, which would rally to the Allied cause certain hesitating nations, such as Greece, Bulgaria, and Rumania. Others advised a landing in the Dardanelles, to force the Straits to get supplies through to Russia. Both plans were put into execution; but, as regards the second, despite heroic efforts and immense losses, the peninsula of Gallipoli defied capture. The Allies had to revert to the sanguinary tactics of frontal attack against fortified positions. To relieve the French army, fiercely attacked at Verdun, the British fought the costly battles of the Somme in 1916. Until June, 1918, fortune was undecided on the western front. The new weapon of tanks, which if used in mass might possibly have broken the German line, was tried too soon and on too small a scale. The tank was the most original invention of the War, and the most effective reply of the shock-troops to the improvement in projectiles. To modern infantry the tank is what armor was to the mediæval warrior. And another new aspect of the war of 1914-1918 was the fourfold part played by the airplane—for reconnaissance, bombardment, pursuit, and direct attack on infantry.

The resoluteness of all the peoples of the British Empire was unbreakable. By voluntary enlistment, then by conscription, they raised eight million men. All the Dominions, and India herself, rallied to the help of the mother-country. Only in Ireland a minority—but, as events proved, a potent minority—showed recalcitrance, although at the outbreak of war Irishmen were moved by the fate of Catholic Belgium. The Easter rising of 1916 in Dublin had to be suppressed by armed force, with considerable loss of life on both sides. The Sinn Fein rebels in years to come became the governing power in Ireland. The cost of the war from 1914 to 1918 came to nearly nine milliard pounds, not reckoning two milliards lent to Allies, whereas the Napoleonic wars, over twenty-two years, had cost only 831 million. Four of these nine milliards were raised by income tax during the war years. The rate of tax rose to six shillings in the pound, and the super-tax on large incomes went higher still. Food had to be rationed. The Government tried to make restrictions weigh equally on rich and poor; war burdens were shared much more equitably than under Pitt; and the common liberties were respected as far as seemed possible. A united nation sustained the war until it was won, not because leaders forced them to do so, but because the people themselves believed it to be a just war.

At first there were justifiable complaints from the army that they lacked munitions. It was primarily an artillery war, and for this none of the belligerents, except perhaps Germany, was prepared. Relations became strained between Sir John French, commanding the expeditionary force, and Kitchener, the War Minister at home. A coalition Cabinet formed in 1915 intrusted the Ministry of Munitions to Lloyd George, who succeeded Asquith as Prime Minister after a later Ministerial reconstruction. The conduct of the war was handed over to an inner War Cabinet of five members, presided over by Lloyd George. An Imperial War Cabinet was also summoned which brought together the Dominion Premiers and Indian representatives. These innovations did not outlast the war itself.

The strength of Germany, the courage of her armies, and the danger of her power and ambition to the independence of other European nations, are clearly visible when one reflects that in 1918, after four years of war with the most powerful of these, she was far from being vanquished. Possibly she would not have been beaten at all without the intervention of the United States against her. The German command's attack on the point of juncture between the French and British armies in March, 1918, nearly succeeded in separating them and driving the British back to the

Channel coast. On March 26th, at Doullens, Marshal Foch was given supreme command of the Allied armies. The German onslaughts were still formidable, but the rapid arrival of the American divisions afforded relief to the Allies and made possible the formation of important reserves. The failure of the German attack in Champagne (an onslaught outwitted by a maneuver in which Pétain was inspired by the memory of Wellington at Torres Vedras), followed by Mangin's attack at Villers-Cotterets on July 18th, marked the moment when "hope changed sides." On August 8th began the counter-offensive of the British, Canadian, and Australian forces, and thereafter until November 11th, when an armistice was declared, the forward movement of the Allies was continuous, their triumphs uninterrupted. Defeat in the field and revolution at home drove the Kaiser into exile in Holland. In the German fleet, where orders had been received late in October to make a last desperate sortie, the sailors mutinied and refused to obey the order. Rather than leave their ships in British hands, the German officers sank their surrendered vessels at Scapa Flow, and England was rid of that nightmare, a rival fleet in Europe. This, to her, was a prime objective of the war. She had achieved others: Mesopotamia, Palestine, the German colonies in Africa had all been conquered by her armies or those of her Allies, and these territories would now, in various guises, be incorporated in her Empire or gravitate around her.

It was natural enough that so complete a victory, rounding off so stern a war, should open the doors to an "orgy of Chauvinism." The "khaki" election soon after the Armistice gave Britain a House of Commons elected on a program of retribution. Lloyd George, by adding to claims for war damage a claim for the cost of war pensions, raised the reparations demanded from Germany to a ludicrously swollen figure. He was also the first to promise his Parliament the punishment of "war guilt." In order to induce their peoples to sustain cruel sufferings and inhuman losses, all heads of Governments had been forced to overstimulate men's minds to the pitch of folly. It was no longer easy to calm them down. The Peace of Versailles was a bad peace. On the pretext of the self-determination of peoples, the so-called Big Five sliced up Europe with little or no regard to its traditions, history, or economic life. France, refused the Rhine frontier by Lloyd George, found herself promised in compensation a treaty of alliance which was never ratified. Italy, who had been given definite pledges when she entered the war on the Allied side, was treated by British and Americans with an ill-will which bordered on enmity. And Germany herself, by a treaty too indulgent for its sternness and too stern for its indulgence, was cast into desperation. This, certainly, was not the Pax Britannica which had concluded other struggles.

CHAPTER XI

The Post-War Years

THIS conflict had disturbed the world more widely and deeply than even the Napoleonic wars. Ancient States had vanished, new ones been brought into being. The treaties of 1815 may have neglected the forces of nationality, but those of 1919 resuscitated nationalist forces which had seemed extinct. Races and languages emerged from the tombs of the centuries. In their anxiety to respect ethical frontiers, the negotiators neglected economic lines of division and laid the world open to universal economic crisis. While Russia became a Communist State, Italy and Germany fell under dictatorships, and corporative or totalitarian States supplanted the parliamentary regimes. These transformations affected England less than might have been thought possible. Too original in character to be susceptible to external influences, she found for the problems of the time solutions suited to her own nature. Nevertheless, she underwent profound political and economic changes.

In domestic politics the most conspicuous of these changes was a new Representation of the People Act which made adult suffrage really universal. Passed during the war years, a symbol of national unity, the Act of 1918 gave the Parliamentary vote to all men over twenty-one and to all women over thirty, thus bringing eight million new voters on to the register, six million of whom were women. This was supplemented by another measure passed a few years later which made the voting age the same for women as for men. What suffragette militancy had failed to obtain, had been won during the war by the devotion and hard work of English womanhood. Fifteen years' experience of female suffrage has shown that, although women are eligible to sit in Parliament, they are seldom chosen; that the electorate becomes more mobile and moves in bulk towards those parties which seem to offer the best safeguards for the tranquillity of the home; and that the female elecorate is pacifist and susceptible to the conception of collective security.

A second political fact of importance was the virtual disappearance of the Liberal party, which, counting its Whig forerunners, had endured for three centuries. In the election of 1924, the Labor party became preponderant over the Liberals. After that date the latter dwindled continuously, and by 1936 it could muster only a handful of members. At least three causes could be found for this phenomenon: firstly, the system of single, direct voting by constituencies does not enable opposition parties to divide their forces. A system of proportional representation might have preserved the Liberal party. But such a voting system, more equitable though it may be in theory, would have tended to bring weak Governments into office, and England had no liking for such. Secondly, the Labor party, although originally Socialists and working-class, was not a revolutionary party. It was open to many of the Liberal intellectuals. Socialism proper, in England, is found only in the advanced wing of the Labor party. And in the third place, as the main political problems had been virtually settled to the general satisfaction, it was the problems of labor, unemployment, and the division of wealth that became paramount. The Labor party, buttressed by the trade-union movement, was more representative than the Liberals of the views of the working classes in general.

During the years which followed the war, English politics were dominated by economics. As after Waterloo, the war of 1914-1918 was followed by a serious industrial slump. The causes of upheaval were the same as in 1816: the sudden demobilization of large numbers of men who could not recover their places in an altered economic machine; the phenomenal development of mechanical processes which had been stimulated by the needs of war; and a Budget inflated by collossal debts incurred during the conflict. The slump of 1920-1931, although it did not provoke violence or revolt, was deeper and more dangerous than that of 1816-1821. For some years it almost looked as if Britain were doomed. The running start she had made ahead of her rivals during the nineteenth century had been lost. Her industries were inferior in equipment to those of Germany and the United States, and were furthermore handicapped by higher wage-rates than those of the Continent; the trade unions refused to allow these rates to be touched. Her trade was affected by the disappearance of consumers in an impoverished world which tended to make its units more and more self-sufficing; and on account of this shrinkage in international trade her merchant marine lay idle. In order to preserve her rôle as the world's banker, Britain tried until 1931 to maintain the gold value of the pound sterling; and this monetary policy, theoretically defensible but in practice harmful, was responsible for increasing unemployment still further.

The unemployment problem in England is complicated. The number of men and women actually at work did not diminish, but really increased, after the war. In 1911 there were 12,927,000 men in employment, and 5,424,000 women. In 1921 there were 13,656,000 men and 5,701,000 women. But the total number of citizens seeking work was greater, and there was also a displacement of hands. Between 1923 and 1933, over a period, that is, of ten years, nearly 1,000,000 workers *less* were employed in the following branches of industry: coal, engineering machinery, naval shipbuilding, iron and steel, railways, cotton and wool. But over the same period, *more* hands were required, to the total extent of 1,327,670, in the following occupations, among others: wholesale and retail trading, sports, hotels and amusements, building trades, electrical trades, road transport, book trade and manufacture, motor cars and bicycles, artificial silk.

Unexpected migrations of labor took place, corresponding to the changes in the general nature of the industries thus affected. At the time of the industrial revolution the center of gravity shifted from the south of England to the north; now the spread of electric power and the petrol engine brought the population southward, especially to the neighborhood of London itself. The use of these new forces accounted for the serious unemployment among coal-miners, which was due also to the increased coal production achieved in other countries, particularly in Poland. In 1926 an attempt to lower miners' wages led to a general strike. Newspapers ceased to appear, and the Government issued a small official newspaper, the *British Gazette*, and for the time being annexed the wireless broadcasting service. Thus controlling public opinion, supported by the majority of the country, and helped out by numerous volunteers who coöperated with the police and insured the food supply for the large towns, the Conservative Government defeated the strike movement.

With the numbers of unemployed standing at over one and a half million, the unemployment-insurance system broke down and had to be replaced by a subsidy method of relief, known as the "dole," which threw heavy burdens on the budget. A Labor Government under Ramsay Mac-Donald, which returned to power in 1929, was no more successful than the Conservatives had been in overcoming the slump and the problem of the workless. In both America and Europe capitalists were losing faith in Britain's future. There was a flight of gold from London. At this pace, bankruptcy was not far ahead. MacDonald came to feel that a National Government would inspire more confidence, and without having been defeated in Parliament, which in any case was not sitting, he tendered his resignation (1931). He was at once intrusted with the formation of a coalition Cabinet with a strong Conservative element, over which he presided until 1935, when the Conservative leader, Stanley Baldwin, took his place, retaining the National form.

Between 1931 and 1935 the rapid re-establishment of British economic stability surprised even the most optimistic. It was due in great measure to the cool heads of the people themselves, but also to an energetic Chancellor of the Exchequer, Neville Chamberlain. The methods used were simple. Firstly, Britain abandoned the gold standard of the pound. This was not followed by any important rise in wage costs. Prices in England dropped to levels lower than those of countries still on the gold standard, and thus favored export trade. The fluctuations of the pound had been followed by the Scandinavian countries, South America, and to some extent by the United States, and a sterling bloc thus came into existence within which London was able to continue as a supreme banking center. Secondly, Free Trade was finally abandoned. At the Ottawa Conference in 1932, British statesmen invited the Dominions to make economic agreements with the mother-country. But the Dominions were not enthusiastic, and this failure obliged British Ministers to look elsewhere for a solution of their problems in an internal reorganization. Protective tariffs enabled manufacturers in many fields (at heavy cost to France and Germany) to recover British markets; and great efforts were made to revive home agriculture and stock-breeding. Thirdly, the Budget was balanced, thanks to the courageous acceptance of economies in expenditure and of fresh taxation. A policy of cheap money enabled the building trades to enjoy a period of great prosperity. Two million new houses were built between 1919 and 1933. And all these measures had fortunate results. Unemployment was still far from being vanquished, but the evil began to dwindle.

Has the time come, then, to record the death of the individualist, Free Trade, Imperial England? And the birth of a new England, self-contained and protectionist? The truth is simpler. In the nineteenth century the different level of European civilization from that of the rest of the world had caused a large, steady flow of trade, which had fostered the fortune of a continent and of a doctrine. The force of this current was bound to diminish, and the World War hastened the change of conditions. When England suddenly encountered an economic hurricane, she took in sail. In a time of world-wide confusion, she found it advantageous to bring production and consumption into a compact and controllable group. It was a compromise rather than a conversion.

By compromise also England was able to preserve her Empire, the disintegration of which was proclaimed by many Continental observers about 1925. During the war, Canada, Australia, New Zealand, and South Africa had poured forth men and money to help the mother-country. But they had agreed to do so as separate States. In the newly founded League of Nations they demanded representation distinct from that of Great Britain. The second Statute of Westminster in 1931 declared that the British Parliament would no longer be entitled to legislate for the Dominions; that the rights of making peace or war, as also of negotiating treaties, would appertain to the Dominions in so far as their concerns were in question; and that the Dominion Prime Ministers would derive their authority direct from the Crown. The Crown was thenceforth the sole official link between Britain and the nations composing the British Commonwealth. By the treaty of 1921 Ireland likewise had been given a separate status, as the Irish Free State, although northern Ireland was excepted and retained a close British connection. Between 1922 and 1931, under Cosgrave's presidency, Ireland accepted this position, but when Eamon de Valera succeeded him, the bonds were gradually loosened. Ireland no longer acknowledged the link of the Crown, was not represented at British ceremonies, and acted as an independent State. In 1936 Britain signed a treaty with Egypt which assured that country her freedom, and British troops, leaving the fortress of Cairo, defended only the Suez Canal.

British foreign policy since the war has conformed to the country's traditions. England still strove, as for four centuries past, to maintain the balance of power in Europe. Just as she upheld France against the Continental allies after Waterloo, so, after 1919, she was afraid of enfeebling Germany excessively, and in the international conferences frequently fought Germany's battle. French demands that the League of Nations should be organized to defend its decisions, if need be, by force, were countered by successive British Governments with the idea of moral constraint. Meanwhile fervent propaganda, carried out all over

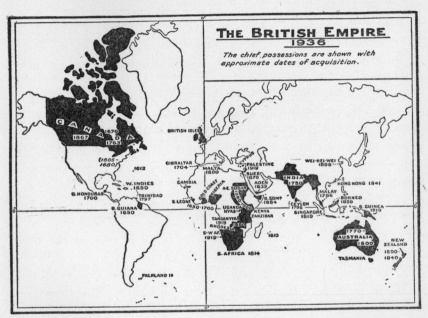

THE BRITISH EMPIRE
1936
*The chief possessions are shown with
approximate dates of acquisition.*

the country by the League of Nations Union and supported by the Churches, gradually engendered a mystical concept known as "Geneva." When Italy in 1935 overran Abyssinia, a wave of sentiment rose in England, reinforcing a sudden revival of the Imperial sense, and then, for the first time, it was Britain who proposed the application of the sanctions provided for by the pact. These measures failed; Italy succeeded in her African enterprise. And as progress in aviation has lessened the value of naval bases such as Malta, or even Gibraltar, a compromise between Britain, France, and Italy will doubtless be necessary to insure peace in the Mediterranean. Besides, the mastery of the air will speedily become more important than that of the sea, and this completely transforms the problems of Imperial defenses. Probably for a few decades longer, the navy will be able to protect Britain's distant possessions; but any colony near Europe will be at the mercy of enemy air forces. Two results ensue: Britain, whether she likes it or no, will find herself more and more involved with the Continent of Europe; and she will find herself forced to acquire, by her own efforts and those of her allies, that margin of security in the air which she has so long kept on the seas.

The shift from rural to urban life had caused much suffering in the earlier part of the nineteenth century; a hundred years later the growth of road transport and of working-class leisure brought about a revival of rural or open-air life. The great new roads of the country were filled with motor-cars, large and small, motor-cycles, pedal bicycles, to an extent that showed unmistakably a leveling of social classes. The seaside, the riverside, the swimming-pool saw something like a resuscitation of the old "Merry England," with gramophone and wireless taking the place of lute and virginal. Relaxed conventions enabled young men and young women to enjoy these delights together. Novelists, playwrights, and scientists combined to emancipate a large proportion of England's youth from the Victorian repressions. The London theater nowadays is as bold as in the days of Wycherley or Congreve. Novelists like D. H. Lawrence and Aldous Huxley exhibit the frankness of the new Georgian age, and also the Puritan inheritance of seriousness, the transformation of religious radicalism into a radicalism of politics, pacifism, and sexual morality. But it should not be overlooked, in commenting on such writers, that their books are read only by a minority, and that throughout the Empire vast numbers of men and women remain loyal to the religious and moral standards of the past century.

If modern England, more than any other country, remains a free country, and can tolerate extremes of thought without imperiling the national order, this is because she accepts certain established frameworks, certain age-old traditions. The King and the royal family retain their prestige intact, and throughout a century it was enhanced by the mythical industry and care of the old Queen Victoria, by the common sense of Edward VII, by the noble simplicity of George V. The Labor party and the Conservative party are at one in their recognition of the constitutional monarch as a useful and respected arbiter. Every night in places of entertainment, "God Save the King" is listened to by standing, silent audiences, a reminder of collective discipline. At Christmas, thanks to wireless, King George V was able to address his people in their homes in every part of his realm and Dominions. His Jubilee in 1935, and his death in January, 1936, gave opportunities to all the peoples of the Empire to demonstrate their loyalty and appreciate their own unity.

How concrete and powerful this traditional England was became manifest in the uprising of public opinion which, in December, 1936, suddenly brought about the abdication of King Edward VIII. His father, George V, and his mother, Queen Mary, had enhanced the prestige of the monarchy by the simplicity and dignity of their life. King George's jubilee in 1935, and his funeral early in 1936, had enabled all the peoples of the Empire to demonstrate their loyalty; and Edward VIII himself, at the outset of his reign, was invested with an almost universal sympathy. England seemed to rejoice at finding in him a modern and vital sovereign who, on the day of his accession, had come to his capital by airplane and had shown no less interest in visiting the homes of the unemployed than the mansions of the great. But the day came when *The Times* applied to him the phrase of Tacitus: *"Omnium consensu capax Imperii nisi imperasset."*

Before the reign of Edward VIII had lasted ten months, his subjects at home and overseas became aware, by persistent rumor and through the American newspapers, that their King proposed to marry an American, Mrs. Ernest Simpson, who was about to obtain her second divorce. The Prime Minister, Stanley Baldwin, was beset by messages of warning and anxiety. He requested an audience of the King and laid before him the dangers of any such decision. The sovereign's right to marry a foreigner, as so many of his ancestors had done, would not have been questioned, but a vast majority of his subjects refused to admit the idea of his marriage with a woman twice divorced. The King himself, alive to these difficulties, suggested a morganatic union. But English law did not admit of this expedient, and neither the British Government nor any Dominion Government was prepared to pass legislation for that purpose. It was considered by them all that such a marriage would gravely impair the authority of the Crown. Irreconcilable factions would come into being. Far from remaining a universally accepted arbiter, a link between the

Keystone View Company

EDWARD VIII

GEORGE VI

component parts of the Empire, the King would actually become a cause of dissidence and scandal.

Early in December, 1936, the dispute was brought out into the open, and for a day or two public opinion wavered. Popular newspapers accused the Government, the Church, and the aristocracy of hypocritically defending an outmoded moral code, and demonstrators were seen in the streets shouting "We want our King!" But even in London these crowds were insignificant, and the great silent masses in the provinces, in Wales and Scotland and the Dominions, soon made it plain to their representatives that they shared the view of the British Cabinet. A majority of British and Imperial citizens required the King to choose between his crown and this marriage. Parliament showed admirable self-discipline during the crisis, and supported the Prime Minister's firmness with no reservations. Edward VIII himself desired abdication. "I am ready to go," he had told Baldwin. He made no attempt to transform this emotional drama into a political intrigue. After his abdication on December 11, 1936, when he was succeeded by his brother under the title of George VI, he broadcast a message to his former subjects from Windsor, in which he explained his action and, in moving terms, declared his loyalty to the new sovereign. "God save the King, although I be not he," Shakespeare had written in "Richard the Second."

This strange drama, the like of which England had not seen before, showed that the monarchy was still important enough for the public to require the royal family to have the representative virtues, that parliamentary institutions were still capable of insuring that great changes should be carried out with dignity, order, and sound sense, and finally that, in grave circumstances, the mother-country and the Dominions could take concerted action with ease, speed, and secrecy. Just as a sick man sometimes finds himself more vigorous than he was before his illness, so the British Empire emerged from this crisis with increased confidence in its laws and in itself. The strength of the roots was all the more manifest for the violence of the storm that shook the tree.

CHAPTER XII

Conclusion

THE history of England is that of one of mankind's outstanding successes. It is the history of how certain Saxon and Danish tribes, isolated on an island on the outer rim of Europe, merging with the Celtic and Roman survivors and organized by adventurers from Normandy, became with the passing centuries the masters of one-third of this planet. It is instructive to probe the secret of a destiny as fortunate and impressive as that of ancient Rome.

The racial blend was aptly measured, the climate healthy, and the soil fertile. Local assemblies had implanted in village communities a sense of public debate, and also of compromise. But these customs would doubtless have fallen into desuetude, as happened elsewhere, had it not been for the conquest by the Normans. To the strong authority of the Conqueror and his successors, both Norman and Angevin, the English owed the benefits of sound justice and their heightened respect for law. Shielded by the sea from their Continental neighbors, and thereby set free from the fears which paralyzed so many statesmen in France, they were able with comparative safety to improve upon their original institutions. By a sequence of fortunate chances they slowly discovered certain simple conditions which assured them at once of their security and their liberty.

In the time of the Saxon Kingdoms, the English sovereigns collaborated with a Council, and strove to obtain for their acts the approval of the most powerful men in the land. Their successors did likewise, and England never knew an absolute monarchy. When the effective forces shifted from their proper place, sovereigns or skillful Ministers consulted and rallied the several "estates" of the realm. The best ecclesiastics were their Ministers; the barons, then the squires, became their officials; the burgesses and notables became their "faithful Commons." As political maturity advanced, the lords, knights, smaller landowners, merchants, artisans and farmers were in turn called upon to participate in the responsibilities of power, until at last, not many years ago now, the working-class party itself became "His Majesty's Opposition," and then assumed power. Having thus transmuted successive groups of potential malcontents into active collaborators, the rulers of England were able to grant the people a measure of freedom which expanded as their sense of security deepened.

Two supremely valuable virtues insured a tranquil evolution in England —continuity, and flexibility. Balfour once remarked that it was better to do something absurd which had always been done, than to do a wise thing which had never been done before. Today as always, England is ruled by precedent. After ten centuries the landed aristocracy remains a benevolent magistrature. The monarchy, Parliament, the universities, are all faithful to mediæval tradition and usage. But the adaptive powers of the English people are equal to their conservatism. The ancient institutions always acknowledge and accept the newer powers. There has never been a real revolution in England. The short-lived risings which mark the stages in her history were only passing waves on a great sea, and the "glorious Revolution of 1688" simply an exchange of signatures.

Chance results have been made use of by England's statesmen, rather in the way that great artists seize and perpetuate a fortunate expression or feature. We saw how the association between knights and burgesses, and then the deliberate abstention of the clergy, led to the formation of a Parliament composed of two distinct Houses. Before long the kings depended for their financial resources on that Parliament's goodwill. In France or Spain sovereigns might forcibly raise taxes imposed without consent. But the English soon realized that their freedom was bound up with the maintenance of two protective axioms—no perpetual taxation, and no royal army unduly strong. Touching these two points, they clashed with, and defeated, the Stuart dynasty. With Parliament here victorious, it remained to find a means of drawing forth an executive power from this legislative assembly. An opportune chance, in the accession of the

Hanoverian dynasty, here made possible the system of a Cabinet responsible to the Parliamentary body. Finally, the prudence of the aristocracy and the political shrewdness of its leaders, made possible the peaceful transformation of a country gentlemen's club into a great national assembly. Thus came about the slow formation of a mode of government which is not, as Europe often believed it was, an abstract system with universal validity, but an amalgam of devices which, in that particular country and for particular historical reasons, have proved successful.

An insular and remote situation, and perhaps climatic influences, brought about a religious breach with Rome; and this rupture was in its turn an initial cause of the formation of a British Empire. Prolonged religious conflict created a type of courageous, resolute Protestant, who yielded to nobody, and preferred to quit his own country and settle in distant lands to which he gave an Anglo-Saxon population. The survival of this Empire was assured by the mastery of the seas, which England wrested from Spain, France, Holland, and Germany in succession, gaining that supremacy because, thanks to her geographical position, she was able to concentrate so much of her resources upon her fleet. That Empire might well have disappeared, at one time or another, if not by conquest from without, at least through explosion from within. But the loss of the American Colonies gave home Governments a lesson in moderation. England had evolved Parliament and the Cabinet; encountering by chance the idea of an Imperial federation of free States, she applied it by common sense. Within the Empire, as in its home boundaries, the British Government now hardly desires to maintain its authority save by consent of the peoples governed. The difficult problem of India, and later that of the colonies, will probably be solved by progressive solutions of similar kind.

Will the success of English compromise endure? Can a mode of governance based on the amicable struggle of rival parties survive in the face of totalitarian States, where unity of command bestows more swiftness in decision? To answer that question is not for the historian, whose task it is to describe the past, not to forecast the future. But he can observe that the clash of class or faction, deadly in other countries, is less perilous in England, because there the habit of disciplined assent to the decisions of a majority is as old as the juries of the Norman Kings, and also because, beneath surface conflicts of opinion, the deeper unity of the nation appears to be indestructible. Classes are sundered by fairly reconcilable interests, not by memories or passions. Intellect and eloquence, so potent in dividing other countries, have less hold on the English spirit than an instinctive, traditional wisdom. Respect for the past is widespread amongst Englishmen, and their history, crystallized in numerous customs, lives in their midst. On sea and land and in the air, England has great armaments; but the strength of her people springs equally from the kindly, disciplined, trusting and tenacious character molded by a thousand years of happy fortune.

BIBLIOGRAPHY

SOURCES

[This is in no way intended to provide the bibliography of so extensive a field of study. The books listed below are simply those of which the author has made particular use in preparing and writing this work.]

A

GENERAL SOURCES

EUROPEAN HISTORY

H. A. L. Fisher: *History of Europe*
L. Halphen and P. Sagnac: *Peuples et Civilisations*
E. Lavisse and A. Rambaud: *Histoire Générale*

ENGLISH HISTORY

The Cambridge Modern History
J. R. Green: *History of the English People*
G. M. Trevelyan: *History of England*
A. F. Pollard: *History of England*
Dictionary of National Biography

HISTORY OF INSTITUTIONS

W. Stubbs: *Constitutional History of England*
W. Stubbs: *Select Charters*
W. Bagehot: *The English Constitution*
F. W. Maitland: *The Constitutional History of England*
E. Boutmy: *Développement de la Constitution en Angleterre*
A. de Tocqueville: *L'Ancien Régime et la Révolution*
A. F. Pollard: *Factors in Modern History*
G. B. Adams: *Constitutional History of England*

[487]

ECONOMIC HISTORY

Thorold Rogers: *Six Centuries of Work and Wages*
R. E. Prothero: *English Farming, Past and Present*
W. Cunningham: *Growth of English Industry and Commerce*
W. J. Ashley: *Introduction to English Economic History*
S. Dowell: *History of Taxation and Taxes in England*
C. Waters: *Economic History of England*

SOCIAL HISTORY

H. D. Traill: *Social England*
E. Wingfield-Stratford: *History of British Civilization*
M. B. Synge: *Short History of Social Life in England*

ENGLISH LANGUAGE

L. Pearsall Smith: *The English Language*

LITERARY HISTORY

The Cambridge History of English Literature
E. Legouis and L. Cazamian: *History of English Literature*
H. A. Taine: *History of English Literature*
A. N. Whitehead: *Science and the Modern World*

FOREIGN POLICY

The Cambridge History of British Foreign Policy
E. Bourgeois: *Manuel Historique de Politique Etrangère*

B

OTHER SOURCES

BOOK I

Mackinder: *Britain and the British Seas*
C. W. C. Oman: *England Before the Norman Conquest*
H. Belloc: *The Old Road*
F. J. Haverfield: *The Roman Occupation of Britain*
The Anglo-Saxon Chronicle
The Venerable Bede: *Ecclesiastical History*

Sources

Beowulf
B. Lees: *Alfred the Great*
H. M. Chadwick: *Heroic Age*
P. Vinogradoff: *The Growth of the Manor*
M. Bloch: *Caractères originaux de l'histoire rurale française*
E. A. Freeman: *William the Conqueror*
E. A. Freeman: *History of the Norman Conquest*

BOOK II

H. W. C. Davis: *England under the Normans and Angevins*
C. Petit-Dutaillis: *Monarchie féodale en France et en Angleterre*
P. Vinogradoff: *English Society in the Eleventh Century*
F. M. Powicke: *Mediaeval England*
F. W. Maitland: *Domesday Book and Beyond*
C. W. C. Oman: *The Art of War in the Middle Ages*
A. F. Pollard: *The Evolution of Parliament*
J. H. Round: *Feudal England*
J. Calmette: *La Société Féodale*
G. G. Coulton: *Social Life in the Middle Ages*
L. F. Salzmann: *English Life in the Middle Ages*
C. Bémont: *Vie de Simon de Montfort*

BOOK III

K. H. Vickers: *England in the Later Middle Ages*
F. M. Powicke: *Mediaeval England*
G. M. Trevelyan: *England in the Age of Wycliffe*
A. F. Tout: *Edward the First*
Mrs. J. R. Green: *Henry the Second*
J. Gairdner: *History of Richard the Third*
The Paston Letters
The Canterbury Tales
Abram: *English Life and Manors in the Later Middle Ages*
G. G. Coulton: *Chaucer and His England*

BOOK IV

A. D. Innes: *England under the Tudors*
K. Garvin (edited by): *The Great Tudors*
A. F. Pollard: *Henry the Eighth*
A. F. Pollard: *Cranmer*
J. E. Neale: *Queen Elizabeth*

[489]

Consulting your

Lytton Strachey: *Elizabeth and Essex*
G. A. R. Callender: *Naval Side of British History*
Cobbett: *Drake and the Tudor Navy*
R. Hakluyt: *The Principal Navigations . . . of the English Nation*
Trotter: *Seventeenth-Century Life in Country Parish*
C. W. C. Oman: *The Sixteenth Century*
M. St. C. Byrne: *Elizabethan Life in Town and Country*

BOOK V

G. M. Trevelyan: *England Under the Stuarts*
S. R. Gardiner: *History of England, 1603-1642*
Earl of Clarendon: *History of the Rebellion and Civil Wars*
E. Dowden: *Puritan and Anglican*
Charles I: *Letters*
Charles II: *Letters*
C. H. Firth: *Cromwell and the Rule of the Puritans*
F. Harrison: *Oliver Cromwell*
J. Buchan: *Oliver Cromwell*
O. Cromwell: *Letters and Speeches*
A. Bryant: *Charles the Second*
John Hayward: *Charles the Second*
H. D. Traill: *Shaftesbury*
Samuel Pepys: *Diary*
Dorothy Osborne: *Letters to Sir William Temple*
Carola Oman: *Henrietta Maria of France*
A. Bryant: *The England of Charles II*

BOOK VI

Queen Anne: *Letters*
Winston Churchill: *The Duke of Marlborough*
W. Sichel: *Bolingbroke*
J. Morley: *Walpole*
F. S. Oliver: *The Endless Adventure*
F. Harrison: *Chatham*
Earl of Rosebery: *Pitt*
Basil Williams: *Pitt*
B. Dobrée: *John Wesley*
A. T. Mahan: *Influence of Sea Power upon the French Revolution and Empire*
J. L. Hammond: *Charles James Fox*
C. Grant Robertson: *England Under the Hanoverians*

Sources

Sir C. Petrie: *The Four Georges, a Revaluation*
Shane Leslie: *George the Fourth*
J. Holland Rose: *The Revolutionary and Napoleonic Era*
A. Sorel: *L'Europe et la révolution française*
J. L. and B. Hammond: *The Village Labourer*
P. Mantoux: *The Industrial Revolution in the 18th Century*
Adam Smith: *The Wealth of Nations*
A. S. Turberville: *English Men and Manners in the Eighteenth Century*

BOOK VII

Elie Halévy: *Histoire du peuple anglais au 19e siècle*
J. A. R. Marriott: *England since Waterloo*
G. M. Trevelyan: *Lord Grey of the Reform Bill*
G. K. Chesterton: *William Cobbett*
Queen Victoria: *Letters*
Lytton Strachey: *Queen Victoria*
Edith Sitwell: *Victoria of England*
W. F. Monypenny and G. M. Buckle: *Life of Disraeli*
J. Morley: *Life of W. E. Gladstone*
B. Disraeli: *Life of Lord George Bentinck*
Sidney Lee: *Edward the Seventh*
A. Maurois: *Edward the Seventh and His Times*
Lady G. Cecil: *Lord Salisbury*
Lord Crewe: *Life of Lord Rosebery*
Basil Williams: *Cecil Rhodes*
A. Duff Cooper: *Haig*
Harold Nicolson: *Lord Carnock*
Harold Nicolson: *Lord Curzon*
Harold Nicolson: *Peacemaking*
G. M. Young: *Early Victorian England*
F. J. C. Hearnshaw: *Edwardian England*
J. A. R. Marriott: *Modern England, 1875-1932*

Index

Index

Index

Index

Index

Index

Set in Linotype Granjon
Format by A. W. Rushmore
Manufactured by the Haddon Craftsmen
Published by HARPER & BROTHERS, *New York and London*